LET THE RECORD SHOW

LET THE
RECORD SHOW

A Legal History of Ingham County

Richard Frazier

David Thomas, editor

Michigan State University Press
East Lansing

All Michigan State University Press books are produced on paper which meets the requirements of American National Standard of Information Sciences— Permanence of paper for printed materials ANSI Z23.48-1984.

Michigan State University Press
East Lansing, MI 48823-5202

Printed in the United States of America

02 01 00 99 98   2 3 4 5 6 7 8 9 10

Library of Congress Cataloging-in-Publication Data

Frazier, Richard, d. 1996.
    Let the record show : a legal history of Ingham County / Richard Frazier ; David Thomas, editor.
        p.   cm.
    Includes bibliographical references.
    ISBN 0-87013-425-6 (alk. paper)
    1. Law—Michigan—Ingham County—History. 2. Ingham County Bar Association—History. I. Thomas, David, 1944-   . II. Title. KFM4799.I54F73 1997
349.774'26—dc21   97-23218
                                                            CIP

CONTENTS

Friends and Patrons of the Ingham County Bar Association

Listed below are those individuals whose financial support for this work we are pleased to acknowledge.

Richard D. Ball

Kenneth W. Beall

Ronald W. Bloomberg

John Brattin

Judge Thomas L. Brown

Henry Clay Campbell

Michael E. Cavanaugh

Charles E. Chamberlain

Elaine H. Charney

Judge Patrick F. Cherry

Allan J. Claypool

David C. Coey

John L. Collins

Gerald M. Conley

John L. Coté

Rollin Dart

James R. Davis

Jack C. Davis

D. Michael Dudley

Stuart Dunnings Jr.

Robert & Jean Earley

Rodger T. Ederer

Quentin A. Ewert

Ida Rose Farhat

Virginia Farhat

Joseph A. Fink

Joe C. Foster, Jr.

Richard B. Foster

Archie C. Fraser

Ruth Tuttle Freeman

Byron P. Gallagher

Karl L. Gotting

Charles G. Hayden

Donald A. Hines

Mrs. Harry Hubbard

Raymond Joseph

Frank J. Kelley

Mary P. Kerr (Barnard Pierce)

William N. Kritselis

Steven T. Lett

Lawrence B. Lindemer

William L. MacKay

Charles R. MacLean

Jonathan E. Maire

Susan L. Mallory

Judge Pamela J. McCabe

Polly Person McKouen
  (in memory of Justice Rollie H. Person)

Neil A. McLean

Gary J. McRay

Lloyd D. Morris

Fred C. Newman

Michael G. Oliva

Judge Donald S. Owens

William D. Parsley

Donald L. Reisig

Maurice E. Schoenberger

Stephen O. Schultz

Raymond L. Scodeller

Peter S. Sheldon

Webb A. Smith

Louis A. Smith

Judith A. Snyder
  (in memory of Donald G. Fox)

Michael R. Spaniolo

Frederick L. Stackable

William J. Stapleton

Norman Otto Stockmeyer

Ted W. Stroud

Theodore W. Swift

Allison K. Thomas

George R. Thornton

David VanderHaagen

Eugene G. Wanger

Jack W. Warren

Judson M. Werbelow

James A. White

Wiliam S. Wilkinson

Charles F. Willingham

FOREWORD

When the Ingham County Bar Association committed to chronicle its history, initial thinking was that it would be just that—a history of the association. After discussing the scope of the project, however, it became apparent that the county's legal tradition consisted of more than its bar association's activities, due principally to the fact that the county's largest city had been the state's capital for 150 years. Accordingly, it was agreed that we would produce a definitive history of the county from a legal perspective. Included would be a history of the Ingham County Bar Association.

Leo Farhat and Allison Thomas were appointed co-chairs of the Ingham County Bar Association History Committee and were asked to find an author for the work. Early on, it was suggested that Dick Frazier, then recently retired from the Lansing State Journal, and his wife, Jean, would be ideal for the task. They were offered the opportunity and accepted eagerly.

Shortly after work on the manuscript commenced, Dick and Jean agreed that Dick would handle the "lion's share" of the research and the writing; it would be Dick's work. For Dick this was a labor of love. It sustained him during his last years while he fought through a series of health problems. Shortly before he died, he presented a manuscript consisting of more than 700 pages that formed the foundation of what you will read in this book.

Dick was assisted in a number of ways by a number of people—but several deserve special mention.

His wife, Jean, was a historian in her own right and her counsel regarding things literary was always available. More important, her loving support and encouragement enabled Dick to see this project to its successful conclusion. Jean graciously acknowledged Dick's devotion to this project by insisting that he be identified as its sole author.

David Thomas, the ICBA editor for the manuscript, provided helpful suggestions and assisted in correlating chapters and events into the final product; and Gil Wanger organized, assembled and provided introductions for the appendices. Their dedication to the project and their enthusiasm for it was probably exceeded only by the author's.

And, of course, the contributions of our association's recently retired executive director, Jean Earley, and her successor, Brad Hobbs, were invaluable—even though not visible to the casual observer. Thanks to them, all of our bills were paid and many other logistical details competently completed.

Still, the work would not have been completed without our co-publisher, Michigan State University Press. Special thanks to Fred Bohm, director, and Laura Luptowski and Julie L. Loehr, editors, for their enthusiastic endorsement of the project. The ICBA could not have picked a better partner.

Space commitments preclude us from mentioning the names of others who contributed to this effort—including individual patrons and law firms who contributed their histories—but we do wish to extend our heartfelt thanks to all who helped in this endeavor.

Finally, know that the author and our committee recognize that every attorney who has practiced law in this county has contributed to its history. Many are mentioned in this book but logistical considerations dictate that a good number are not—although they are fine lawyers and credits to the profession. If there were oversights, rest assured they were unintentional.

Enjoy the book!

Ingham County Bar Association History Committee

Peter S. Sheldon	Allison K. Thomas
Co-Chairman	Co-Chairman

Other Committee Members who served at sometime or throughout the course of this project were:

Judge Robert Holmes Bell	Judge Michael J. Harrison
Allan J. Claypool	Rose A. Houk
John L Coté	George W. Loomis
Jeanette Disbrow	William L. MacKay
D. Michael Dudley	Susan L. Mallory
Leo E. Farhat	Daniel E. Nickerson, Jr.
Joe C. Foster, Jr.	Jack W. Warren
Richard B. Foster	Eugene G. Wanger

Three members of the Committee, Leo E. Farhat, Richard B. Foster and William L. MacKay, died before this book was published. We are indebted to them for their helpful counsel and support. While in the active practice of law each also exemplified what a good lawyer is and what a young lawyer today ought to strive to be.

1

THE EUROPEAN LEGACY

When the Territory of Michigan's Third Legislative Council, guided by Governor Lewis Cass, voted on November 5, 1829, that a portion of inland wilderness be set aside and named Ingham County, it was adding one more detail to an adventure that had begun almost three hundred years earlier. This 550-square-mile area near the geographical center of a mitten-shaped peninsula had already been ruled by four nations, survived several wars, and provided shelter, sustenance and a transportation route for Native Americans and European explorers. And yet, in the mid-Michigan woodland, it would be another six years before a permanent resident would arrive.

That Third Legislative Council, meeting in the Council House at Detroit, the Michigan Territory's capital city, was aware of the history of the land. Many of the thirteen members and Governor Cass had participated in events that changed forever the political status of the area they named Ingham. None of those present could have foreseen that, within twenty years, the county they established would no longer be on the edge of the frontier but the center of political and legal activities for a state that was then only an embryo.

The legal history of this land began shortly before the French explorer Jacques Cartier sailed from North America for his homeland on October 5, 1535. Before embarking, he did three things that set into motion events that eventually led to the action taken that autumn day at Detroit. First, Cartier claimed for his emperor, Francis I of France, massive tracts of land from the mouth of the St. Lawrence River westward to infinity. His expedition members never saw the inland peninsulas or the enormous lakes. Their journals note that the Wyandotte Indians told the explorers that to the west were great waters (Lakes Erie, Huron, and Michigan), a freshwater sea of which no one had ever found an end (Lake Superior), and a country called Sequenay (Saginaw). This area was included in the claim that Cartier named New France. Second, he placed the royal shield of France on the North American shore to signify that

French law ruled New France. Finally, a wooden cross was erected to proclaim that Roman Catholicism was the claim's official religion.

A small group of colonists remained in New France when the expedition departed in 1535, but one winter's survival experience caused them to return to France before the completion of a single year's residence. It was not until 1608, under the leadership of the Frenchman Samuel Champlain, that a permanent colony was established in New France. This colony's government set policies that affected Michigan. Champlain, the second governor of New France and founder of Quebec City, declared that Indian law was to be honored unless the offense involved a "white" person.

Indian law was an unwritten set of rules and regulations that varied from tribe to tribe, but was always severe, dictated by the tribes' religious beliefs and enforced by a tribal council, chief, or shaman. It was usually the tribal council that decided on boundaries, declarations of war, and selection of a chief. The chief settled family disputes, determined time for migrations, and led the council. A shaman—or medicine man—could be all powerful, determining if good or evil spirits were controlling a person's body. The part of the body responding to evil was destroyed and often resulted in the death of the victim.

If an offense involved a white person, French rule took precedence. The British continued this French legal policy, which appears to have been satisfactory for both Native Americans and Europeans during the 186 years it existed. Local chiefs displayed an eagerness to surrender an offender to fort authorities. The Native American who committed an illegal act involving a white explorer, hunter, merchant, settler, soldier, trader, trapper, or voyageur was often an intruder from a non-Michigan tribe. By cooperating with the European's law, the Native Americans were able to inform the enemies within their own nations that Michigan was off limits.

Justice William Renwick Riddell of the Supreme Court of Ontario related an incident in his book, *Michigan Under British Rule: Law and Law Courts 1760-1796*, which illustrates this logic. In 1762, Michigan's Native American leaders arrived in Detroit with a Pawnee man and woman claimed to have murdered a Fort Pitt merchant returning to his home after a visit at that Michigan settlement. The fort commandant, Colonel Donald Campbell, accepted the prisoners and heard the captors' recommendation that the couple be burned at the stake. Prior to the English trial, the Pawnee man escaped, but the woman received a trial, was convicted of murder, and publicly executed by hanging at Detroit.

This dual legal system also proved to be acceptable to both the French and British who discouraged the interior colonization of Michigan. The foreigners' primary interest pivoted around the fur trade, believing inland settlements would disrupt the environment that attracted fur-bearing animals.

During the time of foreign rule, only Native Americans lived in what would become Ingham County. The heavily wooded land had a number of clearings, a network of creeks, small lakes, acres of wetland, and the Grand and Red Cedar rivers that provided surroundings the wildlife sought. It was also a setting that easily sustained Native Americans. Clearings suitable for gardens, swamps rich in natural foods and medicinal herbs, good hunting grounds, and fish-laden water attracted Suak, Chippewa, Potawatomi, Ottawa, and Fox tribes.

Radical changes in the legal system occurred in Michigan during the final years of British reign. This brief period, beginning in 1789 and ending in 1796, changed the court structure, negated Indian law, and caused residents to question their rights and representation.

The Revolutionary War had ended seven years earlier. A new government was being formed by elected officials in Philadelphia and New York City. The Northwest Ordinance of 1787 had been approved by the Confederate Congress and was being implemented. English rule had officially ended in the United States when the well-entrenched British in Canada reorganized their political and judicial system. At the beginning of 1788, Canada continued to claim Michigan as part of the Province of Montreal.

Civilian criminal trials were conducted at the British forts under military supervision. Fort commandants were encouraged to transport prisoners under guard to Montreal for trial at the King's Bench. Leaders at the remote forts of Detroit and Mackinac found this a hardship when adverse weather conditions and dwindling manpower made following the law a dangerous undertaking. Civil cases, excluding those under Indian law, were also to be heard at Montreal. Unless the plaintiffs had time, funds, or a strong dedication to furthering their legal interests, the case often was not pursued.

The Loyalists who had left the United States began pressuring Canada's governor, Sir Guy Carleton, to give settlers more rights. They wanted writs of habeas corpus, trial by jury, British commercial law, and an elected assembly. Aware of the revolt in the colonies south of Canada, Carleton realized that the demands could develop into a serious confrontation. He responded by establishing four more administrative districts in the vast North American holdings that the British continued to claim. Each district had a court of common pleas, an appointed sheriff, and justices of the peace.

One of the new districts, the District of Hesse, included a portion of what is now southern Ontario and all the territory west of Lakes Huron, St. Clair, and Erie. Michigan residents were designated by Canadian authorities as living in the District of Hesse, but many people living in and around Detroit were dissatisfied with this arrangement. Most of them were not of English descent and claimed that law enforcement officials and the courts judged them unfairly. Historical records tend to support their claims.

Just prior to the establishment of the District of Hesse, Colonel Henry Hamilton, the appointed lieutenant governor of Detroit, had performed several acts of questionable legality that upset Michigan residents and disturbed the

Canadian authorities at Montreal. On several occasions, Hamilton had held court at Detroit, impaneled juries, acted as judge, and issued cruel and unusual punishment.

Court records of that time detail two trials that were heard by the same jury. A Frenchman was found guilty of stealing furs from a Detroit merchant and hanged for the offense. Ann Wyley, a former slave, fared no better. The black woman, found guilty of stealing a purse that contained six guineas, was hanged in Detroit's public commons.

The British Parliament passed the Canada Act in 1791, establishing Upper and Lower Canada and revamping the court system, and organizing the election of representatives to the assembly. Residents in the District of Hesse sensed an opportunity for more representational rule, but were later disappointed. The newly organized court system consisted of a Court of Common Pleas and Prerogative Court to handle the civil cases. Serious crimes were judged in the criminal court "of Oyer and Terminer and General Gaol Delivery." In the District of Hesse the same judge, William Drummer Powell, presided over each court.

Powell, a former Bostonian and Loyalist, was considered an honorable person whose character was seldom questioned by Michigan citizens. The legal principle that irritated the residents on the west side of the Detroit river was that the same judge sat on two different courts and passed judgment on his own decisions when a case was appealed to the higher court.

Along with an unsatisfactory court system, the District of Hesse lacked practicing attorneys. The area, also known as Michigan, had one lawyer— Detroit resident Walter Roe. Not until late in 1792 did another lawyer appear, and he was the appointed attorney general.

Outside the sparsely settled lake shore areas, Michigan's interior remained a land for Native Americans and the European trappers, explorers, and traders. Thoughts of lawyers and courts probably were furthest from the minds of Hugh Heward and his French-speaking guides as they paddled their heavily laden canoe into a widening section of the Grand River.

Heward, a clerk and bookkeeper for the Askin and Robertson fur interests in Detroit, was history's first recorded visitor to the area that became Ingham County. There is little doubt that his journal entries are describing the first trip through Lansing by a European. It was April 24, 1790, when Heward's exploration party passed through what was to become Michigan's capital city more than half a century later. The earliest description of the site of Lansing went into his journal that night: ". . . the banks of Red Land from thence came to a River from the East & a little lower two Cabins of Indians from Sagana they were providing Cannots (canoes) for their departure the course to this Time nearly Nore West by Nore from then high broken Land & some pine & Cedar about 11 oclock came to an Island in the Middle of the River & along Rapid. . . ."

Heward was in the Michigan portion of the Northwest Territory of the United States of America, so decreed in that body's Ordinance of 1787, four years after Britain had ceded the area in the Treaty of Paris. But the British steadfastly refused to relinquish their fur trading posts, knowing that the fledgling United States lacked the money and military might to enforce the treaty.

British fur merchants at Detroit sent Heward's party into the Michigan interior with instructions to trade guns for furs with the Native Americans. An ulterior motive, some historians believe, was to arm the Indians against the United States in order to back up a plan by the English merchants in order to obtain a grant of twenty million acres covering the entire Lower Peninsula of Michigan and the northern parts of Illinois, Indiana, and Ohio.

The great plan collapsed when General "Mad Anthony" Wayne defeated the British-supplied Native Americans at the Battle of Fallen Timbers in Ohio in August 1794. Two years later, convinced that the Americans could now capture Detroit, facing a decline in the fur trade and again at war with France, England signed the Jay Treaty and on July 11, 1796, lowered the Union Jack at Detroit. The Stars and Stripes flying over Detroit represented the fourth nation to rule this land. Native American nations were forced to cede ultimate authority to France, then the British, and finally the United States of America.

2

A COUNTY NAMED INGHAM

The exodus of the British from Detroit did not mean that statehood would follow immediately. The new territory on the western frontier underwent several boundary changes, occupation of Detroit by the British in the War of 1812, and an involved border dispute with the state of Ohio, before statehood became a reality. In the end it was the completion of the Erie Canal with a speedy, safe, and inexpensive means of transporting family members and possessions that heralded Michigan's acceptance as the twenty-sixth state.

Michigan was governed first as part of the Northwest Territory with its center of government at Marietta, Ohio. In 1800, the Michigan "mitten" was split by a north-south line, the eastern part remaining in the Northwest Territory and the western half joining Indiana Territory, which encompassed all of present-day Indiana, Illinois, and Wisconsin.

When Ohio became a state in 1803, all of Michigan became Wayne County, Indiana Territory. Michigan's growing cadre of pioneer citizens were unhappy with this arrangement because Indiana, then in the initial stages of territorial government, was awarded all the territory's representatives in the Congress and Michigan again fell under the rule of a federally appointed governor and judges. The Indiana Territorial Capital, located at Vincennes in the southwestern portion of the area, was even more remote for Michigan residents than Marietta.

In an act signed by President Thomas Jefferson on June 30, 1805, Michigan acquired full-fledged territorial status. Its southern boundary was a line from the southern tip of Lake Michigan drawn due eastward to the Lake Erie shore.

By 1818, with Indiana and Illinois already states, Michigan Territory was expanded to include Wisconsin and the Upper Peninsula west of Whitefish Point, with the territorial capital at Detroit. The eastern tip of the Upper Peninsula was already part of Michigan. That configuration continued until Michigan officials determined they had sufficient population in the "mitten" to apply for statehood.

The population boom had been gaining momentum since the end of American-British hostilities in 1814, when settlers, chiefly from the New England states, started moving into the territory. In 1800, the census showed Michigan had 3,106 residents, and approximately 4,000 in 1810. By 1820, there were 8,765 citizens. Ten years later, the population had jumped to 31,640. The opening of the Erie Canal can be credited for this influx of people into Michigan.

Much of Michigan law is rooted in the Northwest Ordinance and its companion Ordinance of 1785, which established division of western lands into townships six miles square, each divided into thirty-six numbered sections of 640 acres apiece. Land would be sold by section at government auctions at a minimum price of one dollar per acre.

The Ordinance of 1785 is recognized as one of the most important legislative measures in American history, chiefly because it established the basic policy for disposal of all of the country's western lands and for a land survey before settlement. The consequences of this land ordinance are enormous, seen today in the orderly checkerboard pattern east-west and north-south dividing lines between Michigan counties and the crisscross layout of the state's rural roads, farms and fields parallel to the base and meridian lines of the public land survey. Michigan's meridian and base lines intersect in Ingham County, a few miles southeast of what is today Leslie.

Equally important to Michigan history is the Ordinance of 1787 or The Northwest Ordinance, dividing the "western lands" into territories and spelling out the procedures for territories to gain statehood. In an 1887 address reprinted in the *Michigan Pioneer and Historical Collections*, Michigan Governor Cyrus G. Luce referred to the Northwest Ordinance as "good law, good patriotism and essential to the preservation of the freedom of the people and the enjoyment of civil liberty a hundred years ago, and is equally so today." The framers of the Northwest Ordinance, Luce said, also declared that "the inhabitants of said territory shall always be entitled to the benefits of habeas corpus, of a trial by jury, of a proportionate representation of the people in the legislature and of judicial proceedings according to the course of common law. No cruel or unjust punishment shall be inflicted, no man shall be deprived of his liberty, or his property, but by the judgment of his peers or the law of the land."

Another section of the 1787 Ordinance, hammered out a full two years before the Constitution of the United States was ratified, was its "crowning glory," Luce told his audience. "Article Six . . . has often been quoted and righteously revered by lovers of freedom everywhere," he said of the principle that welded the northwestern states during the nation's tragic trial in 1860-64. "It reads, 'There shall be neither slavery nor involuntary servitude in the said territory, otherwise than in the punishment of crime, whereof the party shall have been duly convicted.'

"The adoption of this one single provision," Luce stressed, "has changed the whole past, present and future of the empire. It has established freedom as the cornerstone of American civilization. No wiser thoughts were coined into words or law than these. If the fathers had neglected to have placed this one single provision . . . the whole character of our people, of our institutions . . . would in all human probability have changed . . ."

Luce emphasized that when the Ordinance was framed, there were no representatives in Congress from the five states eventually formed from the Northwest Territory. "Doubtless if it had not been for this prohibitory ordinance," Luce continued, "slavery, with its blighting influence, would have crossed the Ohio and entrenched itself in this territory dedicated forever to freedom and its blessings."

The Northwest Ordinance established ground rules for how the western lands would acquire statehood, providing for a division into at least five states and requiring a population of at least sixty thousand for a territory to apply for admission to the Union.

At first, the population requirement kept Michigan Territory from even hoping for state status. The War of 1812 kept new settlers away, since the territorial capital at Detroit was occupied by British forces and the Lower Great Lakes were the scenes of recurring naval battles. Michigan also had the reputation as a swampy, infested wilderness. One report from government surveyors claimed the area had so much inferior land it wasn't worth a survey.

One of the best things that occurred to further Michigan statehood was the appointment of Lewis Cass as territorial governor by President James Madison on October 29, 1813. Cass, a U.S. Army general who had served briefly as commandant of Fort Detroit earlier that year, headed an 1820 expedition that resulted in a report bringing considerable attention to Michigan and eventually helped persuade Congress to appropriate funds for roads. Cass remained as governor until 1831, leaving to serve as President Andrew Jackson's secretary of war.

Completion of the Erie Canal in 1825, coupled with a revised land act, progress on the land survey, the road building activity, and assurance that the Native Americans were not a threat, spurred settlement of southern Michigan's rural areas. For as little as $10.00, farm families could finance a trip from the state of New York to Detroit by using the waterways. A Michigan pioneer with as little as $100.00 could purchase title to 80 acres at $1.25 an acre. By 1825, land sales were booming. The Detroit land office sold 92,332 acres that year. The wooded lands and prairies in southern Michigan began to be dotted with farms.

With the population steadily increasing, it was time for the establishment of local government. Governor Cass had organized Wayne County in 1815. Within six years, Monroe, Macomb, Oakland, and St. Clair counties were added to the list. Washtenaw and Lenawee counties joined in 1826. Seven more, including Ingham, were established in 1829.

The establishment of four of the seven so called "cabinet counties"—each named for a member of President Andrew Jackson's cabinet—was accomplished by the Legislative Council of the Territory of Michigan on November 5, 1829, and Ingham was the first one mentioned. The county was named for Samuel D. Ingham, Jackson's secretary of the treasury.

Cass, an astute lawyer, politician, statesman, and staunch Jackson supporter, was anxious to curry any favors he could with those in Washington for help in Michigan's bid for statehood. Publicizing the Jackson cabinet members by attaching their names to Michigan counties only a few months after they had taken office was a masterpiece of public relations.

Most of the established cabinet counties were not organized for another nine years—two years after statehood had been attained—but by that time, several townships in the county already had organized with complete rosters of officials carrying on local government functions. "Establishment" of a county meant merely that its borders were officially delineated according to surveying terms and it was given a name; "organization" came when qualified residents (free, adult, male taxpayers) were allowed to elect their own county officials. The voting right was granted by Congress in 1825 at Cass's urging.

"Michigan fever" spread rapidly in the mid-1830s. The federal land offices sold over four million acres of the mitten peninsula in 1836, a significant increase compared to the 1833 sales of 447,780 acres.

Michigan's first official try at statehood came on December 11, 1833, when congressional delegate Lucius Lyon presented a petition to Congress asking it to pass an enabling act. The House of Representatives turned down the request and the Senate tabled it mainly because of a border dispute between Michigan Territory and the state of Ohio, both claiming a strip of land that included present-day Toledo.

The rejection out of Washington, D.C., prompted the acting governor of Michigan Territory, Stevens T. Mason, and the Michigan Territorial Council to take action. They framed a motion to form a state government and demand admission to the Union. They contended that the Northwest Ordinance provided that a territory was eligible for statehood once its population reached sixty thousand. The council had ordered a census taken in October 1834 and found that over sixty thousand people were living in the Michigan mitten. At an election held on April 14, 1835, delegates were chosen for a state constitutional convention scheduled the next month at Detroit.

Mason had been officially in Michigan's limelight for four years, starting as an assistant to his father, John T. Mason, the territory's appointed secretary. Young Mason was nineteen at the time his political career began. When the elder Mason left for a mission to Texas that was never fully explained, he persuaded President Jackson to appoint his son as secretary. Then, when appointed Governor of Michigan Territory George B. Porter died unexpectedly, Stevens

T. Mason became full-time acting governor in mid-1834 and soon won the enthusiastic support of the people in spite of his tender age of twenty-three.

The young Democrat leader by then had an additional qualification to offer the citizens he served. He had just become a lawyer. Some historians credit him with being Michigan's youngest lawyer, but that is questionable. Mason was qualified, however, to practice law through a series of self-taught courses.

Michigan's first constitutional convention was called to order on May 11, 1835, with ninety-one elected delegates from the seventeen districts. Forty-six of the delegates were from three counties surrounding Detroit. Democrats were in the majority and Ingham County had no delegates. It was an established county but at this time not an organized county with a formal government. Several of the delegates would later move to Ingham County and become influential politicians.

One outspoken convention delegate was William Woodbridge, the former secretary of Michigan Territory, the territory's first elected delegate to the Congress of the United States, ex-territorial supreme court judge, and a Whig. At age fifty-five, Woodbridge was considered by many as the best legal mind in the territory. Woodbridge insisted that the state constitution include a minimum age requirement of thirty years of age for the office of governor. Democrat delegates complained that the old politician was attacking Mason's age, being vindictive and unfair to the prime candidate for Michigan's first elected governor. Woodbridge lost his point that year in a decision that became a political party vote; but succeeding Michigan constitutions included an age requirement for the state's top executive.

A convention highlight was a surprise visit by Cass on June 2. He brought along from Washington a gift for "the State of Michigan." Cass had designed a Michigan state seal, with the help of an artist in the U.S. Treasury Department, which included the Latin motto "Si Quaeris Peninsulam Amoenam Circumspice" that Michigan has retained through the decades.

To this day, the date on the seal is a.d. MCDDDXXXV (1835), although statehood did not materialize for another eighteen months. The discrepancy caused confusion during Michigan's centennial in 1937 and sesquicentennial in 1987.

While Cass and Michigan Territorial Congressional Delegate Lucius Lyon worked feverishly back in Washington to convince Congress to recognize Michigan, the residents of the "new state" pushed for an early ratification of their constitution. It was approved by a five-to-one margin on October 5, 1835. Mason was elected the state's first governor the following day, defeating Major John Biddle, 7,508 to 814.

The new self-declared state soon learned it could not bluff its way into the Union. When the three newly chosen representatives and senators arrived in Washington in December, they were not permitted to assume congressional seats. United States Representative Issac Crary and Senators Lyon and John Norvell had to be content with sitting in the galleries to learn first-hand what Congress intended for Michigan's struggle for statehood.

Meanwhile, the First Michigan Legislature was called to order on the first Monday in November but moved cautiously, aware that Michigan citizens had created a tangled political mess. The twenty-three-year-old state governor, Stevens T. Mason, gave his inaugural address and advised that first legislature to do nothing. The lawmakers adjourned thirteen days later.

During 1836, insistence on Michigan retaining the Ohio border strip (the bloodless Toledo War in 1835 was "fought" over the disputed boundary) began to diminish and even Mason was showing signs of wavering. Cooler heads were realizing the state's success depended on economic growth, new settlers, and an adequate transportation system. The politically underdog Whigs, however, opposed a boundary compromise from the start and for a time so did the more conservative Democrats, led by Senate President Pro Tem John S. Barry. He discussed the situation in letters to Congressman Lyon, saying he feared Michigan should not accept the federal version that gave Ohio the narrow strip of land because he was certain it could never be regained through the courts. Two days after writing that assessment, Barry dashed off a follow-up message to Lyon, suggesting, "If Congress gives us the usual bounty given all new States, as one of the people I shall give my assent to the alteration of the boundaries . . ."

Lyon, an astute politician from Grand Rapids, decided to lobby with his constituents. In a March 31, 1836, letter to the editors of the *Detroit Free Press*, the congressman explained how Henry Schoolcraft, as a federal commissioner, was then wrapping up a treaty purchase with the Ottawa and Chippewa Indians that would place the upper half of Michigan's lower peninsula and two-thirds of the Upper Peninsula in American ownership. "Of the country purchased," Lyon wrote, "about 4,000,000 acres extending from the Grand River north is known to be fine land for settlement, and within a very few years we shall no doubt see towns springing up at the mouths of all the rivers flowing into Lake Michigan, for a hundred miles north, if not all around the lower peninsula. The Upper Peninsula is known to contain vast forests of the very best pine, which is even now much wanted in Ohio, Indiana and Illinois and the southern part of Michigan and Wisconsin, and must very shortly furnish the material of a highly valuable trade."

By June, word reached Detroit that Congress had passed the Northern Ohio Boundary Bill. That legislation offered Michigan statehood and the western two-thirds of the Upper Peninsula (the original state of Michigan included only the eastern portion of the Upper Peninsula) in exchange for relinquishing its claim to jurisdiction over the Toledo strip. There was one other condition: Michigan must convene a popularly elected convention to approve the compromise offer.

The Michigan reaction was predictable. Residents of the new state resented the congressional action. In late September, elected delegates gathered at Ann Arbor and turned down the offer by a vote of 28 to 21. Prospects of losing up to $500,000 in federal land sale revenues available only to states, however, plus the realization that resistance no longer made much sense, led Michigan to hold a second convention in December 1836. Mason called the elected delegates into a special session at Ann Arbor on December 14 in what became labeled by detractors as the "Frost Bitten Convention." After two days, the assemblage unanimously ratified the compromise.

The fever pitch that Michigan's citizenry had reached, even in backwoods areas, is reflected in two petitions circulated in central Ingham County on December 2, 1836, two weeks before the convention, imploring an end to the local anarchy in which the pioneer residents were mired. Covering all bases and wishing to avoid having to duplicate their efforts, the circulators addressed the petitions "To the Honourable Legislature of the Territory or State of Michigan."

They read:

> We the undersigned petitioners respectfully represent ourselves as being without any organized form of transacting business or enforcing law, feeling ourselves much embarrassed for want of roads, schools and officers to transact town business legally, do humbly request your honourable body to organize us who are the inhabitants of or have interests in the four surveyed towns or either of them, including Town 2 North of Range 1 East Town 3 North of Range 1 East Town 2 North of Range 2 East and Town 3 North of Range 2 East comprising one town entitled East Ingham, for our mutual and present benefit, in judiciary purposes, until it shall become expedient for each to transact business in their own respective capacities as individual towns. Dated at Ingham Dec. 2, 1836.

The two petitions contain fifty-two signatures, including that of Caleb Carr, who would become an elected justice of the peace in the township and a "law and order man." These documents may now be viewed in the Michigan State Archives.

The legislature took the proper action before its session ended. The area that eventually included all of Ingham, Wheatfield, Leroy, and White Oak townships was organized as Ingham Township early in 1838. An earlier act dated March 3, 1837, had created Ingham Township and also formed Aurelius Township from all townships west of the meridian line.

Historic Michigan, Volume III, edited by George N. Fuller, chronicles the first Ingham Township meeting at the home of Caleb Carr in the spring of 1838

with twenty-five voters present to organize the township and elect township officers. A lengthy discussion occurred over the need to elect a justice of the peace.
The recorded minutes say "some wanted no judiciary or justice as there was no
county seat or county judge."

Prior to the political activity in Ingham County in January 1837, Congress
had again taken up Michigan's statehood question as one of its first orders of
business in the new year. The matter dragged on through several debates before
Michigan's admission to the Union was finally approved on January 26. Late
that afternoon, the bill was signed by President Jackson.

Only six hundred miles separated Detroit from the nation's capital but it
took a horse-mounted courier two weeks in the dead of winter to bring the
news of statehood to a waiting Michigan. The celebration began that night,
February 9. Michigan was no longer a state in limbo.

3

COURTS AND PROSECUTING
ATTORNEYS

The surveyors who crossed the land that would become Ingham County saw the miles of swampland, heavy forests, and undulating prairies. They must have had thoughts about the possibilities of the area for its future inhabitants. Many settlers would purchase land sight unseen.

The area required people who were willing to give up the luxuries of their native towns in eastern states, were unafraid of howling wolves and roaming bears, and would labor beyond the usual day's work. Men, women, and children would be required to pull together without the restraints of age or sex determining their capabilities.

Such people did settle in Ingham County to homestead not only the farms but a government with law and order. The majority of the county's first families were, or would become, identified with the courts and the bar. The Lowes, the Tuttles, the Montgomerys, and the Lindermans came before statehood. Because they settled in separate townships it is possible they never knew each other until the county organized in 1838. These families had the necessary fortitude to be successful. So did the second wave of Ingham County settlers—the Cases, the Burchards, the Danforths, the Kilbournes, and the Longyears. It was a courage they were able to pass on to their offspring; a resolve to make the county not only productive and pleasant but to make law and order a primary requirement. From these families came sheriffs, lawyers, prosecutors, judges, and justices whose decisions and actions have impact on Ingham County life today.

Of the men who settled in the county and founded the villages and cities in the first decade land was available, there were two who could be called the "grandfathers" of the Ingham County Bar Association. One was Joseph Kilbourne, Ingham County's first member of the State House of Representatives and the father of the Bar Association's founder. The other was John Burchard, Ingham County's first prosecuting attorney, Lansing's first resident, Lansing

Township's first lawyer, and father of the woman whom the Bar Association's founder took as his bride. Neither was a county resident when Ingham County was organized by a legislative act on April 3, 1838.

By then, the county's population was more than eight hundred. Later that spring, 159 voters from seven organized townships elected a temporary slate of county officers, including a three-man commission to conduct county business until permanent officers could be chosen in the autumn election.

From the outset, partisan politics was part of government in Michigan's counties, and Ingham County was no exception. Even in that organizational meeting in 1838, party lines were tightly drawn. In at least one office, brother opposed brother. The Whigs nominated Peter Lowe for sheriff and the Democrats nominated his brother, Richard. Richard Lowe won the short-term office, but was replaced in the November election by Amaziah Winchell, who held the office for the Democrats for four years. Peter Lowe was not without a job. He was elected county clerk in the fall, replacing short-termer Valorous Meeker. Lowe retained that office for the Whigs for fourteen years.

The meeting place for the canvass of that initial county election was specified in the organization act: ". . . at the dwelling house nearest the county seat of said county, on the Thursday next after said election." Two years earlier, on April 7, 1836, Acting Territorial Governor Stevens T. Mason was sent a report of a three-man commission he had named to locate a seat for Ingham County. Mason confirmed the location in a June 15, 1836, proclamation. The land was owned by Charles T. Thayer of Ann Arbor. He quickly laid out a village on his acreage about two miles due east of Mason and named it "Ingham." But neither the village nor the county seat ever developed there.

County histories agree that there was immediate dissension over the county seat site and several petitions were sent to the legislature to change it, a process that consumed four years.

So it was that the first meeting of Ingham County Board of Supervisors in October 1838 was held at the home of Hiram Parker, his house being the closest dwelling to the phantom county seat location.

Section 3 of Ingham County's organization act decreed that, "The Circuit Court for the county of Ingham shall be held on the first Tuesdays of June and November, in each year, and, until convenient buildings be erected at the county seat, at such place in said county as the supervisors or commissioners thereof shall direct." Finally, Ingham court sessions would be held in the county and not at Jackson in Jackson County. Ingham County had previously been judicially attached to Jackson County.

Another section of the act provided that all Ingham County lawsuits and criminal cases then pending before Jackson County judges "shall be prosecuted to the final judgment and execution." The remoteness of justice prior to the organization of Ingham County caused hardships on residents who were required to attend court sessions. They either made the laborious trip to Jackson on horseback, by ox-drawn conveyance, or on foot.

The situation did produce its humorous moments. One constable presented a bill for taking a suspect to the jail in Jackson; it included use of six oxen to haul the prisoner, service of four men for two days, and hire of two horses for the officers. "When they delivered the prisoner and arrived at home," related the account based on Michigan Pioneer Society reports, "the first man the officers met was the prisoner, who had paid his fine and arrived at home ahead of his captors."

Ingham County early court quarters were humble. Sessions were held in the log schoolhouse situated at what a century later were Jefferson and Oak streets, several blocks south of downtown Mason. The first session, on November 12, 1839, is recorded in the court's initial volume of court journals. The meager details of the proceedings are written in a flowing hand with pen and ink by the county clerk, Peter Lowe. Supreme Court Justice William A. Fletcher, the judge assigned to Ingham County, presided and was assisted by Associate Judges Amos Steele and William Child. The first order of business was the swearing in of a panel of grand jurors and a panel of petit jurors who would hear the cases.

The first criminal cases involved Elijah Woodworth and Ezekiel Critchett, charged with disturbing a religious meeting in Leslie Township. In a companion action, Woodworth and Amos Workman were defendants in a civil suit in which James Leek, apparently the owner of the home where the prayer meeting was held, was claiming damages of $158.21.

John W. Burchard, in perhaps his first jury case, represented "The People" and Phineus Farrand of Jackson represented Woodworth, and perhaps Critchett. And, in an arrangement that would later be disallowed in Michigan's court system, Burchard also represented Leek in the civil action. The criminal case had a ring that became familiar to later generations of lawyers and court followers. Both men pleaded not guilty and their cases were adjourned after Woodworth posted bail of $100.00 and Critchett, also charged with assaulting an officer, put up a $500.00 bond.

The cases were again adjourned in 1840 but on May 4, 1841, Woodworth was convicted, as was Critchett at a later date. Both were fined $5.00 for disturbing the prayer meeting as assessed costs of prosecution. Leek was subsequently awarded a $158.21 judgment against Woodworth.

A postscript to the Critchett case found its way into the Michigan State Archives, which has ninety-six volumes of Ingham County Circuit Court records from 1839 to 1927; the records were turned over to the state when the county ran out of storage space. Most of the early criminal files are missing, but one containing the arrest warrants, justice court appearances, bond documents, subpoenas, and jury summonses for the Critchett trial is in the archives. It also contains a tabulation of the state's costs at the trial, submitted by Prosecutor

Burchard and signed "J.W. Burchard, Notary Public." The bill lists filing fees for various court documents, fees for serving subpoenas on witnesses and notices on jurors, and Burchard's pay, listed under "Pros. Atty. fee—$7." The total cost of the trial was $23.17.

Requirements for practicing law in the nineteenth century were not as demanding as they would be one hundred years later. Several of the important political leaders carried the title of "Judge" with their name although they had little legal training, were not lawyers and, at least in some cases, had been appointed rather than elected to their judicial posts. State law at that time did not require that a probate judge hold a law degree or be a member of the bar.

Prosecuting attorneys, too, were appointed by the governor and there apparently was no residence requirement. *The State of Michigan Executive Acts 1835-1846* in the Michigan Archives lists Daniel Parkhurst's appointment by Governor William Woodbridge as prosecuting attorney for Ingham County. Parkhurst resided in Jackson County. Furthermore, qualifications for admission to the bar—while not necessarily vague—were certainly not so imposing that a man who had "read law" could not gain permission to practice with little effort.

There were no newspapers in those years of the early 1840s, and there was no organized bar association. As a result, most of the early history accounts, based on interviews with "old timers" and Pioneer Society verbal recollections, many of them forty or so years after the fact, leave confusing and sometimes erroneous impressions. A century later, some modern historians perpetuated the errors.

One early history boldly asserts, "The first attorney admitted to practice was Augustus D. Hawley." The same history mentions the Critchett case (although the defendant's name is spelled Critshell) and lists his attorney as "P. Farrand." Still another early account refers to Hawley as "Ingham County's first lawyer," an honor likely bestowed through a loose interpretation of the earlier Hawley reference.

Hawley is never mentioned again in any Ingham history, and the only additional Farrand mention is in an 1880 history that listed him as the plaintiff in one of several civil suits in which he represented a man named Simeon Ford. But, according to a Jackson County history, Farrand settled there before 1838 and was among the first three or four attorneys in Jackson County. The same volume lists Hawley among a half-dozen lawyers who arrived in Jackson in 1839. One of the others, listed only as "Mr. Parkhurst," had a role in Burchard's interrupted career as the Ingham County prosecutor, although none of the Ingham history books ever mention his name.

Information from volume 1 of the *Ingham County Circuit Court Journal, 1839-1855* and other sources suggest that Burchard may have been Ingham's first attorney. Under the date of November 12, 1839, the court's first day in session, is a notation in Clerk Peter Lowe's steady hand: "On the application of A. D. Hawley for admission as an attorney of this court and on reading and filing his papers ordered that P. Farrand, J. W. Burchard and L. Chapman be appointed a committee of examination."

As it turned out, Burchard was on a committee to interrogate a Jackson lawyer seeking admission to the Ingham bar. One of Burchard's fellow examiners was another Jackson lawyer who opposed Burchard in the county's first circuit court criminal case. Justice Fletcher admitted Hawley to practice.

Ironically, a third Jackson lawyer, Daniel Parkhurst, was listed with Chapman and Burchard on the lawyer examination team considering Julius C. Smith's admission to the Ingham County Bar on May 4, 1841. It was Parkhurst who later was appointed to replace Burchard as Ingham County prosecutor, although he never served in the post.

The sketchy story of that first circuit court session held on Ingham County soil in the Mason schoolhouse is contained in one of a half-dozen leather bound volumes of handwritten journals that two Ingham County circuit judges in the 1980s took special care to preserve. Circuit Court Judge Peter Houk keeps the volumes in his chambers. They were rescued from the courthouse attic by Houk's predecessor, former Circuit Judge Robert Holmes Bell, now a United States District Court judge.

One of the salvaged volumes is volume I of the *Book of Common Rules*, containing the original seventy-five court rules of the Ingham County Circuit Court, adopted February 16, 1839, as Justice Fletcher prepared to open the court's first term. The rules, each numbered, were recorded into the book by court clerk Peter Lowe. Tailored to the conditions of their day, the rules reflect such problems as communication. One rule specified that any attorney residing or maintaining an office more than two miles from the court must appoint a local agent to act as a contact person in case the court needed to summon the lawyer.

The early journals contain frequent mentions of Burchard, who could claim the title as Ingham County's first resident lawyer and the first attorney in Mason and later in Lansing Township. Burchard was twenty-four or twenty-five years old when he moved to Mason early in 1839. He had arrived in Lenawee County earlier that year after leaving his native New York State for the Michigan frontier and the opportunities he saw offered by the new state. Born in Scipio, Cayuga County, in 1814, he grew up in the village of Moscow, New York, helping his father in the saddle and harness-making trade. John Burchard began the study of law in Rochester, New York, in 1836, his widow recalled years later, and was admitted to practice early in 1839 in Lenawee County before he moved to Mason.

On April 17 of that year, Judge E. B. Danforth, one of the Ingham County associate judges, asked Governor Mason in a letter to appoint John Woolsey Burchard, "an attorney and counsellor at Law in the village of Mason, the present county site of this county," as Ingham County prosecuting attorney. Danforth and ten fellow townsmen signed the letter.

Danforth's petition appears to have been effective. Nine days after the letter was sent, on April 26, an entry appears in volume 8 of the *State of Michigan Executive Acts* preserved in the State Archives: "On this day, the following appointment was made by the executive [Stevens T. Mason] J.W. Burchard, prosecuting attorney, Ingham County."

At that time, the state constitution, ratified in 1835, was the ruling document for the recently organized county of Ingham. The constitution specified that the elected governor appoint county prosecuting attorneys. Almost immediately flaws appeared in this procedure for selecting county chief law officers. The next constitutional convention (1850) would recommend elimination of that procedure.

Justice continued to move slowly in Ingham County, delayed in large part by the fact that it had a county seat in name only. Dissatisfaction was expressed at the Ingham village site even by the commissioners who selected it. A new candidate for the county seat location surfaced when Jefferson City, about three and one-half miles north of Mason, was suggested. That village already boasted having thirteen houses, a saw mill, and a schoolhouse.

But Mason Centre, as it was first called, had more to offer. Judge Danforth had settled there in 1836 and built a saw mill on Sycamore Creek the next year and a grist mill in 1838. On March 6, 1840, the state legislature in Detroit settled the county seat question. It passed an act vacating the location of the village of Ingham and decreed that the "seat of justice shall be permanently located and established at the village of Mason . . . provided that the proprietors of land in said village shall deed to the county commissioners or supervisors . . . at least five acres of land within said village, for the use and benefit of said county."

The five acres were deeded by "Charles Noble and wife," according to Durant's *History of Ingham County*. Noble and Danforth together owned about seven-eighths of the land in the original village plat.

Within a month, the county commissioners were busy providing a temporary location to conduct county business. The commissioners resolved to build a county clerk's and register's office and specified its completion by September 15. Emmons White was named as the contractor and agreed to build the office for $325.

The office was completed on time; but the structure, sixteen by twenty-four feet, was too high off the ground, a problem solved when Judge Danforth agreed to build a porch and steps for $9.00, "making the total cost $334," according to Durant.

Not everyone doing business with the county fared as well as the judge. The first item of business at the initial meeting of the three-man county board of commissioners on November 20, 1838, was a certificate and affidavit by Native American Wo Non Quit, proving he had killed a wolf within the county and was claiming the bounty of $8.00 offered by the state and $2.50 by the county.

A half century later, Durant wrote, "The board thereupon magnanimously allowed him the state bounty . . . but paid him no county bounty. At the same time, Mr. William Dewey presented his certificate and affidavit showing he had taken five wolf scalps and the board at once allowed him both state and county bounty . . . but then, possibly the Indian never knew the difference. The discrimination was a delicate one."

By 1842, Ingham County officials were anxiously looking for a place to hold court. The new board of supervisors resolved to erect a courthouse "at a cost not exceeding $800" and to pay for it by appropriating that amount, $600 of it to be paid in state bonds and $200 in county-owned real estate. The building was erected the next year by William Hammond & Co. James Turner was paid $100 for painting and $42 for furnishing and installing stoves and stove pipes. John Coatsworth was allowed 74¢ per rod for building a wooden fence around the new court house. Hiram Smith painted the fence yellow, with white trimmings, for $3.75.

Even with the seeming economies—and the fact that the total bill included painting and a fence—some of the supervisors apparently were not satisfied. When it came time to accept the new court house, the vote was eight in favor and seven against.

To pay the county's share of the construction bill, the supervisors in June 1843 authorized J. W. Burchard "to sell the lots belonging to the county," Durant recorded, noting, "Mr. Burchard was at that time prosecuting attorney for the county." The explanation was necessary because Burchard's term as prosecutor had ended abruptly on January 7, 1840, when William Woodbridge, a staunch Whig, took the oath as Michigan's governor. Burchard, realizing a scandal involving Governor Mason had spelled the "boy governor's" political doom, had arranged to be nominated in the fall primary for Ingham County treasurer and won the election in November, serving in that post during 1841.

Meanwhile, Woodbridge, only thirteen months into his term, resigned to become a U.S. Senator on February 23, 1841. The next day Lt. Governor James Wright Gordon became acting governor of Michigan.

Woodbridge had appointed a Jackson County man, Daniel Parkhurst, as Ingham County prosecutor, but there is no record that he ever served in the office. By the end of the year, Ingham County officials were desperate for a prosecutor. And in Detroit, a new governor, Democrat John S. Barry, took office on January 3, 1842.

Burchard, with no assurance he could return to the prosecutor's job, had become interested in another venture. Up north a dozen miles was Lansing Township, in the northwest corner of the county, where the Red Cedar River met the Grand River. The name "Lansing" for the extreme northwest corner of Ingham County was first used in the act authorizing organization of the township, passed February 16, 1842. The name was suggested by Joseph E. North

Sr., one of the area's original settlers, named after the township in the state of New York from where he had emigrated.

A friend of Burchard's, James Seymour, owned much of the land on both sides of the Grand River, including that around a rapids just north of where the river made a wide swing as it flowed westward toward Eaton County. Seymour had acquired from the original owner what many considered a perfect mill site when the latter became ill and left the state.

Burchard started negotiating with Seymour for the Lansing dam site. County records show that Seymour sold the southeast quarter of Section 9, which included land on both sides of the Grand River, to Burchard on October 13, 1841. Seymour provided Burchard with a warranty deed and Burchard mortgaged the property to Seymour to secure part of the purchase price. Like many of his fellow attorneys, Burchard also became a businessman with ideas of supplementing his meager lawyer's income.

The young lawyer/miller-to-be had more mouths to feed than his own. Soon after he became county treasurer, on April 7, 1841, Burchard married Miss Frances Haynes. She was carrying their first child when they decided to move to the wilderness site as soon as they could build a house and start erecting the dam. But the energetic Judge Danforth, who found time to erect and operate saw and grist mills and build porches and steps for the county office building, figured a man of Burchard's youth could mix prosecutor's duties with those of establishing a dam and mill twelve miles from the county seat. So, once again, he talked Burchard into making himself available for prosecutor and sent him off to Detroit with a letter to Austin E. Wing, an established Michigan elder statesman. The letter, dated at Mason on January 7, 1842, somehow found its way into the State Archives. It reads:

> Dear Sir
> This county is destitute of a prosecuting att. Ex Gov. Woodbridge dur-
> ing his reign did not see fit to reappoint [word not legible] our Mr.
> Burchard, the barer of this. He is a young man of fine law talents and
> every way worthy of the appointment. Mr. Parkist [Parkhurst] the man
> appointed by Mr. Woodbridge, resided at Jackson. He has left the coun-
> try. Please give us your influence to secure the appointment of J. W.
> Burchard of this village.

Judge Danforth obviously had not seen "Mr. Parkist" in his court and apparently did not know his first name. Forty years later, the Jackson County history writer acknowledged that Daniel Parkhurst was one of a handful of lawyers who settled there before 1838. But, he recorded, "Mr. Parkhurst remained in Jackson but a year or two, and went away."

Could that have been early in 1840? Volume 8 of the *Executive Acts* in the Michigan Archives reveals this information under the date March 17, 1840: "By Gov. William Woodbridge, Daniel Parkhurst, appointed prosecuting attorney for the remainder of the term of [Mr.] Chapman of Jackson County and also prosecuting attorney for Ingham County." Anxious to appoint yet another Whig to county office in Michigan's interior, Woodbridge likely stretched his gubernatorial powers in making Parkhurst prosecutor of two counties with the same stroke of the pen. Parkhurst may have left the area before he had a chance to establish an early political record as the prosecutor of two counties simultaneously.

Within a week, a clerk noted on page 22 of the *Executive Acts* ledger: "February 14, 1842. On this day, the following appointments were made by and with the advice and consent of the Senate—J. W. Burchard, prosecuting attorney, Ingham County, commencing the first day of March next—by Gov. John S. Barry." Once again, John Burchard was the Ingham County prosecutor.

Within a year, Burchard was making plans to erect a cabin at the mill site and was lining up workmen to help him build his dam. Both structures would be "firsts" in what was to become the city of Lansing by the end of the decade. The only other residents of the entire Lansing Township in 1843 were the Jacob Cooleys, who lived in a cabin on the south side of the Grand River just east of the Ingham-Eaton counties line (today it is just east of the intersection of West Mt. Hope Avenue and Waverly Road in Lansing) and the family of Justus Gilkey on the north side of the river just west of the Ingham County line (near the entrance to Capital City Airport). Both homes were outside the village limits when Lansing was incorporated. Gilkey lived up to his given name and became Lansing Township's first justice of the peace.

The simple Burchard cabin of logs chinked with mud was started in early summer. But the family apparently delayed moving in until Frances gave birth to their second child. It was August 1843 before Lansing's first permanent residents settled into their rustic dwelling. A replica of the structure, constructed as accurately as possible by twentieth-century craftsmen, was built in 1959 and for several months graced the plaza of Lansing's new city hall. It was then moved to the northwest corner of Fenner Arboretum.

With his family moved in, Burchard and his hired men began building the dam that would back up the Grand River and turn the mill wheel. They completed the job before freeze-up and the family braced themselves for the winter.

The tiny cabin was surrounded by dense wilderness. At night, Burchard's widow recalled forty years later, they could hear wolves howling. The only humans they saw, except the hired men, were three families in crude river scows floating downstream.

As spring approached, Burchard made a quick trip back East to order mill-irons, pulleys, a power train, and other equipment for his mill. He obtained most of the needed equipment at Auburn, New York, in Cayuga County, and returned with the machinery, prepared to erect the sawmill as soon as the weather broke. But, as often happens in the Grand River Valley, winter hung on that spring of 1844 and there was still frozen ground and a crust of snow late in March. Then the warm winds came into Michigan from the southwest, along with early April rains—and suddenly it was spring. Just as suddenly, the Red Cedar River and the Grand River hit flood stage and a washout occurred on a portion of Burchard's dam, near the west bank.

Burchard and three hired hands—William Pierce, Alonzo Baker, and Coe Jones—ventured into the river below the dam to examine the break. As they struggled to keep the canoe steady in the churning water, it slid in a backwater too close to the falls and was carried under the sheet. The canoe quickly filled and upset and the four men were dumped into the icy waters. The three workmen managed to struggle to safety, but Burchard did not surface. Ten days later the body of John Woolsey Burchard was found on a sand bar four miles downstream at Ingersoll's mill in Delta Mills.

The former Ingham County prosecutor, Lansing Township executive, Ingham County and Lansing Township pioneer lawyer was drowned on his third wedding anniversary at thirty years of age. A few days before his death, Burchard had been elected Lansing Township supervisor. After his death, Burchard's widow left Lansing and the property again reverted to James Seymour, who completed the mill and sold the site. Frances Burchard eventually remarried and moved to Jackson. Her son, John W. Burchard Jr., grew up to become a Leslie Township farmer; her daughter, Louisa, became the wife of Samuel Kilbourne, a noted Lansing attorney and founder of the Ingham County Bar Association.

4

FINALLY, A COUNTY SEAT

As the decade of the 1840s approached its mid-point, Mason had become a bustling community on the Ingham County frontier. New Englanders emigrating westward, with the Erie Canal providing a relatively inexpensive and rapid means of moving, brought their businesses with them or started anew in Michigan. Mason quickly boasted general stores, a sawmill and gristmill on the dammed Sycamore Creek, a physician, shoemaker, a blacksmith shop, and an ever-growing ring of prospering farms being cleared out of the wilderness. Public buildings were being erected. Already there was a schoolhouse, a log jail that cost $331, the wooden county office building and, in 1843, the pride of the county—the new two-story, $800 courthouse took shape on the south side of the town square. Some historical accounts indicate the courthouse was first used that year, but the circuit court's official journal mentions that the fall term of court opened on October 17, 1843, in "the school house," with Justice Charles W. Whipple presiding. Whipple opened the next term of court on April 16, 1844, with the court clerk noting the session was held "at the courthouse."

The courthouse was built on a county-owned lot on the south side of what is now Ash Street. In the 1880s, the building was moved on bobsleds to a location between South and Cherry streets. It is still serving as a residence, thanks to several additions and remodelings, nearly one hundred fifty years after it was built. A modern Ingham County Historical Commission pamphlet says the early Ingham pioneers not only held court in the structure, but gathered there for political rallies and for Sunday worship until local churches were built.

Justice Whipple was the third judge from Michigan's high court to preside over Ingham County court sessions. The first was Justice William Fletcher, who was succeeded in 1842 by Justice Alpheus Felch of Ann Arbor. Felch was to have a profound impact on Ingham County a few years later. As governor of Michigan during the 1847 session of the legislatures, he was instrumental in heading off a failed effort on the part of a number of lawmakers attempting, on the sly, to buy up several hundred acres in what eventually became downtown Lansing. A few days after Lansing became the capital site, Felch was appointed Michigan's U.S. Senator by the legislature and resigned as governor.

Felch's signatures may be found on various court documents in the 1842 and 1843 Ingham County court sessions. Tracing the judges from the clerk's notations at the beginning of each day's session can be difficult because the daily logs frequently began with the date and the notation "Present, same judges as yesterday."

Although Ingham County was still sparsely populated in the 1840s (the census showed 2,401 residents in 1840, and 8,606 a decade later), U.S. citizenship applications, hearings, and admissions were frequent. In each case, the court clerk laboriously copied into the record the entire citizenship oath administered by the presiding judge, even when several such oaths were spoken on a given day.

The case of John Norris, a native of Northumberland, England, was typical of a score or more recorded in the court's original journals. Norris's application for citizenship was recorded on October 15, 1844. It is not clear whether he had applied then, or in 1827, when he first came to the United States. But the journal says he "renounced allegiance to every foreign prince, potentate, state and soverignty [sic] whatever, especially the Queen of England [Victoria] and the govt. of Great Britain, to whom he has hitherto been a subject." Norris's admission to citizenship was recorded later in the court term.

During those early years, a number of non-lawyers served Ingham County as associate judges. They attended to jurors, signed some court documents, and generally assisted the presiding judge. Associate judges during the 1838-39 session, when the court was still held in Jackson, were Ephriam Danforth and Amos Steele. Steele and William Child served during the next term. Other associate judges included John R. Bowdish, David Johnson, Benjamin Davis, Joseph E. North, and Joseph Hunt.

In a short-lived court revision by the legislature in 1846, a new system provided for the election of a "county judge" and "second judge" in a court that had original jurisdiction of all claims above that of a justice of the peace court, and under five hundred dollars. The "county court" also had appellate jurisdiction over justice of the peace court cases. "County courts" were abolished by the state Constitution of 1850. Davis, William H. Chapman, and Mason Branch were elected Ingham County judges; Horatio Forbes and Orrin Sharp were elected as second judges. Steele and Chapman later served as Ingham probate judges.

In those pre-Lansing years, Mason was the business and legal hub of Ingham County. But after John Burchard left the county seat and attempted to extend civilization another thirteen miles into Lansing Township in the late summer of 1843, lawyers were scarce in Mason. Possibly the only resident attorney in Mason was Daniel L. Case, who came to the county seat in 1843.

Case's arrival was actually the third time he had made Michigan his home. He came to Pontiac first as a seventeen-year-old from Monroe County in New York, where his family had moved from Canada. After a brief stay in Pontiac, young Case took a job with the crew that made the original survey of the city of Jackson. In less than two years, he was back in New York studying law under Judge William J. Moody. But when Moody decided to move to Jackson, Case followed him, continued his law studies with Moody as his tutor and in 1834 married Miranda Brown, Mrs. Moody's sister. In 1836, Case again left Michigan and for the next seven years practiced law in Iowa, Louisiana, and Texas. When he arrived in Mason in 1843 and was appointed prosecuting attorney the next year to replace Burchard, it seemed to underscore the fact that qualified lawyers were scarce in Ingham County.

Case's admission to the Ingham County Bar is noted on page 65 of the initial circuit court journal under the date of August 18, 1843. "The court met pursuant to adjournment. Present the same judges as yesterday," reads the entry. "The committee appointed to examine into the legal qualifications of Daniel L. Case reported that they had discharged that duty and find that the said Daniel L. Case possesses sufficient legal knowledge and ability to discharge the duties of an attorney and counselor at law. It is therefore ordered that the said Daniel L. Case be licensed to practice as an attorney and counselor at law in the courts of this state upon filing the oath of office."

In the courtroom that day, waiting for the arraignment of one of his clients on a charge of assault with intent to murder, was a young Jackson attorney by the name of Austin Blair. Politically, he was a Whig and a few years earlier, while living near Eaton Rapids, had served a term as Eaton County clerk. Blair and Case, an avowed Democrat, would eventually battle in court on numerous occasions. Still later, Case would switch his political philosophies to the new Republican Party and join the forces promoting Blair as Michigan's governor during the Civil War period.

Governor John S. Barry first appointed Case as Ingham County prosecuting attorney on March 6, 1844, replacing Burchard, whose term had expired after he moved to Lansing. Governor Alpheus Felch reappointed Case on January 30, 1846, to a two-year term and on March 12, 1848, he was appointed to a third term by Governor Epaphroditis Ransom.

Case lived an eventful and useful life as a lawyer, flour mill owner, and mercantile business owner both in Mason and Lansing. He also served in the legislature from Ionia County and as Michigan's auditor general. He became an early leader in the Republican Party in the state and in 1862, narrowly missed being nominated to Congress "through the petty pique of one delegate," according to a news obituary in the *Lansing Republican* the day after his death on Thanksgiving Day, November 24, 1898. "But for this he would no doubt have attained great influence in public life, for no man in the state was better equipped for brilliant work as a statesman than our honored pioneer." He was eighty-seven when he died, and at that time was Ingham County's oldest resident.

Although Case outlived most of his contemporaries in the legal circle of Ingham County prior to the Civil War, others were also making history. Foremost in the effort to encourage the development of Lansing Township was James Seymour, who had purchased several hundred acres of Sections 8, 10, 15 and 17—sight unseen—in 1836. Seymour learned of the financial potential of purchasing land in Michigan's interior from his position as president of a bank in Rochester, New York. His cousin, Horatio Seymour, was a former New York governor, and historians believe the latter may have had a financial interest in the early Lansing land purchases. As late as 1880, Horatio Seymour was listed on the city's assessment rolls as owner of several vacant building lots valued at $6,900.

At Burchard's death, Seymour again became the owner of the mill site, the empty Burchard cabin, and the flood-damaged dam across the Grand River. He relieved Burchard's widow of the mortgage, and by letter from Rochester he summoned Joab Page, a carpenter, builder, millwright, tavern owner, Methodist church organizer, and jack-of-all trades.

Page, a native Vermonter, had built an iron works in Clinton, New York, and other structures in Orleans County and was known, at least by reputation, to Seymour. In 1832, Page had brought his family to Jackson County and erected the first two sawmills there in addition to two taverns near Grass Lake. When Seymour's letter caught up with him, Page was clearing a 160-acre farm in Vevay Township. The developer offered Page and a crew—which eventually included Page's son, Isaac, and his three sons-in-law—fifty cents a day per man to repair the dam and complete the mill construction. The in-laws were Whitney Smith, George Pease, and Alvin Rolfe.

The workers and their families could barely fit into the Burchard cabin; the first order of business was to enlarge the dwelling. Their intent was not to relocate in Lansing but merely to repair the dam, build the sawmill, and return to their farms.

Nearly forty years later, Page's daughter, Cornelia Page Smith, recalled those early days in pre-capital Lansing at the first annual meeting of the Ingham County Pioneer Society. Lumber for the sawmill, she said, was rafted downstream from Eaton Rapids. A large crew of men worked with her father's family group, most of them eating on the job and sleeping in the cabin at night. Her mother cooked and she baked eighteen loaves of bread each day in the open fireplace, Smith told her audience.

In the spring election of 1845, "Squire" Page was elected a Lansing Township justice of the peace and thus became the first judge in what became the city of Lansing. The germ of jurisprudence that had permeated the Burchard/Page cabin when Ingham County's first prosecutor lived there was still alive. The Page living room frequently doubled as Lansing Township Justice Court.

5

P. O. MICHIGAN, MICHIGAN

Sounds of axes and cross-cut saws were being heard more frequently in the little village taking shape between the sweeping curves of the Grand River in the northwest corner of Ingham County. The ring of the blacksmith's hammer occasionally punctuated the coarse shouts of workmen assembling homes, stores, office buildings, and millworks among the stumps in Lansing, Ingham County's newest township.

It was the summer of 1846 and there was a reason for the flurry of construction activity.

Down in Detroit, the Michigan legislature, now nearly ten years into statehood, was starting to feel pressure to establish a permanent capital city for the twenty-sixth state. And James Seymour, the young New York entrepreneur who had invested considerable money in Lansing Township frontier real estate, decided he would do everything he could to entice Michigan's lawmakers into selecting his village as the state's new seat of government.

The original constitution of 1835 had fixed the capital "at Detroit, or any other place prescribed by law, until the year 1847," when the legislature was to fix a permanent site. Agitation to make a move developed over a series of Detroit newspaper articles censuring two lawmakers for opposing the granting of some special favors to the Michigan Central Railroad Company. The result was a wave of public opinion against Detroit as a permanent capital.

The Detroit-versus-outstate fuss was fanned by the defeat of Epaphroditus Ransom of Kalamazoo by Gov. Alpheus Felch of Ann Arbor in a Whig caucus contest for one of Michigan's seats in the U.S. Senate. The legislature, which in those days selected U. S. senators every six years, subsequently chose Felch over the incumbent, Senator William Woodbridge. Politicians in both state houses blamed Detroit's political influence for Ransom's defeat and there was soon a decided majority in both legislative houses against Detroit. Within a matter of days, the final question became, "Where, outside of Detroit, will the new capital be situated?"

In a last-ditch effort to preserve Detroit's claim, a select committee headed by Representative George Throop favored delaying the decision for another ten years. Throop was the only legislator to sign the report, possibly because the others realized the constitution mandated an 1847 decision. Two other committee members signed a report opposing Detroit. The reasons for their opposition included the dangers of foreign invasion across the Detroit River, a claim that state officials could not afford to live in Detroit, and a belief that sale of the Detroit capitol would net enough funds to build an outstate capitol large enough to last at least twenty years.

Flint legislator Enos Goodrich advanced the plan that was most acceptable to the legislators. Goodrich argued for locating a permanent capital somewhere north of the Michigan Central Railroad, which then ran east and west through Jackson, to encourage rapid settlement of the state's sparse areas. He recalled the locating of Ohio's capital in the wilderness of Columbus and hailed the move as one that had welded a great state's people together.

A number of established communities, large and small, quickly made offers of free land for capital sites and use of existing buildings while new structures were being built. Among the self-appointed candidates were Ann Arbor, Albion, Battle Creek, Byron, Corunna, Dexter, Eaton Rapids, Grand Blanc, Jackson, Lyons, and Marshall. Owosso, Charlotte, Caledonia, DeWitt, Flint and even Ingham (the non-existent original county seat east of Mason) also were nominated.

Before the vote was taken in the House of Representatives, Seymour decided it was time to play his cards. He had left New York and was then living in Flushing. His holdings in Lansing Township, where his sawmill was already operating, were ideally situated for the state's capital, Seymour reasoned. He bought nearly one hundred copies of the *Farmer's Map of Michigan* and on each one of them he drew conspicuous red lines fanning out from a star he labeled "Michigan" on his town plat to most of the important communities in the state. On each line, Seymour marked the distance from the Ingham County settlement to the place connected. A copy of the map showed up one morning on the desk of each of the sixty-five representatives and twenty-two senators who made up the 1847 legislature.

A quick glance showed "Michigan" was within ninety miles of most population centers and was centrally located to Detroit, Saginaw, Grand Rapids, Kalamazoo, and Jackson. Seymour, in an accompanying letter to the lawmakers, made an offer of twenty acres of free land in the new capital city and promised "to erect on an adjoining lot, suitable buildings for the temporary use of the legislature and public officers, and lease them to the state without charge, till permanent buildings are erected." The offer was backed by a $10,000 bond. Seymour would become Lansing's first state government landlord.

As astute a politician as he was a promoter and businessman, Seymour quickly became acquainted with the influential members of both legislative houses. He especially sought out Livingston County Senator Charles Bush, president pro tem of the senate, and lawyer George W. Peck, also from Livingston County, and speaker of the house. Peck, Seymour certainly knew, already owned considerable land in Lansing Township. And he did not overlook two Ingham County lawmakers—Senator Danforth, the Mason miller and associate circuit judge, and Joseph Kilbourne, the Meridian Township farmer who represented Ingham County in the House. Both were promoting the proposal to move the capital to the Lansing Township wilderness. So was attorney William W. Upton of DeWitt, one of the youngest members of the legislature. Born in Victor, Ontario County, New York, a village that provided a name for one of Clinton County's townships, he was educated at Genesee Wesleyan Seminary at Lima, New York, and spent his collegiate summers with engineers making surveys for the Auburn and Rochester Railroad. He also signed up for law classes with a Canandaigua, New York, attorney. But around 1842 and still in his teens, he "was induced to survey and lay out a canal in northern Indiana," according to a biography in Durant's *History of Ingham County*.

That brought the future Lansing attorney closer to Michigan, and within a year he had purchased land in what became Victor Township, Clinton County, and "had cleared up a farm." In the meantime, he continued law studies (with) Levi Townsend of Dewitt, and was admitted to practice about 1845.

Decades later, Upton recalled that he met Charles P. Bush on his way to the 1847 legislative session and they immediately struck up a friendship. Bush and Upton's father-in-law, Joseph Hollister, had been boyhood friends and neighbors back in New York. Bush, president pro tem of the Senate, took the freshman representative under his wing and even proposed that they room together in Detroit.

Upton tells the intriguing story of the in-fighting, caucuses in smoke-filled rooms, rumors of attempted vote buying, and other political chicanery in an article, *Locating the Capital of the State of Michigan*, first published by the Michigan Historical Commission in the summer 1939 issue of *Michigan History Magazine*. William Upton was just beginning his exciting public career when he stood up in the old State House on January 28, 1847, and introduced the bill that finally became the law permanently locating Michigan's capital at Lansing. In his version of the capital-moving legislation, Upton says he was selected to introduce the bill in the house and to outline Seymour's offer "probably by the advice of Mr. Bush." He also suggests his choice may have been because "I lived closer to this unheard of place—Lansing—than any other member." (Kilbourne's Okemos farm was probably about seven miles away, and Upton's property approximately six miles.)

During the House debate, Ann Arbor, Byron, Detroit, Dexter, Eaton Rapids, Grand Blanc, Jackson, and Marshall all lost out in roll call votes. Lyons actually won 30-28 in one balloting but the House later reversed itself. Lansing's winning margin on the first vote was 35-27 and by the third vote was 48-17.

When the Senate got the bill, even greater confusion prevailed. Marshall, Jackson, and Lyons each won—and then lost on subsequent reversals. DeWitt, Onondaga (proposed by Danforth), and Caledonia Township in Shiawassee County were among other sites proposed. Senators took fifty-one votes on March 8 without reaching a decision, but finally approved the House bill the next day. With Acting Governor William L. Greenly's signature affixed on March 16, Lansing became Michigan's new capital, effective December 1, 1847. That date was fixed in legislation passed by both houses in naming the new capital "Michigan" and directing Governor Greenly to make arrangements to provide necessary offices for state agencies, to arrange for moving the state archives and library, "and to cause suitable rooms to be prepared for the next session of the legislature . . . before the first Monday of January 1848." Greenly, following another legislative edict, immediately appointed a three-man commission to go to the frontier village and choose the precise site of the capital "containing not less than 20 acres of land . . . and procure conveyance of same, free of all encumbrances, and cause the same to be recorded in Ingham County." Legislators appropriated ten thousand dollars for temporary buildings to be completed by December 25, 1847.

The law under which the capital was selected (No. 60, Session Laws of 1847) reads, "The seat of government of the State shall be the township of Lansing, in the county of Ingham." In an unusual relaxation of his normal objectivity, Durant added this comment: "If brevity is the soul of wit, then the Michigan Legislature of 1847 was the most witty of any ever assembled. It would be well if all law-making bodies were as sensible and as witty."

Greenly named James L. Glen of Cass County, Benjamin F. H. Witherall of Wayne County and Alonzo Ferris of Genesee County as the site committee. They were required to take an oath that they were "not directly interested, and would not be so while in office, in any lands or land speculation in the counties of Ingham, Eaton, Ionia, or Clinton growing out of or connected with the State Capital." The oath probably was well advised, for several attempts had been made to purchase lands in the new capital village whose value had increased considerably once the choice appeared imminent.

Immediately after the House passed the site bill, Upton wrote, he was invited to join several representatives and senators who were selling shares in a $2,670 speculative venture to buy Section 16 (the "school section" of Lansing Township) with the intention of selling the lands later at a huge profit. Upton declined, considering the plan "too questionable." As it turned out, the land officer in Marshall refused to sell the school section.

It was twenty-six years later that ex-Governor Felch revealed why. Felch figured that 640 acres in the center of the new capital city would become extremely valuable and decreed the profits should go to the state's educational fund as provided by law. So, he penned a quick note to Judge Abiel Silver, the land commissioner, ordering the lands in question withdrawn from sale. Felch recalled the story in an 1873 talk to the Michigan Pioneer and Historical Society.

When the train left Detroit, both Felch's note and the legislators' messengers were aboard. At Marengo, an accident delayed the train, so it pulled into Marshall several hours late and the land office was closed. Fortunately, Judge Silver's mail was taken to his house that evening. When the land office opened the next morning, the agent was waiting and immediately applied for purchase of the land. But Silver informed him the tract had just been removed from sale.

The school section contained 640 acres in a one-mile square that became downtown Lansing. As early as 1880, its sale to private owners had netted the education fund $93,731.

The wilderness that was Michigan's new capital was vividly described by Augustus F. Weller, who accompanied the commissioners appointed to locate the building site for the seat of government. It took the party three days to reach "Michigan" from Jackson. At Mason, they had to cross Sycamore Creek on a fallen log because a dam and a bridge had been washed out. A team was "driven through the torrent," as Weller wrote, on a Mason-to-Lansing road that "was simply horrible . . . corduroyed . . . more or less [with] logs afloat in many places." Arriving at Joab Page's place (the former Burchard cabin), the party put up in a boarding house Page had fashioned in anticipation of the village's new role in state affairs. It was Weller who wrote that "William Townsend cleared a space about an acre where the capitol now stands [at the rear of the present Cooley Law School] and on this cleared spot a game of ball was played."

The site committee members early on made the acquaintance of one of the area's first settlers who had become one of its staunchest citizens and civil servants. He was not trained in the law, but by his name alone was destined to leave his mark on the legal history of Lansing from its very beginning. Justus Gilkey was to serve the site commission in more ways than one. Gilkey, who came to Ingham County in 1839, had purchased land in the remote northwest corner of the county, in Section 5 about a mile downstream from James Seymour's dam. He attended the first town meeting in Lansing Township on April 4, 1842, scarcely two months after the legislature in Detroit authorized organization of the township. Gilkey was elected inspector for the initial election at which eleven voters filled twenty-two township offices. He was elected justice of the peace, assessor, overseer of the poor, and overseer of highways for the township's second district.

A year later, voters selected him township clerk and in 1844, at a special election, he again won office as justice of the peace when the original winner failed to qualify. Township records do not reveal if Gilkey was ever elected to any post in subsequent elections, but he seemingly continued to serve as a justice of the peace until he left the area in 1849.

It was in a non-judicial, unofficial capacity that Gilkey endeared himself to the members of the capital site commission as they boarded in the home of staunch Methodist Joab Page. In Durant's account, he mentions that the commissioners soon learned that "Justus Gilkey, who lived in Section 5, down the river, was the only man who had whiskey for sale by the quantity within reasonable distance of the capital, and it was in constant demand."

When they had completed their task, the commissioners drew up an inked document dated June 22, 1847, which is recorded in Liber 7, page 593, in the Register of Deeds office in Mason. The certificate formed Section 16 and parts of Section 9 and 21 into the original plat of the Town of Michigan, Michigan. It was signed "Justus Gilkey, Justice of the Peace" and recorded in Mason the next day.

The committee daily encountered transportation problems, including having to cross the Grand River twice a day in boats because there were no bridges. After one such crossing, the man who handled the boat lost control as he returned alone and was swept over the dam and drowned. Page's daughter, Mrs. C.M. Smith, recalled years later that the commissioners, after a few minutes, went on with their work, "giving no further thought to the poor man who lost his life in their service."

As the new capital was taking shape and hotels, boarding houses, mercantile firms, mills, and artisan shops were being erected in the soon-to-be new seat of government, William W. Upton decided to move six miles south and become part of the excitement. Almost as soon as the final session of the legislature in Detroit ended in mid-March, Upton moved from DeWitt to Lansing and, in partnership with Henry Jipson, built the first house on the west side of the Grand River. He also "engaged actively in the construction of the . . . capitol and other prominent buildings, which were erected on contract," Durant wrote.

Upton resumed his law practice in Lansing in the fall of 1847 and became the second attorney to live in Lansing. He promptly ran for Lansing Township clerk and was elected. In the fall of 1850, the first time that Michigan citizens were allowed to vote for their prosecuting attorney as a result of a provision in the recently ratified new state constitution, Upton was elected Ingham County prosecutor. He continued in that capacity for the first year of a two-year term, but in the spring of 1852 was bitten by the "go west" bug. Still in his twenties, Upton took his family and moved to Sacramento, California, where he practiced law for twelve years. He served in the California legislature and from 1861 to 1863 was district attorney of Sacramento County. Again, it was time to move on. Before his death in 1896, Upton practiced law in Oregon, became chief justice of the Oregon Supreme Court, was appointed as second comptroller of the U.S. Department of Treasury by President Rutherford B. Hayes, and set up a law practice in Washington, D.C.

6

A LEGAL COMMUNITY
EMERGES

When Michigan's state government opened for business in January of 1848, reference to Ingham County's "legal community" probably would have drawn as many snickers as did the mere mention of "Michigan, Michigan" as the capital city. Both concepts were soon to change.

As lawmakers gathered for the first legislative session outside of Detroit, there was talk that something had to be done about the town's name. And some of those who appeared disinterested in a name change were openly advocating a move of the seat of government away from the mid-Michigan wilderness. Even though rail service had been established through Jackson, it took some lawmakers four days to reach the capital.

Four primitive hotels had been hastily erected in the latter part of 1847, but rooms were still at a premium. Several lawmakers, including Senator Charles Loomis of St. Clair, found Lansing housewives willing to provide them board, but they were obliged to set up beds in the capitol. A janitor who had living quarters in the basement of the wooden structure kept a fire going day and night, maintaining temperatures in the ground level House chamber from his "fiery furnace . . . at an undurable pitch," according to a Detroit newspaper report of the day. Describing the meager capitol furnishings, the same reporter wrote that the building was "not finished with half the cost or magnificence of the business offices of many young lawyers barely started in their profession."

Communities that had been 1847 rivals as locations for the new capital continued to hope it was not too late for the seat of government to be moved once again; at the same time, townspeople in the rapidly growing village made every effort to woo the lawmakers and make them feel welcome and comfortable in their new wilderness work place. Returning from the capitol at night to Jim Seymour's hotel in "lower town" (now North Lansing), the legislators walked by the light of tin lanterns on a sidewalk of two planks laid on a foundation of mud and tree roots. It was a mile from the capitol to the hotel, and the discussions over a glass of whiskey or tankard of rum once they had arrived probably weren't too complimentary. Frequently, someone would introduce a bill the next morning to move the capital to a more ideal location. None of the measures ever passed.

The new town's name of "Michigan, Michigan" did not fare as well. Legislators quickly saw that the unimaginative name for their capital city would only lead to confusion. Numerous suggestions were made for changing the name to honor presidents, Michigan elder statesmen, national heroes, historic figures, and Native Americans. The suggestions included Houghton, Cass, Washington, Harrison, Franklin, Marcellus, LaFayette, Bushridge, Tyler, Pewanogowink, Swedenborg, Kinderhook, El Dorado, Thorbush, Huron, and Okeema. Finally, Joseph E. North Sr., one of the township's original settlers, petitioned the legislature to select the obvious and name the state's new capital for the place where it was located, a township he had named a decade before after his old hometown in New York. The name honored a famous Revolution-era judge.

A joint resolution approved the measure on the last day of April, 1848. Entitled simply, "an act to change the name of the town of Michigan," it contained only a single sentence decreeing that ". . . the name of the town of Michigan, in the county of Ingham, be and the same is hereby changed to Lansing." A few letters mailed from the new capital in the early part of 1848 and bearing the confusing "Michigan, Michigan" postmark still exist.

By the time the town of Lansing was created, there were perhaps eight lawyers living and practicing in Ingham County, although some of them depended on earnings from pursuits other than the practice of law. In 1848, their ages ranged from 21 (Ephriam Longyear) to 37 (Daniel Case, the county's last appointed prosecuting attorney and "old man" of the Ingham County bar). The others in this handful of pioneer Ingham lawyers were John W. Longyear, 28, Ephriam's brother and mentor of several notable Ingham County attorneys; William W. Upton, 25, destined to be the county's first elected prosecuting attorney; George Peck, 30, the former House speaker who, along with Charles P. Bush, president pro tem of the 1847 State Senate, had moved from Howell to Lansing and set up a mercantile business; David E. Corbin, 34, Upton's law partner; William H. Chapman, 28, a "county judge" and later judge of probate; and George I. Parsons, 28, who later served as Ingham County prosecutor and Lansing city attorney.

If these law-trained pioneers are to be considered as the group that brought jurisprudence to Ingham County, two other men who settled in the county soon after statehood was accomplished should also be mentioned. Neither was a lawyer, but both Joseph H. Kilbourne of Meridian Township and John J. Tuttle of Leslie Township started families that produced stellar lawyers. The pioneer godfathers themselves had a profound influence on the history of the legal system in Ingham County.

Tuttle and Kilbourne both personified the pioneer spirit that prompted people to leave their eastern roots and holdings behind and venture into the unknown that was Michigan's frontier at the time the territory was winning its battle for statehood. That same pioneer spirit was indeed present in their offspring a generation or two later. And in Tuttle's case, it lasted yet another generation when two of his great-granddaughters became well-known Lansing lawyers in an era when female attorneys were scarce.

Joseph Henry Kilbourne was born in 1809 near Bennington, Vermont. He farmed until he was twenty-seven, moved to Canada before the Patriots' War, and joined that conflict as a captain. Captured by the royalist forces in March of 1838, Kilbourne was imprisoned by the British at Toronto at the time his son, Samuel, was born in 1839. The elder Kilbourne managed to escape from the wartime prison and, in disguise, took charge of a drove of cattle the British wished taken to Sarnia to feed their troops. Arriving in Sarnia "after many harrowing adventures," according to an obituary printed in the 1892 annual meeting report of the Michigan Pioneer Society, Kilbourne boldly delivered the cattle and drew his pay from the redcoats. Then the man who was destined to be known as the "founder of Lansing" borrowed a rowboat and calmly rowed himself to freedom across the St. Clair River. He walked from Port Huron to Detroit and took a job in a blacksmith shop for two years until his family joined him in a move to Northville, where they opened a general store.

The Kilbournes had come to Ingham County in 1843, buying land on which later became the village of Okemos. Kilbourne prospered as a farmer, served as one of Meridian Township's first supervisors and, in 1846, the same year his wife died, ran for and was elected to the legislature that voted favorably on his motion to move the capital to Lansing.

As the new wooden capitol was being built, Kilbourne moved into Lansing to manage James Seymour's hotel, mill, and real estate interests. He defeated the Whig candidate, Mason lawyer John W. Longyear, by a single vote and represented Ingham County in the first legislature seated in Lansing.

In the prime of life at age forty-two, successful in farming, business management, and state and local politics, Kilbourne was again overcome by the pioneer spirit in 1851. Attracted by stories of the discovery of gold at Sutter's Mill, he disposed of his Lansing interests, put the Okemos farm in temporary hands, and led a wagon train party across the plains and mountains to California. Kilbourne was soon back in politics. He ran for a seat in the California legislature but was defeated by a narrow margin; he and his family returned to the Okemos farm in 1858.

Joseph Kilbourne possessed a large measure of that intangible, the "pioneer spirit," which he apparently willed to one of his sons, Samuel L. Kilbourne, who was to found the Ingham County Bar Association at the peak of his long legal career. Samuel Kilbourne was born near Toronto, Ontario, on April 15, 1839—about the same time the first session of the Ingham County Circuit Court was being held in Mason.

Young Sam began his education at home and was already thoroughly familiar with *Webster's Spelling Book*, a grammar and arithmetic text, when he entered school soon after the family arrived in Meridian Township. He attended primary school in Okemos and in Lansing.

History has not preserved the identity of who cared for the well-being of teenager Sam Kilbourne when his family left for California in 1851, but as early as 1854, at age fifteen, he was attending Albion College. And when Michigan Agricultural College (MAC)—now Michigan State University—opened its doors in 1857, Sam Kilbourne was one of the first to enroll. He also taught school for three months while keeping up with his college class work but eventually was required to drop out of MAC because Ingham County was over-represented with students. That seeming ill fortune may have been a blessing in disguise for jurisprudence, for young Kilbourne, accustomed to self-education, decided to "read law" by himself. Later, he was tutored by Delos Wiley, a leading Lansing lawyer. Before long, Kilbourne was allowed to practice in the local justice courts as sympathetic lawyers ignored the fact he had not been admitted to practice. By the time he was twenty-one in 1860, he decided on the law as a lifetime vocation.

Sam Kilbourne, learning that the University of Michigan was about to open a law school in Ann Arbor, was accepted in the first class. When he graduated in 1861, his entire class was admitted to the bar in Washtenaw County. Kilbourne returned to Lansing and opened a practice—this time with a "shingle" and full-fledged acceptance as a member of the Michigan bar.

The Civil War was well under way by that time, and Kilbourne threw his oratorical talents into the Union cause. His fiery speeches at war meetings quickly stamped him as a promising political orator. The energetic young attorney became his own best listener, "took the war fever," and was on the verge of enlisting in the army when his brother, Henry, who had originally agreed to remain at home, yielded to patriotic pressure and went instead.

Kilbourne tried his hand at several endeavors. He was a regular contributor to several newspapers, ran unsuccessfully for circuit court commissioner, edited the *Michigan State Journal*, a Lansing Democratic weekly, and for a time was deputy clerk for the Michigan Supreme Court. He remained a fiery Democrat despite the fact that many of his contemporaries were caught up in the Republican fever after the party was organized in Jackson. He traveled through mid-Michigan during the war, making impassioned speeches designed to recruit soldiers for the Union cause. He apparently tried his hand at elective office only once and was elected to the Michigan House of Representatives from Ingham County's first district in the fall of 1874. Although he was the youngest member of the House, Kilbourne was named chairman of the Democratic minority and was chosen for a special committee on liquor traffic. He authored a bill that repealed the prohibitory law on intoxicants and installed in its place a new system of taxing liquor sales, a practice that was still in place more than a century later.

Early in his legal career, Kilbourne served as an Ingham County assistant prosecutor. He was also a member of the Lansing Board of Education and served as Lansing city attorney. Later in his career, he was appointed by Governor Cyrus Luce to the advisory board for pardons, serving as its chairman for several years.

Kilbourne married first in 1862, the year after he got his law degree and license. He took as his bride Louisa F. Burchard, the daughter of Ingham County's first lawyer, John W. Burchard. One of their children, Mary L., followed the lead of her mother in choosing a successful Lansing lawyer for a mate when she became the bride of James Harris.

In his law practice, Kilbourne was known as an outspoken practitioner, although none of the history books or biographic accounts credit him with plowing any new legal ground. He was considered a good teacher and counted among his successful students Alva M. Cummins, who read law in Kilbourne's office and himself became a credible Lansing lawyer. Cummins said Kilbourne "had one of the keenest legal minds" he had ever known. "No one could go into a suit with Sam Kilbourne without knowing a real legal battle was on."

Kilbourne was one of the few opponents to get a courtroom advantage over Delos C. Wiley, who during the 1860s and early 1870s was on one side or the other in many of the cases being tried in Ingham County's one-judge circuit court. Wiley had the reputation of being a fast talker; one chronicler remarking he would have been "a terror to stenographers if the court had been favored with their services in those [early] days." Years before, Wiley had tutored Kilbourne before the latter attended law school. It was part of the crafty Wiley's strategy to offer clerks from his office as witnesses, qualifying them as having read, viewed, or filed evidence and getting the favorable facts before a jury without risking having an untrained witness muff the presentation by saying too much or cracking under cross-examination. Wiley had used several clerk-witnesses in one case in which he was opposed by Kilbourne. So when Kilbourne began his arguments to the jury, he sought their sympathy by remarking, "I labor under a disadvantage trying cases with my brother Wiley, for I keep only a law office while he keeps a law and evidence office."

Over the years that he practiced in the courts of Ingham County, Kilbourne was associated with hundreds of cases, the majority of them routine divorce actions, property disputes, run-of-the-mill crime defenses, and damage cases. One attracted news attention in the latter part of 1898 when Kilbourne took on the Michigan Southern Railroad in a damage claim suit involving the skeletal remains of a prehistoric beast. The plaintiff, Kilbourne's client, was a Dr. Kost. He apparently was so well known in the community that the *State Republican* chose never to use his first name in any of nearly a dozen reports it ran before and during the trial, which attracted sizable crowds. Kost, claiming the railroad extensively damaged a shipment of mastodon bones he had shipped from his former home in Ohio to Lansing, sought damages of ten thousand dollars.

Dr. Kost testified at length as to how he had unearthed the remains of the elephant-like beast in a Florida swamp several years before and had stored them in his Ohio home. They were in good condition, he said, when he shipped them from Ohio. But when they arrived in Lansing, the bones were in shambles. It was clear to him that the railroad had ruined his valuable collection. The railroad's agent, George Mask, testified the freight shipment had received normal railroad care. The defense also brought to the stand a University of Michigan geologist who testified about the properties of old bones. He hurt Kilbourne's case when he estimated the value of the bones, even before they were broken, at between $75 and $200. The verdict was a mixed bag for Kilbourne and his client. They won, but Dr. Kost collected only $125.

In another case in the 1880s, Kilbourne came out the loser in a confrontation with Professor Robert Kedzie, the renowned MAC scientist. The suit concerned an Ohio firm that was marketing a "Farmers Favorite" fertilizer in Michigan without a license and without having had its product analyzed according to terms of an 1885 statute. Kedzie conducted his own analysis. "It was made of powdered furnace slag and common salt, the slag . . . a waste material found in abundance around furnaces where iron ore is smelted," Kedzie decreed, ruling the "fertilizer" had no commercial value. The Ohio firm was selling the fertilizer for $22 a ton and its value, Kedzie computed, was actually 34¢ a ton.

Kedzie exposed "the bare-faced fraud" in a letter published by the *Detroit Free Press* and widely copied by other newspapers across the state. Company agents were soon calling at Kedzie's laboratory on the MAC campus, demanding retractions and threatening damage suits. He agreed to meet with them in Lansing one afternoon, knowing they had brought along two lawyers from Cleveland and had engaged the services of Kilbourne as a local back-up. On the way to the meeting, Kedzie secured Richard Montgomery, a Lansing lawyer, as his counsel.

A "spicy conversation" ensued, Kedzie recalled in a sketch of the case printed in his biography in the *Michigan Pioneer* collection. Kedzie acknowledged his exposé but refused to retract a word. The fertilizer people said they had 1,800 tons of their product in Michigan and, with sales halted, stood to lose $36,000, the wholesale value of their stocks. Kedzie said his retort was, "If I have saved the farmers of Michigan $36,000 in cool cash, I am glad of it." Kilbourne, attempting to forge a compromise, asked Kedzie if he could modify "or change his statements in some respect so that my clients can dispose of the stock they now have in the state, saving them from heavy loss and yourself from all the trouble and litigation?" Kedzie refused to budge and the Ohio lawyers said they would return to Cleveland and prepare the lawsuit. Kedzie said his reply was, "Well, you will find me at the college." The suit was never filed, and Kedzie said a dealer confided to him a year later that dealers had been instructed to dump the material into the street and keep the bags as pay for their trouble.

When the 860-page *Pioneer History of Ingham County, Michigan*, a collection of talks and business at fifty years of Society meetings, was prepared in 1923, accounts of Kilbourne-related tales were sprinkled throughout the thick volume. They indicate that Kilbourne had an intense interest in people, whether they be politicians, friends from the upper crust of Ingham society, or old-time cronies of lesser means.

The book contains an account of the July 18, 1917 homecoming celebration held at School District No. 5 in Meridian Township, the old Mullett School. "Automobilists" passing the picnic in the school-yard grove looked on with envy, according to the account, which said the "most unique part of the whole thing" was the presence of Jerusha Doyle (Mrs. Charles J.) Mullett, then eighty-four, who had taught in the district's original school. Sam Kilbourne, whose father had bought a tract of land that had been occupied by Chief Okemos and three hundred Potawatomi Indians, was there, too. He was seventy-eight, only six years younger than the teacher he came to help honor.

In the final three weeks of his life, Kilbourne, who had been ill for more than a year, became too much of a burden to be nursed at home. Reluctantly, his wife and other family members had him "taken from the home" to the state mental hospital in Kalamazoo, where he died June 14, 1925. Thus ended the life, at age eighty-seven, of the founder and seventeen-time president of the Ingham County Bar Association.

For John J. Tuttle, life on the Ingham County frontier appears to have been considerably more rigorous than it was for Joseph Kilbourne, especially in the early, pre-statehood months and the first few years that followed his 1836 arrival in Leslie Township, although both men had agricultural backgrounds and similar educational advantages. Tuttle was born on June 14, 1812, at Mentz, New York. His father, Jabel, fought in both the Revolutionary War and the War of 1812. In his late teens, John Tuttle apprenticed himself to a blacksmith in Auburn, New York, but ran away to Weedsport and served as an apprentice in the tanner's and currier's trade. He then operated his own tannery for two years before signing a government contract at the outbreak of the Black Hawk War, calling for him, as a butcher, to supply friendly Indians in the Chicago area with meat. Meanwhile, he searched for some good farming land but, disgusted with the low, marshy country he found at Chicago, returned to New York in 1834 and farmed there for two years before buying eighty acres in Section 7 of Leslie Township, Michigan Territory.

In 1837, Tuttle brought his bride, Emma Warren, to Michigan, along with "a very meager outfit for housekeeping, a good axe and $3," according to lawyer/historian A. E. Cowles. Tuttle also brought his robust constitution, a keen sense of humor, and an indomitable will. Decades later, the old pioneer would tell audiences at annual meetings of the Pioneer and Historical Society that it was five years before a team passed the door of his log cabin or before he saw smoke from a neighbor's fireplace.

Those early years were bone-wearying. John and Emma Tuttle would spend their winters rolling the great logs he had felled from his forest into heaps and then set fire to them, collecting the piles of ashes. The ashes were then placed in hollowed-out sycamore "gums," or barrels, rendering the gray mess of lye into what was called "black salts," used as the chief ingredient of soap. That and the maple sugar from their trees were the only commercial crops the Tuttles could produce those first few years to use as barter for their household needs.

John Tuttle would entertain audiences a half century later with the tale of his first sugar crop. During the winter, he cut three-foot-long sections of big sycamore logs, split them in half, and then hollowed out the sections to make troughs in which to catch the sap from maple trees on his farm. He also whittled out the wooden spiles—tube-like spouts driven into holes bored in the tree trunks to carry the sap to the troughs. And he cut the fire wood needed for boiling down the sap; about forty gallons of the sweet nectar was needed to make one gallon of syrup. But where on the Leslie Township frontier could one get a kettle in which to evaporate the sap? Tuttle finally located a "five-pail kettle" (it would probably hold about twenty gallons) in the village of Jackson. Unable to purchase the vessel, Tuttle borrowed it and carried it home on his back, a distance of nearly twenty miles.

When the first bright, thawing days of mid-February arrived, Tuttle tapped as many trees as he figured he could attend to, carted the sweet sap on foot to a holding tank, and depended on Emma to keep the fire going beneath the kettle while he continued to haul sap. Their entire crop, save for a few gallons they kept for sweetening Emma's cooking, was hauled on foot to Jackson County and exchanged for supplies needed in the Tuttle pantry.

Tuttle was also active in politics. He attended the Jackson meeting "Under the Oaks," where the Republican Party was founded. He was supervisor of Leslie Township during the Civil War, later served as justice of the peace and was county coroner for approximately twenty years. Emma Tuttle died September 2, 1887, at age seventy-five. John remained on the farm and continued his active life as a widower until a few days before his death at age ninety on January 20, 1903.

Thus, the jolly old pioneer never knew his great-granddaughter, lawyer-to-be Ruth Beatrice Tuttle, the elder daughter of John's grandson, Arthur Tuttle,

himself one of Ingham's ablest attorneys. Ruth was born March 21, 1904, fourteen months after her great-grandfather died. But it's easy to see where the
lawyer Tuttles—Judge Arthur and his daughters, Ruth and Esther—acquired the
fortitude, drive, and vigor that helped emblazon their names across the pages of
Ingham County's legal history.

7

TWO SEATS OF GOVERNMENT

By the middle of the nineteenth century, it became evident that the Ingham County bar had advantages and disadvantages that lawyers in Michigan's other counties would never experience. An Ingham County attorney's opportunities increased and the fields of legal expertise became more varied when the state capital moved to Lansing. After the people approved a new state constitution in 1850, attorneys from outside the state and from other Michigan counties gravitated to Lansing, where a good living could be made in the law profession. Prior to this time, Ingham County attorneys had supplemented their income with a variety of work, including merchandising, farming, and teaching.

The 1850 constitution emphatically stated that the state capital would be in Lansing and that the state's supreme court would sit there. Lawyers were lured by the political action, the potential for a political appointment, and the opportunity to be near lawmakers whose actions could affect popular business enterprises. Railroads, lumbering, and mining ventures required lawyers knowledgeable in law, land use, and easements.

Activities in Lansing, the boom town, were in contrast to those occurring at the county seat in Mason. There, the population was diminishing. Local residents referred to it as "the great exodus." Attorneys moved to Lansing or opened a second, more spacious office in the capital city.

The legal profession was forced to adapt to a unique situation. In all other states, the capital city was also the county seat, allowing state business requiring a prosecutor, clerk, or lower court to be done at least in the shadow of the statehouse. Only in Michigan did state officials have to travel more than twelve miles to complete such legal business.

In 1850, that distance became a distinct hardship. Transportation in and out of Lansing was limited. The nearest railroad was at DeWitt, but that line was used chiefly for moving farm products. The closest practical connection to travel outside the mid-Michigan area was at Jackson. Only the stagecoach provided direct public transportation to and from Lansing, and service was limited. An item in the June 19, 1855, edition of the *Lansing Republican* indicated, "Two coaches leave this place daily for Detroit, morning and evening. There are also two coaches a day, each way, on the Jackson route. These, with the daily lines to Marshall, Ionia and DeWitt, relieve in a measure the feelings of our uneasy community. There has been a decided improvement, and one which the increase of travel will fully warrant." The newspaper did not clarify that the two stages a day to Jackson were not over the same route. One coach went by way of Mason, Leslie, and Stockbridge. The other stage went through Eaton Rapids, Onondaga, and Tompkins Center.

In 1850, eight lawyers were practicing in Ingham County; by the time the Civil War began in 1861, twenty-seven men occupied or had once maintained law offices in Lansing alone. A number of the attorneys in both Lansing and Mason had young men studying law in their offices. Youth dominated the legal profession in those early days. Except for fifty-five-year-old Orange Butler and two attorneys in their mid-thirties, those in that early group were under the age of thirty when they opened their law offices in the county.

The emergence of Lansing as the state capital quickly initiated a rivalry that continues today between Lansing and the out-county area. Mason was the larger of the two at first, but it did not take long for the capital city to catch up. At the time of the capital move, there were approximately eighty residents in what became the village of Lansing, while Vevay Township boasted approximately 700 residents, many of them in Mason. By the 1860 census, Mason Village had 363 residents and Lansing close to 3,600.

As 1848 began, Ingham prisoners still had to be housed in the county jail at Jackson if they could not provide for pre-trial bonds. On January 6, the Ingham County Board of Supervisors passed a resolution appropriating one thousand dollars to be raised by taxes, and a like amount in the form of a loan, to erect fireproof offices and a jail in Mason. The jail walls were constructed of brick, but the cells were of hewn timbers. Sheriff Joseph L. Huntington, fearing that fires lit inside the jail to hasten drying of the mortar might set fire to the structure, directed his son to sleep there for a time as a safety precaution. The offices were soon erected on the site of the original office building, which was sold at auction for seventy-five dollars and moved a few rods to the east. The jail and sheriff's residence were erected on a lot at the rear of the first courthouse, the two-story frame structure built in 1843.

It was not long before pressure started building for a new Ingham County courthouse. The original wooden structure was only twelve years old, but in a county that boasted Michigan's capital city in addition to the ever-growing communities of Williamston, Stockbridge, Dansville, Leslie, and Okemos, and a handful of smaller villages, it was inadequate even by 1854 standards.

The lawyers from Lansing, forced to ride the stage or their own mounts when they had circuit court business in the county seat, no doubt joined the lobby for new court facilities that reached a fever pitch at the January 1855 meeting of the supervisors. The board approved a resolution to submit a proposition to county voters raising five thousand dollars through taxes, spread over two years, and to borrow another five thousand dollars to finance a new, more commodious courthouse. The action was finalized at the board's December meeting that year and the question was placed on the county ballot in April 1856. Both issues were approved by substantial, if not overwhelming margins—the taxation question passing by a vote of 1,090 to 665, and the loan by a 1,088 to 652 vote.

A committee of supervisors selected the center of the public square in Mason as the site for the new building, but it was more than a year before a contract was let for construction of what was to become the county's most magnificent structure, except for the state capitol itself. The board of supervisors had to go to Lansing to find a contractor capable of submitting plans and specifications for such a building.

Matthew Elder was awarded the contract on June 20, 1857, for $11,700, and he started construction almost immediately on a two-story brick structure with four tall fireplace chimneys and an ornate cupola. The building was completed within a year and was accepted by the county board on April 10, 1858, after supervisors approved cost overruns of about $500.

The new colonial-style brick courthouse was an imposing structure, built in the prevailing style of the pre-Civil War period. It was described in an Ingham County Historical Commission brochure 130 years after its construction as having a wide first-floor hallway extending the length of the building and leading to various county offices. The wide hallway helped provide ventilation on warm, humid days. The entire second floor was devoted to the circuit court room, judge's chambers, and jury room. The chimney locations near the building's corners suggest that the courtroom was heated by two fireplaces, the others heating the judicial chambers and jury quarters.

Mason residents, justifiably proud of the new courthouse, took it upon themselves to finance the landscaping of the building. In the autumn of 1858, Mason citizens raised approximately $1,700 and donated it to the county to provide for grading of the grounds, sidewalks, shade trees, a wrought-iron fence, and park benches. Watering troughs for horses were installed at the front corners of the courthouse block and special features in the front yard included an artesian well and a bandstand. A croquet court was laid out on one of the side yards and a large woodshed was properly situated at the rear. The building was to serve the county for forty-five years.

The new courthouse brought mid-1850s judicial elegance to Ingham County. For eighteen years, lawyers in Ingham had plied their craft in dingy, Spartan surroundings—initially in the log schoolhouse in Mason, then in the cabin homes of various township justices of the peace, such as the dwelling of Joab Page near the dam in North Lansing.

The justice of the peace courts, however, weren't always held in homes. The *Ingham County Pioneer History* contains one account of a justice court trial conducted in the wagon shop of Hale Granger in Dansville in the late 1840s. The trial was recalled by D. L. Crossman in an 1889 letter replying to an invitation to recite some of his boyhood experiences. It was in 1847, Crossman wrote, that the Granger shop had served as the site of the Dansville School District's first meeting. Crossman recalled:

> The wagon shop . . . also served as a hall of Justice for those primitive people, the jury sitting in line on the workbench while the justice of the peace occupied a splint chair in the corner. Lawsuits were not frequent but when they did occur, general interest was manifest, everybody being active on one side or the other of the case. I remember one case which involved an accounting between the parties. One item charged was the pasturing of a yoke of oxen over night, and a witness was called to prove the value of the pasturage. He was very reluctant to set the figure, but when pressed by the attorney said, "It's worth two and six a week, you've got your pencil and you can figure it up to suit yourself."

By the time Ingham's new brick courthouse was ready for use in 1858, Michigan's court system had undergone several stages of evolution. The county's first judges in the circuit court had been Michigan Supreme Court justices, assisted by locally elected "assistant judges." Then, under terms of an 1846 revision of the judicial statutes by the legislature, the circuit court in each county was presided over by a "county judge" and a "second judge," both elected locally for four-year terms. The court had original and exclusive jurisdiction of all claims above the jurisdiction of a justice court. It also had appellate jurisdiction over the justice court. But that system lasted only four years, being abolished by the constitution of 1850. Benjamin Davis was elected county judge for 1846-50, but resigned in 1849 and was replaced for the final year of the term by William H. Chapman, who was elected to fill the vacancy. Horatio N. Forbes was elected as second judge.

Under terms of the 1850 reorganization, Ingham County was placed in the Fourth Judicial Circuit, along with Washtenaw and Jackson counties. The arrangement continued until 1877, when Washtenaw was paired with Monroe County in a new district, leaving Ingham and Jackson in the Fourth Circuit.

8

EARLIEST TRIALS

In an era devoid of organized sports and electronic entertainment and in a frontier area too far from the large centers of civilization to attract theatrical presentations and musical concerts, the courts quickly became the best show in town for many Ingham County residents. Even before court observers were lured to the spacious new brick courthouse at the county seat, trials and lawsuits were drawing crowds. When circuit court convened at the log schoolhouse at Jefferson and Oak streets, the village's population was inflated as judges, lawyers, witnesses, jurors, and spectators gathered for the show.

Just reaching court was a sizable task in itself for many early Ingham lawyers. If they lived in Lansing, Stockbridge, Williamston, or Leslie, attorneys faced a horseback or buggy ride of an hour or more. After the capital came to Lansing, the Lansing lawyers could opt for a horseback trek or a bumpy stagecoach ride to court in Mason. The rigorous ordeal of reaching court was described half a century later by one of Ingham's most competent probate judges, Mason D. Chatterton, who filled the position from 1873 to 1880. Speaking at the 1898 annual meeting of the Ingham County Pioneer Society, Chatterton described the early bench and bar of the county, especially praising the first seven probate judges who "had no precedents to follow and were obliged to strike out for themselves, [leaving] a trail of blazed trees through the virgin forest of the law."

Chatterton could also have mentioned that, for the most part, Peter Linderman, Valorous Meeker, Henry Fiske, Amos E. Steele, Richard Ferris, Griffin Paddock, and William H. Chapman performed their services to the county without benefit of college law degrees or previous legal experience or training. All of the seven were deceased by the time Chatterton was praising them. He pointed out that the probate courts "are closer to the people than any other court in the state" and that the pioneer probate judges were "quasi-guardians for the incompetent, the widow and the fatherless" and were noted "for their probity of character, honest construction of the law and attention to duty."

Chatterton recalled that in the early days, the opening of the circuit court term "brought the Judge and the lawyers with their satchels filled with briefs and law books" on the stagecoach from Lansing and Jackson to Mason. Often, the satchels also carried a change or two of socks and shirts, for most of the attorneys who had more than one day's business with the court stayed in one of Mason's rustic inns for several nights. "Court opened on the first day of the term at ten o'clock and [the judge] held three sessions each day until the calendar was disposed of," the retired judge told his 1898 audience." The stenographer was unknown and the only law book then furnished for the court was a copy of the *Michigan Statutes*.

"There were exciting trials where witnesses and spectators flocked to the court," Chatterton said.

After the first few years, trials were held on the second floor of the wooden courthouse across Ash Street from the present court facility. Cases were decided rather rapidly, partly because court opened regularly at 8:00 A.M., adjourned briefly for dinner at noon and supper at 6:00 P.M., and then resumed until a 9:00 P.M. adjournment.

Although Chatterton spoke of the early court procedures from first-hand experience, it was as a spectator and not a participant. A native of Vermont, he came to Meridian Township in 1851 as a teenager and was the first student examined and admitted to Michigan Agricultural College when it opened in 1855. After three years at the college, he entered the University of Michigan law school and graduated with its first class in 1861. When his active judicial career ended, he wrote the two-volume *Chatterton's Probate Law*, which became the bible of probate judges in Michigan and was widely used in other states. He died in Lansing in 1903 at age sixty-five.

One of the earliest criminal trials—probably the county's first murder trial—occurred in 1844, a few weeks after what is known in the local history books as "The Jefferson City Murder." Unfortunately, existing court files in the Michigan State Archives fail to produce a trace of the trial record. All that remains in print are the recorded recollections of an elderly pioneer woman, recounted thirty years after the slaying, at an 1874 meeting of the county Pioneer Society. And by the time she told her version of the story, she had forgotten the name of the unfortunate victim of the bloody slaying although she thought the man convicted of the deed, "if I remember aright, was a man by the name of Hyde."

The woman said she thought the killing took place on the Alaiedon Township farm then (1874) owned by Isaac Drew. She said the suspect, captured at the scene by neighbors or friends of the victim, was tried in Mason, convicted, and sent to the penitentiary. In commenting on the conviction, she was quoted in the *Pioneer History of Ingham County* as saying, "I don't see how in the world they could bring him in guilty of murder in the second degree without he killed tew men." The story was attributed, simply, to "a pioneer."

In 1915, the *Ingham County News* carried an obituary notice about the demise of eighty-year-old Levi Ketchum of Mason, who claimed to have been a witness to the slaying when he was nine years old. Ketchum was reported to have recalled details of the murder shortly before his death. In the obituary, young Ketchum was said to have been "present when the murderer rushed in with his bloody axe, and went with a band of men to look for the body of the man he had killed." The boy attended the ensuing trial, and heard him convicted and sentenced to life-long imprisonment at "The Tamaracks," as Jackson Prison was then known.

A diligent search of files of the *Lansing State Journal* and the *Ingham County News* failed to turn up the original Ketchum recollections. And without an 1844 trial record or any court notice of a murder charge or trial, the name of the victim and the identity of his slayer remained uncertain. But a search of the state archives' file of persons incarcerated in the state's prisons since 1837 at least established the slaying occurred. The first card in the file under the name of "Hyde" reads: "Hyde, Almerin (Almeron), 5', 8", light, age 51, white male, [convicted] 22 Sept 1848, Ingham County, murder second degree, term 8 years, died 18 July 1854." His demise came apparently while he was still in prison after having served five years and ten months of his sentence. On the reverse side of the card was the notation "physician—born in England." The "Jefferson City Murder" still lacks some details, but the prison card seems to document that it did occur.

A series of trials in Mason that attracted attention in both Ingham and Eaton Counties were held in the early part of 1851. With no newspapers carrying stories of the trials at the time, details quickly became obscured. But in 1895, the *Leslie Local-Republican* recalled the legal excitement in a review of the early history of Onondaga Township. Part of the story was then included in Adams's *Pioneer History of Ingham County* and deserves repeating:

> During the term of the Ingham County Circuit Court, which was held early in 1851, a large portion of the cases were criminal and had come from the township of Onondaga. Those legal giants, Austin Blair and Henry H. Shaw, were arrayed against each other in contests, the earnestness and bitterness of which must make them long memorable. Then it transpired that this accumulation of criminals from one township was not accidental. According to the confession of Peter Waggoner, he belonged to a gang organized for the purpose of robbery and theft. But the trials ended without a single conviction. They were not, however, without their result. They broke up the organization that had so terrorized the community. They furnished local history that has been narrated with zest for more than fifty years.

Both Blair and Shaw (it was actually Henry A., not Henry H.) were frequently in the courts of Ingham County. Shaw later served a dozen years as
Eaton County's probate judge and was speaker of the house during his stint in
the Michigan legislature. But how they could have opposed each other in the
organized gang trials poses a question since neither was an Ingham prosecutor.
Perhaps one of them represented Waggoner, the confessor, and the other was
attorney for defendants not so willing to talk.

Many years later, Shaw was in the Ingham Circuit Court representing a
Leslie man charged with slander. The prosecutor was Henry P. Henderson, who
had once read law under Shaw and who was getting the better of his mentor as
he cross-examined some of Shaw's witnesses. Angered, Shaw, in an effort to
recoup, objected strenuously to Henderson's line of questioning but received no
help from the judge, according to Dr. Frank N. Turner, author of Volume III of
Fuller's *Historic Michigan*. Turner, who was visiting the court that day, wrote that
Shaw finally arose, leaned over the table, shook a bony forefinger in the prosecutor's face and exclaimed, "Young man, I taught you all the law you ever
knew!" The explosion, accentuated by Shaw's tall, lean frame, his obviously
crossed eyes, and fringe of red hair, "produced such a comic effect" that the
judge, jury, and both attorneys broke out laughing and forced the bailiff to
restore order.

By the time Lansing finally got a permanent newspaper, the *State
Republican*, in April of 1855, public drunkenness had become a problem that the
township government was hard pressed to control. Consequently, a new liquor
law went into effect later in the year, aimed at controlling consumption of spirits. Daniel Case, after three terms as county prosecutor and having spent several years before and after his public service as a practicing attorney, and a term
in the legislature as a representative of Ionia County, had returned to Lansing
and was participating in several business ventures. He was promptly elected
Lansing Township justice of the peace, probably the first time a trained lawyer
had held that position.

Case seemingly took enforcement of the new liquor law seriously. Hardly
an issue of the Lansing weekly was without a court news item reporting some
tippler running afoul of the new liquor regulation. An October 2 item told of
two men convicted in Case's court of "selling intoxicants to habitual drunkards"—S. D. and Eugene Newbro. Both men were fined ten dollars and assessed
costs. And early in November, the newspaper reported "another bootlegger" had
been fined ten dollars for an illegal sale of liquor.

It was on a Sunday morning, October 18, 1857, that a series of events
occurred in Lansing's Middletown that could have put an end to the ten-year-old
village. Just before 2:00 A.M., the Moore Block, owned by lawyer George W.
Peck, was discovered to be on fire. The block and most of its contents, including
the offices and shop of the *Michigan State Journal*, a Democrat weekly newspaper,

were destroyed. Citizens managed to keep the flames from the office and print shop of the *Republican* and the state bindery. But while that fire was raging, it was discovered that five other buildings, including three downtown barns and a marble shop, also had been torched and were ablaze. Lansing almost had a lynching at this point when a man was caught in the act of torching the new United Brethren Church, under construction at Kalamazoo Street and Capitol Avenue. But the culprit was rescued by two citizens and jailed, along with his brother, in the county's first big arson case.

News of the fires, the arrest of the "incendiaries," and their "diabolical attempt to burn the town for plunder," was announced in headlines two days later by the *Republican*, which assured readers that regular issues of the competing *Michigan State Journal* "will appear in a week or two." The *Republican*, which managed to publish on time, also carried an almost verbatim account of a hastily arranged preliminary examination for one of the defendants, Edmund Bobier of Alaiedon Township. His brother, William, was apparently charged later.

In a statement at the hearing, Edmund Bobier said he and his brother came to town about 2:00 p.m. on Saturday and "drank freely during the day," disposed of some wheat they had brought to market, and then separated. Edmund said he rented a bed at the Travellers' Home, then "entered a saloon kept by a colored man" and joined a card game. After an argument with one of the card players and upon notification by the proprietor that Sunday had arrived, Bobier said he left the saloon. He heard a cry of fire and noticed the Moore Block ablaze. He said he helped carry merchandise from the burning dry goods store and had started toward another reported fire when some men pointed at him and said he had set the fire. He tried to run and was stopped.

William Bobier claimed he stayed at a different hotel and did not hear the fire alarms. The newspaper concluded its report of the arrest of Edmund Bobier by reporting the defendant had been committed to the county jail at Mason in lieu of a $5,000 bond and added, "We earnestly hope that when he leaves the custody of Sheriff Lowe he will be incarcerated in the state prison for the full extent of time provided by our statutes."

Then, the *Republican* seemed to lose interest in the case. Its next report came in the April 26, 1858 edition, when it said, "Ed Bobier, the principal incendiary, in the fire in this village in October last, had his trial last week before Judge Lawrence. He may think himself fortunate that his fate is no worse. His brother William is having his trial this week for the same offence [sic]." And a week later, this item closed the big arson case: "William Bobier has also been convicted of arson in setting the fire here last fall, and both the promising brothers have ten years of service to the state before them. The way of the transgressor is hard."

Ingham County court watchers had experienced four years of business in the new circuit court facilities in the two-story brick courthouse in Mason by the time the state's first big government scandal since the move of the capital to Lansing had occurred. And about the only way the locals could learn the details of the case was to sit in the courtroom and watch and listen. James V. Campbell, a former Michigan Supreme Court justice, described the situation years later in his *Michigan Political History*:

> The Legislature of 1861, which was very strongly Republican, met under unfavorable circumstances for State prosperity. John McKinney, the outgoing State Treasurer, was found to have embezzled the public funds, and left the treasury empty, and liable for large outstanding and pressing debts.

The *Republican* first noted the scandal in its February 13 edition with a brief item that read:

> Mr. McKinney came to Lansing on Wednesday evening last [February 6], having been summoned before the joint committee of the legislature. On Friday, he refused to be sworn before testifying. Contempt proceedings were instituted against him Saturday. He was arrested and brought to the bar and jailed in the city lockup on February 12. He told his bondsmen "It will all come out right." Mr. McKinney appears unexcited and cool and speaks with great circumspection.

One of the charges against McKinney, who had served two terms as secretary of state before he became state treasurer, stemmed from letting a contract to the firm that was repairing the St. Mary's Ship Canal, forerunner to the Soo Locks. The funds involved amounted to between $55,000 and $70,000, according to the investigative report by a joint legislative committee that was carried verbatim in the *Republican*. Other monies in question included $20,000 advanced to the contractors, $1,580 in orders to the city of Lansing, $23,000 in state railroad taxes collected but not entered in the account books, $500 in a draft signed by McKinney, $2,100 in missing "office monies," and $50,000 "loaned to the bonding company." The total of the funds mentioned in the report was $97,180. In a seeming disclaimer, the report noted that, "The committee, however, after all, are compelled to say that, within the last two years, no very great amount of the public monies can have been lost."

Ingham County Prosecuting Attorney Stephen D. Bingham, however, thought sufficient public funds had been lost and the next day, May 7, 1861, authorized a warrant for McKinney's arrest. The former state senator and state representative from Van Buren County, who had refused to answer any questions put by the legislative committee, was arraigned and released on $14,000 bond after he pleaded not guilty before Circuit Judge Edwin Lawrence to embezzlement and neglect to deliver monies. According to court records now in the Michigan Archives, lawyers Whitney Jones and William H. Chapman arranged for the bail at the request of Orlando M. Barnes, whom McKinney had engaged to handle his defense.

The next circuit court term began the second Tuesday in September but it was mid-November before a jury was drawn to hear the McKinney case. Prosecutor Bingham was assisted by Attorney General Charles Upson and John W. Longyear, one of Lansing's most brilliant lawyers engaged as a special prosecutor. McKinney was defended by Barnes and Chapman, and Judge Lawrence presided.

The *Republican* did not cover the trial and did not have a reporter present on November 14 when the jury returned a guilty of embezzlement verdict against McKinney. Almost a week later, in its November 20 edition, Lansing's first substantial newspaper reported the news with just over one line of six-point type headed "Criminal Matters." The item read, "People vs. John McKinney. Tried-verdict guilty."

The conviction was immediately appealed to the Michigan Supreme Court, the defense claiming, among other things, that Deputy Treasurer Theodore Hunter actually kept the state's books and that they were all in his handwriting. The defense objected to the introduction of the books as evidence against McKinney. Barnes and Chapman also argued that the jurors were confused by a complicated method whereby the Detroit and Milwaukee Railway Company had arranged with McKinney to pay their state railroad taxes. The railroad's tax bill of $23,257.49 was made in quarterly payments by the railroad's New York bank and deposited in another New York bank used by the state of Michigan. A financial officer of the railroad in Hamilton, Ontario, eventually handled drafts for the tax amounts and they were then sent to McKinney at the state's New York bank, endorsed by McKinney and deposited in the bank. But the bank's bookkeeper had testified that McKinney had withdrawn the $23,257.49 before the end of his term as state treasurer.

A venue problem had also turned up when Judge Lawrence instructed jurors "that the embezzlement must have occurred in the county of Ingham" for McKinney to be convicted, backing up Barnes's and Chapman's argument that the money never reached Ingham County or the Michigan treasury. Justice Campbell wrote, "I am very strongly inclined to the opinion that where a public officer is bound to have his office in a certain place, and to keep his accounts there, an official embezzlement may always be charged in law to have been committed there—at least when it is of money unaccounted for."

In a split decision, Justices Martin and Manning voted to uphold the conviction and Justice Campbell voted to overturn it. Campbell's main objection was that McKinney was not charged under an indictment but, instead, as a result of "information," which he said "can only be filed after the party had an opportunity for a preliminary examination." He termed the information "fatally defective."

The justices, meeting in Detroit for that term, handed down their decision on April 26 and McKinney, still protesting he was innocent, was sentenced on May 7, exactly a year after his arrest. According to archives' records for Ingham County Circuit Court, Judge Lawrence decreed that John McKinney "be confined at hard labor in the state prison at Jackson in this state for the period of seven years from and including this day."

It was sixteen months before McKinney was back in the news. On September 17, 1863, the *Republican* reported:

> The Governor [Austin Blair] issued the necessary papers to release ex-State Treasurer John McKinney from State Prison, on Wednesday last, while in this city, and they were at once forwarded to Jackson. Thus, after something over a year's confinement at hard labor in the penitentiary, Mr. McKinney is once more restored to freedom. We presume this act of leniency on the part of the Governor will meet with no denunciation from any quarter. All things considered, we think the law has had sufficient course in the case of Mr. McKinney, and the precedent fully established that Michigan will hold to rigid accountability any of her public servants that violate against her statute laws at any time in the future.

People v. McKinney was finally history.

9

BIGGER THAN LIFE

By the time the Appomattox Courthouse surrender ended the Civil War in 1865, Michigan was known nationally as a dependable and economically sound state with outstanding legal minds practicing law and ruling in its courts. Ingham County was productive in agriculture, criss-crossed with railroads, and no longer considered a frontier area. Lansing had outgrown its wilderness image and was a city where government, business, industry, and merchandising afforded an attractive place to practice law. The county's law community had obtained upper-class status with six incorporated law firms in the capital city at prestigious addresses. Fine offices, impressive libraries, and young men reading law under their tutelage made Ingham County lawyers proud.

Complex patterns began to develop in the law firms as an attorney became known as an expert on a particular phase of the law. Although most lawyers continued to be general practitioners, the specialist became evident during this period of Ingham County history. The growing railroads, mining and lumbering industries in the sparsely settled northern areas of the state retained lawyers knowledgeable on specific subjects. Most of these growing businesses retained an attorney to represent their interests at the capitol. This early lobbying technique, combined with a growing number of legislative acts that resulted in volumes of law, contributed to the country and frontiersman lawyer fading into history. Lawyers on retainers from the big industries were able to put many extra dollars into a law firm's coffers, bring prestige to the office, and live beyond the means of many of their clients.

Three lawyers who were foremost in raising the status of attorneys and developing a positive attitude toward the profession among the citizenry were Ephriam and John Wesley Longyear, and Orlando Mack Barnes. Their ability to attain this status must be largely credited to their practicing law in the correct locale at the right time in history. Their bigger-than-life status came about in part because they gave a public impression of amassing wealth, displayed flamboyant social habits, and owned ostentatious houses. The Longyear brothers were cautious conservative Whigs who were at Jackson when the Republican political party was formed in 1854. Barnes was a devotee of Andrew Jackson and Democratic politics that ardently promoted the common man as the backbone of the country.

The legacy of these men begins at almost any well-established Michigan library. The bound volumes of the Michigan Pioneer and Historical Society, where each man's talks recall pioneer life in Ingham County, detail their preparation for law professions, and preserve their earliest court cases. Their later accomplishments and activities were documented in the local newspapers and have since been preserved on microfilm. Their personal papers are safeguarded at such institutions as the Bentley Historical Library at the University of Michigan, the John M. Longyear Research Library at Marquette, Michigan, and at Michigan State University.

The Longyear and Barnes homesteading experiences have many parallels. Teenager Ephriam Longyear arrived in Alaiedon Township in 1843. His family's first order of business was felling timber with which to erect a log cabin, and young Ephriam pitched in and helped.

Ephriam's brother, John Wesley Longyear, did not accompany the family to Michigan. He had earlier obtained a seminary diploma at Lima, New York, and was teaching at an academy and reading law in his free time. At age twenty-four, he decided to visit his family in the Michigan wilderness. Years later, his account of the journey was a portion of a program he presented at a meeting of the Michigan Pioneer and Historical Society. His trip from New York State to Alaiedon Township was routine with no unusual events or exciting encounters. That alone makes it a valuable piece of history, for the ordinary is seldom recorded.

Longyear left New York late in March of 1844 on a Lake Erie steamer that arrived at Detroit on April 5. The following morning, young Longyear boarded a railroad coach and rode as far as Dexter. He wrote, "From Dexter, I footed it through sparsely settled country to Stockbridge, and staid all night with John Dubois." Longyear walked the trail for over nine hours before arriving at the Dubois Inn in Ingham County's earliest settled village nearly thirty miles from Dexter. The next morning John continued his journey to the Alaiedon Township homestead by walking the fifteen or so miles. An often-used word in his account is "fatigue."

Longyear was never to return to New York as a resident. Although farming was not an attractive livelihood to Peter Longyear's eldest son, he was attracted to work in education and law. John readily saw that both fields had potential for him to develop in this frontier county. In January 1845, he opened a Select School in Mason and was invited to read law in the office of Daniel Case.

A tragic accident on June 11 of that same year sealed John W. Longyear's future plans. His father was killed while felling a tree. The twenty-six-year-old son became the head of the family that included five younger brothers, a sister and their widowed mother. Two older married sisters lived nearby. The Longyears were a well-organized, successful farming clan but John was not the planter and reaper of the family. He handled the business details and brought home extra earnings from his own activities. He invited his brother Ephriam to read law in the now-established Longyear office in the county seat.

In 1848, John Longyear became the Whig candidate for the State House of Representatives from Ingham County. His opponent, Joseph Kilbourne of Okemos, was highly respected, especially since he had the year before introduced the bill that moved Michigan's capital from Detroit to Ingham County. Longyear made an exceptional showing against the more experienced lawmaker, but lost to Kilbourne by a single vote.

Meanwhile, a few miles to the southwest of the Longyear place, Orlando Mack Barnes had put together a plan that took him away from the farm to earn a livelihood. A native of Cato, New York, twelve-year-old Orlando had arrived in Aurelius Township in 1837 with his parents, John and Anna Abbott Barnes. It was the most primitive era of the county's history when wilderness and wildlife dominated the interior of the state. In later years, Barnes frequently kept audiences spellbound by relating his pioneer experiences, which included such activities as walking to Jackson and back the same day.

By the late 1840s, Barnes was a student at the University of Michigan, where he displayed his knack for recognizing investments with a lucrative future. It would take Barnes nearly a decade to get through the university because his finances were meager and he several times left school to work. Selling farm machinery, particularly plows that could turn the rich soil of newly logged-off forests and rolling prairies of mid-Michigan, became Barnes' method for paying his tuition, room and board in Ann Arbor. Riding on horseback from farm to farm, he discovered that he enjoyed the banter as well as the sales. The banter at one farm near Albion became even more important to Barnes when he discovered a mentally bright, physically attractive young woman operating the spread. Amanda Fleming eventually became Mrs. O. M. Barnes, wife of Lansing's wealthiest business baron. She accomplished, established, or suggested numerous projects for the betterment of Ingham County.

Barnes graduated from the university in the Class of 1850. He had majored in literature and became an avid devotee of Shakespeare's writings. Soon, his pursuit of law studies began in earnest. He was admitted to the bar after reading law in a variety of law offices in the state of New York and at Jackson.

It was not long before Barnes opened a law office in Mason, became active in Democratic party politics, and acquired the reputation as *the* lawyer in the county seat. Young men vied to study under his tutelage because the holder of a law certificate with experience in the Barnes office carried weight and prestige.

Barnes's political career began with a governor's appointment as prosecuting attorney of Ingham County. He used that experience later to win election to the post when the legislature changed the method of choosing prosecutors. It was Barnes's term as a state representative during the Civil War, his convincing oratory to raise money and troops for the Northern cause, and his unwavering championing of railroad development that provided opportunities and contacts that brought riches into his life.

The careers of Ephriam and John Longyear had taken paths similar to that of Orlando Barnes. They were recognized as excellent attorneys, were prominent in party (Republican) politics, took advantage of offers from their business contacts, and accumulated considerable wealth. Unlike Barnes, the Longyear brothers moved their law office to Lansing in 1847, shortly after the legislature voted to move the capital from Detroit to an interior site. Earlier historians refrain from crediting the Longyears with establishing the first law firm in Lansing. If they were not first, however, it is unclear who was. The Longyears are identified in county histories as "among the earliest of the bar to locate in the capital city."

John Longyear's marriage to Harriet Munro, a sister of Mrs. James Turner and Mrs. Daniel Case, placed him in a family active in politics, legal matters, and industrial developments. James Turner became a railroad magnate, using the Longyear legal expertise along the way. The land holdings that were accumulated are impressive, with the state's lumber-covered and ore-rich Upper Peninsula probably being the most lucrative. John Longyear's son, John Munro Longyear, eventually became a prominent citizen in the Marquette area.

The son, when just out of college, wrote *A History of the City of Lansing* under the pseudonym "M. Dash." (A "one-em dash" in typography jargon of the era was the horizontal character in the type case, similar to "—" on a typewriter keyboard.) The pocket-sized volume, published in 1870, includes a vivid description of a situation profitable for the lawyers. J. M. Longyear writes that in 1859, immediately after Lansing received its first charter, "a force of men was set at work upon Washington Avenue with plows, scrapers, shovels, and wagons and straightway the irregularities of that thoroughfare began to assume a different aspect . . . By this change some residences were left so high above the street that it became necessary to construct flights of stairs from the sidewalks (boardwalks) to the houses above, while others were left so far below the level of the street that in order to be able to look upon persons passing by, the inmates were obliged to gaze from the second story." The account concludes that "The troubles arising from these grades were particularly edifying to lawyers and civil engineers, as they were litigated and surveyed several times over . . . after two or three years of controversy the final assessment has been made."

The Washington Avenue problem, it turned out, wasn't quite so handily solved. As late as 1871, a distinguished visitor to the city made what may still stand as downtown Lansing's best-ever put-down. The visitor was being shown Washington Avenue during a walk the morning after he had given a lecture at the opera house. The guide commented on the avenue's width, to which the visitor replied, "Yes, it is the widest—and deepest—street I've ever seen," according to that evening's *State Republican*. Later that year, that visitor, Mark Twain, published his famous *Roughing It*.

Court records from this period reveal that most cases—and the Barnes and Longyear firms had the majority of them—dealt with land surveys and rights, misuse of horses, cattle foraging in neighbors' yards and gardens instead of at the "common grounds," and theft from woodpiles and unsecured dwellings. A surprising number of divorces were granted and again the division of the live-stock was a major concern.

When the abolition movement began to heat up and war became imminent, both Orlando Barnes and John W. Longyear turned the bulk of their legal work over to associates and jumped into the boiling political cauldrons. Barnes, aligned with the Democrats, shone at the state level. Ephriam Longyear accept-ed city of Lansing positions and appointments; President Lincoln appointed him Lansing postmaster. Later, Ephriam was elected mayor. Brother John W. Longyear was elected representative to Congress from the Third District in 1862 and re-elected in 1864. As a member of the Thirty-eighth and Thirty-ninth Congresses, he witnessed the devastation of America's bloodiest war, the trau-ma of Lincoln's assassination, and the mass confusion that existed as Congress tried to guide the nation's reconstruction.

Longyear's widely recognized refined legal mind is reflected in an address he delivered in the House of Representatives on April 30, 1864, on "Reconstruction of the Union." In that lengthy talk, he presented the answers that reflected the position of the Republican Party on the questions "What is a state?" "What is it to become and to be a state of the Union?" "What are the relations of the State in rebellion to the General Government while they are at war with it?" "And what will be those relations when those states are subdued by force of arms?"

Longyear became entangled in the controversial extension of United States land grants to the Amboy, Hillsdale, Lansing, and Traverse Bay Railroad. Many assessors of the political scene believe it cost Longyear his seat in Congress.

When the war ended, the county's young lawyers who had survived the bat-tles returned to Michigan. Congressman Longyear further developed his Lansing law practice with a new partner, Schuyler Seager, who had begun his law education in the same office. Ephriam Longyear was by now a banker with his own bank on the ground floor of the Longyear Building on the northeast corner of Washington and Michigan avenues. The prestigious Longyear & Seager law firm occupied the second floor.

Schuyler Seager was undoubtedly the first law specialist in the Ingham County bar. Resolutions presented November 3, 1883, by fellow lawyers at the time of Seager's untimely death at age forty-two attest to his specialty in corporation law. Seager was well known in the courts of Michigan's Upper Peninsula, where he represented lumbering and mining companies.

The day after Seager's death, an informal meeting of the Ingham County bar was held in the circuit courtroom at Mason. Stephan D. Bingham's remarks to the court included, "He seldom practiced in this court, yet he had connection with cases of very great magnitude, involving interests of millions, and he carried them to a successful conclusion."

On February 18, 1870, President Ulysses S. Grant commissioned John Wesley Longyear as judge of the United States District Court for the Eastern District of Michigan. To mount the federal bench in May of that year required the Longyears to move to Detroit. The stay was just short of five years, for on March 11, 1875, Judge John W. Longyear died without warning. This leading Republican's funeral from the wooden First Presbyterian Church at Washington Avenue and Lapeer Street and his burial at Mt. Hope Cemetery was thoroughly covered by Lansing's newspapers. Eulogies praised his intellect and fair interpretation of law, and the cortege of over a mile in length was a final expression of endearment to Ingham County's first federal judge.

By the 1880s, Ephriam Longyear was in poor health, living in California in the winter and in Lansing during the warm-weather months. His spacious, imposing, and elegant home on North Capitol Avenue was a showplace. Some visitors to Lansing even mistook it for the Capitol before the present seat of government was completed in 1879.

Orlando Barnes withdrew from active participation in his law office sometime in 1871 when he began to devote all his working time to the Jackson, Lansing, and Saginaw Railroad Company. Since its organization, Barnes had been secretary of the company, its legal counsel, and general attorney. Then came his opportunity to become land commissioner for the expanding transportation system. These new responsibilities provided Barnes with capital that he invested in downtown Lansing real estate. He also formed the State Savings Bank and bought into a number of the county's industries. Barnes, the risk taker, was enjoying his wealth and was becoming an example of a poor farm boy rising to the top of the social pyramid.

Other dreams became realities for the Barnes family between 1875 and 1880. Work began on a new home situated at the south end of Capitol Avenue, with its back yard along the north bank of the Grand River. The Mason office was closed and the dwelling there was sold. The family toured Europe for a year while awaiting completion of their new house.

On their return to Lansing, the Barneses learned "the castle" was causing an awesome reaction from the citizenry. The 17,537 square feet of living space was divided into twenty-six rooms, eleven halls and landings, and six stairways. The three-story building was in the center of four acres of lawn and gardens sloping to the river. No other place in town rivaled it except the new state Capitol six blocks to the north. A gardener, housemaid, cook, and liveryman were employed to maintain the mansion. Lansing residents were welcomed into the home on numerous occasions and the populace appear to have revered Orlando and Amanda. He was elected the city's mayor the year he moved into the big house. Two years later, the state's Democrats prevailed on him to be their candidate for governor; but it was not to be. Michigan, a Republican stronghold, elected Charles M. Croswell of Adrian.

Although his counsel was sought by many, Barnes never opened another law office. He continued as land commissioner, continued developing his vast library, continued managing his various investments, and accepted an appointment to the state prison board. His contribution to the state penal system is still recognized.

The Barnes fortune began to have difficulties as the century's final decade approached. In 1893, a bank panic occurred and two of the banks Barnes had established—the Ingham County Bank and the Central Michigan Bank—failed to survive. A bleak period set in for Orlando Mack Barnes and his son, Orlando Fleming Barnes; the latter lacked his father's discernment in business.

Orlando M. did not live into the new century for death came at age seventy-five on November 11, 1899. His finances were in worse shape than anyone realized, with over $200,000 in outstanding debts. Second mortgages had been taken out on many of his properties, except the mansion, which he had separated from his estate. An article in the February 7, 1901, *Lansing Journal* stated that the Barnes estate was settled. All remaining properties were divided among the creditors with most of them receiving only about seventy cents on the dollar.

As the attorneys and courts moved rapidly forward into the twentieth century, the pioneer lawyers were left in their graves. Eventually, their offices and their resplendent homes that silently spoke of their success at the bar were razed. The contrasts they experienced from holding court in a log cabin to a more sophisticated setting in a courthouse was now a record in a Pioneer Society paper. They had walked into a wilderness as youths; as men, they guided a new transportation system and rode in plush railroad cars. They recognized the need for a brotherhood in their profession and that was the living legacy they left as each took pride in helping establish, and being a member of, the Ingham County bar.

10

MICHIGAN'S "BIG FOUR"

As the war between the states focused national attention on Michigan—where President Lincoln's Republican Party had been born a few years before—the Wolverine state was also getting its share of attention for its judicial reforms. Especially at the supreme court level, a new system of four elected justices, unfettered from their previous dual duties as judges in the state's circuits, appeared to be working well. In 1858, for instance, the Michigan Supreme Court decided ninety-six cases; not a large number, perhaps, for a state whose population was approaching 750,000 but significantly more than the average of thirty-two cases per year for the period from 1852 to 1858, when the justices spent most of their time presiding on the circuit court benches in the state's four circuits.

The Michigan Constitutional Convention of 1850 changed all that, providing for the eventual establishment of a supreme court independent of the circuit court system. But the reform didn't occur all at once. There was considerable controversy in the 1850 constitutional convention over the organization of the state judicial system. About the only concept on which there was general agreement was the need to abolish the combined circuit judge-supreme court justice arrangement which allowed "circuit judges to assemble together and persist in their errors," in the words of Justice William E. Potter. In 1934 speeches before bar association meetings in Grand Rapids and Detroit, Potter presented detailed analyses of the Michigan Supreme Court from its earliest days and included some interesting court stories. The Potter history turned up in 1990 in an apartment formerly occupied by Hazel Bray, a supreme court secretary in the 1930s who died in 1989 at age ninety-nine.

The 1850 constitutional convention established eight circuit judges with supreme court powers instead of four supreme court judges with circuit powers. It also provided authorization for the creation, after six years, of a separate supreme court, according to Justice James V. Campbell's 1876 *Outline of the*

Political History of Michigan. All state and judicial officers were made elective, subject to impeachment for misconduct.

In 1857, the legislature provided for four supreme court justices to be elected to an independent court, nominated by congressional districts and serving eight-year terms. Another provision of the constitutional convention stated there would be no revision of the Michigan statutes, although a compilation of existing laws was permitted. That job was tackled, and successfully completed, in 1857 by an up-and-coming young Lenawee County attorney, Thomas M. Cooley. He was hired for the task by the Republican legislature upon the recommendation of his Adrian law partner, Charles M. Croswell, a former law student of Cooley's and secretary of the Jackson convention that founded the Republican Party. Croswell later became Michigan's governor.

It took nine months for Cooley, who had publicly broken his ties to the Democratic Party in the election of 1856, to produce the *Compiled Laws of 1857.* His early work for the state was described in a 1987 *Wayne Law Review* (vol. 33, no. 5) article by Professor Edward M. Wise, an associate dean at Wayne State University.

Legislative leaders quickly recognized Cooley's talents. One of their first actions as the 1858 session opened was to appoint him to the new supreme court staff as reporter of its decisions. Justice Campbell said later:

> We selected him because we had noticed in his management of cases, even in his early standing at the Bar, a very great discrimination in picking out and enforcing the strong and important points in a case. He was able to select from . . . a confused mass of material . . . the key to every transaction with a clearness of mind that [made] him . . . one of the best reporters . . . we ever had in the United States.

Reporter Cooley kept that job for seven years, Wise wrote, editing eight volumes of the *Michigan Reports*, even though he was appointed on March 30, 1859, as one of the original three professors for the University of Michigan's new law school. The other two law professors were Justice Campbell and Charles I. Walker, a Detroit lawyer. Cooley moved to Ann Arbor and as the only resident member of the law faculty, took on the day-to-day task of running the school, although he was not formally designated as its dean until 1870.

An Attica, New York, farm was the birthplace of Thomas McIntyre Cooley on January 6, 1824. He was his father, Benjamin's, tenth child and the thirteenth offspring of the father's second wife, Rachael. The shy, studious Thomas Cooley graduated at age eighteen from Attica Academy. He then studied law at Palmyra, New York, under a former Democrat congressman and later a New York Supreme Court justice, Theron Strong.

Cooley was nineteen when he headed to Michigan, settling at Adrian and completing his law studies under three Adrian lawyers in 1845. He was admitted to the bar in January 1846 and soon moved to Tecumseh to join C. A. Stacy, a probate judge and avid Democrat, in a law practice. But within a year or so, he was back in Adrian and in partnership with Fernando Beaman, one of his ex-teachers. Together, they organized the Free-Soil Party in Lenawee County and backed Martin Van Buren for president.

In 1850, Cooley moved to Coldwater but was back in Adrian in partnership with Beaman and a lawyer named Beecher. He rejoined the Democratic Party and was elected circuit court commissioner.

Professor Cooley was forty and had been on the law school faculty for nearly five years when he decided to run in the fall of 1864 for a Michigan Supreme Court vacancy created by the death of Justice Randolph Manning, who had served since the 1857 election with Campbell and Justices George Martin and Isaac P. Christiancy. Democrat Alpheus Felch, the former governor and U.S. senator, was Cooley's opposition; but Cooley won handily in his first try at a major office.

Three-quarters of what was to become known as "the ablest state court that ever existed," in the words of Irving Browne, editor of the *Albany Law Review* at the time of Cooley's death in 1898, was now intact. And the court approached its full stride on January 1, 1868, when Benjamin F. Graves, a hard-working circuit judge, replaced Justice Martin, who did not run for reelection and died two weeks before his term was completed. Justices Campbell, Christiancy, Cooley and Graves were soon to become the "Big Four" and put Michigan on the nation's legal map. Of the four, Justice Christiancy, because of his earlier career and a post-court stint as one of Michigan's U.S. senators, probably was better known to the general public. To fellow lawyers and academicians, Cooley and Campbell probably were more familiar because of their long tenures at the University of Michigan.

Isaac Peckham Christiancy was a native of Johnstown, New York. He was born March 12, 1812, the son of a blacksmith/farmer who was disabled by a serious accident when the future judge was twelve. With what education he had absorbed at two local academies, young Isaac became the family breadwinner, teaching school at intervals and studying with a local attorney. Christiancy was twenty-four when he came to Michigan, settling at Monroe, serving as a clerk in the federal land office, completing his law studies, and quickly becoming one of the town's foremost lawyers. By 1846, he had served three terms as Monroe County prosecutor.

Originally a Democrat, Christiancy was opposed to slavery and joined the Free Soil movement in 1848. He first came to Lansing in 1850 to serve in the state senate and was defeated as the Free Soil candidate for governor in 1852. In 1856, Christiancy, now a member of the new Republican Party he helped found, purchased the *Monroe Commercial* and the next year was elected to the supreme court, remaining until 1875, when he resigned to become U.S. senator. For a short time during the Civil War, he served on the staff of General George A. Custer. For most of the twenty years that he was on the high court bench, Christiancy lived in a splendid mansion he built on a bluff in the southeast part of Lansing. Christiancy Elementary School was later constructed on the site of the home.

James Valentine Campbell was born on February 25, 1823, at Buffalo, New York. His father was a successful merchant, county judge, and a prominent Episcopal layman when the family moved to Detroit when James was a toddler. The boy was educated at a private boarding school in Flushing, New York, studied law under a pair of Detroit attorneys, and was admitted to the bar in 1844 when he was twenty-one.

A Whig until he became a Republican, Campbell was a member of the Detroit Board of Education as a young man and continued his interest in education throughout his life. When elected to the first "independent" supreme court, he was its youngest member at age thirty-four, and also was the youngest member of the University of Michigan's original law faculty in 1859.

Even before Graves joined the court, it had acquired a semblance of a national reputation with a series of opinions that had impact outside of Michigan. One of these was the famous case of *Twitchell v. Blodgett* (13 Mich. 127) which had its oral arguments in Lansing on January 26, 1865, only a few weeks after Justice Cooley joined the court. The question involved the Soldiers' Voting Law, hastily passed by Michigan's 1864 legislature. The statute allowed Michigan soldiers in the Union Army to file absentee voter ballots in the November general election when President Abraham Lincoln was returned to office for another four years, along with a host of Republican state officials, state legislators, and county officials. The problem was that the constitution provided for places and means for voting but did not mention absentee voting. Opponents of the law questioned whether a special class, such as soldiers in active service outside their home voting precincts, could legally vote.

The decision could have had an immediate effect in Michigan. Twitchell, a challenger for the office of prosecuting attorney in Washtenaw County, had received a majority of what his lawyers termed the "legal vote." But if the "soldier vote" was considered, the incumbent won handily. As it turned out, the Washtenaw County canvassers decided to disallow the "soldier vote" and certified Twitchell's election. Attorney General Amos C. Blodgett then ruled that the 1864 legislation permitted the counting of the absentee soldier ballots, giving the election to the incumbent and forcing Twitchell to file suit. If the law was overturned, and the votes of the absentee soldiers were removed from the final tallies, it could result in the unseating of numerous Republican electees. The case was one of the first to be heard by the supreme court, whose four members—in those days before "non-partisan" judicial elections in Michigan—had all been elected on the Republican ticket.

Lansing, now a city of close to twenty thousand, was bustling with Michigan's leading politicians that cold January day, recalled lawyer/State Senator Hugh McCurdy of Corunna years later in a courtroom eulogy at the time of Campbell's death. McCurdy said "excitement ran high on the fate of the issue involved, and everything was done that could be to induce the Supreme Court to sustain the law and save the party."

McCurdy was boarding at the American Hotel, as was Justice Campbell and at least two of his benchmates, while the court was in session. Because office space was at a premium in the capitol, the justices frequently held evening debates and wrote opinions in their hotel rooms. The oral arguments on *Twitchell v. Blodgett* continued through January 27 and the court set the next morning for making its decision.

Campbell and McCurdy left their rooms on the same floor at the same moment on the morning of January 28, Campbell cradling "a bunch of papers" as McCurdy commented, "Now, judge, comes the tug-of-war," to which Campbell replied, "Yes, senator, and I am going to do what I believe is right, and let the consequences take care of themselves."

Justices Campbell, Christiancy, and Cooley rendered decisions declaring the law unconstitutional. Justice Martin dissented, holding that the legislature had the right to allow soldiers to vote in absentia because of the emergency. Campbell closed his opinion with these emphatic words: "And I am, therefore, compelled to declare that in my opinion the act of the Legislature authorizing voting on a different basis is invalid. Public duty will not permit me, as a magistrate, to offer excuses for performing an unavoidable office. If our constitution deprives the privilege of voting a class of men to whom we are largely indebted for having the right preserved to ourselves, the only remedy is to invoke the people to amend a restriction which has become too narrow for complete justice."

Several Republican incumbents lost their offices as a result of the supreme court decision, which had a domino effect in a number of northern states that had followed Michigan's lead a few months before and had passed their own soldier voting laws. The courts in a majority of those states also followed the Michigan example and found the legislation unconstitutional. The end of the war in 1865 made the question moot. But the decision did trigger new legislation, or referenda, to finally permit absentee voting that is now commonplace in a mobile United States.

Benjamin Franklin Graves had twelve years of experience as a Michigan trial judge when he joined the supreme court in 1868. He also had the "prerequisite" for being a member of the "Big Four"—a New York birthplace and training as a young man in a law office in that state. Graves was born on October 18, 1817, near Rochester, New York. He worked on his father's farm as a youth but was disabled by illness and began to study law at age twenty, first in nearby Albion and later in Rochester. He was admitted to the New York bar at Rochester in 1841 and spent the next winter as journal clerk of the New York State Senate. He moved to Kentucky in 1843, then to Battle Creek, Michigan, where he practiced law and served as justice of the peace.

In 1857, Graves was elected judge of the Fifth Circuit, which included Eaton, Calhoun, Kalamazoo, Allegan, and Van Buren counties, and would have taken office on January 1, 1857. But before that term began, he was appointed to fill a supreme court vacancy for the remaining months of 1857. He opted to return to the circuit bench where he was known for nine years to have worked hard, even to the extent of holding night sessions, to keep court dockets clear.

Graves resigned early in 1867 when he was threatened with paralysis, but was elected to the supreme court the next year and joined "the three Cs" at the beginning of 1868. Critics of the Cooley-Christiancy-Campbell-Graves court— and there were some—occasionally noted it seemed to lean in favor of big business, especially the railroads. The criticism reached a fever pitch as an aging Cooley prepared to run for re-election to the supreme court bench in 1885 and was opposed by both the *Detroit Free Press* and *Detroit Evening News*, both fiercely Democratic at the time. In a 1964 *Wayne Law Review* article, former Michigan Supreme Court Justice George Edwards, then sitting on the U.S. Sixth Circuit Court of Appeals bench in Cincinnati, reproduced a *News* editorial urging Cooley's defeat.

The editorial, in part, responded to Cooley's defense of the court's rejection of an appeal request in a libel suit in which the *News* had been hit with a $20,000 judgment, sizable in those days. It had been awarded to a Canadian husband who claimed his ailing wife had been "debauched" by a University of Michigan physician. The *News* claimed Cooley was prejudiced against the paper. Then it reported that in a five-year period the supreme court had decided ninety-three corporation cases in favor of corporations and only nineteen against, including seventy-two in favor of railroads and only sixteen against.

Over the years, the "Big Four" court handled dozens of cases involving railroads. But the ruling in *People v. Salem* in 1870 probably attracted the most criticism—and the decision was against railroading. In that case (officially listed as *The People ex rel. The Detroit and Howell Railroad Co. v. the Township Board of Salem*, 20 Mich. 452) the court was asked to decide whether public aid to railroads was constitutional. In those days of expanding frontiers and promoting trade and faster, more comfortable transportation, both the federal and state governments were accustomed to favor any legislation that would help "progress."

At issue was whether the township, in Washtenaw County, could defy state law and refuse to issue bonds to help pay for construction of a railroad crossing the township. The township board had passed a resolution providing that "no bonds, or other certificates of indebtedness shall be issued by said township to aid in the construction of the Detroit and Howell Railroad, unless the ties shall be furnished and delivered on the line of the road; and the road-bed thereof, including all bridges, culverts, cattle-guards and road crossings, shall be fully completed and ready for the iron, within the limits of the township of Salem, on or before the first day of July, a.d. 1868." A Washtenaw County jury ruled in favor of the railroad, and when the township refused to post its contribution, the railroad sought mandamus relief from the supreme court. The township attorneys' response was that townships have no power, either at common law or under Michigan statute, to pledge their credit or make donations to private corporations.

The high court ruled during its April 1870 term in *People v. Salem* (20 Mich. 452) that it was unconstitutional for the legislature to authorize municipalities to aid financially railroad construction through taxation. Justices Cooley, Christiancy, and Campbell voted in the majority. Justice Graves dissented in a lengthy opinion he conceded "is longer, much longer, than I intended . . . I have written to justify myself, not to convince others [and] I have this consolation, that if I am in error, my mistake can work no public mischief."

Professor Wise noted the decision "met with mixed expressions of respect for the court's integrity and outrage at its perversity in impeding progress." But in the end, opposition to railroad aid proved popular with the citizenry and eventually became a central issue in railroad regulation reform.

It was in what the history books term the "Kalamazoo Case" that the Big Four court probably rendered its most famous decision. Officially, the case was entitled *Stuart v. School District No. 1 of the Village of Kalamazoo.* The suit was originally brought by Charles E. Stuart and others who objected to an attempt by the school district to establish a free, tax-supported high school and staff. More specifically, should public funds be used to teach teenagers such subjects as French, German, advanced arithmetic, history, surveying, bookkeeping, Latin, Greek, and rhetoric? Labor unions fought for the establishment of the secondary schools, but taxpayer groups everywhere erected barricades.

Kalamazoo residents voted in 1872 to give the free high school concept a try. Stuart and his co-plaintiffs responded with an attempt to restrain the collection of that portion of the school taxes assessed for support of the high school and for payment of the superintendent's salary. The Kalamazoo Circuit Court had issued a decree dismissing the Stuart complaint, and the taxpayer group then appealed *Stuart v. Kalamazoo* (30 Mich. 69) to the supreme court. After lengthy debate and two days of oral arguments in its Lansing quarters, the high court rendered a unanimous decision, penned by Justice Cooley. The landmark decision provided a legal foundation that envisioned free, tax-supported schooling from the earliest grades to the university.

Wrote Cooley:

We content ourselves with the statement that neither in our state policy, in our constitution, or in our laws, do we find the primary school districts restricted in the branches of knowledge which their officers may cause to be taught, or the grade of instruction that their officers may cause to be taught, or the grade of instruction that may be given, if their voters consent in regular form to bear the expense and raise the taxes for the purpose.

In arriving at his decision, Cooley went all the way back to the Northwest Ordinance of 1787, the first "constitution" of what became Michigan Territory, pointing out that Congress originally donated lands for educational purposes. Later, he wrote, territorial authorities "accepted in the most liberal spirit" the ordinance's requirement that "schools and the means of education shall forever be encouraged."

Cooley also noted the 1850 constitutional convention, ratified by Michigan voters, provided for establishment of free schools. "The inference seems irresistible," he wrote in his opinion, "that the people expected the tendency towards the establishment of high schools in the primary school districts would continue until every locality capable of supporting one was supplied." After the Michigan decision, there was no stopping the free high school movement. State after state followed the Cooley court's lead and struck down attacks against tax-supported secondary education.

Widespread as was their fame in judicial circles, the Big Four justices were together for just over seven years—January 1868 to February 1875—when Christiancy resigned to accept the U.S. Senate appointment after seventeen years on the bench. Graves was next to leave, in 1883, after serving fifteen years. Cooley resigned October 1, 1885, after twenty years on the court; Campbell remained the longest, thirty-two years, until a heart attack ended his life at sixty-seven years of age on March 26, 1890.

Contemporaries and later historians agree that in addition to native intelligence and an intense love of the law, the members of the Big Four court acquired a sizable share of their reputation through hard work. When court was in session, the justices regularly commenced work at 7:30 a.m. Arguments were heard from 9:30 a.m. to 12:30 p.m. and from 2:00 p.m. to 5:30 p.m. The judges frequently remained at the Capitol until 10:00 p.m. reading records, writing opinions, and reading each others' opinions. And frequently, contemporaries reported, Cooley and Campbell took work home.

Cooley, who taught in the law school throughout most of his judicial career, also turned out a series of major legal textbooks. His *A Treatise on Constitutional Limitations* was the first (1868) and most famous and went through six editions. An early, systematic analysis of the legal restrictions on state legislative power, it was largely responsible for his national fame and reputation.

Graves, Cooley, and Campbell were joined in 1875 by appointee Isaac Marston, who had just completed a nine-month period as Michigan attorney general after four years as Bay County prosecutor and a short stint as a fill-in state representative for a special session in 1872. The court lineup that included

Marston—a student of Cooley and Campbell at Ann Arbor—continued to enjoy the "Big Four" reputation for another eight years but never reached the heights of the original quartet. Marston resigned in 1883 to enter private practice in Detroit.

Within two years, the Democrat resurgence in Michigan had gained momentum and Cooley was defeated for re-election in 1885 by Allen B. Morse of Ionia, the first Michigan Supreme Court justice to have been born in Michigan. Psychologically whipped by the Detroit newspaper attacks, Cooley decided not to complete his term and resigned.

He was not finished with public service, however. In 1887, President Grover Cleveland appointed him to the newly created five-man Interstate Commerce Commission; he served two years as its chairman, resigning in 1891. In 1893, although he was a semi-invalid, he was elected president of the American Bar Association.

As his life neared its end, Cooley, despondent over his wife's death in 1891, suffered a brain disorder and was taken to an asylum near Flint. He rallied briefly and was brought back home, where he recognized some friends and family members. When Cooley died in Ann Arbor on September 12, 1898, there was an outpouring of praise for him in the nation's press and spoken eulogies in courts across the land.

The *New York Times* said that during his time on the bench, "There was, perhaps, no lawyer in the United States so universally conceded to be of the first rank, as Judge Cooley." The *Chicago Tribune* printed an obituary that was two full columns long. It called his work "brilliant, profound and of lasting effect on the intellectual life of his country" and said "many held him to be the greatest constitutional lawyer" in the country.

Christiancy had a sad life after he left the court. He was recently widowed when he went to Washington in 1875 to replace Zachariah Chandler in the Senate. According to the lurid tale, a young woman in the boarding house where he lodged twisted a casual remark into a marriage proposal and threatened Christiancy with a breach of promise suit. To quell the scandal, he married the woman, who left him the day after the wedding. Embarrassed publicly, he eventually wrangled an appointment as minister to Peru from President Rutherford B. Hayes. He returned to the United States in 1881 and finally "succeeded in shaking off his tormentors" by obtaining a divorce. But he moved back to Lansing a dejected and broken man, spending his final years in comparative retirement with his books and "mingling little with his fellow men." He died at his Lansing home on September 8, 1890.

Justice Campbell, as noted earlier, died in 1890 when he was still on the bench. And Justice Graves, who had retired at the end of his term in 1883, moved from Battle Creek to Detroit in 1894 and died there on March 3, 1906.

When the State Bar of Michigan was completing its new Lansing head-quarters in the mid-1960s, bar officials sought a fitting art object for the new structure at 306 Townsend Street. They settled on a portrait of Michigan's "Big Four" and had likenesses of Justices Cooley, Christiancy, Campbell, and Graves recreated, as a group, in a courtroom setting. The painting occupies a prominent spot in the State Bar Building board room, only a block or so from where the famous legal quartet wrote sparkling pages in the *Michigan Reports* nearly a century before they were relegated to canvas.

11

MORE AND MORE LAWYERS

In the years immediately following the Civil War, Ingham County's legal ranks were swollen by the return of lawyer/soldiers who had fought for the Union cause, and by the emergence of a new breed of attorney—the university-trained lawyer. University of Michigan's law school was well into its first decade of existence and, while a great majority of its graduates had taken jobs with firms in Detroit, several others were attracted to the ever-growing state capital in Lansing. The 1860 federal census had counted 17,398 residents of Ingham County. Perhaps thirty of them were lawyers. The population total had dipped slightly to 17,128 at the time of a special state census in 1864, probably reflecting soldiers absent—or killed—in the war and other individuals who left the state on various war duties. But the Ingham population quickly increased to 25,268 in the 1870 federal census.

In addition to the surge of college-trained lawyers, Ingham County's existing cadre of veteran lawyers—headed by the Longyear brothers, Delos Wiley, Sam Kilbourne, and Orlando M. Barnes of Mason—was also doing its share of instructing students in the intricacies of the law and preparing them for acceptance into the bar.

One lawyer/soldier was Henry B. Carpenter, a New Yorker who came to Lansing in 1860 and was admitted to practice the next year after studying in the Longyear office. Carpenter enlisted in the Union army within the year, was quickly promoted to corporal, and was commissioned a second lieutenant in May 1863 and promoted to captain after being wounded at the Battle of Cold Harbor in mid-1864. He survived the war, returned to Lansing, and served two terms as Ingham County prosecutor and also as Lansing city attorney. Carpenter was still practicing law well into the twentieth century.

Among the University of Michigan-trained Ingham lawyers of the 1860s was Mason D. Chatterton, who as a teenager had settled in Meridian Township with his parents in 1851. Like Kilbourne, he was in the first class at Michigan

Agricultural College in 1855 and accompanied the eventual Ingham County Bar Association founder to the University of Michigan law school, graduating with the first class in 1861. Although he first entered politics as an Ingham circuit court commissioner, probate judge, and village president of Mason, Chatterton was a more gifted writer than Kilbourne, who was an adequate public speaker and better at telling historical accounts than writing them. After his death in 1903, a Chatterton volume titled *Immortality of Man from the Standpoint of Reason* was published.

Chatterton was drafted into the Union Army during the waning days of the Civil War but was sent home on an indefinite furlough after reporting to the provost marshal in Jackson and was never called to service. He remained in Mason until moving to Lansing in 1886, serving as probate judge from 1873 to 1880.

Another early Michigan law school graduate was Albert E. Cowles, who in 1905 authored *Past and Present of the City of Lansing and Ingham County, Michigan*, one of the best of the early histories of the community. All Cowles could manage to print about himself was a simple, one-sentence autobiography: "Albert E. Cowles was admitted to practice with his University of Michigan Class at Ann Arbor in March 1862, now living in Lansing." Cowles allotted biographical space to 34 men whom he termed "early attorneys"—those who joined the Ingham County bar before the Civil War. Then he listed the names of 164 lawyers who joined the Ingham County bar and practiced in the area between 1862 and 1905.

Some of those early practitioners started their careers in the Lansing area but, still influenced by the call of the pioneer spirit, moved on to other locations. A few, such as William W. Upton, whose busy career was detailed earlier, achieved true national greatness in distant legal realms. Others included Daniel L. Case, who left Ingham County twice but always returned; both Longyears; George I. Parsons; John G. and Thomas J. Ramsdill; and Rollin C. Dart.

Parsons, a New York native, came to Lansing in 1848. He was prosecutor from 1857 to 1860 and Lansing city attorney the next two years before moving to Winona, Minnesota, where he died in 1884.

The Ramsdills, possibly Ingham County's first Michigan-born lawyers, both served as deputy clerks in the Michigan Supreme Court and both left for northern Michigan. John, born in Wayne County on January 10, 1830, arrived in Lansing in 1856, studied under Longyear, served in the high court office for a short time and then moved to Grand Traverse County, where he practiced law and served as circuit judge. Thomas, born three years after his brother, was admitted to the Ingham bar the same day as John—October 6, 1858—and moved to a practice in Manistee in late 1859. But he returned to Lansing in 1861 to take the deputy clerk job for the supreme court and later served in the legislature as a representative of Manistee and other counties.

Dart, a New York state native, arrived in Lansing in 1856, studied under the Longyears, joined the bar in 1858, and practiced in Ingham County until 1882, when he moved to Petoskey and practiced there for another quarter of a century. While in Ingham County, Dart was a justice of the peace for eight years, Ingham prosecuting attorney for four years, and a Lansing third ward alderman.

For eleven of the years in Lansing, Dart was in partnership with Delos Wiley. The Dart and Wiley firm was a prominent one and Wiley, who came to Lansing in 1857 from DeWitt, was probably the stronger of the pair. Cowles said about Wiley: "He gave and took hard knocks but did not allow them to break friendships between knocker and knockee." Dart & Wiley continued until Wiley died on May 5, 1874.

There was another lawyer in that early group who defies categorization— George W. Peck. He had as much to do as anyone with the capital being switched from Detroit to Lansing. With his gifts of public speaking, debating, and political maneuvering, he probably could have been elected to any office he desired in those pre-Republican years. He was also an astute businessman and at several times excelled in commodities and newspapers.

Peck was born in New York City on June 4, 1818. He attended primary school and an academy there, then studied law and came to Michigan in 1839 with every intention of practicing law in Oakland County. But for the first two years on the frontier, he followed mercantile pursuits in Oakland and Livingston counties. Then, in 1841, he resumed his law studies and was admitted to the Livingston County bar the next year, opening a practice in Brighton.

Unable to make an adequate living during three years of lawyering, Peck tested the political waters and was elected to the legislature as a Democrat. He immediately distinguished himself as a debater and framer of laws, was reelected in 1847, and was selected as speaker of the house for the session that was to choose the site of the new capital. Still with an eye for a good business deal, Peck looked into some land in Lansing Township and managed to buy considerable acreage near the confluence of the Grand and Red Cedar rivers. As Lansing's first postmaster and the man who canceled those now-valuable "Michigan, Michigan" covers, Peck set up the capital city's first post office in the Bush & Thomas general store near what later was the corner of Main and South Cedar streets.

Governor Epaphroditus Ransom still recalled Peck's stirring farewell address that had closed the old capitol in Detroit. As one of his first acts of office in 1848, Ransom appointed the thirty-year-old Peck as secretary of state. Two years later, Peck temporarily left active politics for business and in 1852 became proprietor of the *Lansing Democrat*, a newspaper that shouted the party cause. The sheet was at least partly financed with proceeds from Peck's related job as official state printer.

Meanwhile, Peck had established the first Masonic Lodge in Lansing and when he traveled around the state, he could talk enthusiastically about

Michigan's new constitution, business opportunities in the capital city, political news of the day, Masonry, or the Democratic Party. It surprised nobody who knew Peck when he announced he was running for the U.S. Congress in 1854.

Despite the euphoria in Michigan over the new Republican Party formed in the summer of 1854 and notwithstanding Michigan Democrats' stand that residents of territories that had not yet attained statehood should decide the slavery extension question themselves, Peck was elected to Congress. He lost his seat two years later when Republican DeWitt Clinton Leach, editor of the newly founded *Lansing Republican*, accused Peck and his party of being followers of the southern extremists who fostered slavery. Although he was a loser at the polls, Peck remained a hometown favorite, sold his newspaper and plunged back into the business and legal world.

As the war clouds gathered, Peck joined other northern Democrats in abandoning the party's southern wing and pledging themselves to the Union cause. He also began to agree with his old journalistic nemesis, Leach, when hostilities broke out and together they gave stirring speeches about the Union cause, although both men remained fiercely partisan.

Peck became concerned when the *Lansing Journal*, his old paper under new ownership and a new name, stopped publishing in 1861. Feeling there should still be a Democratic voice in Michigan's capital, Peck and some party associates purchased the *Journal* and Peck was again an editor.

By 1867, the public office bug had again bitten Peck. He ran for mayor of Lansing and won. But lawyering was still in Peck's blood and on January 9, 1868, the opposition paper, the *Republican*, reported that "Mayor Peck has formed a law partnership in East Saginaw. Lansing will still be the home of his family and meetings of the common council will be held every two weeks, when he will preside as usual." But the arrangement proved cumbersome and Peck, in the prime of his life at age fifty, had to admit he had spread himself too thin. Judge Jessie Tenney was appointed to fill out Peck's unexpired mayoral term.

Little was heard of Peck after the abrupt departure. In 1875, news reached Lansing that he had moved to Missouri. By 1880, he had moved to Arkansas, and was chief attorney for the St. Louis and Iron Mountain Railroad. It was twenty-two years before George W. Peck was heard from again in Michigan. On March 2, 1902, Peck's old *Lansing Journal* carried a story that the one-time political giant was crippled, destitute, and living in near poverty at the Masonic Home in Grand Rapids. His lodge brothers planned one last fete for the old man and made him guest of honor at a December 16, 1903, celebration at Lansing Capital Masonic Lodge. At eighty-five, Peck received visitors at the Hotel Downey and for one last time was the center of attention. He died in Saginaw on July 1, 1905.

Unlike Peck, most of the early attorneys remained in the county for their entire careers, although some of them entered business as a second vocation.

Others used their legal expertise as justices of the peace or in government-related positions such as city aldermen, city attorneys, or as members of city and state commissions. They included:

William H. Pinckney—A New York stater, he come to Ingham County in 1850 and practiced alone until 1857. He later was an aide to Attorney General Jacob M. Howard, served for a time as Lansing city recorder, and for many years as a justice of the peace. He died in 1901.

Orange Butler—Another New Yorker, he came first to Adrian, served in the legislature in 1837, moved to Lansing in 1849, and practiced for many years. He died in 1870.

William H. Chapman—He came to Lansing in 1848, a year after being admitted to the New York bar. Chapman held the offices of county judge, probate judge, and mayor of Lansing; he died in 1895.

George M. Huntington—Also from New York, he grew up in Mason and was admitted to the Ingham County bar in 1857 after studying law under Barnes. He soon joined Barnes as a law partner and was elected circuit judge in 1875. Huntington died in 1889.

Henry L. Henderson—Located in Mason in 1857, he was admitted to the Ingham County bar the same year. He practiced for nine years, then formed his own bank, later was cashier of Mason's First National Bank, and was president of the State & Savings Bank when he died in 1897.

In the years immediately following the Emancipation Proclamation and, eventually, the end of hostilities in the war between the states, most Michigan citizens could be said to be "anti-slavery." But that does not mean that they were all ready to accept southern blacks as equals. Lawyers, as a group, probably were as "liberal" in that area, or perhaps even more so, than the general population because of their strict belief in the U.S. Constitution and its amendments guaranteeing equality under the law.

The Ingham County bar—still an informal collection of legal practitioners but frequently united on important issues—must have been shocked to its core by the events of late August 1866. One evening, a frightened, near-destitute former slave from Kentucky was dragged at gunpoint from the county jail at Mason by an angry mob, lynched, and beheaded. Historical accounts of the lynching and the events that led up to it vary, just as did the newspaper accounts at the time. Even juries empaneled to try the alleged perpetrators of the bloody mob kidnapping disagreed. One trial ended with a hung jury after considerable deliberation, and Circuit Judge Edwin Lawrence was forced to declare a mistrial. And a second trial got underway only after more than one hundred jurors were questioned before an impartial panel could be seated.

The central figure in Ingham County's only lynching—William Taylor— was sixteen years old when he fell in with soldiers of a Lansing infantry company of the Union army as they boarded a troop train that brought them home from Kentucky at the close of their service in the war. Taylor, who had been a camp follower with the company, had shined shoes, polished brass on uniforms, and run errands in exchange for bites of food and a comfortable place to bed down.

Jobs for a teenaged, illiterate former slave were scarce in Mason in the summer of 1866, but some of his soldier friends secured a hired hand try-out for Taylor on the farm of Daniel Buck and his family. Taylor was found by Buck to be "lazy, ignorant and vicious," according to an account written nearly seventy years later by Dr. Frank N. Turner for George N. Fuller's *Historic Michigan*, and Buck ordered him off the farm with only his room and board as pay for what work he had done. He next moved in with a black family in Lansing and later with another black family near Bath. The latter also turned him out, hungry and wearing only the tattered rags he had worn on the farm. Taylor went back to the Buck farm and again tried to collect some wages. Rebuffed, Taylor returned later that night—probably just before midnight on August 22, 1866—with the idea of burglarizing the house to get enough clothing so he could enroll in school and get an education.

That was the way the story was recalled nearly half a century later by an aging D. B. Harrington, editor of the *Ingham County News* in Mason at the time of the tragedy. His 1911 recollection was reprinted in the *Pioneer History of Ingham County*, published in 1920. Harrington prefaced his account by writing that as editor of the Mason weekly, he "took unusual pains to obtain and publish the facts."

The story continued. Fearing Buck might resist his efforts, Taylor picked up an ax from Buck's woodpile in case it became necessary to defend himself. He went to Buck's room but found the bed empty. Sensing a trap, he started for the front door but in his haste aroused Buck's eleven-year-old daughter, who jumped up from the lounge where she was sleeping and hit her head on the ax, causing "a slight wound." Her screams were heard by her mother, who "pounced upon the Negro." Taylor, defending himself, struck Mrs. Buck "a slight blow with the side of the weapon." At this point, Mrs. Buck's mother entered the fray carrying a lamp and also received a blow with the side of the ax. In the excitement, Taylor managed to run from the house and escape on his horse.

Buck, it developed, had gotten up, realized it was sprinkling outdoors, and went to a nearby field to cover a partly erected oat stack. Summoned by the women's screams, he had returned to the house too late to confront the boy. He quickly alerted neighbors, who summoned Sheriff Frederick P. Moody. A posse was on Taylor's trail within minutes and he was captured within three hours at Bath.

Taylor was brought back to the jail at Mason by Sheriff Moody. In the August 19, 1866, edition of his paper, Harrington reported the prisoner was at first locked up in the Lansing city jail, where Moody "found the street and the area around the jail filled by an infuriated mob, intent on lynching the assassin on the spot." That story referred to Taylor as "the assassin" and "the murderer" because initial reports were that all four members of the Buck family had been hacked to death. The original story reported Mrs. Buck "in a very low condition but [her mother] is considered out of danger." Why Harrington did not correct the impression that Taylor had killed them is still unexplained.

Three days after Taylor's capture, the Mason paper reported, a large mob of about two hundred, most of them from Delhi Township, collected at approximately 10:00 p.m. around the jail and demanded Taylor be turned over. When Sheriff Moody refused, "they broke down the jail doors and took Taylor from the cell to a tree near the depot and hung him," the paper reported. "After the rope was passed around his neck and over a limb, Mr. Buck came forward and questioned him about the butchery. He acknowledged the deed but denied ever having murdered before. He expressed a desire for prayers, and prayed for himself, after which he was drawn up and expired without a struggle."

When Harrington was recounting the "Horrible Tragedy!" (an 1866 headline) in 1911, he said he went with Dr. Wing, the local physician, to the Buck home the morning after the attack was reported and learned that "not a drop of blood was shed from those reported butchered except from the little girl, and so far as we could see no one was seriously injured."

On October 2, 1867, more than a year after the lynching, the Mason paper reported a hung jury in the trial of William Cook "for hanging the Negro, Taylor." Prosecutor Rollin Dart, the story said, was assisted at the trial by Austin Blair of Jackson, who had completed two terms as Michigan's governor. The prosecutor was opposed by two of the best defense lawyers in the area, H. H. Shaw of Eaton Rapids, and Delos Wiley of Lansing. Dart announced immediately after the mistrial decision that he would try Cook again at the next term of court.

The second trial began and ended on February 13. The *Ingham County News* reported that the jury, after a short deliberation, returned a not guilty verdict and that Cook was immediately released. The brief story on the acquittal mentioned that William Pinckney assisted Prosecutor Dart the second time around. The report concluded, "Thus endeth the matter of lynching the Negro, Taylor."

Shocking as it was, the lynching case and the two trials that resulted were quickly forgotten in Ingham county in the late winter of 1868 because the capital city was abuzz with debates about the proposed new Michigan constitution. The question of a constitutional revision, according to a provision of the state constitution re-written in Lansing in 1850 and overwhelmingly ratified by Michigan voters, had to be submitted to the state's voters in 1866 and every sixteen years thereafter. It had taken more than two years to get the new constitution on the ballot.

In explaining to its readers that the November 1866 general election could offer voters a proposition for the holding of a state constitutional convention, the *State Republican* wholeheartedly encouraged a "yes" vote. An October 10 editorial stated emphatically, "We do not believe there is a sensible man in the state who does not believe that we should have a new Constitution . . . there were in [the 1850 Con-Con] a few able men, but the good they attempted to accomplish, was so tinkered and amended by committees and old fogies that nobody would own it as their offspring after it was born."

Early in the legislature's 1866 session, the constitutional revision had been brought up. But the Senate and House could not agree on how delegates should be selected. The *State Republican* reported on February 20 that the House favored naming one delegate per House district and paying five dollars per day while drawing up a new document; the Senate wanted two delegates named for each senatorial district, with an additional three delegates representing each congressional district and another eighteen delegates appointed at large. That would result in a total of one hundred delegates, each of whom would be paid four dollars per day.

Various other convention configurations were discussed before Michigan voters decided in the fall election by a vote of 79,505 to 28,623 to hold a Con-Con and to elect one hundred delegates. Ingham County was allotted two delegates, apparently on an apportionment geared to the 1860 census, and in April of 1867 elected attorney John M. Longyear, and cabinet maker and businessman Lemuel Woodhouse.

Delegates met in Lansing on May 15. Key constitutional issues were salaries for state officials, government financial aid to railroads, absentee voting for soldiers on active duty out of the state (the state's supreme court had outlawed it four years before), a provision that state officers be required to attend personally to the duties of their office, and a prohibition on state funding of denominational institutions by grants of money or lands (the legislature had granted building lots to several Lansing churches to attract them to the new capital).

Included in the judicial changes proposed by the Con-Con were: adding a fifth supreme court justice; providing for four supreme court terms per year, one to be held in each of the judicial districts; and giving the high court the right to establish and modify its own rules "necessary for the exercise of its appellate jurisdiction." But by far the most controversial concept discussed by the convention delegates was one that would have given black males over twenty-one years old the right to vote. The 1850 constitution restricted the vote to male citizens of the United States, foreign-born male adults who had lived in Michigan at least two and one-half years, and "civilized" male Indians not living on reservations.

The final tally of the April 6, 1868, vote showed 110,582 in opposition to the proposed document and only 71,733 in favor. Supreme Court Justice and University of Michigan law professor James P. Campbell, probably one of the best political minds of the time, said the defeat was due to "an enormous majority, composed in great measure of the aggregate of the opponents of single parts of the instrument, which were not all obnoxious to the same objectors." He suggested that "it is entirely manifest that the faults of the present constitution are found in some of its details and specific provisions, and not in its general plan . . . logrolling and swapping measures are more easily carried through select bodies than through a popular election."

Seven years later, the legislature thought the time was ripe for another constitutional revision attempt. Legislators authorized the governor to appoint a representative "constitutional committee" of eighteen members, draft a general revision of the 1850 constitution, and submit it to voters.

Ingham County did not rate any direct representation on the committee, which Governor John J. Bagley appointed to do its work at an extra session in 1874. The draft was submitted to voters on November 4 and was resoundingly defeated, 124,034 to 39,285. A major objection, Justice Campbell wrote in his political history, was a feeling that the legislative function of proposing amendments did not extend to framing a wholesale revision and that a constitutional convention should be representative and not appointed. The constitution of 1850, eventually revised thirty-eight times out of seventy-one attempts, remained in force until January 1, 1909.

12

TRAINS, TRIALS, AND
TEMPERANCE

With its population over the 25,000 mark, Ingham County in 1870 had achieved a respectable size for a capital county. And with the 1870 U.S. census showing Lansing had 5,243 residents, Michigan's capital city—though considerably smaller than neighboring state capitals Columbus, Ohio, and Indianapolis, Indiana—had come a long way since some eighty residents had welcomed the seat of government twenty-two years before. Ingham County had quickly gone through the plank road/stagecoach era, which decreased in importance when Lansing's first railroad connection was completed to Owosso in 1859. Since 1864, when the Jackson-Lansing section of the Jackson, Lansing & Saginaw Railroad was opened, Lansing area residents, especially the Lansing lawyers who had business with the county courts and other offices at the county seat, could hop a coach to Mason twice each day and be assured of a speedy, comfortable, safe trip home in time for supper.

Ingham boosters were so willing to assist the railroads that they convinced the county to donate $40,000 to the J. L. & S. Railroad. The city of Lansing, not to be outdone, chipped in with $22,400 in city bonds and pledged a similar amount to the Peninsular Railroad's Lansing-Flint section, which would complete an east-west link between Port Huron and Lake Michigan.

Industry was starting to boom in Lansing. The state's nearby agricultural college was also prospering and agriculture was continuing to out-produce itself every year, with the railroad hauling out surplus crops and timber. Already, as the decade of the '70s began, there were plans for three additional railroads crossing the county. All that should have spelled a prosperous future for bankers, industrialists, businessmen, and lawyers alike.

But despite the seeming economic security, there was the nagging fear in the minds of some Lansingites that the whole thing could blow up if "outside" forces somehow managed to manipulate the state legislature into moving the capital from their city. Some lawmakers, especially those from Detroit and its neighboring counties, continued to protest the rigorous trip to Lansing and the rustic accommodations they found in the capital in the woods. Their early complaints in the first Lansing legislative session in 1848 had not resulted in a move. They tried again in the constitutional convention of 1850. Delegate John D. Pierce, architect of Michigan's free public school system, offered a motion to move the capital to New Buffalo, but cooler heads prevailed and the motion was defeated, eighty to zero. Pro-Lansing forces succeeded in inserting a provision as Article II of the proposed document—one of the shortest articles, incidentally, to be found in any constitution. It read, "The seat of government shall be at Lansing, where it is now established." The move gave constitutional sanction to Lansing's grip on the seat of government, underscoring what had been a mere legislative action. Voters overwhelmingly ratified the constitution.

That should have hushed the detractors and convinced the doubters that Lansing was here to stay as Michigan's capital city. But the talk continued. Hardly a session of the legislature was held but what some "renegade" would bring up the question of removing the capital from Lansing. The doubters feared it might happen in 1866, when the constitution decreed another constitutional convention should be held to consider amendments or a general revamping.

Probably what served most to quell the move-the-capital talk was the cooperative attitude of the Lansing citizenry in striving to make their city a comfortable place for legislators, state government officials, and visitors with state business. From the start, Lansing housewives had opened their homes to lawmakers, offering room and board during legislative sessions for nominal fees. The whole citizenry seemed to pitch in to spruce up the town for legislative sessions.

In his December 28, 1858, edition of the *Lansing Republican*, editor Rufus Hosmer reported, "The busy note of preparation has been the prevailing sound in and about Lansing for a week past. The great event of two years is about to happen . . . everybody's new clothes are kept 'till session . . . houses are painted, carpets renewed, walks prepared, beds renovated, cellars filled, wood piles replenished to be in readiness for session . . . delicacies are spared and saved until session and the entire economy of life is disturbed, in order that six score of worthy men may fare well for forty days and go away rejoicing, to say a good word for the comfort, hospitality and liberality of Lansing." Hosmer said he heard one local citizen "inform a neighbor across the fence that he didn't expect his cow to calve till session." He noted that "even churches" got into the spirit and were "painted and whitewashed ready for session." Hosmer said the "old wooden capitol" was cleanest of all, down to the "scrubbing at the old box stoves" and lamented that the portrait of Governor Cass, "looking like a cross between a country Justice and a Roman soldier, gazes mournfully down upon all this expense!"

Ten years later, another *Republican* editor, still concerned that Lansing's grip on the capital was not chiseled in stone, breathed a sigh of relief on the eve of

the ratification vote for a new state constitution. Ingham County had not had a
delegate of its own in the Con-Con that had met the previous year. Annual sessions of the legislature were included as one of the changes to be voted upon,
and editor/publisher S. D. Bingham probably realized that would expose his city
twice as often to legislative complaints about housing. But Bingham was heart-
ened by the fact the delegates again beat down a proposal to move the capital
from Lansing.

In his April 2, 1868, issue, Bingham, in an editorial addressed to "The
Citizens of Lansing," remarked that "the past 18 years has [seen] a continual
war against other localities, and rival interests about us have not only retarded
our growth, but made the retention of the seat of government a serious question." The situation had held down property values and caused some of "the
wealthiest of our citizens to dispose of their property here and remove elsewhere," he lamented.

> For the purpose of putting an end to the complaint that Lansing had
> no hotel accommodations, our citizens subscribed a large amount
> towards the erection of the Lansing House. There was great disap-
> pointment that it was not opened at the commencement of the last
> [1866] session of the Legislature. The prospect was that it would still be
> unfinished at the opening of the Constitutional Convention.   All
> believed that unless this was done, the convention would go elsewhere.
> To prevent this, many of our leading men invested their money, and
> some of them all their property, in the purchase of the hotel, and in fit-
> ting it up for the convention. This saved the Capital in the new
> Constitution.

By "saved," Bingham meant that the constitution was going to the voters without a clause jeopardizing Lansing's claim to the seat of government. The state's
voters overwhelmingly turned down ratification anyway a week later, 110,582
no votes to 71,733 yes.

There's an interesting footnote to the financing of Lansing's first comfortable hotel, which was tied, indirectly, to the assassination of President Abraham
Lincoln. The Lansing House at Washington Avenue and Washtenaw Street—
later to become the Hotel Downey and still later the site of the J. W. Knapp
store—had as its principal owners General Lafayette C. Baker and his cousin,
Lieutenant Luther B. Baker. The elder Baker was head of the U.S. Secret Service
during the Civil War and was placed in charge of the effort to capture actor John
Wilkes Booth, Lincoln's assassin. The actual pursuit by twenty-five cavalrymen
was placed in the hands of Lieutenant Baker. Congress eventually granted the
general twenty thousand dollars in reward money and his cousin five thousand
dollars for Booth's fiery capture. Both immediately resigned their commissions

and placed their rewards into the construction of the Lansing House, which opened in May of 1867.

The four-story structure, with canopied entrances on each street, was considerably more comfortable than the capitol itself. Lawmakers had complained for the past three sessions about the open well water supply in the capitol's back yard and the candle lighting, later replaced by smudgy kerosene oil lamps that only increased the fire hazard and added to the poor ventilation.

Early in the 1870 session, according to the Fuller/Turner *Historic Michigan*, there was again some loud legislative discussion "of moving to a more suitable building in another city." Finally, an act was passed to construct a new building on the original site or on the site of the office building then situated on the west side of Capitol Avenue at Michigan Avenue.

It was not until 1871, however, that the question of whether Lansing would remain as the seat of state government was finally resolved. Said the 1873 *Lansing City Directory*, edited by C. Exera Brown, in a sketch of the city, "The strongest element against the growth of Lansing was the constant fear among many of its inhabitants of the removal of the Capital to some other site . . . it was not until the Legislature of 1871 voted $1,200,000, to be raised by taxation in six years, for the purpose of building a State House, that the question of Lansing retaining that position permanently was regarded as finally settled."

During those early years of the 1870s, there were three major items that seemed to be on the minds and lips of Ingham County folks: the need for a new capitol building, one that would be safer from a fire standpoint for the storage of important state documents; salaries of state officials, especially circuit judges and supreme court justices; and the "liquor problem." The importance of the three items was directly reflected in the amount of news space these issues were allotted in the local newspapers.

The *Republican* decided to devote column after column in its four-page format to the 1871 annual address of Governor Henry P. Baldwin, which was reproduced in its entirety. His reference in the address to "a new capitol" was the first such official suggestion, although state officials and legislators had been grumbling for years about the little wooden structure. The *Republican* had already referred to the structure as "an old rattle-trap" and a "humiliation if not a positive disgrace" and John M. Longyear, son of the county's leading attorney, had said there were "private dwellings in the city of Lansing that would sooner be taken for the capitol by a stranger than the shed actually used for that purpose."

In his address, Governor Baldwin left the best for last when he said:

I deem it my duty to call your attention to the subject of the erection of a new capitol. The present State House was built nearly twenty-five years ago, when the State was comparatively new, with a population about one-fourth as large as at the present time, and with about one-twelfth of the present taxable valuation.

The present building was designed for a temporary purpose only; was poorly built, and is wholly insufficient in size and accommodations even for the purposes for which it is now used. The Legislative halls are small and inconvenient, without ventilation, and without necessary committee rooms. The Library should be steadily increased, but the rooms devoted to that purpose are already overcrowded. The Supreme Court room is exceedingly small, and wholly unfit for that purpose.

Baldwin recommended immediate action to erect a new capitol, including an appropriation of $30,000 for a temporary office building, $10,000 for plans and specifications for the new capitol, and $100,000 for fiscal 1872 toward the construction.

By March 31, the legislature had passed an act providing for a new capitol and for temporary quarters for state offices so that the original brick "state office building"—on the site of what was destined to be Michigan's capitol well into the twenty-first century—could be razed. It was almost a year later—March of 1872—that the legislature accepted Elija J. Myers's design for the new structure and appropriated $1,200,000 for its construction.

At the same time the *Republican* was promoting a new capitol, it was urging legislators, and its readers, to get on the bandwagon for an increase in judicial pay. The 1867 Con-Con had been voted down, partly on the pay increase issue, and the *Republican* had decided it was high time that Michigan started paying its judges fair salaries. The state's circuit judges had met in Lansing twice during 1870—once in July and again after Christmas—to discuss a uniform system of practice. In its last issue of 1870, the Lansing paper reported the December 28 meeting of "the Circuit Judges of this state to take into consideration the dilemma in which they are placed by the refusal of the people to increase their meager salary from $1,500 to $2,000 a year. There is a strong possibility that most, if not all of them, will resign unless the people reverse their decision."

Tacked on to the news report was this editorial plea: "Let a joint resolution provide for the submission of an amendment at the spring election. Then, instead of $2,000 a year, let the people vote upon an amendment to pay them $2,500 or $3,000 a year, or let the amendment give the Legislature power to fix the salary of Circuit Judges as they now fix that of Supreme [Court] Judges. In our view this should be done, and the salary for Circuit Judge should be at least $3,000 and of Supreme Judges $4,000 a year."

The Legislature complied, at least in part. It caused a proposed amendment to be placed on the spring ballot in 1872 calling for a $1000 raise for circuit judges. The proposal failed, 58,987 to 57,326—a closer margin than a vote for a $500 raise lost by in 1870.

Another amendment attempt at an increase to $2,500 was tried in 1876 and again was barely defeated—65,966 to 65,374. Finally, in 1882, Michigan voters decided to give their circuit judges a decent living wage and approved an amendment hiking their pay from $1,500 a year to $2,500 by a vote of 85,705 to 55,638. As it turned out, that $2,500 yearly stipend voted the circuit judges in 1882 didn't apply automatically to judges in the Upper Peninsula. It took another constitutional amendment in 1884 to extend the raise to the U. P.'s judges.

The increases came no easier, although somewhat sooner, for the supreme court justices. Their salaries were also pegged at $1,500 by the legislature when the independent court was organized in 1858. The pay was finally raised to $4,000 in 1874 and by 1889 had reached $5,000, where it remained for more than ten years. The next jump—to $7,000—came by a legislative act in 1903.

By far the most frequent types of local news items in the 1870s were the reports of arrests of saloon keepers for selling hard liquor and the arrests of consumers of spirits who, as a result of their imbibing, became involved in all sorts of debauchery, bar fights, petty thievery, and general mischief. Enforcement could not keep up with the hard liquor consumption, and the city council could barely keep pace by passing new ordinances to quell the flood of "demon rum" that seemingly threatened to inundate the city.

One of the first souls to run afoul of the new laws was Dennis Collins, who was brought into recorder's court on January 23, 1867, and fined eight dollars "by His Honor" for keeping open his saloon and grocery on Sunday, "contrary to the city ordinance." A review of typical criminal arrests and court proceedings from 1870 issues of the *Republican*, most of them containing a taste of liquor, included:

> **April 14**—The Wolf brothers, who took one side of the row in the Star Restaurant on election day, were arrested for disorderly conduct and one was fined $3 and costs, the other proving that what he done was in defense of his property. The Little boys, Frank Drum and others who took the other side of the contest, have disappeared from the city, fearing arrest. But, like bad pennies, they will soon return.
>
> **June 23**—LIQUOR SUIT - Dennis Collins, who keeps a saloon near the Michigan Avenue depot, was arrested on Monday, upon complaint of City Marshal Shafer, for selling liquor. The trial is to take place on Friday before Justice Shubael Greene.
>
> **June 30**—STOLE A WATCH - Last Thursday a girl 13 years of age, whose name we suppress, as it seems to have been the first offense, stole a ladies' gold watch from the store of H. P. Hitchcock. The girl was found after a search by the City Marshal, and the watch recovered and returned to the owner. The girl was taken before Justice Greene, and after a severe reprimand from the justice, and Prosecuting Attorney Carpenter, was allowed to go without further punishment at the request of Dr. Hitchcock. The girl lives some 10 miles northwest of the city.

December 14—"One night last week a woman who has a good husband and a good home was found so drunk that it was necessary to carry her out of the street to a comfortable room, lest she freeze to death." Another woman "was found dead drunk on Cedar Street last Wednesday, and the officers were obliged to take her to her home on a dray. The officers complained of Theo. Walters or, Augusta Ruxton, each claiming the other owns the saloon where the woman says she procured the liquor, and the trial is to come off next week before Justice Campbell."

Continually nudged by local church groups, particularly the women of the Methodist and Episcopal churches in Lansing and Mason, Ingham County and municipal officials in the two towns kept up the drive against saloons that insisted on selling hard liquor and the "drunkards" to which the spirits were sold. Fines at first were moderate, but continued to increase—especially for those convicted on bootlegging charges. Jail sentences for more than a day or two were infrequent and were used mostly for violators with reputations for harming themselves or others until they were sober.

But the temperance folks did not let up, and the *Republican* and *Ingham County News* continued to publish names and escapades of the violators. The editors covered frequent mass meetings of the temperance groups and devoted considerable news space to their preachings. And they lost few opportunities to color the reports of some of the bar-bashings with flowery comments and humorous telling of the stories.

By 1874, the temperance groups were commanding more and more attention. Along with police, prosecutors, the courts, and the press, the anti-liquor forces launched what became known in the weekly editions of the papers as "the liquor prosecutions"—an all-out effort to rid Ingham County of problems caused by over-indulgence in hard liquor. The campaign was kicked off in mid-May after a mass meeting at Mead's Hall with singing, organ music, prayers, and fiery oratory by several "ministers of the Gospel." The "event of the evening," said the *Republican*, "was a temperance song by three little girls, Ida Chase, Ida Ewer and Minnie Murrey, the latter playing the organ."

What probably was Ingham County's first medical malpractice lawsuit occurred in the mid-1870s, although no report of the proceedings was found in newspapers of the day. The case surfaced forty-five years later when the *Lansing State Journal* in 1921 published a series of articles on recollections of some early pioneers. One article about Dr. Orville Marshall, an early practitioner and probably Lansing's first city physician, so infuriated his daughter in California that the newspaper later carried her "correction," a much longer—and, hopefully, more accurate—story of his twenty-four years of practice in North Lansing.

Dr. Marshall, a University of Michigan graduate, served as a volunteer physician in Washington, D.C., during the last year of the Civil War and shortly afterward arrived in Lansing. He soon had a thriving practice out of an office he constructed himself near Washington Avenue and Franklin Street (later Grand River Avenue). His daughter said he owned Lansing's first microscope, with which he studied germs that spread various contagious diseases. Dumping of sewage into the Grand River infuriated him, as did open wells and the city fathers' refusal to uphold quarantining ill patients.

An eccentric old woman who was a city charge was the plaintiff in the malpractice suit against Dr. Marshall. She had broken her arm and refused to submit to his treatment, then sued him when her arm did not mend. It took three days to select a jury, according to the story, accomplished finally when an exhausted judge told a bailiff to go out and not return until he had found someone who was not a patient of the good doctor. Dr. Marshall won the suit.

There was another issue that created concern in the late 1870s. Now that construction of the grand new capitol was nearing completion and Lansing residents were finally satisfied that neither the legislature nor a constitutional revision was going to rob them of the state's seat of government, some business leaders, and more than a scattering of lawyers, thought it was high time that something was done about the "county seat problem."

For nearly thirty years now, Lansing had been the center of state government. It had grown steadily since the capital was moved from Detroit to Ingham County and now rivaled—in population, cultural advancement, city government, transportation facilities, commerce, industry, educational opportunities— any state capital west of the Alleghenies.

What troubled some Lansing leaders was that they had almost every convenience at their doorsteps save one—easy access to their county government, which was still thirteen miles away. Lansingites were painfully aware in 1877 that they lived in the only state capital in the nation that was not a county seat. For most businessmen and citizens, the inconvenience was probably more of a bother than an obstacle to earning their livelihood. The occasional half-day trip to Mason and back probably gave them a welcome respite from the hum-drum life of a merchant, laborer, clerk, or housewife in an era when travel to another city, even in the same county, was an infrequent happening.

But for a lawyer living in Lansing and needing access to the county clerk, register of deeds, treasurer, road commission, prosecuting attorney, and the circuit and probate courts, doing business with Ingham County became a decided hardship. It was no wonder that Lansing attorneys were at the forefront of the movement to bring the county seat to the capital city.

The movement had been a long time gathering momentum. It started even before the capital came to Lansing, when, during the legislative session of 1847, Mason had been proposed as one of a multitude of possible locations for the seat of state government. It continued immediately after the capital move when numerous Mason businesses and several leading law offices moved to Lansing, touching off a rivalry that has continued for nearly one hundred fifty years. The "anti-Mason" forces gained some ammunition when the independent Michigan Supreme Court was established in the late 1850s and claimed the Ingham County clerk's and sheriff's offices for record-filing and bailiff duty. It took high court action to accomplish enforcement of the state statute.

But in October of 1877, the move-the-county-seat issue "fell like a lightning stroke from a clear sky," in the words of the *Republican*, surprising Mason residents and forcing them, in their anger, to resort to "personal vituperation, dire curses and threats, and charges of bribery and corruption . . . all of which was very foolish and lacking largely in the essential element of truth." But it worked. Somewhat unexpectedly, at the October session of the Ingham County Board of Supervisors, a motion was made to place the question of removal of the county seat before the county's voters. Obviously, such a vote, with one-fourth of the voters residing in Lansing, could easily be expected to go in Lansing's favor if more than one-third of the remainder of the county's voters were convinced of the advantages of Lansing as county seat. The townships with the heaviest populations were Meridian, Lansing, Aurelius, and Delhi—all bordering the city of Lansing. Mason won by an eyelash in the board of supervisors' voting. The proposal to place the issue on the ballot needed a two-thirds majority, and it missed by a single vote.

The county seat removal question continued to be a subject of debate for several months. There were special meetings in mid-January in Williamston and Leroy townships and a few days later in White Oak Township, with delegations present from Wheatfield, Locke, and Leroy townships and the village of Williamston, plus a handful of attendees from Lansing and Mason.

Attempting to simplify the meeting's agenda, D. L. Crossman of Williamston said the main question boiled down to "Shall the people be permitted to say where they will have their county seat located?" and whether the removal, if decided upon, could be done without expense to the county. With a decided tinge of sarcasm in his voice, Crossman demanded that Lansing should immediately settle that question "by giving the most undoubted guaranties that this removal should be at her expense." If Lansing failed to make such a pledge, Crossman said, he was ready to vote against the removal.

With less than a year remaining before dedication of the new capitol building was scheduled, Lansing folks couldn't be bothered with the question of becoming the seat of Ingham County, let alone agreeing to financing such a move. For the present, most Lansing residents were satisfied with the assurance that the splendid new capitol gave them that their city would remain, forever, the capital of Michigan. Let Mason have the county seat.

13

MURDERS IN MERIDIAN

It was November 12, 1876, when an event in Meridian Township shattered the relative calm of Ingham County, calling on all the resources the prosecutor's office could muster and awakening the talents of the area's leading defense attorneys. A bloody, late-night gun fight on the farm of John P. and Emily U. Marble left bodies scattered over the grounds and resulted in two slayings and the arrest of three persons on murder charges. The story even made Lansing folks forget for the moment the construction of the state's new capitol and forced the *Lansing Republican* editors to send a reporter outside the confines of downtown Lansing.

In strict chronological style, the reporter wrote in his lead paragraph that "Early Monday morning our citizens were electrified by a rumor of a bloody encounter which took place four miles east of this city on Sunday evening, in which it was said one man was killed and an old resident of the city was so badly wounded that he lay at the point of death. The news was brought by a messenger from the scene of the melee, who reached here about midnight, to procure an officer and a physician. Through the courtesy of Officer Baker, who had early responded to the call, and had returned to the city but a few moments previously, a reporter from this office was at the scene of the bloodshed at about 8 o'clock a.m."

He described the location as being "about one mile northeast of the agricultural college" and nearly opposite District No. 8 (Marble) School. It took another long paragraph of description of the farmhouse and yard before the writer introduced the principals—John Marble, then living in Lansing; his estranged (and allegedly adulterous) wife Emily; her son by a previous marriage, Willard H. Chapman; her neighbor, William Martin, "a married man who deserted his wife about a year ago, leaving them destitute"; John Morley, a private detective hired by Marble to "obtain positive proof of adulterous intercourse between Martin and Mrs. Marble"; and Charles W. Ayres, a Mason saddle-maker and Morley's son-in-law. Marble had previously filed adultery charges against his wife and Martin.

According to the story based on what the reporter learned from police and from testimony at a coroner's inquest held in the Marble living room—which served simultaneously as a temporary morgue, hospital ward, and courtroom— Marble, Morley, and Ayres went in a carriage to the farm on a Sunday evening to spy on Mrs. Martin. Marble testified he, Morley, and Ayres hid their horse and carriage in the woods one-quarter mile from the house and sneaked into the orchard north of the house. Hearing a noise, they crept to the south of the dwelling and at one time heard Martin and Chapman talking about some apples. Suddenly, Marble and his companions, all lying prone, were confronted by three figures coming up behind them from the direction of the house and were fired upon. Ayres was struck by a shotgun blast as he tried to arise. He died instantly. Morley arose, Marble said, and retreated toward the road, followed by all three persons from the house. Near the roadside fence, there was more firing and what Marble figured was hand-to-hand combat. Marble then got up and rushed to Morley's aid and was himself shot in the back. He said the shot lodged just under the skin and he heard his wife tell Chapman, "That's the old man— go for him, Will!" The boy answered that he, too, was shot, Marble said, and Emily Marble, Chapman, and Martin then retreated to the house and locked the door. Marble said he went to a neighbor's for help and sent to Okemos and Lansing for officers and physicians.

The *Republican* reporter said when he arrived at the scene the next morning, "the gory remains of Ayres" lay in the Marbles' parlor. He had been hit in the head by the shotgun blast. In the next room, partitioned off with a quilt, lay "a bloody, mangled human being almost unrecognizable." This was Morley, surrounded by his family. He had been shot and his skull fractured, apparently from a clubbing from a shotgun, the bent barrel of which was found in the house. The splintered stock had been found a few feet from where Morley, who died approximately two weeks later, had collapsed. In an adjoining room was Chapman, lying on a bed with two pistol shots in him, one in the neck and one in his upper right arm. His mother and Martin, under an officer's guard, tended Chapman. John Marble's slight wound had been attended to.

Lansing Justice Ephriam Longyear presided at the Marble home inquest and Prosecutor Henry P. Henderson represented the State. Rollin C. Dart was the only other attorney present, apparently retained by Emily Marble. Four physicians who conducted the autopsy on Ayres testified his death was immediate. Constable Warren S. Abels of Meridian Township testified as to a "collection of firearms" taken from the various participants. The arsenal included a gun for each of the six participants: the smashed and bent shotgun, a four-inch Colt belonging to Marble, a "small, cheap cartridge revolver" taken from Martin; a similar weapon found on a table in Emily Marble's bedroom; a Colt revolver found under Ayres's body, and a small Smith & Wesson found near where Morley lay wounded, "every chamber empty." Late that Monday afternoon, the inquest jury returned from the kitchen to the parlor/courtroom with its verdict—"the deceased, Charles W. Ayres, came to his death from shots fired from a gun in the hands of Willard H. Chapman."

Emily Marble, her son, and Martin were taken to the county jail in Mason yet that night. By Tuesday morning, Morley, brought back to Lansing in a carriage, was reported markedly improved and his doctor entertained a slight hope that he would ultimately recover. The *Republican* reported, "He cannot speak, but writes and is evidently sane," despite a "ghastly wound across the top of his head" and a broken skull from which three bone fragments had been removed from "a cavity nearly three inches in circumference."

At the inquest, Emily Marble had testified her son had been loading apples earlier in the day into a wagon near the road when he noticed one barrel of fruit was missing. She said he later found it several rods down the road and insisted on going back to stand guard and try to determine who came for the apples. Martin and Emily Marble decided to arm themselves and accompany him, she testified, fearing the missing apples were possibly part of a ruse her husband had instigated to get them out of the house. She said as they walked along the driveway toward the road they encountered the spying men in the orchard and that the men fired at them first.

Five days after the shooting, on Friday, November 17, Emily U. Marble, her twenty-one-year-old son, Willard Chapman, and her neighbor and adultery co-defendant, William Martin, were charged with the murder of Charles F. Ayres. The information prepared by Henderson charged Chapman with the fatal assault on the victim and alleged his mother and Martin were present and aided and abetted the killing. The warrant was authorized by Prosecutor Henderson, who undoubtedly felt some satisfaction in the knowledge that there wasn't the remotest chance of the trial starting before he completed his stint as prosecutor on December 31. The task of prosecuting the "Meridian Three" would fall to young Edward Cahill, whom Ingham County voters had elected as their prosecutor only a week before the shooting. The defendants spent the holidays in the county jail at Mason, where a jailor informed Emily Marble that her divorce from John Marble had been finalized on December 29.

It was March 3, 1877, before the next entry in the case appears in the Ingham County Circuit Court Calendar, Volume 94, now in the Michigan Archives. The entire case files from two 1877 trials—one for Chapman and the other for his mother—have mysteriously disappeared from the records of Ingham County cases from 1839 to 1900. The absence of the case files leaves two Michigan Supreme Court opinions and orders, the supporting briefs for those actions, and newspaper clippings as the only first-hand sources of information about one of Ingham County's more fascinating murder cases.

Some of the delay in getting the trials under way probably stemmed from the change of the prosecutorial guard in Mason. Cahill, then thirty-three years old and destined, eventually, for Michigan's Supreme Court, was relatively inexperienced in the county. He had spent most of his early legal career in Chicago—where he was burned out of his office in the great fire of 1871—and in St. Johns and Hubbardston. Cahill was familiar with the surroundings in the capital because he had served as a teen-aged legislative page in the sessions of 1857, 1858, and 1859 while earning money to finance his legal education. He attended Kalamazoo College and interrupted his education to learn the printer's trade at the *Kalamazoo Gazette*. He later worked at the *Kalamazoo Telegraph* until 1862, when he enlisted in an Illinois company and participated in several Civil War battles in Kentucky. Illness forced him to accept a disability discharge and he returned home, started to recuperate, and began studying law in the office of a local firm. That fall, Cahill raised a company of black soldiers for the First Michigan Colored Infantry and led them into the war, becoming a captain in 1865. After the war, he completed his legal training in a law office in St. Johns, where he was admitted to the bar in 1866.

Not wishing to tackle the important Marble murder trials alone, Cahill talked Henderson into assisting him, at least in the "sure thing" prosecution of Chapman, who had clearly been identified by the inquest jury as the prime shooter at the bloody ordeal in the orchard. Defense attorneys Rollin Dart and John C. Shields argued strenuously, to no avail, that Henderson, who had left the prosecutor's office four months before, and Martin V. Montgomery, who was John Marble's longtime personal attorney, had no business assisting in the prosecution. Especially, they insisted, Montgomery should not receive a cent of public funds. Taking the stand at a hearing before the jury was selected, Montgomery testified he had received no remuneration, didn't know if he would, and indicated his presence was more or less a favor to his client. Judge Huntington overruled all the objections and ordered the jury selection to begin.

The trial started on Monday morning, April 9, 1877, in the twenty-year-old Mason courthouse. Although the maple syrup season had just been completed and lambing, sheep shearing and spring planting were occupying most of the county's farmers, there was a packed house. Some probably were attracted by the stellar lineup of legal talent assembled for the trial. The interest had been accentuated when the defense rolled in a big gun of its own—former Governor Austin Blair of Jackson, a veteran of many Ingham County court cases.

It took most of two days to seat a jury. None of the twelve men finally selected was from Meridian Township, and there was only one from Lansing, Morley's home. Before the witness parade began, Dart and Shields convinced the judge to exclude members of Morley's family, and John Marble, from the courtroom except while testifying. Five doctors testified as to Morley's condition at various times after the shooting. One said he was present November 21 for

Morley's "dying declaration," obtained by asking the paralyzed man, unable to speak, to point to letters in an alphabet while a family member copied the message, witnessed by Justice of the Peace Augustus F. Weller, who also testified. The first day's testimony included that of two Morley family members and John Marble.

Still on the stand the next day, Marble testified he, Morley, and Ayres were all armed in the orchard with pistols, his own loaded with five charges. The *Republican* said Marble generally related facts already in evidence and that considerable time was spent arguing the admissibility of Morley's dying declaration. Judge Huntington at first held up admitting the declaration into evidence after having it read into the record, but later admitted it and had the lengthy document read to the jury. The *Republican* spared its readers from having to wade through the declaration, merely summarizing it with the characterization, "It is long and very positive as to facts—seemingly affording a sure evidence of guilt against Chapman. It seemed to make considerable impression on the jury."

Some of the most telling testimony of the third day came from George M. Williams of Eaton Rapids, who was jailed with Chapman while he awaited trial on a forgery charge. Williams said Chapman volunteered that the Marble party was expected at the farm and that he, his mother, and Martin were prepared for them. Chapman, according to Williams, was the first to spot the men in the orchard and fired at the first one who rose up, dropping him. According to Williams's testimony, Chapman then chased Morley as he ran toward the fence, "knocked him off the fence with his gun" and later told Williams they "accomplished what they expected to do, and were glad of it—only felt a little sorry for Ayres."

With that, the prosecution rested its case and the defense called its star witness, forty-seven-year-old Emily Marble. She testified she had "always had trouble with Marble; that he had threatened to kill her several times; and that after hearing prowlers around the house, she'd bought a revolver. She said when she was arrested, with Martin, for adultery, Morley told her to "settle with the old man on any terms you can." Then she told of the missing barrel of apples and said she, her son, and Martin went out to investigate. As they passed the orchard, she saw someone crouching, then saw Marble shoot at her son four times. She said she could identify him "by the [gun's] flash."

The next morning, Emily Marble and Martin repeated their version of the shooting and Marble was recalled to establish he had hired Morley to spy on his wife. The defense called Dr. George Ranney, who testified that additional bone fragments should have been removed from Morley's skull. Leaving them in had caused his death, the doctor said, adding that he considered the treatment the victim received was "defective" and thought that his life could have been saved.

The doctor continued his testimony the next day, the fourth day of the trial, by saying his examination of Chapman the day after the shooting revealed the young man's wounds were severe, and Morley's condition serious. Dr. I. H. Bartholomew confirmed those diagnoses and said the loose bone fragments under Morley's scalp "could have been taken out." He added that Morley should not have been moved to Lansing.

Former Prosecutor Henderson was later sworn as a prosecution rebuttal witness and testified Emily Marble had come to him several times complaining about John Marble. He said he told her he could not protect her as long as Martin was living with her. A brief return appearance by Emily Marble then concluded the testimony and the judge declared that two lawyers from each side would be permitted to address the jury.

Henderson then presented a comprehensive review of the testimony. According to the *Republican's* report, he was "eloquent, forcible, clear and logical." Shields then spoke for the defense, winding up in a voice "fairly tremulous with emotion" as he begged the jury for mercy for the defendant. Austin Blair then took up the defense cause, presenting for two hours "a masterly argument producing a deep impression on the Jury by his eloquence" while emphasizing that to find the prisoner guilty jurors "must deduce from the evidence that he went to the place of conflict with the purpose of murder formed."

The *Republican* said a "breathless stillness pervaded the courtroom, crowded to its utmost capacity," as Montgomery spoke. He told the jury that even if it found that Chapman only entertained the design to kill when he raised the gun "and gave Morley those terrible blows that sent his soul before an eternal God," then their verdict must be guilty.

Judge Huntington gave jurors an hour of instructions at 9:00 A.M. Saturday, repeating the charge that Chapman did "willfully and of his malice aforethought kill John F. Morley" on November 12 in the township of Meridian. It was 10:00 A.M. when jurors huddled for the last time together. They had been sequestered for six days of trial, plus a weekend, in a single room in Mason's Hotel Donnelly.

After a one-hour lunch recess, jurors asked for another reading of Morley's dying declaration and parts of John Marble's and Constable Abel's testimony. Finally, the jury bell rang again at 4:15 P.M. and the jury filed in and its foreman announced the verdict—guilty of second degree murder.

The next week, Chapman was sentenced to sixteen years in prison at hard labor. He was taken to the prison at Jackson a week later. But attorney John C. Shields and appellate attorney W. K. Gibson were not finished. Within a few months, they filed an appeal with the Michigan Supreme Court. The case, *Chapman v. People*, 39 Mich. 357 (opinion filed October 15, 1878), was decided on April 15 by the supreme court, Justice James. V. Campbell writing the six-page unanimous opinion.

In Campbell's words, "the crime set forth in the information is not the same in description as the one the prosecution was allowed to put in proof." The information, termed "very meager in its allegations" by Campbell, set forth that

Chapman "on the twelfth day of November . . . at the township of Meridian, in said Ingham County, with force and arms did make a felonious assault in and upon the body of one John F. Morley and then and there willfully and of malice aforethought did kill and murder the said John F. Morley . . ." Continued the opinion: "The proof offered and admitted against objection was that on the day named . . . Chapman committed an assault on Morley at . . . Meridian. That Morley was subsequently removed to his home in Lansing, where he lived until November 27, 1876, and then died, as was claimed, of the injuries which he had received fifteen days before in the former town." The ruling was simple: On November 12 "there had been no murder" and "an averment of the death at Meridian was untrue." On June 22, 1878, the day after the high court's unanimous ruling overturning the conviction, Chapman—fourteen months into his sentence—was released from the state prison at Jackson, a free man.

The *Republican* reported Chapman's release in its June 25, 1878, edition, blaming his serving of only fourteen months of a sixteen-year sentence on "legal defects in the information." The editor couldn't resist the editorial comment that, "It seems almost a mockery of justice that man can commit the crime of murder and escape punishment after it is proved against him, because an officer of the law made an error in the proceedings."

It was three months after Chapman was sentenced to prison that his mother's trial for the murder of Charles Ayres began in the same courtroom, but before a different judge. Loss of the court records makes it impossible to determine why Circuit Judge Josiah Turner of Owosso, in the Seventh Judicial Circuit, presided instead of Ingham's Judge Huntington. If there were defense motions objecting to Huntington because he had presided at the Chapman trial, no mention of it is made in the voluminous news reports of the trial. Ingham County Prosecutor Cahill again was assisted by former Prosecutor Henderson, and Emily Marble was represented by J. C. Shields and Sam L. Kilbourne of Lansing, and Dennis Shields of Howell.

The week-long trial featured lengthy testimony by both John Marble and Emily Marble, despite defense arguments that John Marble should not be allowed to testify because he was the husband of the defendant. Cahill, however, called Ingham County Clerk John C. Squires to the stand to state that John Marble had been granted a full decree of divorce from Emily Marble. After considerable arguments by both sides, Judge Turner ruled Marble could testify. Both the prosecution and defense finally rested on Friday and Judge Turner announced he would "limit" arguments to four hours for each side. What the *Republican* referred to as "the forensic contest" began at 10:00 A.M.

Former Prosecutor Henderson opened, stating that Emily Marble obviously wanted to draw her husband onto the farm for the purpose of killing him and set up the missing apples incident to excuse herself and her partners for going armed toward the road and making the incident appear to be in self-defense.

"Mrs. Marble is an extraordinary woman, and as cunning as Lucifer himself," Henderson told the jury. He said the adultery charge explained Marble's visits to the farm and that "the old man had a morbid desire to hang around there, where Martin was defiling his bed and desecrating the sacredness of that home around which most holy memories clustered."

After a noon recess, it was Shields' turn to be eloquent. He led the jury through a factual review of the evidence, attempting to show that the Marble party went to the farm to commit a felony. He said Morley rolled the barrel of apples into the road to draw Emily Marble and her friends out and make them easier to attack. Sam Kilbourne then continued the defense relay, holding the jury's attention "in a candid, fair and inimitable manner" as he traced the entire Marble difficulty. His review of the evidence was "acute and caustic and always logical" as he warmed up the jury for his associate, Dennis Shields.

The final defense orator had a near full house when he began his plea at 5:00 P.M., presenting several important points in a new light and obviously "wielding great control" over the jury. When Shields finished at 6:20 P.M., the *Republican* reported, "everyone was convinced he had ably defended the prisoner." Court then adjourned until the next morning.

It was not unusual for circuit court to be in session on a Saturday, especially when a jury trial was in progress. And since Saturday was go-to-town-day for Ingham County farmers and those who lived in the small rural communities, the wind-up of an exciting murder trial on a summer Saturday was a natural attraction. The second-floor circuit courtroom was packed when the bailiff pounded his gavel promptly at 9:00 A.M. as the timely visiting judge mounted the bench. The bailiff puffed himself up sufficiently for the important, brief address it was his duty to deliver and intoned for all to hear: "Oyez, oyez, Circuit Court for the County of Ingham is now in session for The People versus Emily U. Marble, Circuit Judge Josiah Turner of the Seventh Judicial Circuit presiding." A hush came over the audience as Judge Turner nodded toward the prosecution table, announced that the jurors were all in place and said, "Mr. Cahill, you may begin your rebuttal."

Reporting the summation to its readers the next week, the *Republican* said, "That Mr. Cahill was equal to the occasion was plain to all after his first eloquent sentences . . . in reviewing the [previous] arguments, he was unsparing and caustic and gradually gained a strong fortification for his points in the minds of the attentive jury, and in rebuking some of the allusions made to parties concerned, living and dead, with a solemn voice and indignant mien, he exhibited a deep earnestness, and an eloquence impressive and grand." Emily Marble's guilt, he said, hinged mostly on which party the jury believed fired the first shot. His words appeared to cast a spell over the jurors, the *Republican* said, and as the argument continued, "the chances of acquittal for the prisoner grew less and less." Cahill talked for just short of two hours and by the time he finished, "the last hope of the prisoner had been swept away."

Judge Turner used only twenty minutes to charge the jury. He stressed that Emily Marble was being tried for murdering Ayers, not for cohabiting with William Martin. Then he launched into the jury's duties in deciding facts based on evidence and testimony, the differences in the degrees of murder and how to weigh circumstantial and positive evidence. After they were sworn, the jurors retired to their room, in charge of Deputy Sheriff Harry O. Gall.

Throughout the long afternoon, most of the court watchers remained in their seats, in anticipation of a verdict. But as the day wore on, some of those present began to whisper about the possibility of a hung jury. At 5:00 P.M., some of the spectators started to leave. So did the judge, since he intended to board the train soon leaving for Lansing.

The crowd was more than halfway to the depot when the warning of the courthouse bell announced the jury had come to a decision. From all directions came the shouts of "The jury has agreed!" reported the *Republican*, and the depot-bound crowd, including Judge Turner, turned around and scurried back to the courthouse. It was 5:20 P.M. when Turner told the bailiff to summon the jurors and the defendant to the courtroom. The jury foreman announced the verdict—guilty of second degree murder, with a recommendation for mercy—which, the *Republican* reported, was received by a stoic defendant "as emotionless, apparently, as a marble statue."

In an afterward, the newspaper reported Emily Marble would be sentenced the next Saturday and that William Martin's trial was scheduled for October 1877. As it turned out, Emily Marble was not sentenced the next Saturday. Shields immediately filed with the Michigan Supreme Court for leave to appeal the conviction on the grounds that Judge Turner improperly allowed the jury to consider the testimony of John Marble. In his brief, filed in the high court on October 10, Shields contended (38 Mich. 117, decided January 15, 1878) that "a husband cannot testify against his wife after divorce, either at common law . . . or under Michigan statutes." He also claimed there was judicial error in allowing testimony and evidence about the shooting and eventual death of Morley and argued the judge did not sufficiently stress that presence at a crime's commission does not necessarily make one an accomplice. There was also an exception taken to the judge's explanation of "reasonable doubt."

Attorney General Otto Kirchner argued for the state, citing several cases in which divorce had been ruled to remove "the want of capacity to testify as between married persons." Justice Graves wrote the majority opinion.

"No part of (John Marble's) testimony consisted of matter exposing anything written or spoken under the protection of matrimonial association," Graves wrote, noting the Marbles had been estranged for several months before the shootings. He also said the multiple attacks on the three men consisted of continuous violence—"There was no intermission"—and that the various parts of the fray "reciprocally served to color and characterize each other," indicating the testimony about Morley's wounding was proper.

As to facts of the shooting, Graves said Judge Turner properly outlined to the jury that the versions of the opposing parties to the shooting contained contradictory facts and that the judge properly instructed the jury that it must decide which version to believe. The justice said a "careful examination of the record discloses nothing of which the defendant has anything to complain." He said the exceptions should be overruled and judgment on the verdict entered. Justices Cooley and Campbell concurred. Justice Marston did not sit on the case.

Before sentence could be pronounced, Sam Kilbourne rejoined the defense effort for a new trial and a second application for leave to appeal was filed with the supreme court (38 Mich. 309, submitted and denied on January 29, 1878, two weeks after the first appeal was turned down). In the second appeal, Kilbourne and Shields said their grounds for a new trial was newly discovered evidence "and other reasons." The court noted a Michigan statute provided a new trial in a felony case could be applied for only "at the same term [of court] or at the next term thereafter." Since more than one term had intervened, the high court ruled a new trial was "now barred by lapse of time" and the motion was denied.

On Monday, February 11, 1878, Judge Turner sentenced Emily U. Marble to seven years in Jackson state prison for her part in the death of Charles Ayres. In the meantime, John P. Marble had died and a nolle prosequi (will not prosecute further) was entered in the murder case against William Martin, who was present for Emily Marble's sentencing. Martin remained free on bail on the adultery charge, which also was nolle prossed on March 6, 1878.

Emily Marble's prison index card in the Michigan Archives says she was released from the prison at Jackson on July 10, 1879. The Ingham County Circuit Court Journal in the same repository explains the "release." She was moved to the new Detroit House of Correction (July 14, 1879 entry) and presumably served the rest of her sentence there.

As late as the 1990s, the old Marble farmhouse at Burcham Drive and Hagadorn Road—across the street from the site of Marble School—was still known as the "Haunted Marble House," though it was serving as a child development center for Eastminster Presbyterian Church.

14

MR. DODGE TAKES THE CAKE

Completion of Michigan's splendid new Capitol late in 1878 and its inspiring dedication ceremony on January 1, 1879, seemed to calm the controversy over whether Lansing or Mason should be the county seat of Ingham County. And, as the decade of the 1880s arrived, the possibility of removal of the state government was no longer a thing to which Lansingites gave a second thought. Even *Harper's Weekly*—the epitome of periodical publications—had run a major story on Michigan's governmental jewel, illustrating it with exquisite line etchings of the building's exterior, its state library, and its state-of-the-art supreme court quarters. Certainly, *Harper's* would not give Lansing such a mention if its fixtures were not Gibraltar secure.

The county seat question aside, lawyers in Lansing and the townships along the northern edge of Ingham County were far from satisfied with the logistics with which they had to contend in practicing law. Maintaining offices in Lansing was a must, because that is where the mass of the population was located. And more and more often, citizens and businesses were having legal difficulties involving the state, and it was convenient for lawyers to be situated near their clients and their adversaries. But when matters reached the courtroom stage, it meant a train ride to Mason and back or, especially in bad weather, the expense of an overnight stay in the county seat. Why couldn't a plan be worked out, some attorneys began to wonder, whereby a session or two of the circuit court could be held in Lansing?

Enter Frank L. Dodge, a young Ohio-born Eaton County lawyer, described by one of his biographers as a "pillar of strength . . . a tower of community leadership . . . a first citizen." Son of a New England cabinetmaker, Dodge was born at Oberlin in 1853 and early in his adulthood worked for a railroad in Cleveland and in an older brother's hotel business. Still in his twenties, Dodge moved to Eaton County and soon began studying law under Isaac M. Crane, one of Michigan's leading lawyers. He was admitted to the bar in Charlotte and lived in Eaton Rapids in the late 1870s while maintaining a law partnership with Crane.

Dodge moved to Lansing in 1879, admired Michigan's shiny new capitol, and decided it might be a good place to spend some of his working hours. He was elected to the Michigan House of Representatives in 1882 and was appointed to committees on the judiciary and state affairs. Those positions provided Dodge with an adequate vantage point from which to launch a piece of legislation for which every Lansing attorney for centuries to come should be grateful.

As a lawyer in Eaton Rapids, Dodge knew the rigors of traveling from there to the county seat of Charlotte for court sessions. Early in the 1883 legislative session, Dodge introduced a brief bill of three sections that stipulated that at least two of the regular terms of the Ingham County Circuit Court be held in the city of Lansing during the remainder of 1883 "and during each year thereafter." The lone requirement was that the Lansing City Council "shall furnish and provide, free of expense to said county, a suitable place for holding court within said city, and transacting the business thereof, and a suitable and sufficient jail for the incarceration of prisoners during the sittings of said court, both to be inspected and approved by the judge of said court, or the prosecuting attorney . . ." The bill's second section gave the judge of the Fourth Judicial Circuit ten days to decide and post which two court terms would be held in Lansing that year, and the third section commanded him to choose the Lansing court term dates two years ahead of time for ensuing years.

Introduction of the bill had the effect of firing off a field cannon aimed directly at courthouse square in Mason. By the time the *Republican* took note of the "Dodge Bill," it had already cleared the House and was in the Senate, "being eagerly watched by its friends and enemies." The newspaper argued in a heavily weighted news-editorial that "It . . . has been shown beyond question that nearly four-fifths of the business of the circuit court comes from the northern part of the county, and the expense of this litigation would be reduced nearly one-half if the court were sitting at the capital, where there are abundant facilities for coming and going at all hours."

Within three days, the *Ingham County News*, as anticipated, had thrown itself "in a delirium of excitement," according to the *Republican*. The Mason paper had tossed "wholesale abuse" at House members who had voted the bill's passage and unfairly reported the approval came "in spite of the written remonstrance of more than 3,000 taxpayers representing every township in the county," the *Republican* asserted. If the question were put to a fair vote, it would win by two thousand votes, the Lansing paper predicted.

The Senate quickly passed the bill. By May 3, almost open warfare had broken out between Lansing and Mason forces. The latter, "not content with its passage through both houses . . . immediately lay siege to the executive power and so persistent have been their pleadings that Governor Begole finally granted them audience," reported the *Republican*. "For nearly three hours, the governor turned himself into a court and listened patiently to . . . both sides."

Former Ingham Prosecutor H.P. Henderson, still a Mason fixture, fired the first salvo by telling Governor Begole that the Dodge Bill was unconstitutional because it virtually allowed removal of the county seat. He denounced the legislation as an unwarranted interference with local affairs; and he said it did not provide suitable machinery for holding court in Lansing. The proposed law, Henderson insisted, was passed merely in the interest of the people of Lansing. He cited the three thousand out-county signatures against it and urged the governor not to sign it into law.

Lansing wheeled in its big gun, lawyer Martin V. Montgomery, to the front and he assured the governor that the question of constitutionality had been studied by the judiciary committees of both houses. He stressed that the county's government machinery was not being removed to Lansing and that the proposal merely allowed people in the northern part of the county to transact court business nearer their homes. He asked the governor to study the facts and decide the issue on its merits. Mason backers shoved scholarly lawyer William P. Wells of Detroit into the fray. By the time he ended, the Republican reported sarcastically, "It looked exceedingly doubtful as to whether even a circuit judge had the right to step outside the city of Mason" during a regular court term. But Lansing's Orlando M. Barnes "completely annihilated" Wells' argument by proving the proposal was not a removal of the county seat, the paper told its readers. And he answered the argument "that the bill was only for the benefit of a few Lansing lawyers by showing that a majority of the people of the county would be accommodated [and it] would tend to prevent a bitter contest over the question of removing the county seat."

The *Republican* reported in its May 12 edition that, "On Friday morning, Governor Begole signed the bill providing for two terms of the Ingham circuit court to be held in Lansing. The law is a just one, and despite . . . our Mason friends, will be of benefit to a majority of the people of this county." The story went on to compliment Representative Dodge and praise Governor Begole for his nine days of patience in listening to the various arguments.

Fanned chiefly by the Mason paper and its readers, the flames of the controversy failed to die. By August, the feeling was so intense that the entire Lansing portion of the Ingham bar, joined by prominent non-lawyer citizens, addressed an open letter to all citizens of the county and asked the *Republican* to publish it. The letter began with a printing of the entire law and added,

> We [believe] the people of the south Part of the county have been gravely misinformed as to the scope, intent, purpose and effect of this legislation . . . it is not proposed to remove the circuit court for the county of Ingham to the city of Lansing . . . [nor] to remove . . . the

county seat from Mason to Lansing. It is proposed simply to require the Ingham circuit court to sit twice a year at the city of Lansing to allow the people of the northern part of the county to transact their legal business at home, leaving the circuit judge to hold at least two, and as many more as he pleases, terms of court at Mason . . .

For many years it has cost the people of this part of the county thousands of dollars annually to be compelled to transact their court business at Mason. Trains on the railroad have been for years so run that we cannot reach the county seat until eleven o'clock in the forenoon, and if we return the same day, we are compelled to leave at half past five, and before court has adjourned in the afternoon. The result is that litigants, lawyers, and witnesses, in order to do a day's work in court at Mason, are compelled to go the night before, and remain two nights and one day.

The letter continued for a full column. It said the writers were confident the two-city court would result in a decided savings for all county citizens, that the new law would quiet the county seat controversy, and that the city of Lansing was prepared to withstand the entire cost of furnishing court facilities. It cited a June 18 resolution by the Lansing City Council to loan its council chambers for the courtroom, three committee rooms, and a vault, all in the Barnes Block on Michigan Avenue, in addition to use of the city jail, "without a dollar of expense to the county." Among the twenty-six prominent citizens—Republicans and Democrats—who signed the letter were lawyers Martin V. and Richard A. Montgomery, John C. Shields, Albert E. Cowles, E. C. Chapin, Sam Kilbourne, H. R. Carpenter, Edward Cahill, Jason E. Nichols, Frank L. Dodge, and Ephriam Longyear.

A month or so passed. Then Ingham County Clerk John W. Whallon received a notice from Circuit Judge G. T. Gridley, dated September 19, stating that he planned to hold the October term of his court in the city of Lansing, as provided by law, in facilities provided by the city and commencing on the second Monday of October. The order informed Whallon that he was "required and directed" to appear at the opening of court "and to act as clerk thereof during the sitting of the same" and to bring with him "ready to be used in the business of said court the law and chancery journals thereof, the common rule book and special motion book kept in your office, and all the files and papers in your office, in each and every case that has been, or may be hereafter, placed upon the calendar of said court, for hearing or trial at the next term thereof. . . ." Clerk Whallon, with some learned legal assistance, answered Judge Gridley's order with a petition politely, but firmly, announcing he was "greatly embarrassed by said orders, which seemed to him in clear violation of the constitution and laws of this state" and requesting that the orders be vacated. The Whallon petition was probably written by William P. Wells, the Detroit lawyer who argued Mason's case before Governor Begole, and former governor Austin Blair, both of whom had been engaged by the Mason bar to fight the court-move question to the bitter end.

Actually signed by Wallon, the petition asked Gridley to withdraw his orders for four reasons: because the Dodge law was "null and void" since Mason was the county seat and only the board of supervisors, under the Michigan Constitution, could move it; because the constitution and statutes require the clerk and sheriff to hold their offices in Mason, not in Lansing; because the act did not authorize the judge to require the clerk or sheriff to move their offices to Lansing; and because the legislature has no authority to require holding of courts at any other place than the county seat. To attempt to remove their offices, papers, and records from the county seat would cause "great inconvenience and confusion," Wallon's petition concluded.

Judge Gridley denied the petition on September 26 and Whallon immediately filed a mandamus petition with the Michigan Supreme Court—*John W. Whallon v. Ingham County Judge* (51 Mich. 503)—asking the court to force Gridley to retreat. The arguments officially reached the high court on October 4 and the clerk had his answer—"petition denied"—the next day in a unanimous opinion written by Justice Thomas R. Sherwood and extended to eighteen pages by the time Justice James R. Campbell added his written assent a few days later. Wells and Blair presented the Mason arguments and the Lansing cause was upheld by a trio of stalwarts—John C. Shields, Schuyler F. Seager, and former Supreme Court Justice Isaac Marston.

To refute the Mason claim that the terms "county seat" and "seat of justice" were synonymous, Sherwood went back to the Northwest Ordinance and Michigan Territorial statutes. And he pointed out that the 1850 constitutional convention did not alter the situation or require holding court only at the county seat. Justice Campbell stressed that counties infrequently, in their own right, are interested in litigation. But he noted that the state has required special legislation to enable it to resort to this very circuit court [Ingham's] not only as a forum of litigation, "but also to review some action of state officers of an administrative and not judicial character." Justice Campbell noted the legislature hadn't yet insisted on state cases being tried in Lansing for the convenience of state employees and agencies, but opined that it might not be such a bad idea. Campbell wrote, in summary, "I do not think the [Dodge] law invalid." The other justices concurred. At last, Lansing had a circuit court.

It was a grand day on Monday, October 8, 1883, when the first term of the circuit court ever held at Lansing opened in the common council rooms. The October 10 *Republican* said the legal fraternity and a council committee started fitting out the rooms immediately after the decision was announced and worked all weekend to attain a proper judicial atmosphere. The paper reported:

New and elegant desks for the clerk and judge have been placed . . .
tables and chairs provided . . . the mayor's room neatly carpeted and
furnished. . . . Just previous to the arrival of the Jackson [to Owosso]
train, Mayor Barnes and a number of attorneys, accompanied by representatives of the press, drove to the depot in carriages, where a large
crowd of citizens had assembled to welcome the arrival of the court
officers. As the train drew up at the platform there was a momentary
hush of expectation which was almost immediately followed by a bus-
tle, almost amounting to a cheer, as Judge Gridley was seen to emerge
from a coach, and was soon followed by Clerk Whallon, and
Stenographer Daniel. The gentlemen were conducted to the carriages
and conveyed to the hotels where everything was done for their comfort that experience could suggest. Sheriff McKernan was also on
hand, accompanied by Deputy Sheriff Squires, and six prisoners, who
were conveyed to the lock-up.

In the meantime a number of ladies, wives of the members of the bar
of this city, had assembled at the new courtroom, awaiting the arrival
of the court. Beautiful basket bouquets adorned the desks of the judge
and clerk. Just in front of the bench was a stand, upon which was a fine
pyramid cake, decorated with wreaths and flowers, surmounted by a
small card which bore the legend, "Mr. Dodge Takes the Cake." They
had also provided a large number of boutonnieres, with which everybody was decorated who came inside the bar. After a few moments
spent in informal chat and congratulations, Judge Gridley took his seat
on the bench, and was introduced by Representative Dodge, to the
company. The judge briefly thanked the bar and citizens for their
expressions of friendship, and Sheriff McKernan then formally opened
the court. At 10:30 A.M. the usual preliminary business of the court
was in progress, with a very full attendance of the bar.

That seemed to settle the biggest internal court battle the Ingham County
Circuit Court ever had, and the thirty-year-old author of the legislation that
made it possible, quickly got the attention of the bar. In his first legislative session, Dodge introduced forty-one bills and resolutions while maintaining an
almost spotless attendance record. One clever piece of legislation he introduced
and ushered through to law involved an appropriation of state funds for the
Lansing police and fire departments, on the theory that the services they rendered the state for protection of state property and employees should not be
entirely shouldered by Lansing taxpayers. The state "rebate" in lieu of city taxes
more than made up for the added expense Lansing had accepted in furnishing
quarters for its "own" circuit court—but since it was state money being spent,
the out-county forces didn't seem to mind.

Within two years, Dodge was appointed a United States court commissioner, the duties of which he performed for ten years "with marked ability," according to his biographer, fellow lawyer Albert E. Cowles. When he left the legislature in 1885, Dodge began a successful statewide law practice. He did not, however, neglect his home duties. For more than a dozen years, he served on the Lansing City Council, part of that time as council president, and on the Ingham County Board of Supervisors, which had opposed his court-splitting legislation. He was also a city police and fire commissioner and school board member.

In the autumn of 1888, Frank L. Dodge, then thirty-five and one of Lansing's most eligible bachelors, was married to Abby Turner, daughter of "Big Jim" Turner, the Lansing railroad magnate. Not only did the marriage provide a permanent historical name for their mansion at 106 North Street—the Turner-Dodge House—but it also helped perpetuate the railroad business in central Michigan. Following in the footsteps of his late father-in-law, Dodge became the original promoter of the Lansing, St. Johns and St. Louis Railroad Company and helped push the line to St. Johns. Dodge showed his true colors as the twentieth century dawned and there was a clamor for yet another new courthouse for Ingham County. The author of the law that took half of the circuit court away from the county seat voted, along with other Lansing members of the Ingham Board of Supervisors, to construct the edifice that became Mason's most significant landmark.

According to Cowles, Dodge's rationale for supporting the new courthouse was a simple one. It had been agreed upon when Governor Begole signed the court-splitting bill, and was "an act pre-eminently fair to do." Dodge's reward for his forthrightness was an appointment to the building committee named to draft the resolution and contract for the new courthouse. For his efficient labors in drawing up the necessary legal papers, the citizens of Mason presented Dodge with a handsome gold-headed cane and numerous other gifts. The state capital and the Ingham County seat, at last, were in tune.

15

THOSE FRIVOLOUS GAY NINETIES

In most areas of the United States, the period that ended the Victorian era—the final decade of the nineteenth century—was known as the "Gay Nineties." It was a period when the cares of war were few and living was considerably easier, thanks to inventions during the industrial revolution that had simplified problems of transportation and communication and had removed drudgery from many home, factory, and marketplace tasks. Leisure time, at least for some, was a reality. The more carefree lifestyle was reflected in the literature, music, and drama of the times. It was a good time to be alive—especially if you were a person of means.

The gaiety probably was not as apparent in Lansing and Ingham County as it was in other parts of the country. Some local bank closings and failures that reflected an 1893 dip in the national economy didn't let up until 1898. Furthermore, Lansing and the rest of Ingham County were still behind the times as far as "modern" conveniences were concerned. Manufacturing, like the railroads, was late in coming to mid-Michigan; that undoubtedly accounted for the tardy appearance of home telephones and electric lights in Lansing. Telephone service was available in Lansing during most of the decade of the eighties, but many of the subscribers were hotels, small factories, and a few of the larger businesses. The first telephone company had so few customers that an operator could memorize all the telephone numbers. The city did not get a telephone directory until 1893, when the Citizens' Telephone Company was organized. Electric lights illuminated Lansing streets beginning in 1883. Sixteen miles of water mains were installed in 1886, but many homes still depended on private wells and gas lights. Transportation was slightly better. The Lansing City Railway Company had been hauling passengers on the main downtown streets with horse-drawn streetcars since 1886. When the firm changed hands in 1890, the new owners electrified the line, but maintenance was poor.

As the decade of the nineties began, the rosters of most categories of skilled craftsmen still outnumbered practitioners in the legal and medical professions.

By 1896, the Lansing City Directory listed 50 lawyers and 44 physicians in the city of approximately 21,000. But it also numbered 96 carpenters, 22 black-smiths, 2 coopers, and 7 harness makers.

For entertainment, Lansing had Buck's and Mead's opera houses and several lecture halls that frequently attracted leading performers and speakers of the day. But there were those who insisted that the justice, circuit, and supreme courts and the state legislature were still the best shows in town. In the nineties, the court trials seemed to become more numerous, more risqué, and more "much ado about nothing." On the drop of a hat, it seemed, a Lansing attorney would take almost any case to the Michigan Supreme Court, frequently with satisfactory results for his client.

By actual count, a total of 112 Ingham County cases went to the high court and were reported in Volumes 81 through 120 of *Michigan Reports* between 1890 and 1899. Research of that entire decade was done in 1991 by Keelyn Friesen, a student intern with the Lansing law firm of Fraser, Trebilcock, Davis and Foster. Joe C. Foster, Jr., one of the firm's senior partners, then scanned each of the case sketches without finding a single landmark case and labeled the 1890s as "the trivia decade" in Ingham County law. "I was impressed again," Foster remarked, "as to how often dog cases used to get to the supreme court . . . and I concluded the sidewalks and roads were as bad in the 1890s as one hundred years later."

It must also be remembered that in this era, there was no such thing as a court of appeals. A losing attorney had only the Michigan Supreme Court to resort to if he felt justice had not been done—and for Lansing lawyers, Michigan's highest court was just across the street or, at worst, only a few blocks away. It was easy to rationalize paying a modest filing fee for a possible reversal or a chance at a new trial.

The Friesen hunt turned up numerous cases with legal questions that, a century later, seem almost humorous. Others were deadly serious but involved money claims that today would appear hardly worth going to court to resolve. But it must be remembered that in the 1890s, one could buy a fashionable lady's hat for under one dollar or a satisfying meal with thirty cents. A year's subscription to either of Lansing's daily newspapers was five dollars. Thus, a personal injury award of twenty-five hundred dollars was worthy of a sizable story in the paper and a laborer could readily justify suing for forty dollars in withheld wages, the equivalent of close to three weeks of work.

Several of the appeals uncovered in the search dealt with railroad operations, including one in which a widow was again denied a claim that her husband, killed while operating a handcar that collided with a locomotive, died as a result of a negligent foreman. In another, a lower court judgment against the Detroit, Lansing & Northern Railroad Co. was reversed when the supreme court ruled the plaintiff's husband did not exercise proper caution when he approached a crossing in a horse and buggy with his son. Both were killed. Testimony had indicated the father tried to race the train to the crossing, but the jury found the railroad at fault. A new trial was ordered.

One case involved a local farmer and an insurance company that had insured his egg-pickling business. A fire destroyed one thousand dollars worth of eggs, and the high court ruled that the phrase "in pickle" meant that only eggs in vats—not those ready for processing—were covered by the policy. An actual dog bite case was reversed by the supreme court in favor of the dog owner and a new trial was ordered. Ex-governor Austin Blair, attorney for the defendant, convinced the justices the circuit judge erred in four instances, including allowing testimony from a physician that if the dog had been rabid, rabies could have resulted, even though the plaintiff did not develop the disease.

Most of the lawyers involved in those seemingly trivial appeals were among the leading Ingham County attorneys of their time. They included several who had been or were destined to become supreme court justices themselves. There were at least two Lansing mayors in the group, several former or future Ingham circuit judges, at least three ex-prosecutors and numerous lawyer-citizens who held important state, county and city appointive positions.

Brothers Martin and Richard Montgomery, for example, were probably as well known a law firm as Ingham County had in its first half century. They were among the county's first Michigan-born attorneys since both were born on their father's farm near Eaton Rapids—Martin on October 20, 1840, and Richard on the same date in 1845. Both died of chronic ailments at age fifty-eight, cutting short careers that had just reached their prime.

Martin Van Buren Montgomery attended Eaton Rapids public schools and began teaching there when he was seventeen years old, starting to read law about the same time. He tutored with Judge Isaac Crane and in 1865 was admitted to the bar in Eaton County and joined Crane in a law practice. Martin moved to Jackson for a short time but returned in 1871 and was elected to the state legislature from Eaton County. In 1874, he was an unsuccessful Democratic candidate for attorney general. The next year, he and his brother began their partnership in Lansing.

Martin was still only forty-four years old when his work for the Democratic Party at the state level and at national conventions was recognized by President Grover Cleveland, who appointed him U.S. Commissioner of Patents. He served well in that capacity but the job—and its constant demands for patronage—became distasteful to him and he resigned and was promptly appointed to the supreme court of the District of Columbia. He gained considerable distinction there and his resignation in October 1892 was accepted with deep regret. Judge Montgomery immediately returned to Lansing, renewing the partnership with his brother. The Montgomery brothers, as before, took on all comers during the next six years, both in Ingham County and wherever else their reputations took them. They were well received by their colleagues in the profession. Judge Montgomery was honored by the Michigan State Bar Association in 1894-95 by being elected its president. It was with deep regret that Judge Rollin Person's courtroom opened the morning of November 14, 1898, with the formal motion that the court observe the death of Judge Martin Van Buren Montgomery, who had died the previous Saturday.

Richard A. Montgomery lacked the national acclaim that his brother had achieved, but in the supreme court, Ingham County circuit and probate courts, and the justice courts of the county, his reputation was excellent. Known as "Dick," he was a stickler for following the rules but was a whiz before a jury and a tiger on cross-examination. He tried numerous cases throughout Michigan. Just before his death on August 27, 1902, he was counsel for Michigan Central Railroad and other Michigan railroads. Montgomery received his courtroom baptism at age twenty-six when he was admitted to the bar after studying under his brother and Judge Crane. He joined his cousin, Robert M. Montgomery, in a practice in Pentwater for four years before coming to Lansing, and once served as city attorney.

One of the prominent firms of the time, Dodge and Black, had as its partners a pair of "naturals," Frank L. Dodge and Cyrenius P. Black, both sons-in-law of James Turner, the pioneer financier and railroad builder. Dodge's early career was sketched in a previous chapter that recounted his legislative work in securing a circuit court in Lansing. Black, a native New Yorker and son of a farmer, began his legal career in Bay City in 1867 after serving two years as United States assessor there. He was recorder for West Bay City for two years and then moved to Marquette, where he was the county prosecuting attorney and city attorney. He then returned to Tuscola County and was elected to the Michigan House of Representatives for two years. From 1885 to 1890, Black was United States Attorney for the Eastern District of Michigan. After his first wife died in 1889, Black met Eva Turner, one of the daughters of James Turner, and they were married in 1891. Black served twice as Lansing city attorney and as Ingham County probate judge. After his partnership with Dodge was dissolved, he was associated with Charles H. Hayden and with his son, Allan Black.

No lawyer ever left this earth in more of a blaze of glory than did Judge Black. It was Friday, October 13, 1916, when Black faced the assembled Michigan Supreme Court in its chambers. He arose, cleared his throat, gave the customary salutation "May it please the court . . ."—emitted a gasping groan and toppled to the courtroom floor, dead of a heart attack.

Word of the seventy-two-year-old veteran attorney's death gripped Lansing "with a shock of sorrow" said that evening's *Lansing State Journal*. At the time of his death, he was a vice president of the American Bar Association and secretary of the commission compiling Michigan statutes.

Charles B. Collingwood, who became a prominent Lansing attorney and eventually an Ingham County circuit judge, started his law career in 1894 as a partner of Harris Thomas. Collingwood was forty-four years old at the time, having spent his early years as a cowhand in Colorado, a student, a railroad surveyor in the west, a school teacher in Pewamo, Michigan, and a chemistry professor at the University of Arkansas.

Albert E. Cowles, lawyer and historian and one-time Ingham County probate judge, chose to describe his own career in a single sentence in his *Past and Present of Lansing, Michigan and Ingham County*, a volume which carried biographies of most of the early Ingham lawyers who practiced before 1905. Cowles's historical writings may be his greatest legacy. Anyone researching the capital city's beginnings is indebted to Cowles, who knew many of the pioneers—especially those involved in the court system—and drew heavily on his personal recollections in writing his history. His descriptions of the second Ingham County courthouse and the wrangles that went into the planning, financing, and engineering of the one that replaced it at the turn of the century are particularly helpful to the modern historian.

Cowles was five when he and his family moved to a farm in Alaiedon Township from Greene, Ohio, where he was born May 14, 1838. The family moved to Lansing in 1848, and young Cowles enrolled in Michigan Agricultural College's initial class in 1855. Cowles began his law studies at the University of Michigan just before the outbreak of the Civil War, in which he served for about a year with the 20th Michigan Infantry Regiment. He continued his studies after his discharge for a disability. Cowles did not enjoy courtroom work, one of his partners, Judge Edward Cahill, recalled at the time of his death. But he once served a term as Lansing city attorney, another as city clerk, and in 1892 was elected for four years as Ingham County probate judge. Cowles, in failing health, had moved to Los Angeles, California, soon after his history was published. He met a tragic death there on November 23, 1906, when he was run over by a streetcar.

Two of Lansing's most prominent attorneys confronted each other in Ingham County's first civil rights case in 1892 when a "colored" woman charged that on the Fourth of July a Lansing restaurant refused to serve ice cream to her and a Grand Rapids couple that was visiting. Restaurant owner Harry Graves and his wife were arrested for violation of a recently passed statute and retained Sam Kilbourne to defend them. Jason Nichols represented Maria Dorsey in filing the complaint, and trial was set for August 15. A justice court found the Graveses not guilty, according to a brief report in the August 16 *Republican*.

In the nineties, as now, lawyers could not always trust their clients. The *Republican* reported on December 5, 1896, that an accused pick-pocket tried to lift his attorney's wallet during a justice court hearing. Reports of petty crimes were often detailed. The *Ingham County News* carried a story on January 2, 1896, on a hearing before Justice Squires in which W. W. Rector charged his Alaiedon Township neighbor, James Heathman, with stealing "four fine, fat turkeys, one of which was blind in one eye."

Divorces often were reported in story form, frequently with an editorial comment. The January 2, 1896, *Republican* said Judge Person disposed of three such cases by granting decrees, one of them to "Lorin S. Buck . . . from his wife, the notorious Jessie Buck, on grounds of adultery."

Inadequate toilet facilities in the brick courthouse in Mason were involved in one defendant's request for a new trial. A man named Frank Hopkins was convicted on a charge of illegal parentage in the days when bastardy was considered as much a crime against the state as it was against the unfortunate "fatherless" child. Hopkins charged misconduct on the part of the jury, alleging that C. J. Loomis, the deputy in charge of his jury, permitted jurors "to leave the courthouse unattended, and to mingle with various persons in the courtroom while they were supposed to be in the jury room." He also charged that juror O. J. Lewis left the courthouse and wandered the streets of Mason for more than an hour "unattended by any officer."

The charges created such a fuss that the *Lansing Journal*, in its January 21, 1899, edition, felt obligated to explain that Deputy Loomis "was in no way to blame" for Lewis's temporary absence during jury deliberations. "The arrangements of the old ramshackle courthouse at Mason are responsible for all the difficulty," the *Journal* explained, "and if the county is put to the expense of a new trial it should force the Board of Supervisors to make some needed improvements . . ."

The *Republican* explained a couple of days later that "[Juror] Lewis has made affidavit before Prosecutor [Arthur] Tuttle that . . . he was excused to go to the toilet room in the rear of the [probate] courtroom downstairs and was gone not to exceed five minutes." Before the century closed, the quest for a modern courthouse—with toilets on upper floors—was underway.

If the decade produced a typical Gay Nineties court case, it had to be the trial of Catherine (Mrs. Levi) Ketchum, charged with threatening the morality of all Lansing by posing for a pair of itinerant photographers in the "all-together." It took the camera only an instant to record Mrs. Ketchum's image on the glass plate negative in 1893. But it took close to three years for the case to be resolved.

Ingham County readers of the *Republican* first heard of Catherine Ketchum on Monday, September 11, 1893, when her arrest the previous Saturday was detailed in a front-page story. The headline read, "Stuck On Her Shape" and a sub-head said Ketchum "had her picture taken dressed only in a pair of shoes and a smile." The camera operators, J. N. Wigle of Detroit and W. W. Webb, of St. Thomas, Canada, were charged with procuring an obscene picture for sale.

Catherine (Mrs. Levi) Ketchum, the story said, came to Lansing with her husband about 1888 and moved into a house at 812 East Michigan Avenue. She soon became involved with the work of the Women's Christian Temperance Union (WCTU) and was a leader in the movement to reform the nation's drinking habits. But as time went on, her fellow WCTU members "began to question her sincerity," the Republican reported, "Men were seen to leave her house at unseemly hours and soon ugly rumors were afloat. . . ." Finally, neighbors "decided to oust her from the neighborhood" and Detective Horace Dresser was appointed to procure evidence against her.

After working several weeks, the newspaper said, Dresser completed his labors and put before the police and Justice Dolan "one of the most disgusting pictures that was ever produced by a photographer." Numerous people recognized the face in the picture, the story said, so warrants were obtained for Ketchum and the photographers, who had been in Lansing for several weeks taking pictures of public buildings and points of interest. A search warrant brought to light a large number of nude pictures in the rooms the photographers had leased at the Irving House. They denied any connection with the nude photos and said other pictures showing naked women were copies of oil paintings.

The news story reported, however, that "besides the likeness in the face and form," the photograph's background "is beyond doubt one of the corners of her [Ketchum's] parlor" showing several decorative furnishings and, "what is most absurd of all, a copy of the WCTU constitution and by-laws." The report said Ketchum admitted the picture "unmistakably" showed her parlor but quoted her as saying "they must have got some woman in there during her absence." Levi Ketchum also confirmed the setting but would not concede the image was of his wife.

The *Republican* said that, since the arrest, many stories were circulating about Mrs. Ketchum's previous life in Leslie, "which . . . does not seem to have been very virtuous." In fact, the story said, "the record of the Ketchums in Leslie was unsavory, to say the least."

On September 13, the *Republican* carried two front-page stories on the scandal, one a detailed correction/apology titled "The Reverse Side." That story said that in reporting the "unfortunate matter" that placed Mrs. Ketchum "in a very unfavorable light before the community," some statements were published "which might be construed, possibly, as reflecting somewhat upon the reputation of her husband, L. O. Ketchum. The *Republican* does not believe this was intentional, and disavows such a purpose upon its own part." The story went on to print Ketchum's version of one reported Leslie affair and added that Ketchum had an "excellent reputation" in Leslie and that his conduct "has been above reproach" in Lansing.

Another story the same day reported photographer Wigle was bound over by Justice Dolan to Ingham County Circuit Court after hearing testimony from two witnesses—Irving Cary and detective Horace Dresser. Cary, a young local photographer, said he loaned some frames to Wigle and Webb and later retrieved them from the men's hotel room. Later, he said, he was in the room looking over their negatives, found the one of the nude Mrs. Ketchum and took it to his gallery. Cary testified he "knew the neighbors wanted evidence against her" and so he made a print. Still later, he said, the city marshal demanded the plate and he gave it up. Then the day before the arrest, Wigle and Webb came to him and demanded the negative, saying Ketchum "was on to him." Detective Dresser then testified as to similarities between the furniture in the picture and in the Ketchum parlor. Webb was examined the next day and both picture takers were bound over for trial. Justice was still fairly quick in those days of the mid-nineties, and Wigle's trial began on schedule on October 3 in a crowded Lansing courtroom.

The room was full of spectators, "all of the male order, eager to hear all the testimony . . . [even though] the atmosphere of the room was unbearable . . . ," reported the *Republican*. The prosecution evidence came in testimony from seven witnesses "and a few dozen of the most obscene pictures upon which mortal eyes could gaze. . . ."

The defense, conducted by Jason E. Nichols, "tried hard to show . . . that although the pictures had been taken, they were not distributed, sold or loaned by [the] defendant . . . this technical point did not go, for the intent and purpose for which the pictures were taken was clearly shown by the prosecutor [L. B. Gardner] to be criminal."

Wigle was convicted by the jury after a brief deliberation and was sentenced to a short term in the county jail. His partner, Webb, was tried in Mason in January on the same charge and was acquitted, "doubtless due to the fact that the evidence showed that the [Ketchum] picture was taken by Wigle . . . ," the *Lansing Journal* reported on January 16.

Scheduling the main event—the Catherine Ketchum trial—for Mason in January probably produced more prospective jurors who hadn't been exposed to hearsay, cigar store and barbershop scuttlebutt, and pre-trial reports on the defendant than if it had been staged in downtown Lansing. But it did little to cut down on the size of the crowd that showed up, some of them no doubt taking the early train from the capital to the county seat. The trial began on a Thursday and consumed three days. But since most of the defense case—and the guilty verdict—came on a Saturday, and there were no Sunday papers in those days, it was Monday before the *Republican* could inform its readers of the outcome. By that time, most Lansingites would be expected to have known the result, so the paper gave the conviction only two paragraphs.

Judge Person told the jury, according to the report, that to convict her, they must find that the pictures put in evidence were of Mrs. Ketchum and that they were made for the purpose of loan, exhibition, or sale. The jury pondered about three hours before rendering its guilty verdict.

The case was appealed to the supreme court.

The appeal was argued on October 25, 1894, and decided unanimously January 4, 1895, with Justice Frank A. Hooker writing that Person should have directed a verdict of not guilty. The conviction was set aside and a new trial ordered. The high court ruled that the purpose for which the picture was obtained was an essential element of the case and that no such purpose was proved. "She is not shown to have done more than to sit for a negative," the opinion said.

Some might be disappointed to learn the photograph of Mrs. Ketchum "wearing only her shoes and a smile," as the *Republican* described it, was not preserved in either the circuit court or supreme court records.

A few days after the supreme court decision was filed, Prosecutor Gardner moved to nolle pros the Ketchum case, conceding that with the witnesses he had for the first trial "the prosecution couldn't even hope to produce . . . any further evidence upon the question of intent."

Why did she pose for the picture? Catherine Ketchum took that answer to her grave.

16

THE BAR ASSOCIATION IS

CREATED

It was a summer day in 1894 when Sam Kilbourne met the Montgomery brothers on a Lansing street and suggested it was time to start thinking seriously about forming a professional lawyers' association that could speak for its members in court matters, set some standards for attorneys, monitor fee schedules, and sponsor an occasional social event for lawyers and their spouses.

The Montgomerys offered their ample offices in the Hollister Building for the organizational session and July 19 was agreed upon as the date. Word of the meeting spread and a sizable turnout of Lansing lawyers and a few from Mason and other localities showed up. Before the meeting adjourned, the Ingham County Bar Association was born.

The organization received only moderate attention in the *State Republican* the next day, July 20, 1894. In a short story in the lower left corner of the front page, headed *Lawyers Getting Together*, the newspaper reported:

> The attorneys of Ingham County met in R. A. and M. V. Montgomery's office yesterday and organized a county bar association. There has never been in this county an organization of this kind and considerable discussion had been had among the lawyers lately about the advisability of organizing. Pursuant to a general understanding, R. A. Montgomery called the meeting of yesterday afternoon. S. L. Kilbourne was elected president, M. D. Chatterton vice-president, Harris Thomas secretary-treasurer, H. B. Carpenter, Fred Day and Lawton Hemans of Mason were elected a committee to prepare the constitution and by-laws for presentation at the next meeting.

> The objects of this association are those usual to such organizations. The promotion of friendship and sociability among the members will

be one of the aims. An annual banquet is proposed. While the association is not political, it will doubtless exercise a strong influence on the nomination and election of county officers.

It was not long before the bar association proved it was more than a social organization. The heavy workload of circuit judges prompted action. An ICBA meeting was scheduled for the evening of January 28, 1895, to discuss a plan for relief of the circuit judges and to mull over another idea that was beginning to receive some backing in legal circles—a superior court in Lansing. The meeting was held in the offices of Smith, Lee & Day, but "attendance was so small," the *Republican* reported, "that the matter was not taken up." Those present agreed that creation of a superior court, with jurisdiction concurrent with the circuit court "of causes arising within the city, would be the proper thing." A suggestion that Ingham County seek a second circuit judge was opposed because that would require a constitutional amendment, the paper said. That meeting did, however, accomplish one thing. Steps were taken to incorporate the bar association, and by-laws were adopted.

Approximately twenty lawyer-members showed up in the Smith, Lee & Day offices for the second meeting on February 1. Articles of incorporation were signed and steps taken to establish a permanent organization. Samuel L. Kilbourne was elected president, M. D. Chatterton vice-president, and Harris Thomas secretary-treasurer. By-laws prepared by H. B. Carpenter were thoroughly discussed. Objectives set out in the articles of incorporation were to maintain the honor and dignity of the profession, to secure the enforcement of law, and to promote communication among its members.

Richard A. Montgomery told the *Republican* that the bar was not in favor of the superior court idea. Chatterton said a bill was being introduced in the legislature requiring judges in out-state circuits to hold court in Wayne County to help pare down that county's case load. The state constitution gave the legislature power to provide additional permanent judges for Wayne, Saginaw, and Kent counties. The new bill would provide for temporary substitutes for the larger counties, presumably at a salary savings for Wayne taxpayers. Chatterton suggested if such judge-loaning legislation could be passed for Wayne County, "it was equally possible for Ingham." It would be eighty years, however, before an arrangement for Ingham County to be allotted seven circuit judges in exchange for acting as the Michigan Court of Claims would finally help alleviate Ingham's court case load.

Another ICBA meeting was called for February 11, resulting in a recommendation that a committee be named to study the matter of judicial relief. That committee eventually suggested making a new circuit of Livingston and Shiawassee counties, thus leaving Ingham as a one-county circuit and considerably cutting Judge Person's work. It also suggested that since Ingham County naturally received more than its share of court cases because it contained the seat of state government, a second circuit judge would be appropriate.

On April 18, an ICBA contingent—Richard Montgomery, Russell Ostrander, Cyrenius Black, Frank L. Dodge, Quincy A. Smith, Sam Kilbourne, and C. F. Hammond—appeared before the senate judiciary committee to plead the ICBA recommendations. They reminded the senators that Ingham's circuit court case load on March 11 stood at ninety-two cases marked ready for trial, not including chancery issues. And Judge Person faced another eighty-two Livingston County trials beginning that very week. The delegation also stressed that Person was required to hear numerous "state cases" in which the only connection with Ingham County was that the capital was situated there. Some Ingham County cases that had been ready for trial more than a year before were still waiting to be heard, the lawyers explained.

The lobbying effort of the ICBA apparently worked. On May 8, as the legislature was approaching its adjournment, Livingston County was moved into a circuit with Shiawassee County and designated as the Thirty-fifth circuit. Ingham retained the designation as the Thirtieth circuit and Genesee County became the Seventh, each with one circuit judge. Through a special arrangement, the supreme court said Judge Charles Wisner of Genesee County could be temporarily assigned to Ingham to help Judge Person clear up his mounting docket of jury trials.

The ICBA also had wanted a second judge added permanently for Ingham County. Its objective had been to have such a proposal placed on the April 1 ballot in the form of a proposed constitutional amendment.

Ingham County succeeded in getting the proposal for a second judge on the ballot, but the issue lost in the state-wide election, 60,567 yes votes to 97,278 no. Ironically, a similar constitutional amendment to allow a sixth circuit judge for Wayne County was approved, even though a fifth had been added just two years previously.

The bar association, by its ability to influence legislation and to get a proposed constitutional amendment on the ballot, had demonstrated remarkable effectiveness for a newly created organization. It is doubtful that a handful of lawyers, even though they were respected individually by their legal peers, could have generated significant interest in Ingham County's problem and helped produce so rapid a solution. But with the lobbying strength of an association, they were able to convince the lawmakers that conditions in the court of the state's capital county were reaching the critical stage.

Politics became an official ICBA activity in 1895. On February 13, the ICBA had gone on record as backing the Michigan Supreme Court candidacy of Judge Edward Cahill. That action was taken at a meeting in the office of Cahill's partner, Russell C. Ostrander. Cahill had served a brief appointive period on the supreme court in 1890 and had indicated a willingness to run for election to the high court. Apparently it was felt that Cahill's past exposure on the supreme court, plus the backing of the recently organized Ingham County Bar Association, would be pluses to such a candidacy. But Michigan Republicans nominated Circuit Judge Joseph B. Moore of Lapeer County, and he won a resounding April victory over the incumbent, Chief Justice McGrath.

Some ICBA activities were more ceremonial than political. On January 4, 1897, for example, the new circuit courtroom in the Lansing City Hall was dedicated. As soon as court was called to order, President Sam Kilbourne of the Ingham County Bar Association was recognized by Judge Person and offered the following resolution:

> Resolved, that the thanks of the association are hereby tendered the City of Lansing for the handsome and commodious rooms in the new city hall building furnished for the use of the circuit court of the county of Ingham and that Hon. Rollin H. Person, judge of said court, be requested to direct the entry of this resolution and the following order on the journal of said court.

The ICBA often showed its sensitive side by turning out for funerals and memorial services in large numbers for its deceased members. In early 1895, when attorney Albert F. Rouse died, the *Republican* reported that "six gentlemen of the bar association" had been chosen as pall-bearers. In late 1899, after businessman and attorney Orlando Mack Barnes died, ICBA President Sam Kilbourne gave an extensive eulogy at the special memorial service and dozens of bar association members were in attendance.

The ICBA could also come quickly to the defense of its members when it appeared they had been wronged. After Governor Hazen Pingree attacked Arthur Tuttle and Howard Wiest for their role in investigating alleged state government corruption in late 1900, the *Lansing Journal* reported that ICBA membership believed Pingree "richly deserved punishment for his scandalous utterances." But the county's lawyers decided not to make a plea for criminal proceedings.

Bar association president Sam Kilbourne called a meeting of members on January 25, 1901, to make arrangements for the local celebration of John Marshall Day on February 4, marking the centennial anniversary of the appointment of the revered chief justice of the United States Supreme Court. Kilbourne appointed R. C. Ostrander to present a paper on Marshall's distinguished thirty-four-year career as chief justice. Kilbourne urged members to encourage their non-attorney friends to attend the celebration in the city hall courtroom. He also announced that the ICBA's annual banquet would be held the evening of the fourth and said Governor and Mrs. Bliss, the justices of the Michigan Supreme Court and their wives, and circuit judges Wisner of Flint and Peck of Jackson had been invited to the dinner.

The *Republican* out-did itself in observing the Marshall Day celebration, devoting most of its front page and three inside pages to a lavish report of the bar's activities of the day, a lengthy report of Ostrander's speech, a complete biography of Justice Marshall, and a detailed summary of the toast-accented banquet. The package was illustrated with photographs of nearly twenty of the county's leading lawyers.

The *Republican's* description of the courtroom festivities caught the spirit of the day:

> The circuit courtroom is handsomely decorated with flags, bunting and flowers. The portrait of John Marshall which hangs on the wall [behind] the judge's desk, is draped with flags and smilax. Flanking it are portraits of Judges Thomas M. Cooley and James V. Campbell. On Judge Wiest's desk stand two large boquets [sic] of carnations and grouped at the foot are many potted plants.

The banquet that evening was a more informal affair—but with even more speeches, assigned, apparently, by Kilbourne. In his own remarks, Kilbourne mentioned the bar association was seven years old and "that he had the honor of being elected its first president." As he was still holding the position, the *Republican* said, Kilbourne "began to believe he had clear title to it." Kilbourne introduced Jason Nichols as toastmaster "and Nichols had a little fun with Kilbourne by declaring that no new president of the association had ever been elected because the president had never called a meeting for such purpose."

Alva M. Cummins outlined the history of the Ingham County bar. H. B. Carpenter, a bachelor attorney, made a humorous response in a toast to "the ladies" and Cyrenius P. Black, speaking on *The Lawyer and the Layman*, said that "the impression among some people that a lawyer was not always honest was decidedly wrong, and declared that the lawyers of Michigan were honorable, upright men to whom no man need be afraid to trust his affairs." Judge Cahill, speaking on *The Qualities of a Good Lawyer*, said the first quality of a good lawyer "was to live in Ingham County." In many instances, Cahill said, lawyers make their living "by keeping lawsuits out of court."

There was one sad note to the Marshall celebration—the death of Judge William H. Pinckney on January 24 at age seventy-seven. A New York native, Pinckney was born March 18, 1824, and was admitted to practice by the New York Supreme Court in 1848 after studying law for four years under two Auburn, New York, attorneys. He came to Lansing in 1850, opened a law office, and practiced until 1856, when he was elected Ingham County probate judge, a position he held until 1864. For ten years, Pinckney was a justice of the peace after resuming his private practice. Kilbourne called Pinckney "the pioneer of the present Ingham County bar and one of the leading lawyers of earlier

Michigan." He said Pinckney got his start in Lansing "by clearing 40 acres of land for the state buildings." He lived for fifty years at 118 North Grand Avenue in a house built on land he had cleared.

Although the bar association's lavish observance of the John Marshall centennial was probably the most energetic project it had undertaken since its founding seven years before, it was by no means the only activity in 1901. On January 31, the ICBA helped organize a petition drive, asking the legislature to increase the roster of the Michigan Supreme Court to seven members. Since the 1850 constitutional convention, four justices had done all of the high court's work and lawyers throughout the state thought the court's case load demanded more bodies on the high bench. Twenty-four bar association members signed the petition. It was two and one-half years later, on June 18, 1903, that Governor Aaron T. Bliss signed the bill adding three justices to the high court.

ICBA members seemed to be skilled at alternating serious business with good times. An early June newspaper item told how the entire membership acquired a sunburn during an all-day picnic at Pine Lake (now Lake Lansing). One of the day's features was the "skillful manipulation" of the fiddle by Probate Judge Jason Nichols. "While the judge charmed from his instrument old time airs of the hoe-down variety," said the *Republican*, "his listeners glided about McGiveron's dance hall with an abandon which bespoke utter forgetfulness of conventionality." Activities engaged in by bar members who "laid aside their artificial cloaks of dignity" included "such trifling pleasantries" as croquet, quoits (horseshoes), "and the standing broadjump."

But the fun never seemed to last long. On September 19, 1901, former prosecutor Alva Cummins and Judge Cahill were appointed by ICBA president Kilbourne to give the eulogy at Lansing's community memorial services for President William McKinley, who was fatally wounded by an assassin in Buffalo, New York, the previous week. The outdoor services, attended by a large throng, were held on the capitol steps.

Between Christmas and New Year's Day, the State Association of Circuit Judges held its annual meeting in Lansing, and the Ingham County Bar Association voluntarily acted as official hosts for the convention. Many of the judges visited the circuit courtroom in city hall. Before they left the city, the judges elected Judge Wiest as their secretary-treasurer.

On their final night in town, the judges were guests of the ICBA at its annual banquet at Plymouth Congregational Church. A feast was prepared and served by women of the church. The 76 guests, including Governor and Mrs. Bliss and the supreme court justices and their wives, were seated at tables decorated with cut flowers. President Kilbourne, in a gracious welcome as he was introducing the toastmaster, C. P. Black, mentioned it was Wiest's idea to join the judges' association meeting with the annual ICBA banquet. Kilbourne, ever the smooth politician, mentioned that the association had on other occasions "had with us the gentlemen of the supreme bench whose residence here and hearty entering into all that tends to the betterment of the city's moral, religious and social life has endeared them to our people." No wonder he continued for more than a decade and a half as ICBA president.

The Ingham bar was saddened on August 27 by the death of Richard A. Montgomery after an extended period of stomach trouble. Considered one of the foremost lawyers of Ingham County, Montgomery was adept in both criminal and civil law. He was attorney for the Michigan Central Railroad when that line was one of the most important carriers in Michigan. Almost the entire membership of the ICBA met in the attorneys' room of Lansing City Hall on August 28, 1902, to observe Montgomery's passing; they attended the funeral as a group the next day at the Montgomery home on South Washington Avenue.

Early in 1903, members of the Ingham County Bar Association were busy trying to get Lansing's four justice courts replaced by a recorder's court with jurisdiction, concurrent with the circuit court, in actions involving less than $500 in civil matters and presided over by an elected judge who was a licensed attorney at a $2,000 annual salary. President Samuel L. Kilbourne of the ICBA announced on February 20 that he would name a five-man committee to draft a bill for state Representative Nottingham to introduce in the house.

Within 24 hours, it became apparent that the thrust of the reform, from the standpoint of most attorneys, was to replace the justices of the peace with lawyers. The next day, Kilbourne announced he was calling a special meeting of the entire bar membership "to discuss changes in the character of the municipal courts" instead of naming a committee. He wanted to give the county's lawyers a chance to discuss necessary changes "in the interest of justice in view of the large advances made in population, which seems to render the present system inadequate to demands." Most attorneys also felt the reform should do away with the fee system, abused by both justices of the peace and process servers.

Kilbourne appointed a drafting committee after all, but at a meeting in Edward Cahill's office, the five members could not agree as to the legality of some of the provisions. As late as March 3 the ICBA had no document to submit to the legislature for its March 16 deadline in order for passage to have immediate effect. If no new law was passed before the spring nominating convention, justices would be elected in April for another four years.

When the bar committee did complete its bill draft, the recorder's court idea was dropped in favor of a municipal court presided over by a salaried judge qualified as an attorney. Constable fees were abolished. The court's civil jurisdiction would be raised from $300 to $500. A salaried clerk would be provided. The entire bar met on March 9 and endorsed the bill after setting the judge's annual salary at $1,200 and providing that all fees were to go to a salary fund to pay the judge, clerk and constables.

Kilbourne said the new court would cut the number of civil cases appealed to circuit court. The $1,200 judge salary "means that much clear ['take-home' pay]" he said, representing as much as $2,000 to a "regular practitioner" who pays such expenses as office rent and a clerk's salary. "Many a man who has risen to distinction has begun at the lower courts," he said.

The bill passed the house on March 19 and the senate on the 26th. Governor Bliss signed it into law the evening of March 31, even while the city Republican convention was selecting candidates for the spring election. The convention nominated Lewis M. Miller to become Lansing's first municipal judge. Miller, then completing a term as justice of the peace, was a veteran Lansing attorney. He lost the election in April to Simon B. Roe, the Democrat candidate, by 182 votes.

The Ingham County Bar Association's first decade was instrumental in defining its future, and the next ninety years followed the pattern set by Sam Kilbourne and his colleagues—determined efforts to improve Michigan's legal system, and increased communication opportunities among Ingham County lawyers.

17

SCANDALS UNDER THE DOME

Early in 1894, as Governor John T. Rich began the second year of his first term as Michigan's titular head, he made a startling discovery while going over returns of a vote in the spring of 1893 on a constitutional amendment concerning the salaries of several high state officials.

The official returns, as certified by the Board of State Canvassers, showed a total of 127,023 votes—64,422 for the amendment raising the salaries and 62,601 against—indicating the amendment passed by 1,821 votes. But when Rich tallied his copy of the returns, the numbers showed a total vote of 129,989—59,217 for the amendment, 70,772 against, meaning the question was defeated by 11,555 votes.

The offices affected by the constitutional amendment were lieutenant governor, secretary of state, commissioner of public lands, superintendent of public instruction, state treasurer, and attorney general. The "passage" of the amendment had the effect of raising the treasurer's salary from $1,000 to $2,000 and the attorney general's from $2,500 to $3,000. It also upped the salary of the public instruction superintendent from $1,000 to $2,000, and those of the secretary of state and land commissioner from $800 to $2,000. The pay of the lieutenant governor was increased from $3 per day during the legislative session to $1,200 a year. With the exception of Attorney General Adolphus A. Ellis, the officials affected were Republicans serving their first terms as state officials. Ellis was a Democrat holdover from the administration of Governor Edwin B. Winans, the only Democrat to hold the gubernatorial reins from the mid-1850s until well into the twentieth century. In the 1892 fall election, Ellis had defeated the Republican candidate, Gerritt Diekema, 223,471 votes to 222,149.

In a page-one story on January 18, 1894, the *Lansing State Republican* said Lieutenant Governor J. Wight Giddings, Secretary of State John W. Jochim, Public Instruction Superintendent Henry R. Pattengill, Land Commissioner John G. Berry, State Treasurer Joseph F. Hambitzer, and Ellis had been drawing their salaries at the increased rate since the previous April. Making the revelations especially suspicious was that three of the increased salaries went to constitutional members of the Board of State Canvassers—Jochim, Hambitzer and Berry. The newspaper reported that the governor's private secretary "intimated" that Rich would ask for the resignations of the three men. Questions were also raised about the counting of votes on an 1891 constitutional amendment that had increased the attorney general's salary from $800 to $2,500 a year.

Hambitzer and Berry denied any wrongdoing and Jochim "courts the fullest investigation," the *Republican* reported, adding that the three-man board of canvassers was already poring over the returns and that as soon as the corrections were made, Ellis "will petition the supreme court for an order to set aside and nullify the old returns and recognize the corrected copy."

As things turned out, it was not quite that simple. Before it was over, Jochim, Hambitzer, and Berry were indicted by an Ingham County grand jury, charged with felonies in Ingham County Circuit Court, and, in a separate action, removed from office by order of the supreme court at Governor Rich's instigation. Ellis and Jochim both had lengthy trials, but Ellis retained his office after paying the state back for paycheck overages he had been collecting for more than two years. Interestingly, as the *Republican* pointed out, it had been twenty-five years since a grand jury had been called in Ingham—in 1867 to look into the lynching of John Taylor by an angry mob.

Ingham County attorneys and judges played major roles in the next two years. Circuit Court Judge Rollin Person called the grand jury and later heard the criminal cases in his court. Ingham County Prosecutor Leonard Gardner, with assistance from the Montgomery brothers, Richard and Martin V., and former Michigan Supreme Court Justices Cahill and Ostrander, prepared the original grand jury indictments and assisted with the prosecution in both the grand jury and later criminal trials. Sam Kilbourne defended Attorney General Ellis. One of Ingham County's classic legal confrontations came at the end of Ellis's criminal trial when Sam Kilbourne presented final arguments for the defense and Edward Cahill argued for the prosecution.

The *Republican* later reported that both men were scholarly and eloquent in their presentations. It was apparently an even match as the jury deliberated forty-four hours before announcing to Judge Person that it was irrevocably locked, six to six. Person ruled a mistrial.

Ellis returned to his Ionia home and his train was greeted by Company G of the National Guard and nearly one thousand townspeople. Two days later, Ellis returned to his office in the capitol and announced he was prepared to run for reelection. There was even talk he might seek the governor's office.

Prosecutor Gardner had different ideas, saying he was ready to retry the case. And Ellis' party was not certain the no-verdict end of the trial meant vindication for the attorney general. In convention in Grand Rapids on June 29,

Michigan Democrats nominated James O'Hara of Muskegon as their attorney general candidate for the fall election.

The Jochim criminal trial also ended in a hung jury, but it was not until New Year's Eve of 1896 that the fraudulent vote cases of the early 1890s were finally over. In one of his final acts before leaving office, Prosecuting Attorney Gardner filed a nolle pros action dismissing felony charges against four elected state officials and others accused of wrongdoing, telling Judge Person he did not believe convictions were possible and the charges should be dropped.

In November of 1899, shortly before he left office, Judge Person called another grand jury, this time to probe possible irregularities in the administration of Governor Hazen Pingree. The probe focused on several instances of improper use of state funds, but gave most of its attention to a scheme to buy and sell military supplies that bilked the state out of approximately $40,000. Approximately $50,000 of military supplies were sold by state officials to a bogus Illinois firm for $10,500 and eventually sold back to the state for $62,000.

The eventual outcome saw the resignations of several top state military officials, numerous indictments, criminal trials, and eventual gubernatorial pardons for two of the convicted generals. But while the military uniform scandal and subsequent trials provided much fodder for the newspapers, they also provided turning points in the careers of three of Ingham County's most influential attorneys—Arthur Tuttle, Rollin Person, and Howard Wiest.

Twenty-nine-year-old Tuttle had been Ingham County's prosecutor less than a year when he also assumed the grand jury's prosecuting duties. The Leslie resident was known as a fiery, flamboyant, and competent attorney. He quickly proved the descriptions were accurate, both winning indictments and refusing to back down from the pressure of hostile state officials.

In one instance, Tuttle confronted a breakfasting Hazen Pingree at the Hotel Downey, requesting the governor to appear before the grand jury. When Pingree abruptly left for the train station, Tuttle quickly filled out a blank subpoena he carried in his pocket, gave it to a deputy sheriff and had the governor served before he boarded the train.

Tuttle was beginning to develop a talent for getting his name in the newspaper. On February 2, the young prosecutor went into the county treasurer's office and collected all the pay he had earned since joining the county payroll—twelve months of 1899 and one month in the new year, for a total of $1,825. Then he went back to Leslie and applied the entire amount on the purchase of the Bailey homestead, considered, the *Republican* reported, to be "the mansion of Leslie." Arthur Tuttle was just starting to do things in a big way. He was also constantly on the move. He lived in Leslie, had an office in the Mason courthouse and three leased rooms in Lansing's downtown Hollister Building. Eventually, Tuttle would be appointed a United States District Attorney and then a federal judge by President William Taft. Veteran Lansing attorney Roy Conley remembered Tuttle as a no-nonsense federal judge. "Judge Tuttle was an autocrat, and was lord and master of his courtroom."

While Tuttle's years on the bench were still in the future, Person was concluding his tenure as a circuit court judge. Person's final day as judge was December 30, 1899, before the grand jury had completed its duties. He was actually in mid-career when he left the bench at age forty-nine to resume private practice. He would enjoy fifteen years of successful practice in Ingham County after he retired from the circuit bench. He served for nearly two years on the Michigan Supreme Court (1915-16), replacing an elected justice who died before his term commenced.

Known as a tough jurist, he was also respected and liked by almost everyone who knew him. On that final circuit court day, thirty members of the ICBA arrived early to decorate the bench with a bouquet of roses and carnations bearing a card that wished the judge a happy new year on one side and a "We welcome you back to active practice" on the other. Person was also led into the jury room where the entire grand jury had quietly assembled to wish him well and present him with a "handsome leather chair."

Two months after leaving the bench, Person addressed a convention of Royal Templers of Temperance. An active Presbyterian, he was proud of how he cut down the number of liquor violations cases before him early in his career as a circuit judge. Tavern owners had been in the habit of pleading guilty to Sunday and after-hours violations and paying only $25 fines. Person handed out tougher penalties and the violations decreased. Then, facing several Fourth of July liquor violators, Person recalled warning the defendants not to plead guilty unless they were guilty. Each pleaded guilty. "I fined them $200 each and you ought to have seen their faces," the judge said. "The violations suddenly ceased."

Howard Wiest, a thirty-five-year-old attorney who took over Person's grand jury duties in early 1900, was just beginning twenty-two years as an Ingham County circuit judge. He could probably be described as slightly eccentric, never purchasing an automobile, said to enjoy walking from the capitol to his Williamston farm, and preferring to read by gas rather than electric light. But his competency in the law was rarely questioned.

Wiest, a strong supporter, and sometimes organizer, of ICBA activities, eventually became a justice of the Michigan Supreme Court, filling that position for twenty-five years.

East Lansing attorney Allison Thomas remembers the annual ox and corn roasts hosted by Wiest. He told an ICBA gathering in 1994:

A great moment for me occurred after I passed the bar exam in 1939 when I was invited to attend the Ingham County Bar Association annual ox and corn roast hosted by Supreme Court Justice Howard Wiest at his country home near Williamston. [The country home] was called Shagbark, for the many shagbark hickory trees on the property.

Judge Wiest walked about the property in an old battered straw hat and corn cob pipe warmly greeting all the lawyers and judges in attendance. After playing horseshoes and baseball we quenched our thirst with a libation from his well which Judge Wiest claimed was the coldest water in the county. Many years later, Joe Planck, one of Ingham County's great scholars (and a highly respected attorney), told me the judge spiked the well with blocks of ice a few hours before the festivities. We were called to the feast by an old farm dinner bell hung from the bell tower.

About 5 P.M. we assembled in front of the pillars of Judge Wiest's colonial "mansion" and stood at attention while the flag was lowered and we all sang one verse of "America the Beautiful."

Many Ingham County attorneys who practiced during the first half of the twentieth century had Wiest stories. Former Ingham County Prosecuting Attorney Richard B. Foster, in a 1989 interview, recalled his father, Walter Foster, also a former prosecutor, discussing the popular judge. "I remember my father talking about trying cases before Judge Wiest," said Foster. "He [Wiest] loved to smoke cigars and my dad said his recess always depended upon how fast he finished his cigar."

During the 1899 grand jury probe, Tuttle, Person, and Wiest, like Ingham County legal officials of later years, were sometimes unpopular with state officials. Pingree, unhappy that county officials were investigating his administration, used both legal action and state newspapers to battle the three. There were also constant battles between the state and the county over which entity should pick up the bill for grand jury expenses. Pingree used the term "the boy," "the little cuss," and "that kid" to refer to Wiest, and suggested the judge be impeached. He showed similar contempt for Tuttle and Person. Little did Pingree know he was attacking two future Michigan Supreme Court justices and a federal district judge.

18

A NEW COURT HOUSE

As Ingham County settled into the twentieth century, the condition of the courthouse in Mason increasingly became the subject of conversation among lawyers. The brick building was only forty-four years old, but it had been constructed before the advent of central heating, running water, forced air ventilation, and electricity. There were constant complaints that the structure was not a safe place in which to store valuable county and court records. Opening of Lansing's modern city hall—complete with electric lights, running water, indoor toilet facilities, and even an electric elevator—served to underscore the inadequacy of the Mason courthouse. Yet, Mason residents, especially rural Ingham County supervisors, hesitated to mention the building's condition lest it touch off another round of speculation as to whether the county seat should be moved to Lansing.

On October 26, 1901, the building committee of the board of supervisors was asked to secure estimates for "repair" and modernization of the Mason structure and/or construction of a new courthouse. Those favoring a move of the county seat to Lansing figured it was only a matter of time before they would be in the driver's seat.

Before the first week of the new year ended, the board of supervisors' building committee report recommended the county build a new courthouse in Mason. The committee was headed by Lansing lawyer and city councilman Frank L. Dodge, whose bill in the legislature nearly twenty years before had established an Ingham County Circuit courtroom in Lansing and who, a few short years before, had predicted the county seat would soon be moved to Lansing. The official report stressed the need for safe storage of public documents and court records and mentioned how such provisions had been addressed in courthouses the committee visited at Hillsdale, Ionia, Ithaca, Corunna, and Charlotte. Mason has no such provisions, the report said, and even the hazardous storage facilities now provided are woefully lacking in space.

County offices are also "entirely inadequate," the report noted. Several departments were using rented quarters. The committee avoided mentioning building style and probable costs, but noted the buildings at Hillsdale and Ithaca cost between $40,000 and $45,000.

Supervisors decided not to waste any time. On January 9, 1902, they voted overwhelmingly to submit a proposition to voters in the April election authorizing Ingham County to borrow $40,000 for a new courthouse in Mason, the loan to be repaid with collections of a special property tax at the rate of $8,000 per year for five years. The supervisors' vote came on a motion by Lansing supervisor Shank, seconded by Frank Dodge. It was obvious to many that some healing of the longtime open wound in Mason's pride was taking place and that Lansing officialdom was abandoning, probably forever, any thoughts of attempting to move the county seat to the capital city.

Was Dodge really championing Mason's place as the legitimate center for county government, or was he perhaps taking a calculated risk that voters would turn down a new Mason courthouse, opening the way for a final push to remove the county seat to Lansing? Sam Kilbourne immediately predicted that a big voter turnout in the spring would doom the $40,000 loan. He told the *State Republican* that the estimated cost of a new building was high and said most lawyers and jurymen prefer that court sessions be held in Lansing. The ICBA president stressed, however, that he spoke as an individual and not as the bar association's leader.

Lansing's two daily newspapers were not enthusiastic over the referendum vote, considering the issue a matter of Lansing versus the out-county area. But the press did not openly oppose the issue, perhaps feeling that it did not stand a chance of passing. The *Republican* gave the post-election story a small space on its classified ad page the next day under a heading that read, "Exceeding Great Joy In Mason." The three-paragraph story reported that county voters outside Lansing gave a "majority for the loan of 2,762" while Lansing voters turned it down, 462 votes to 29. Lawyer Lawton T. Hemans, who had worked diligently on the campaign, was on the night train from Lansing that was met by a throng at Mason, which included the city band. Hemans was "lifted to the shoulders of stout men" and carried three blocks to the "old" courthouse, the *Republican* said, as sounds of "bells, whistles, fireworks and firecrackers" filled the night air with "excitement [that] did not abate until midnight."

Three weeks of construction weather were wasted before the county canvass on April 29 showed the proposition passed by 2,188 votes, with only Locke and Williamstown townships voting against it. County offices were moved from the old courthouse that summer (1902), and after several suggestions were made about moving the building to the rear of the square, it was torn down to make way for the new structure.

The replacement procedure was not a rapid one. At a special board meeting, committees were appointed to hire an architect and procure plans and

specifications, to negotiate the necessary loans, and to obtain space for the county offices and courts during construction. Edwyn A. Bowd of Lansing submitted the plans that were finally accepted. But the board cast 108 ballots before it
could agree on his concept.

By the time the cornerstone was laid on May 5, 1903, supervisors were asking county taxpayers for an additional $36,000. The overage was turned down
on an initial vote, but finally passed at a second referendum on November 3 by
a majority of 1,153. Taxpayers had ten years in which to pay the special assessment for the overage. At the 1903 ceremony, a sealed copper box was placed in
the cornerstone containing the day's printed program, a booklet on Mason history, the January term court calendar, directories of several Mason churches,
and histories and membership lists of a host of local fraternities.

In 1905, January 23 was a big day in Mason. It marked the first time the
Ingham Circuit Court held a term opening in the magnificent new courthouse. The
opening was delayed until nearly noon because the morning Michigan Central
train, bearing Judge Howard Wiest and most of the county's attorneys, was
late. Dedication of the new courthouse would be postponed until early in May.

After the crowd was quieted by the gavel pounding and "Hear ye, here ye,"
ICBA President Sam Kilbourne addressed the court at length, concluding with
a declaration that "every lawyer ought to receive new inspiration from his surroundings." Rollin Dart of Petoskey, a former Ingham County lawyer, also was
present and said he was envious of "such a handsome building." Prosecutor
Louis B. McArthur said all of the building's beauty depends on the impartiality
of the justice dealt within its walls. Other brief comments came from lawyers A.
M. Cummins and O. J. Hood of Lansing, and Frank M. Fogg of Leslie. Judge
Wiest promised the doors of the new courtroom were "open to everyone—not
barred to anyone, rich or poor."

No new courtroom ever had a splashier baptism. Lawyers and laymen alike
praised the facilities. But the attention paid to the building in chilly January of
1905 did not deter from the formal dedication on a beautiful, sunny Michigan
May morning four months later. On May 9, an estimated 2,500 Ingham County
residents, including Governor Fred M. Warner and Chief Justice J. B. Moore of
the Michigan Supreme Court, gathered in and around the new structure for a
day-long formal dedication.

The *Republican*, which was marking its own fiftieth anniversary that day
with a fat edition filled with various historical summaries, made the courthouse
dedication its lead story. Approximately 250 Lansing residents came to the festivities by train, arriving in time for a parade led by the Industrial School (later
known as the Boys' Training School) band. After a free lunch served in the courthouse, speeches began at 1:00 P.M. and continued until late in the afternoon.

The principal address was by Lawton T. Hemans, Mason's leading lawyer
and Ingham's representative in the state legislature. He called the new courthouse
"a temple of justice . . . a monument to the genius of our people."

Aware that many county taxpayers were critical of the building's cost—thought to be nearly thrice the original estimates—Supervisor Asa Barber of Mason, chairman of the building committee, set the record straight. He said the total cost, including new equipment and furniture throughout, was $96,678. The board of supervisors chairman, Lawrence Price, invited spectators to scrutinize the courthouse before deciding "whether or not this large amount of money has been honestly and wisely expended."

It was not until 1912 that the four-faced courthouse clock and bell were added, hauled to their lofty position in the ornate tower by horse-powered block and tackle. In 1971, the Ingham County courthouse was placed on the National Register of Historic Places; its renovation began in the mid-1980s.

Another event in the early 1900s with widespread legal ramifications had a profound effect on Ingham County and Lansing. On August 13, 1901, Ransom E. Olds, who had taken his horseless carriage manufacturing business to Detroit a few years before, announced he was planning to move it back to Lansing. A disastrous fire had extensively damaged Olds' Detroit factory and a group of Lansing businessmen, including several lawyers, had seized the opportunity to gain controlling interest of the county fairgrounds along the Grand River west of Washington Avenue. The business group, which included attorney Harris E. Thomas as its vice president, put up $5,000 to cover Thomas's personal note and obtain title to the property.

The Olds Motor works on River Street had been turning out engines for twenty-one years, shipping them to Detroit in 1900 and 1901. The engine business boomed after Olds secured patents in 1894 on the engine he planned to install in his "Curved Dash" model. The firm was then (August 1901) three hundred engine orders behind. Plans called for the engine operation to be moved to the fairgrounds site so the entire assembly—at the rate of thirty automobiles per day—"may be in contiguous buildings." Visions of an automobile assembly line were already dancing in the brain of R. E. Olds.

In 1902, the city council couldn't have anticipated the legal problems that a nation on gasoline-powered wheels would soon face. It didn't take long for automobiles to start running into things, including each other; and frequently, the newfangled machines were themselves being hit. The November 26, 1906, *Lansing Journal*, for example, carried the story of motorist Joseph P. Fillingham after his auto was rammed by a street car on Pine Street. Fillingham turned left to enter his driveway, claiming he looked before he turned and saw nothing. Before he could reach his drive, however, his automobile was rammed by a streetcar turning off St. Joseph Street. Fillingham hired former Circuit Judge Rollin Person to file suit against the streetcar company, alleging the motorman was negligent in not sounding a gong and for running "at a greater speed than the firm's franchise permits"—sixteen miles per hour. Fillingham sought $300 in damages to the automobile and another $200 for loss of its use during the three months required to repair it.

Prosecutor Arthur Tuttle was upset with the Ingham County legal system in early 1902. In addition to the lack of convictions in the bribery cases—not because of poor preparation but because of a quirk in the law that allowed a key witness to avoid testifying—Tuttle felt some guilty parties were going free. He had also "lost" several justice court cases recently, a large share of them because police had obtained warrants directly from justices of the peace. When the cases came to trial, Tuttle frequently was caught without sufficient evidence to back up the charge. That did not help the prosecution's batting average, and Tuttle decided to put an end to trying questionable cases. He announced that beginning in February, all criminal cases would be reviewed by his office before the information was presented to a justice of the peace for issuance of a warrant.

In May of 1902, Ingham County residents learned their young, successful prosecuting attorney might never try a case in the new courthouse. Arthur Tuttle had aspirations of bigger things, and with Judge Wiest firmly seated on the county's circuit court bench, Tuttle decided to make a run for Congress. By May 8, the *Republican* was saying Tuttle would be nominated for the Sixth District seat at the upcoming Republican congressional convention in Fenton. Judge Cahill gave him a boost, telling the newspaper that his young friend and cohort "has good timber in him. . . ." Later that week, the paper reported all seven of Lansing Township's delegates had been instructed to back Tuttle after township Republicans voted 24 to 14 to support him over the GOP incumbent, Sam Smith. Tuttle backers later claimed a "safe majority" of Ingham County's delegates, 111 to 102. As it turned out, Tuttle lacked strength in other areas of the district. The convention gave its nod on May 29 to incumbent Smith, 83 votes to 21, and he was re-elected in November.

Tuttle quickly decided not to run again for prosecutor and announced his intentions on July 10. That same day, the *Republican* carried the prosecutors report on the first half of 1902, showing 653 prosecutions and 606 convictions, including 121 for drunkenness, 380 disorderly cases, 34 larcenies, and 18 for playing baseball on Sunday.

A young Williamston lawyer, Orr C. Trask, was credited in early 1905 with uncovering a cold-blooded murder—the poisoning of a highly respected Wheatfield Township farmer. The lawyer's suspicions set the stage for the first trial held in the new Ingham County courthouse at Mason.

William Joslin, whose farm was four and one-half miles northeast of Dansville, began having attacks of illness in September of 1904. About the same time, he confided to Trask, his attorney, suspicions of an illicit relationship between his wife Carrie, who was thirty years old, and the hired man, Isaac C. Swan. Trask said he advised Joslin to go home and "kick Swan out and if his wife objected, to invite her to go, too." Joslin's illnesses continued, Trask told authorities, and worsened early in December. When he learned Joslin had died at his home on Christmas day, Trask became suspicious "that all was not as it should be" and, at the request of the man's father and brother, did some follow-up investigating.

Three physicians who had attended Joslin all were in doubt as to the exact nature of his malady. On a hunch, Trask went to the Williamston pharmacy of Lesia & Headley and learned that on December 5 Swan had bought four hundred eighty grams of arsenic. Neighbors then told the attorney of rumors of the intimacy of Swan and Mrs. Joslin. Trask conveyed his suspicions to Prosecutor McArthur on December 30. On January 3, McArthur and Sheriff William Steele met at Dansville with the three doctors and then went before a justice of the peace to obtain an order to disinter Joslin's body. The request was signed by the three doctors and by Joslin's father and brother.

Exhumation of Joslin's body "was hastily made," the *Republican* reported the next day, and a post mortem examination was done in the Dansville town hall. "The stomach was removed and sealed in a two-quart jar," the news story said, and was taken "to the agricultural college" by the sheriff. Chemistry professor Robert Kedzie was asked to search for possible traces of poison. McArthur also sent for Mrs. Joslin, who was confronted with the incriminating facts. She "broke down and confessed that she had administered poison to her husband."

According to her story, Carrie Joslin put arsenic in her husband's coffee only once—on Saturday, December 24. He immediately became violently ill, she told McArthur, and died on Christmas morning. The doctors said he must have been "doped" repeatedly because his final illness, a puzzle to them, lasted for two weeks. Authorities determined Swan had left the farm about a week before Joslin died.

Mrs. Joslin was arraigned on a murder charge before Justice of the Peace Paddock of Dansville; then, pending a report on the contents of the victim's stomach, she and her two young children were taken to a Mason hotel in charge of a sheriff's deputy. Later in the day, the suspect's father, who lived near Webberville, went to Mason and took temporary custody of the two Joslin children. Mrs. Joslin was then taken to the jail in Mason. She wrote a letter to her hired man (not Swan, but a man named Alford Hollis), according to the *Republican*, and the sheriff immediately opened it. The letter asked Hollis to bring her some money and clothing and to pay the taxes on the farm. It closed with, "I'm crazy or I wouldn't be here." She also told the jail turnkey that Swan had a certain influence over her "and when he asked her to kill her husband, she couldn't refuse." She said "When I love, I want to be loved back and want to be loved right. My husband wouldn't go to church with me, so I went with Swan."

Swan was arrested on January 7 as he stepped from a train in Detroit. He acknowledged to police he had bought the arsenic for Mrs. Joslin but did not know she had been arrested. Turned over to Ingham County authorities, Swan said Mrs. Joslin exerted a "strange influence" over him. He said she had first tried to administer to her husband a sedative drug—aconite—made from a poisonous plant. Swan told officers he had "laid low" in the east for the past week but was returning to the farm after receiving an all-clear message from his brother. When the prosecutor informed Mrs. Joslin that Swan was in custody, she said, "He was the cause of all our trouble."

Ex-Probate Judge Jason Nichols, just returning to private practice, agreed to defend Swan; Mrs. Joslin retained Lawton Hemans. Swan was arraigned on January 10 before Mason Justice of the Peace Sherwood and was jailed without bond pending a preliminary examination set for January 12.

Dansville's township hall bulged at the seams on January 11 when Carrie Joslin was brought over from Mason by carriage to be examined before Paddock. At least 800 curious (a reporter's generous estimate) jammed the building, reported the *Republican*, and hundreds more gathered outside. They were grossly disappointed when the carriage stopped at the rear entrance and Mrs. Joslin was "hastily escorted" into the basement boiler room. She talked briefly with Hemans, and Paddock then rapped the court into session as he sat at a workman's bench and acknowledged the defendant's wish to waive examination. She was then whisked back to Mason for trial later in the month.

At Swan's examination in Mason the next day in Justice Sherwood's court, William Joslin's brother testified that the victim had begun showing signs of illness in August. Sheriff's deputy Fred Tobias produced a gushy love letter from Carrie Joslin to Swan, mailed by the latter's brother and addressed to Swan in New Jersey. The officer also related Swan's story about buying the arsenic and delivering some of it to Mrs. Joslin. Dr. Charles Culver of Williamston testified he cared for Joslin throughout his illness, which had "all the symptoms of arsenic poisoning." He said he told his suspicions to Mrs. Joslin and predicted if her husband died, she would be accused of causing his death.

On Friday the 13th of January, William Joslin's body was exhumed for the second time in ten days from its grave in the Dansville cemetery after McArthur learned Kedzie had found no trace of arsenic in the stomach. McArthur wanted the search extended to the victim's liver and spleen, which were removed at the undertaking parlor of Isaac Moe and delivered to Kedzie. The body was returned to its resting place a third time.

Swan and Mrs. Joslin were the first persons to be arraigned in a courtroom that a newspaper account described as having "the finest" appointments and furnishings. The story neglected to describe the room's novel double jury setup that made possible simultaneous trials of two defendants charged with different crimes involved in the same incident. Considerable time could be saved by moving separate juries in and out of the courtroom so they hear only testimony applicable to the defendant in judgment of whom they are sitting. Both Swan and Mrs. Joslin stood mute. Wiest entered not-guilty pleas and gave McArthur a week to file further charges on the suspected poisoning.

Carrie Joslin entered a guilty plea to the murder charge on February 15 and Judge Wiest accepted the first degree plea the next day after a lengthy in-chambers consultation with the woman. Before he decided the degree question, Wiest had the prosecution produce its evidence, the most telling of which came from Dr. Robert Kedzie, who testified he found traces of arsenic poison in William Joslin's heart, liver, spleen, kidneys, and skin.

Swan's jury trial began on February 17. McArthur told the jury he would prove Carrie Joslin and Swan were infatuated with each other and wanted to marry. He said he would establish that Carrie's signal to her lover that Joslin was not at home was a lamp placed in a window. McArthur also told the jury he would prove that Mrs. Joslin and Swan attempted during the summer to poison William Joslin with aconite, a quantity of which was found in the house.

As the trial progressed, Kedzie testified as to amounts of arsenic found in the various organs of the victim and said the amount found in a skin sample indicated more than a one-time dosing of the poison. A confession Swan made to a Detroit police captain who arrested him was admitted by Wiest. In the confession, Swan admitted he and Carrie Joslin had been intimate and that she had spoken several times about getting rid of her husband. He said he finally agreed, quit his job as the Joslins' hired man, and purchased the arsenic at Carrie's request. Her love letter was admitted into evidence.

Attorney Nichols surprised the court, the prosecution, and the courtroom spectators when the trial resumed on Monday by announcing he would call no witnesses and make no arguments in Swan's behalf. Informed that one of the jurors was ill and his condition worsening, McArthur said he, too, would forego final arguments to the jury. The courtroom remained packed.

Carrie Joslin was called by the prosecution and admitted putting some arsenic in her husband's coffee on December 10. She said she got the poison from Swan, who told her "that would do the business." She then arose, glanced at Judge Wiest and walked, falteringly, from the courtroom into his office, followed by one of the physicians.

The jury took only fifteen minutes to convict Swan of first degree murder after Wiest, in his charge, said that all murder by poison is first degree. Swan, who was thirty years old, was immediately sentenced to life at the prison at Jackson. Court officers escorted him to the jail for the night and returned with Carrie Joslin, who was given a chair to sit in immediately in front of the bench. She asked to see her lawyer, Hemans, before sentence was passed. Someone went to get Hemans. But Wiest was impatient. After a few moments, he ordered the woman to stand. She asked that one of the doctors stand with her. The young widow Joslin braced for the lecture from Wiest. He told her she had confessed to murdering her husband after plotting to "deliver up" his life "on the shrine of unholy lusts and desires." The judge said her crime was "the coldest kind of a murder." Carrie slumped to her chair as Wiest pronounced the life-without-parole sentence.

19

TRIALS AND TRIBULATIONS

The Ingham County legal scene in the first decade of the twentieth century was a study in change and at the same time provided a cementing of traditions. If ever the old saying, "The more things change, the more they stay the same," had an application, it was in the courts, law offices and professional law association of Ingham County between 1900 and 1910.

One change came in the makeup of the state's highest court. As the decade began, Michigan's supreme court was made up of five justices elected by the people as provided for in an amendment to the 1850 constitution's provision that the legislature would set up the court system. The court had been increased to five members in 1887 after thirty years as a four-judge body. By 1903, legislative action had increased the court to eight justices.

Three new justices were elected to staggered terms in 1904 and were sworn in at the start of the new year. One of the new justices was Lansing lawyer Russell Ostrander, a former mayor considered among the leading attorneys in the capital city.

Ostrander's name was a familiar one to Lansingites from the time he was a teenager in the 1860s. Born in Ypsilanti, he came to Lansing in 1858 with his family. His father was a carriage maker. Young Ostrander was a trusted youth and for several summers daily herded the milk cows of Lansing residents out into the forested farmlands at the city's east edge to graze. Each evening he herded the bovines back into town, making certain each animal was back in its own shed by milking time.

Ostrander completed his public school education and a commercial course and was clerking in Robinson's store when, in 1874 at age twenty-two, he received two letters the same day. One offered him a position in a Saginaw mercantile business and promised an eventual salary of four thousand dollars. The other offered him odd jobs in the office of lawyer Albert E. Cowles and the care of his horse and carriage house. He accepted Cowles offer and soon was reading law under the veteran attorney.

Later that fall, Ostrander entered the University of Michigan law school and graduated two years later. Returning to Ingham County, he served as a circuit court commissioner, prosecuting attorney, Lansing city attorney, state law examining board member and headed a lucrative private practice before his election to the supreme court in 1904.

Another change in the legal scene was the arrival of the "interurban"—an electric-powered, frequent-trip vehicle with comfortable seats. When it began its runs to Mason from Lansing, lawyers, judges, witnesses, and litigants no longer had to wait for the train to get to court. And by the end of the decade, a few in the legal fraternity were even driving their own cars between Lansing and Mason.

The courthouse itself had one noticeable change several years after its completion. In 1903, a gilded copper eagle—the national emblem—had been purchased to roost on a ball surmounting a large weather vane atop the dome of the courthouse. For some unexplained reason, the four-foot wingspan eagle was not placed on the dome when the building was completed. Instead, it was relegated to obscurity in a vault in one of the offices. Some youthful hell-raisers, the story goes, learned about the eagle, sneaked into the vault and made off with the big bird, intending to affix it to the top of the Lansing City Hall. But some young Masonites learned of the dastardly deed, rescued the eagle, and returned it to Mason. In April of 1910, the county board of supervisors decreed that the eagle should finally gain its lofty perch. It landed there on April 8, 1910, thanks to a "human fly" described by the *State Republican* as "a graduate of the Ingham County jail" who volunteered to "risk life and limb" to place it on its roost.

Another decided change was Michigan's new constitution—billed as the first real overhauling of the 1850 document, which had been altered numerous times by amendments but was considered sorely dated by the turn of the century. Voters several times had turned down the opportunity to hold a constitutional convention and on two occasions, in 1868 and 1874, had gone through the tedious process of calling a Con-Con, electing delegates, revamping the document, and then failing to ratify the revision at the polls.

The legislature decided that constitutional convention delegates would be selected by popular vote, each state senate district being allowed three male representatives on the ninety-six-member body; women still could not vote or hold office in Michigan. Of the ninety-six delegates who gathered on October 22, 1907, in the supreme court chambers in the capitol, fifty-nine were lawyers—including Ingham County's lone representative, Lawton T. Hemans of Mason. The other two Fourteenth District delegates were from Owosso. As the convention organized itself, Hemans came to wield considerable power as chairman of two committees.

Delegates plunged immediately into their work, meeting daily, including some Saturdays and even on December 31. But they made mostly brief, often one-word changes in the 1850 document and in no way overhauled it. Rather, it was mostly a revamping of the old document and a regrouping to place similar items under one heading. A large share of the changes were in the judicial section. The delegates completed their work and adjourned on March 3, 1908. A week later, the supreme court ruled the ratification question should be decided at the fall election. It was on November 3, 1908, that the new constitution—which would remain in force until 1964—was ratified 244,705 votes to 130,783.

One major change in the judicial section of the new constitution concerned placing juvenile criminal cases under the jurisdiction of the probate courts. The new constitution, like its 1850 predecessor, was lengthy and detailed, making necessary a constitutional amendment to effect even a minor change. As a result, the constitution was amended seventy times in the fifty-five years before the next rewrite in 1961-62; voters rejected another fifty-seven proposed amendments.

In the same 1908 election, Hemans, largely on the strength of his stellar role in the constitutional convention and in the legislature, ran for governor of Michigan on the Democratic ticket. He was beaten as Republican Fred M. Warner was narrowly re-elected. But the popular Hemans did carry Mason, Lansing, and the rest of Ingham County as many voters split their tickets. Arthur Tuttle was re-elected state senator and Walter S. Foster won a second term as Ingham County prosecutor. Henry Gardner won re-election as county probate judge.

While Hemans was known for his skills at both law and politics, he also had a passionate interest in history, becoming obsessed with the life story of Stevens T. Mason, Michigan's first governor. Bothered that so little had been written about the "boy governor," he eventually authored *The Life and Times of Stevens T. Mason*, still considered a scholarly and very readable contribution to Michigan history. It was largely through Hemans's efforts that Mason's body was removed from an obscure cemetery in New York City and reburied with honors in Detroit.

In the waning days of 1907, the *Republican* gave front-page play to a story announcing the formation of a new Lansing law firm—Tuttle, McArthur and Dunnebacke—occupying an office suite in the Hollister Building. Tuttle was then chairman of the Ingham County Republican Party, president of the village of Leslie, and president of the Leslie bank. The new partnership was destined to give its partners considerable prestige and to serve as a base for Tuttle's political future. L. B. McArthur and Tuttle were recent Ingham prosecutors, McArthur was president of the Farmers Bank in Mason, and Joseph Dunnebacke, a former deputy clerk of the supreme court, was an accomplished writer on corporate law and taxes for legal publications.

Despite the myriad changes, there were a number of happenings on the Lansing-Ingham legal scene that were assuming the status of traditions. One of them was the annual gathering in the capital city of the Association of Judges of Michigan, an organization of supreme court justices and circuit and probate judges. The sixteenth annual session of the association was held on December 29 and 30 in 1908. The dates usually coincided with that of the annual banquet of the Ingham County Bar Association, and for the previous several years the ICBA had invited the visiting judges and their ladies to the banquet. In earlier years, the "feast" was held at the tall-spired Plymouth Congregational Church on Allegan Street across from the capitol or at the Church of Our Father. But those who attended the 1908 joint banquet had a unique treat; Lansing attorney Frank Dodge opened his exquisite North Street home on the bend of the Grand River in North Lansing to 125 of his judicial and attorney friends.

The banquet guests were seated at tables for five and served by twenty-one young men and women from prominent families. In a hallway of the home, an orchestra played dinner music. All the after-dinner speeches were impromptu, reported the *Republican* the next day. ICBA president and spellbinder Sam Kilbourne concluded his "clever remarks" by introducing A. J. Sawyer, a former Lansingite and then prosecutor of Washtenaw County. Sawyer said it was his first experience at attending a banquet with wives present and promised to take the novel idea back to Ann Arbor.

In their business session, the judges' association elected Supreme Court Chief Justice Montgomery as their 1909 president, barely a year before he accepted federal assignment as chief justice of the U.S. Customs Court. But in the interim, Montgomery agreed to run for governor on the Republican ticket— and lost. He left Lansing on April 5, 1910, with the sounds of toasts and acco-lades of members of the Ingham Bar Association still ringing in his ears from a festive banquet in his honor at the Hotel Downey the night before. Fifty ICBA members and other state officials and county leaders gave him a gracious send-off. Sam Kilbourne gave the main address, saying that President William Howard Taft had honored Michigan by naming its chief justice to head up the new judicial tribunal.

It could not qualify as a tradition, but it seemed to have become a habit that every so often another Ingham County grand jury investigation would surface. This one, involving state Treasurer Frank P. Glazier, had its beginning in the closing of Glazier's Chelsea Savings Bank by the state bank examiner on December 2, 1907. By the next day, the newspapers were claiming Glazier had a list of liabilities in the form of loans he was unable to pay from other Michigan banks—totaling $1,978,000. Among the questionable figures was $685,588 of funds of the state of Michigan that Glazier reportedly had deposited the year before in his bank.

Glazier, the stories said, had placed his business affairs in the hands of his friends. By January 16, a deputy was running the department; Glazier was trea-surer in name only because he had failed to file a $150,000 bond. Governor

Warner was expected to demand Glazier's resignation momentarily. Glazier reportedly was broke and had loans from five Detroit banks plus one in Grand Rapids and one in Stockbridge.

Glazier resigned January 20, 1908. Meanwhile, a Wiest grand jury was investigating whether any crime had been committed. The investigation and follow-up took up nearly all of 1908 before Glazier was finally indicted and brought to trial. His arrest warrant, alleging thirty-one counts, was served in his bedroom in Chelsea to a defendant whom the local paper reported was dying. He improved, and the trial opened in the Lansing City Hall on December 17, 1908. Prosecutor Walter S. Foster's opening statement reviewed Glazier's career. He told the jury that one reason Glazier required large sums of money in 1907 was that he had lost $70,000 in the *Ann Arbor News*, which he owned at the same time he was building "a magnificent house" in Chelsea. The Chelsea mercantile establishment in which Glazier held a controlling interest "was in hard shape," Foster said, and "he was using state money" to bolster the firm. Foster said Glazier "borrowed $40,000 from the state." He was also building some brick warehouses and a welfare building for his employees. Once, Foster told the jury, Glazier left the capital with $3,000 to deposit in his bank, "lost $1,000 [of it] on the train" and devoted another $1,000 to his own use, depositing only $1,000. Foster's predecessor, L. B. McArthur, and A. J. Sawyer of Ann Arbor, outgoing Washtenaw prosecutor, defended Glazier. Sawyer's term still had two weeks to go. Ex-Judge Rollin Person assisted Foster.

The defense tried to show by a deputy state treasurer's testimony that Glazier did not commit any crime by depositing state funds in his bank. His lawyers also tried to show that as state treasurer, Glazier was not responsible for loans the bank made. Thus, the theory went, the charge of appropriating state funds to his own use could not be sustained against the defendant.

The trial continued through January of 1909. The defense offered no testimony. The case finally went to the jury on January 27, the thirty-seventh day of trial. After four hours, the jury found Glazier guilty of ten counts as charged—misappropriating state funds for use in the Chelsea bank. He still faced counts of misappropriation for himself personally, Judge Wiest told the jury in his charge. Wiest gave Glazier's lawyers until the first day of the March term to file exceptions. It was November 16 before Glazier's attorneys, Sawyer of Ann Arbor and ex-Ingham Prosecutor L. B. McArthur, filed their appeal with the supreme court. The high court, in a twenty-two-page opinion (*People v. Glazier*, 159 Mich. 528, February 1910) written by Justice Blair, affirmed the conviction.

The supreme court sent Glazier back to Wiest for sentencing. On February 3, 1910, a frail Glazier, flanked by his wife and attorney, was sentenced to five to ten years in the state prison at Jackson. "It is the opinion of the court that you should serve ten years," Wiest told the sobbing ex-state treasurer as he buried his face against his wife's bosom.

By March of 1909, Judge Wiest's civil case docket had piled up to the point that President Sam Kilbourne of the Ingham County Bar Association decided to take matters into his own hands. He called together attorneys who had assembled for the opening of the new term of court on March 9. Kilbourne said he wanted the association "to take some action in an endeavor to get the legislature to relieve Judge Wiest by appointing an assistant judge." Scores of civil cases were backlogged, Kilbourne said, because of an accumulation of criminal and other cases.

Wiest himself got into the act, pointing out that the new constitution did away with the practice of summoning a judge from a neighboring district to help whittle away at log-jammed dockets. For years, Wiest had received temporary help from judges in Gratiot, Genesee, and Jackson counties. It appeared these visiting judge assists had been unauthorized—Wiest would simply telephone a judge to ask for a week's help, and he would promptly show up.

Ingham's legislative representatives were advised of the bar association's move. Senator Arthur Tuttle took up the cause in the state senate; and on May 26, the legislature delivered a two-page document, Public Act Number 136 of 1909, to Governor Warner. His signature gave Ingham County's circuit court immediate permission to place a second judge on its bench. The "relief" posed immediate problems for Lansing and Ingham County and its bar association.

Kilbourne called a bar association meeting for June 3 to make a judicial recommendation for Warner to appoint. Nearly forty ICBA members showed up. Tuttle, who would have been a "natural" for the post, said he was representing his law partner, L. B. McArthur, who did not wish the association to ballot on his name because he was not certain he could accept the appointment if it should be tendered. Both Tuttle and McArthur, however, were named for the balloting. Charles W. Nichols and Jason Nichols were named, along with Edward Cahill, Kilbourne, C. P. Black, and O. J. Hood. Charles Nichols received seventeen votes, Hood nine, Cahill and Black three each, McArthur two, and Kilbourne, Jason Nichols, and Tuttle one each. In a second balloting, Charles Nichols again received seventeen votes and Hood eleven. The association decided the recommendation should have something closer to unanimity and agreed to meet on June 17 to make a final decision. On that occasion, since Nichols (twenty votes) gained and Hood (ten) lost slightly, it was decided the ICBA would make no recommendation to the governor.

Lansing's growing pains were creating another problem. Act Number 136 specified that additional offices, a courtroom, a jury room, and facilities for court workers be provided by the city council in Lansing and the board of supervisors in Mason. The 1880 act, creating a court site in Lansing, still required that two terms of court be held in Mason and two in Lansing each year. The 1909 act did not specify that one Ingham County judge would sit in Lansing and one in Mason, which would have avoided the space problem. In fact, it said the judges could sit together or separately. Only the judge to which a case was assigned, however, could make rulings on that case except in cases of illness or absence from the county. The act also specified that "neither judge shall grant an application which shall have been denied by the other." The Lansing council said it had only one empty room, and Judge Wiest said the third-floor room used for storing voting machines could be made into a jury room. Some councilmen feared the only solution would be an expensive addition to city hall. More realistic officials suggested using the council chamber for a courtroom when two trials occurred simultaneously.

By mid-July, the *Lansing Journal* reported the new judge contest had been reduced to three candidates—Charles Nichols, Hood, and lawyer Charles B. Collingwood, who also was postmaster of East Lansing. Nichols now had forty-four backers in the ICBA, the *Journal* said, and many others in the electorate. Collingwood was labeled the "choice of the politicians" who feared that "neither Nichols nor Hood would be easily controlled if on the bench." The July 16 story concluded with a listing of the eleven Ingham lawyers who refused to sign a petition backing Nichols. The list included Hood and Collingwood.

Knowing the governor would read the story, Collingwood went to the Capitol the next day and had a lengthy visit with Governor Warner. The visit paid off. On August 30, the *Journal* ran a headline across its front page: "COLLINGWOOD WILL BE THE NEW CIRCUIT JUDGE." The story said Warner had confided his plans to associates the previous week after twice offering the appointment to another lawyer who turned it down in favor of retaining his present position.

Collingwood would be required to run in 1910 to retain the job, and again on April 3, 1911, when all circuit judges in the state would be in the final months of their elected terms. Meanwhile, Collingwood would begin his appointed term immediately, the *Journal* reported. Collingwood, a bar member for more than a dozen years, had served as Lansing city attorney and as Ingham County Republican chairman. His 1907 appointment as East Lansing postmaster was made by President Theodore Roosevelt.

Warner announced Collingwood's judicial appointment on September 8. The *Journal* revealed it was Probate Judge H. M. Gardner who had turned down the job. The next day, Collingwood was told his courtroom would be the city council chambers, already undergoing remodeling that included construction of a jury box. Within a week, the "extra" room on the third floor of the city hall was being revamped—just in time for some of the twenty-seven jury trials on the September court calendar, along with sixty-five contested divorce cases.

In the fall election in 1910, Collingwood ran against Arlington Bergman and defeated him 5,054 votes to 4,805. And on April 3, 1911, he received 4,627 votes and Wiest 5,637 to become the successful candidates in a four-man field that included Alva Cummins (3,433) and Bergman (3,528). Members of the

Ingham bar could relax a bit. Two circuit judges now were able to handle the case load without frequent night and Saturday sessions. The county had two highly capable circuit judges in place, at least until 1918.

The political pot boiled overtime during 1910, stirred by a number of attempts by ICBA members to push fellow attorneys into more important jobs. Prosecutor Walter S. Foster began the new year by taking over the reins as president of the newly formed Michigan Association of Prosecuting Attorneys; and Robert Montgomery, for the second year, was named to head the Michigan Association of Judges. In February, Judge Wiest was again brought to the attention of top federal officials when the bar association proposed him to President William Howard Taft as the logical successor to U.S. District Judge Swan of Detroit, who was nearing retirement. A flowery resolution that was vintage Sam Kilbourne, extolling the forty-six-year-old Wiest's accomplishments and talents, was adopted unanimously by the ICBA and sent to the Michigan Congressional delegation.

Lawton T. Hemans, still considered a valuable public servant because of his stints in the legislature and the constitutional convention, ran for governor that year but lost by forty-five thousand votes to Republican Chase S. Osborn. On the Ingham County level, Charles Hayden was elected prosecuting attorney. Wiest did not get the federal appointment, but the other member of his grand jury team—Arthur J. Tuttle—received an appointment that helped put the Ingham bar on the map. Tuttle's appointment as federal district attorney in Detroit was announced on December 23, effective as soon as the new Congress took over in March 1911.

Also in the 1910 election, veteran Lansing lawyer Alva Cummins took on incumbent Samuel Smith of Flint for the Sixth District Congressman post, losing by five thousand votes. Cummins tried again in 1912 and narrowed the margin to about three thousand votes.

One of Michigan's big legal news stories of 1912 broke at the annual late December meetings of the Michigan judges' and prosecuting attorneys' associations in the capital city. The *State Journal*, "born" earlier that year in an amalgamation of the *Lansing Journal* and the *Republican*, gave top play in its December 27 issue to a fiery speech delivered to the convention by Judge Wiest. Referring to suggestions in the recent political campaign that judges and judicial decisions should be recalled, Wiest said the idea amounted to political exploitation of the courts. He denounced such recall as "political heresy absolutely destructive of the constitution, subversive of civil liberty, damned by history and a menace to the very existence of government."

Two businesses that prospered early in the twentieth century by offering to relieve boredom of the populace came in for considerable opposition from moralists and some church groups. The offending businesses were saloons and motion picture houses, both of which continually tried to woo customers on Sundays, the only day of the week in which most folks did not work.

Nationally, the prohibition forces were gearing up for their big push that would come at the end of the century's second decade. The drys enlisted backing from the mainline churches, which in turn applied local pressure in states in which local option had been approved. The drive to dry up Michigan cities was unrelenting, but with women still denied the vote, the success rate was slow. John Barleycorn and Demon Rum were still very much apparent.

By 1909, several Ingham County communities had adopted bans on the sale of alcoholic refreshments on Sunday. Operators of taverns and saloons had to obey the law or risk arrest because their businesses were so visible. But hotels would sometimes serve customers on the Sabbath, the owners figuring skeleton police crews wouldn't notice the violations because it was normal for people to be seen coming and going from hotels at all hours. Sheriff Harvey O. Cline and two of his deputies decided to improve enforcement of the Sunday law in Onondaga, where reports indicated both hotels were serving alcohol illegally on Sundays.

The first arrest was easy. Deputy Eckert and former Deputy Sheethelm merely arrived at the hotel run by Ira Ball and Orrin Blakeley, went to the barroom and asked to purchase a bottle of "Old Coon" whisky. Blakeley acted as lookout, according to a story in the September 14 *Journal*, and passed the men into the barroom where Ball took their money for the booze. Charged with keeping a saloon on a Sunday, the pair demanded examination when arraigned before Justice Lumbard of Leslie. Blakeley had paid a fine of $150 the previous April when he pleaded guilty to a similar charge before Judge Wiest.

Cline figured it would not be quite so easy to catch Robert Sweeney, owner of the village's other hotel, so he and the deputies devised a plan. They borrowed an automobile from a friend (the sheriff's department was still "horse-and-buggy," although Lansing police had a Reo patrol car by 1909). The trio drove to Onondaga early the next Sunday evening. Stopping along the road, they pretended to be repairing the car; a bystander stopped to watch. One of the deputies asked the bystander where they might get a drink, and the local man directed them to Sweeney's hotel. Sweeney was arrested and then bound over to circuit court after waiving examination before Lumbard. Sweeney asked to plead guilty and pay his fine immediately, but was told he must appear before Wiest. His comment: "Well, all I have to say is that the men who secured that booze from me are no gentlemen!"

By 1916, Sunday motion pictures and even Sunday automobile drives were condemned by the General Assembly of the Presbyterian Church. A few weeks later, the *State Journal* reported the Methodists had followed suit and added drinking, dancing, and card playing to the list of entertainment sins. Lansing, by then, had three operating movie houses.

At least one Lansing movie house operator had beaten a city ordinance when he showed a silent picture five years before on October 15, 1911. But it cost Leroy Brown plenty of attorney fees for the case to be taken to three courts before he was exonerated. Brown was convicted in Lansing Municipal Court and the verdict was upheld on appeal by Judge Wiest in circuit court. Sentence was imposed, but stayed, so that Brown's lawyers—Jason Nichols and L. B. McArthur—could appeal to the Michigan Supreme Court. City Attorney C. P. Black represented the People in *City of Lansing v. Brown*, 172 Mich. 50 (1912). On October 1, 1912, the high court reversed the conviction and ordered Brown discharged in a decision written by Justice Ostrander, a former Lansing mayor, and concurred in by five other justices. Chief Justice Moore dissented.

Although Michigan at the time had a statute against Sunday movies, Brown was charged under a city ordinance providing for the licensing of places of entertainment. Ostrander ruled the ordinance did not ban Sunday picture shows and that the warrant charged Brown with operating on Sunday without a license. The city's position was that its license did not permit Sunday showings, an argument Ostrander found "essentially unsound." Moore argued that the ordinance forbade city licensing of Sunday shows, which was, in effect, a prohibition of Sunday showings.

The legality of Sunday movies, however, seemed minor compared to the mysterious murder that occurred in a home a few blocks north of the Lansing business district a fortnight before Christmas 1912. The *State Journal* carried the story of the Friday, December 6 death of "Mrs. Pauline Fingel Pole," on its Saturday edition's front page, and reported the only suspect in the murder by poison—widow Mary Lucas—had been in police custody since a few hours after the victim died. The case was destined, eventually, to shake the neighborhood, the criminal justice system, and the Ingham County bar. A decade before, Mary and John were known as an up-and-coming lawyer team of Lucas & Lucas and she was considered to be Ingham County's first female lawyer.

By the time the citizenry learned of the crime, there were reports that police were digging up the Lucas basement and yard in a search for the remains of John Lucas, who had disappeared fifteen years or so before. The Tuesday headline announcing the investigation read. "'MURDER FARM' IN LUCAS HOUSE, BELIEF OF POLICE." The story said Mrs. Lucas admitted administering poison to Mrs. Fingel, who supposedly had attracted the affections of neighbor John Berenzc in a "modern Lucretia Borgia" entanglement. Mary had been infatuated with Berenzc, described by the newspaper as "the burly, swarthy Pole," when he abruptly turned his attention to Mrs. Fingel. Newly arrived immigrants, she and her husband, Daniel Fingel, had moved in next door to Lucas only four weeks before.

Apparently there had been some deep-rooted suspicions about Mary Lucas. She and her husband had left for Nebraska in the mid-1890s, and she had returned to Lansing within a year, explaining that John had "died out west." Then, in 1910, neighbor Carl Miller "disappeared mysteriously" after being "attentive" to her. She told police she had baked some pancakes for Miller, who put them in his pocket and left. Owners of a real estate firm told authorities that shortly after Miller's disappearance, Lucas came in with deeds to property Miller owned and asked for help in transferring the property over to her.

While investigating the Fingel death, police found that earth in the Lucas basement had been recently disturbed. They also found three shovels and a pick. Digging into the freshly turned dirt, officers encountered quick lime, used to quell odors in outdoor toilets.

Prosecutor Hayden and Police Chief Henry Behreadt interviewed the suspect five times over the weekend. Finally, Lucas admitted she had invited Mrs. Fingel to her home, offered her some hot chocolate, and laced it with one-third of an ounce of aconite, a sedative-type drug. Earlier, a coroner's jury had ruled Fingel died of "causes unknown." In her detailed confession, Lucas said she bought the poison at a north-side pharmacy, invited her victim to her home, and poured the fatal dose into her hot chocolate. The *State Journal* reported she told Hayden and Chief Behrendt, "When she was taken ill, I did what I could to relieve her pain."

Mrs. Fingel, in her death throes, had told attendants, "The woman next door put poison in my coffee [chocolate]." Hayden said Lucas also stole forty dollars in bills from Fingel's bosom. Police found it hidden behind a trunk in Lucas's home. By Thursday, authorities were still looking for more bodies in and around the Lucas house. With few developments to report, the *State Journal* fortunately came upon an attorney—kept anonymous but billed as "one of Lansing's most prominent lawyers"—who told a story about Mary Lucas's past. The following is an edited version of the tale, told in the first person, more than eighty years ago in a newspaper of December 12, 1912:

I went to Ann Arbor in 1872 to study law and [boarded] with Mrs. Buckland . . . found the Bucklands honest, law abiding . . . Baptists. [He] had been probate judge . . . and a wealthy farmer . . . near Howell. I met Mary Buckland, the daughter, who had been Mrs. Lucas. The son-in-law's name was forbidden in the household. He was an attorney . . . divorced . . . had gone west.

In 1875 [after getting a law degree] I went west . . . [and later learned] that Mary had married a man named Ayres. I had some county seat cases to argue . . . on the Nebraska-Kansas line [and later] went to Republican City, Nebraska to act as counsel on more cases . . . I found the hotel full [but] was able to secure a bed in a room with another attorney . . . we began to talk without introductions and found that both of us had been in Ann Arbor. When . . . I furnished the address, the other occupant of the room rose up in bed and exclaimed, "Why, that's where my wife lives—she's coming out here soon."

"What is your name," I asked, "John Lucas?" He replied "yes."

"Don't you know that your wife has secured a divorce and married again and . . . she has a child?"

With this, Lucas jumped clear of the bed and paced furiously up and down the room.

"Look at these," he exclaimed, as he threw a bundle of letters on the bed . . . I found Mary had been writing to Lucas all the time that she was married to Ayres and called him "my dear husband." She repeatedly acknowledged receipt of money and in her last letter told him she would be out soon.

The anonymous teller of the tale said John Lucas then left the room and walked the streets all night. He said they never opened the subject nor discussed Mary again. He continued:

I never knew a man more daring than John Lucas. He practiced law and gambled a great deal . . . he always carried . . . a little pepper-box revolver . . . and on one occasion held three horse thieves at bay until help arrived.

Later I again came east . . . and returned to Howell . . . late in the 1880s and in 1890 I came to Lansing. While walking along Washington Avenue near the Prudden Building I was startled to see a sign bearing the legend "Lucas and Lucas, Attorneys." I went upstairs and was met by John Lucas, who greeted me warmly . . . imagine my surprise when he called his wife, Mary Lucas, who I had known as Mary Buckland and as Mary Ayres. How they got together again or what became of Ayres I never learned beyond a statement that he had died.

I continued to practice law in Lansing and Lucas, still a dandy, continued to practice . . . Mrs. Lucas also did some law business, principally in divorce matters. Her career was ended a few years later, however, when service in several cases was not made and other chaos existed. She was called to the private office of the circuit judge who reprimanded her by saying, "Mrs. Lucas, you know and I know that you are not an attorney and you will have to cease practicing here."

Mary, who had been a fine looking girl and exceptionally neat, became shabbier and the Lucas fortunes waned. Finally [John] Lucas went to [another] attorney and asked that [he] endorse a note for $50. He dis-

appeared and the attorney paid the note. Mary told me that she heard
he had been killed in the west. . . . after this, I saw Mary on the street
occasionally but knew little of her until . . . the papers printed what
seemed to be one of the final chapters of a most checkered and roman-
tic career.

Who was the anonymous lawyer who blew the whistle on Mary Lucas and
caused her to be brought before "the circuit judge" and summarily disbarred? It
was none other than Rollin H. Person, whose biography contains every fact and
date as did the story teller's, including the move from Howell in 1891 after a stint
on the Nebraska frontier. And who was "the circuit judge?" That, also, was
Rollin H. Person, appointed as judge of the new Thirtieth District by Governor
Winans, of Howell, in 1891. Person returned to private practice in 1900.

On December 17, 1912, Mary Lucas's preliminary examination began in
municipal court but was immediately adjourned until December 20. Jason
Nichols appeared for the defense and Assistant Prosecutor William C. Brown
for the People, since Prosecutor Hayden was ill. Brown amended the charge
against Lucas to first degree murder as she "remained calm and wrote notes to
her attorney." Nearly three hundred curious filled the courtroom at 9:00 A.M.
and had to wait until nearly 11:00 A.M. for a glimpse of the defendant, who
arrived by train from the jail at Mason.

Dr. M. L. Holm, state bacteriologist, testified December 20 when the hearing was resumed that his analysis of the victim's stomach revealed aconite in
sufficient quantities to cause death. Nichols, joined by C. P. Black, led Holm
through a lengthy cross-examination on the poison-detecting procedure as a
large crowd in the courtroom and corridors strained for a look at Mary Lucas.

The hearing was set to continue the next day, Saturday, but Nichols
informed the court that his client wished to waive examination. It was Monday,
however, before she was bound over to circuit court for the January term.

The trial opened March 31, 1913, in the city hall circuit courtroom with
Judge Collingwood presiding. The police chief, Henry Behrendt, described how
Mrs. Lucas "confessed" to the poisoning of Pauline Fingel. He emphatically
denied a suggestion from Nichols that the five interrogations of Lucas employed
"sweat-box" tactics. A northside druggist testified he sold the aconite to Lucas,
who said she needed it "for a sick horse." The police chief said Lucas once
called him to her jail cell and admitted she gave Mrs. Fingel a small amount of
the poison in some hot water because she was sick. Later, he said, in the presence of Prosecutor Hayden and a jail matron, Lucas said she gave the victim
half an ounce of aconite. Dr. Holm testified how he determined the victim's
stomach contents bore traces of poison—by the "taste test" and by injecting
some of the fluids into a frog that died in twenty minutes.

The prosecution rested its case shortly after the noon recess on the trial's second day with testimony from Dr. C. V. Russell, who performed the autopsy on the Fingel body. Nichols then opened for the defense, telling the jury that he intended to prove that Mary Lucas was insane at the time she administered poison to Pauline Fingel.

Dr. C. L. Barber testified he examined Mary Lucas on January 24 and again on the second day of the trial and considered her insane the day of the poisoning, December 6, and at the present time (April 2). A St. Johns lawyer, Henry Patterson, testified he had known Lucas for six years through business dealings and characterized many of her actions as "queer." He said he conferred with her soon after her arrest and that Lucas at first denied, then admitted, giving poison to Mrs. Fingel "under the influence of Berenzc." Patterson testified he considered Lucas insane. Several neighbors testified as to Lucas's actions, one saying she was slovenly in her dress. Several said she was always slack in her personal appearance. But on Thursday, April 3, Dr. Oscar Long, superintendent of the state asylum for criminal insane, testified there was no evidence proving Lucas insane.

Final arguments were completed on Saturday and dealt mostly with the question of Lucas' sanity. Collingwood adjourned the trial until Tuesday, April 8, since Monday was election day. The jury was out eleven hours before returning a verdict of guilty of first degree murder. When Collingwood asked her if she had anything to say, Lucas said: "Your honor, I did not willfully give that woman poison. I was under the influence of that Pole, Berenzc. I was under his influence all summer and I have been under a cloud for a number of months as a result."

Collingwood gave Mary Lucas the mandatory life sentence in the Detroit House of Correction, where she was taken the next day.

Fewer than three months later another trial dominated the local news. Double-banner, black headlines greeted *State Journal* readers the evening of June 21, 1931, concerning a scandal involving "fraud, deceit and malpractice" of James H. Thompson, a member of the Ingham County bar. Judge Wiest had acted immediately on a petition signed by six members of the ICBA and containing documented evidence against Thompson. Alva Cummins, a former Ingham prosecutor, headed what the newspaper called "a self-appointed committee of the Ingham County Bar Association." The committee had first presented its petition and evidence to the Michigan Supreme Court on Monday morning and it was not clear whether the documents were taken to Wiest by the high court or the bar committee. In any event, the newspaper report said, Wiest acted "with the same characteristic fearlessness that has marked his entire career on the bench."

The judge issued and signed an order titled, simply, "In re James H. Thompson" at 4:15 P.M. that Wednesday. The order commanded Thompson to appear before Wiest on July 3 and show cause why he should not be removed from his "said office of attorney and counsellor at law and his name stricken from the roll of attorneys and counsellors of law of this court . . ." The *State Journal* reported that Thompson had been collecting fees for representing out-of-state estates in inheritance tax cases. The Michigan inheritance law was first passed in 1899 and amended by subsequent legislatures. It provided for taxing Michigan estates left by non-residents. A former member of the Michigan State Board of Education, Thompson was appointed to the State Tax Commission in 1906 and served until 1911, when, at the request of incoming Governor Chase S. Osborn, he resigned. Thompson had stayed in Lansing in a private practice, specializing in tax law. He became attorney for R. E. Olds and joined the automobile giant's church—First Baptist.

Under the inheritance laws, Michigan would collect a five percent tax of the value of bonds or stocks of Michigan firms left in wills to non-residents. A question arose as to how the tax would be levied against securities such as railroad stocks of lines located in several states. For years, the state collected on the full market value of such stocks, but an attorney general's opinion in 1911 changed the rules so that the state collected such taxes on a pro rata basis. The attorney general and the state accountant worked out a pro rata schedule that they asked the probate court to follow.

Before 1911, the probate court routinely asked administrators of non-resident estates to name their lawyers to act in adjusting inheritance taxes. In 1911, Thomas A. Lawler, an assistant attorney general who handled the state's inheritance tax matters, pushed an amendment through the legislature providing for the probate court to name such representatives locally. The Ingham probate court was designated in nearly every case since all the machinery for administering the law was in Ingham County. Over one thousand such cases were handled in that court between 1911 and 1916.

Since representing a non-resident estate required considerable knowledge of the tax law, Probate Judge Henry M. Gardner began appointing Thompson in each case. In March 1916, when seventy-five inheritance tax cases appeared, Thompson was assigned to each one involving a non-resident estate. Copies of several letters written to attorneys of non-resident clients by Thompson and advising that he was handling the inheritance tax for the non-resident were included in the information filed with Wiest by the ICBA committee. In each case, Thompson explained that "the State of Michigan has universally collected inheritance tax upon the full market value of shares of railroad stock regardless of whether or not the entire mileage of the railroad was located in Michigan." Then he would explain that he took the position that Michigan was due only a pro rata share of the inheritance tax. In one such letter, Thompson said he anticipated "the court would value the Michigan property at $25,570 and determine a tax of $255 instead of valuing it at $65,287 and determining a tax of $3,653. . . ." In a follow-up letter, Thompson explained that he became familiar with the state inheritance tax law as a member of the Michigan Tax

Commission and had since "briefed up" the attorney general on the merits of
the pro rata procedure. Finally, the estate's attorney received a letter that
Thompson had prevailed and that the entire bill for tax, court fees, and
Thompson's fee was $1,700. No lawyer who had just saved a client's estate close
to $3,000 would likely complain. In the cited case, the probate judge had origi-
nally set the tax at $255 and there never was a contest of any kind before the
court.

What Thompson hadn't mentioned in the letters was that Michigan was
automatically assessing such taxes on a pro rata basis and that he actually did
nothing but forward the bill to the out-of-state estate and collect the fees.

It was July 24 when the disbarment proceedings began before Judge Wiest.
The Ingham County Bar Association acted as prosecutor, Alva H. Cummins
carrying the bulk of the load, assisted by Walter S. Foster. Thompson was represented by Edmund C. Shields of Lansing and James O. Murfin of Detroit.
Cummins listed Probate Judge Henry M. Gardner and State Accountant Fred
Hamilton as the main prosecution witnesses while the defense said it would call
only Thompson. As the hearing began early on a Monday afternoon, the temperature on the shady side of Ottawa Street was ninety-five degrees. It would get
much hotter than that in the third-floor courtroom of the city hall before the
week was ended. Bickering between the lawyers reached the point that Wiest
cautioned them that "It is too hot to caution any more." Either address objections to the bench or move on, the judge urged. The defense lawyers contended
that none of Thompson's letters were in any way misleading and that "any fee
he desired to charge was a matter between him and his client."

On Wednesday, as the temperature flirted with the century mark, Lansing's
interest in the Thompson hearing suddenly shot up. Judge Gardner was scheduled to resume his testimony on Wednesday morning, but because state accountant Fred Hamilton's sister had died overnight in Eaton Rapids, Hamilton was
allowed to give his testimony first. Thus, Gardner's absence from the courtroom
was not a matter of concern. When the judge failed to appear, Wiest called an
early noon recess extending it for another hour when Gardner hadn't shown up.

Tuesday's session had been adjourned just after Shields asked Gardner
about a letter he had signed. Holding what supposedly was a copy of the letter
addressed to the tax commissioner of Massachusetts, Shields read a laudatory
evaluation of Thompson and his efforts to obtain the pro rata tax assessment.
But Gardner could not recall the letter and Cummins objected to testimony
about it since the judge could not recall it. Wiest asked Gardner to bring a copy
of the letter from his files in Mason—if he could find it—to court on
Wednesday. Gardner later told reporters he did recall the letter, and said there
were possibly other similar ones.

As the confusion was being discussed Wednesday in the sweaty courtroom,
someone arrived with the report that Judge Gardner had jumped from the

Michigan Avenue bridge into the Grand River. Police looking for the body had so far found only the judge's "skimmer" straw hat. It was identified by a Detroit News reporter, H. N. Duff, who had noticed the judge's initials on Tuesday when he inadvertently mistook the hat for his own. Judge Wiest adjourned court.

The whole story—actually three stories, including Gardner's obituary—made the evening *State Journal's* extra under the largest type banner that paper had ever printed. It read, "PROBATE JUDGE GARDNER SUICIDE." The obituary told readers the judge, sixty-four years old, was born in Meridian Township and grew up with his brother working a small truck farm and selling the produce in Lansing. He saved enough to finance his law education at the University of Michigan. After graduating, he and the brother, L. B. Gardner, a former Ingham County prosecutor, opened a Lansing law office. Active in Republican politics, he was first elected probate judge twelve years before his death. Gardner had then moved to Mason. He had recently announced plans to retire from the bench and re-enter private practice.

The Thompson trial resumed Thursday morning. The courtroom, lawyers' room and hallways were abuzz with speculation about a private note Gardner had written to his wife before his fatal plunge. Wiest and the opposing attorneys were prevented from comments, Wiest saying only that the case would continue without interruption. Cummins offered only the brief observation that "absolutely nothing in [Gardner's] testimony placed any implied criticism" on the judge "further than that he might have been careless in signing a letter someone else wrote."

Defense attorney Murfin announced as court opened that the defense would not insist on having Gardner's testimony stricken—even though there had been no opportunity to cross-examine him. All Murfin wanted was for "attorneys for the court" to agree the disputed letter was "signed and sent" by the judge. Cummins refused to concede Gardner "sent" the letter. (Gardner had admitted off the stand that Thompson had prepared the letter.) Wiest read into the record that Gardner was dead and the defense had not been able to cross-examine him.

Police found a note in an inside pocket of Gardner's vest telling them there was another note in the desk in his Lansing office. The judge's law partner, O. J. Hood, found the note and asked Clinton to deliver it to Gardner's widow. The newspaper said the note referred to the Thompson case as the reason for him taking his own life, explaining, "I am unable to withstand the strain of public criticism in this matter." Curiously, the judge added that no blame could be attached to him for his "many appointments" of Thompson as administrator of non-residential estates.

The letter referred to in Wednesday's testimony was dated March 6, 1913, addressed to William D. T. Trofry, the Massachusetts tax commissioner, and signed by Gardner. It explained that since 1911, Michigan, chiefly through an agreement Thompson had worked out with the attorney general's office and since followed by Gardner's court, was no longer taxing foreign inheritances at full value. It set Thompson up as the champion of out-of-state inheritors' rights. Reading the letter four years later, Gardner presumably felt he had been instrumental in establishing Thompson's lucrative tax practice, a business that later testimony would show netted Thompson over $27,000 in three years. President Frank L. Dodge of the bar association called a formal meeting in the courtroom at 1:30 P.M. to pass resolutions of respect for Judge Gardner. A resolution offered by Walter S. Foster instructed the ICBA to attend the Saturday funeral service in Mason as a body.

On Friday, the thermometer hit ninety-seven degrees in mid-afternoon. Thompson was on the stand most of the day in his own defense. Before the session began, Judge Wiest informed the attorneys that he had read all the notes left by Judge Gardner and felt none of them should be made part of the evidence. The judge's brother, Lawrence B. Gardner, appeared for the morning session and was "visibly pleased" when Wiest read into the record a statement that the notes intimated nothing "reflecting on the official honesty" of his brother the judge.

So certain were Cummins and Foster of their case, they offered to submit it to Wiest without argument, but Thompson's lawyers would not consent. In his final argument, Ed Shields likened his client to "A boy with a new pair of boots . . . Thompson thought he had a big thing, talked about it and boasted about it." Shields, in one of the first big cases he handled before Wiest, was trying to counter the declaration of Walter S. Foster, who asserted: "Thompson, not content with deceiving clients in Boston, [is] now attempting to deceive this court . . . he got $1,700 in one case and should have had but $7 for his work. There came a time when he knew. He still has that $1,700." In his final plea, Foster said Thompson "has besmirched the profession to which he unrightfully belongs. He has betrayed a lovable and upright judge. The purity of the courts and protection of the public demand his disbarment."

Shields and Murfin, his co-counsel, both mildly criticized Thompson's methods of handling the inheritance tax cases, but were more critical of his lack of grasp of the legal matters and argued strongly that he intended no fraud. Murfin said, "We don't disbar men for being fools. Our profession is full of them."

Even before the verdict was rendered, Ingham County had a new sitting probate judge. Jason Nichols, who had served that court before, was appointed by Governor Ferris on August 4 to complete Judge Gardner's term.

On August 8, Wiest handed down his opinion—a victory, albeit a bitter one—for the Ingham County Bar Association. Wiest suspended Thompson from practicing law in Michigan for five years. Wiest said if the charges had been as broad as the evidence, he would have considered permanent disbarment. He said Thompson's handling of the tax matters was "a shame and disgrace to the fair fame of the State of Michigan and to the ethics of the legal profession." The record in the case, Wiest said, "is barren of the least intimation that the late Henry M. Gardner, judge of probate during the whole period under investigation, had any knowledge of the misdoings of respondent."

By the time his suspension was over in 1921, Thompson was managing a developing subdivision on the west side of East Lansing. He was still listed in the 1923 Lansing City Directory, but his address was the R. E. Olds winter home in Florida.

20

A PERIOD OF TRANSITION

Already organized twice—the first time, very informally, in 1894 and again, to be certain it was official, in 1895—the Ingham County Bar Association decided in 1909 that it was time to "organize" one more time. So on November 1, 1909, members of the association met in the attorneys' room in the Lansing City Hall before the start of the day's court activities and officially adopted articles of association. In its front-page story on the meeting in that evening's edition, The *Lansing Journal* noted it was the first time the organization had adopted such articles, "although the association has been in existence for the past 20 years." (Actually, it was only 16 years.)

The news story continued: "The articles provide that all attorneys in active practice and maintaining an office may become members and it is desired that attorneys so engaged sign the articles and become charter members. The annual meeting will be held on the last Wednesday in December of each year and special meetings will be held upon the call of the president. The dues are $3 per annum and new members may be taken upon application signed by two members of the association and voted upon by a membership committee or by the association."

Another *Lansing Journal* item on December 7 reported the ICBA had held its "first annual meeting under the recently adopted articles of association" in its city hall quarters, at which time the articles were formally signed. Sam Kilbourne was elected president for the seventeenth and last time. Edward Cahill became vice-president and heir to the presidency, Harry Silsbee was elected secretary, and John McClellan treasurer.

The articles, a nine-page document, stated that the "object" of the association "is to maintain the honor and dignity of the profession of law, to increase the usefulness of the profession in promoting the due administration of justice, and to cultivate social intercourse among the members of the bar of Ingham County." The articles specified that ICBA meetings be held in the attorneys' room of the Lansing City Hall and that ten members constituted a quorum. The document stated the order of business, explained the conditions of active membership, and provided for retired members "resident in the county" and active members retiring in the future to be admitted to honorary membership by a vote of active members.

The bar association continued to serve as the official voice of lawyers in Lansing and Ingham County. When a position on any of the judicial benches became vacant because of a death or mid-term resignation, the association would be quick to recommend a name for appointment by the governor. And if a judicial or prosecutorial vacancy occurred on the federal level, the association usually found one of its members qualified for the job and did not hesitate to forward the name to the Michigan delegation in congress.

A typical ICBA involvement in 1917 made known the increasing court load experienced by the Lansing Municipal Court. Appointed by Alva Cummins, the association's president, Walter S. Foster became chairman of a special committee to investigate the situation. Other committee members were leading attorneys Joseph Dunnebacke, Edward Cahill, William Brown, and Judge Wiest. The committee was charged with investigating the condition of the single-judge court. It began its work on Monday, May 7. Twenty-two drunk and disorderly arraignments, usually combined with a guilty plea and sentence, faced Municipal Judge C. F. Haight that morning, reported the *State Journal*, along with a dozen jury trials and preliminary examinations and four civil jury trials plus a backlog of non-jury civil cases.

"Such a mass of business could not be handled by even two judges in a single day," declared Foster. Cases involving habitual violators frequently were dismissed a few months later because the judge couldn't otherwise dispose of them, he said.

Supreme Court Justice Russell Ostrander died on September 12, 1919, and the Ingham County Bar Association met hurriedly in the circuit court room in the Lansing City Hall to plan a determined campaign to have Circuit Judge Howard Wiest appointed as Ostrander's replacement on the high court. "Nearly every practicing attorney" attended the meeting the morning of September 17, 1919, reported the *State Journal.*

Even as the ICBA was adopting its resolution, word was received that the Shiawassee County bar had done likewise and was to present its document "at once." Bars in several other circuits adopted similar resolutions later that week. Circuit Judge C. B. Collingwood, Wiest's benchmate, presented the finished version of the ICBA resolution. After it was unanimously adopted, he led the assembled Ingham County lawyers across Capitol Avenue to the office of Governor Albert E. Sleeper, who would make the appointment to the high court. The ICBA was determined.

When the group learned Sleeper was at his home in Detroit and not expected immediately in Lansing, each member signed the hand-written document personally. The association then appointed a three-man committee of Collingwood, Charles W. Foster, and D.G. F. Warner to take the afternoon train to Detroit and deliver the document to Sleeper along with a firm request that he take the recommended action. The newspaper quoted Collingwood, an entrenched Republican, as calling Wiest "Michigan's foremost circuit judge" with experience, ability, and integrity "which come to but few men on the bench." Lansing lawyer Edmund Shields, one of the leading Democrats in Michigan, said, "We all want Judge Wiest appointed to this position . . . and if he cannot be appointed, we want to see him elected to that place."

Shields, apparently already knowing that Wiest would not get the Sleeper appointment, was laying the groundwork for a Wiest candidacy. Within two days, the bars in nine outstate counties had passed resolutions asking Sleeper to appoint Wiest. The governor, in no hurry, waited until September 25 to appoint Judge Nelson C. Sharpe of West Branch to the vacancy. In its front-page news report of the appointment that read more like an editorial, the *State Journal* said Sleeper "slapped the people" in by-passing Wiest for political reasons. Key Detroit Republicans, the paper said, feared Wiest would come down hard on American Telephone and Telegraph Company rate increases and did not want him on the high court, which was due soon to consider a telephone rate controversy. It would be two more years (January 1921) before Wiest would be appointed by Governor Alexander Groesbeck—and subsequently elected—to the supreme court. By then, Wiest—who had been called a "boy judge" by Governor Pingree in 1900—was a mature fifty-seven years of age.

Numerous Ingham County attorneys—especially some of the pioneer lawyers in the 1840s, 1850s, and 1860s—had found time to form, head, and participate in business ventures while maintaining sizable law practices. A few of them even managed to dabble in politics and hold down important state, county, and city positions. After the Civil War, however, two- and three-pronged careers seemed mostly to disappear, though many lawyers were still involved in politics.

But Harris E. Thomas was cut from the same bolt as were some of those earlier pioneer lawyers—men who were somehow able to maintain a law practice, participate in local politics enough to be elected to office, manage a business, and act as a community leader, all at the same time. He was born in Kent County on August 2, 1859, of parents who obtained a large tract of land the year before Michigan attained statehood. Young Thomas was educated in the grade and high schools near Grand Rapids and graduated from Michigan Agricultural College in 1885. He must have already shown some promise because his first job was with Cahill & Ostrander, before either man served on the supreme court. He acquired an excellent knowledge of the role of modern jurisprudence while "reading" for four years under Cahill and Ostrander and was encouraged by them to enroll in the University of Michigan's six-month law short course for exceptional students. He passed the bar examination in 1891, opened a general law practice in Lansing, and was twice elected Ingham County circuit court commissioner as a Democrat. Thomas later was elected to the Lansing school board for two terms and to the Lansing City Council for one.

By the time of the depression of 1893, three of Lansing's four banks had failed and most of the large manufacturing firms were closed or in serious trouble. R. E. Olds' fledgling automobile manufacturing business gave the capital city a brief period of hope, but as the century drew to a close, Olds took his business to Detroit. Early in 1901, some of the business and manufacturing leaders, in an attempt to revive the city's commercial life, formed the Business Men's Association, forerunner to the Lansing Regional Chamber of Commerce. Fifteen directors named Harris Thomas as vice-president and elevated him to the presidency the next year. Thomas was credited with successfully soliciting Olds to return his operation to Lansing after it was seriously damaged by fire in Detroit. By 1907, three automobile firms and several related industries were flourishing and Thomas received much of the credit for placing the community on the industrial map. By 1924, Thomas was vice president of two of the automobile firms and president of three smaller ones. He continued as senior partner and an active lawyer in the prestigious firm of Thomas, Shields & Silsbee. Earlier, Thomas had been a partner in the firm of Thomas, Cummins and (Charles) Nichols.

Whether Thomas and Charles Collingwood were acquainted at MAC was not recorded in either of their biographies. The two men had much in common. Of almost identical age, they both graduated in the class of 1885 after working their way through college. Collingwood, however, had a tougher early life. He was born near Plymouth, Massachusetts, on May 1, 1860, and still a toddler when his father was killed in the Battle of Fredericksburg in December 1861. Young Charles lived with his mother until he was fourteen and then became an office boy for a Boston publisher. Collingwood spent his eighteenth year punching cattle on a Colorado ranch and in 1879 enrolled as a freshman at MAC. After a year, he returned west to earn money, mostly with a Denver and Rio Grande Railroad survey crew. Then he came back to Michigan, finished his college work, and taught school briefly at Pewamo and Howard City. Not much of his experience so far had prepared him for a law career—except, perhaps, a self-taught legal course he pursued in the lonesome winter evenings. In 1888, Collingwood taught chemistry at the University of Arkansas. The next year, he joined the chemistry department at the new University of Arizona.

Still interested in the law, he returned to Michigan and in 1894 passed the bar examination. He was appointed Lansing city attorney in 1897 after joining Thomas in a law partnership that must have provoked some interesting in-office debates, since Thomas was an entrenched Democrat and Collingwood a staunch Republican. Collingwood was elected to the state senate in 1898 and in 1909 was appointed to the Ingham County Circuit Court bench.

In his twenty-five years on the bench, Collingwood twice presided over trials that caught the attention of the national press. The first came early in 1926, when Collingwood was named to preside over a rape trial moved from Calhoun County to Mason on a change of venue. The defendant, the young son of a wealthy Battle Creek couple, was charged with sexually assaulting a teenaged college coed on the grounds of the posh Battle Creek Country Club. Prejudicial pretrial publicity before the original hung jury mistrial was one of the reasons for the move. But some of the publicity naturally followed the proceedings to Ingham County. Collingwood summoned ninety-eight jury panelists to make sure there were enough. The trial, originally set for February 1, was postponed for two weeks by the accidental explosion of a gasoline tank at the home of the chief defense counsel, whose wife died in the blast.

Most of the principals in the case quartered themselves in Lansing hotels. The *State Journal* predicted that a "stream of motor cars" would line the Lansing-Mason road mornings and evenings as the press, court officials, lawyers, trial principals, and the curious went back and forth to the big show. Reporters were expected from Detroit, Chicago, Battle Creek, Grand Rapids, Lansing and from the national news services. Mason prepared by installing telegraph facilities and pay telephones in the courthouse. County-seat housewives put up posters near the courtroom doors offering spare bedrooms and meals—for a price—to the court crowd.

The defendant, Arthur C. Rich, had three lawyers for the start of jury selection on February 15. One of them was Frank L. Dodge of Lansing. The People had an assistant Michigan attorney general, the Calhoun County prosecutor and his chief assistant. During noon recess, the father of the defendant, George R. Rich, wealthy Battle Creek manufacturer, grabbed the camera of a Lansing newsman and tore off its lens before the photographer could snap a picture of him. Male jurors were asked if they had prejudices against the current style of women's dress, "including rolled stockings." None did. During the trial, the charge was referred to as "criminal assault." The words "sex" and "rape" were avoided by both sides.

It was on February 20, the trial's sixth day, that the complaining witness, Louise King, was called as the first prosecution witness. Two weeks later, the twenty-two-year-old Rich finally took the stand. It was another four days before the case went to the all-male jury on March 10. The verdict was guilty and Collingwood immediately sentenced Rich to a life term in the state prison at Jackson.

Collingwood served three terms on the circuit bench with little controversy of a personal nature. He handled all types of cases with dispatch, absorbing his share of higher court reversals but generally avoiding the judicial ruts and skirting the peaks while building a reputation as a better-than-average judge. But late in 1928, Collingwood fell victim to the fallout from a recently passed Michigan statute aimed at helping enforce the federal Prohibition law against the manufacture or sale of liquor. The case involved a Lansing mother of ten who supplemented her meager household finances by selling bootleg "moonshine" whiskey. Over a span of six years, the woman, Mrs. Etta Mae Miller, was convicted three times of liquor sale violations. She had served sixty days in the Ingham County jail for a 1923 conviction, six months in the Detroit House of Correction in 1925, and another six months in the jail at Mason in 1927. Then, on the afternoon of October 3, two liquor law enforcement officers of the Lansing Police Department said they watched Mrs. Miller sell two pints of liquor to two men in a car.

Miller's trial, two weeks before Christmas, attracted national attention because Michigan law carried a mandatory life imprisonment penalty for a fourth offense conviction of liquor sale violations. The officers, called by Prosecutor Barnard Pierce, testified they witnessed the sale in Matt Smith's driveway. Seymour Person, Mrs. Miller's lawyer, summoned two witnesses who swore that Mrs. Miller was inside her home when the sale was said to have been made. Person was allowed to mention the habitual criminal aspects of the case and asked the jury to consider "the facts" before sending the woman to prison for life. The guilty verdict was returned in less than two hours.

Person immediately announced he might ask for a jury trial to rehash the circumstances of the first three convictions and to establish Mrs. Miller's identity as the person previously convicted. That would also give him an opportunity to question the constitutionality of the habitual criminal statute. Collingwood, a week later, set the habitual criminal trial before a jury for December 31. It was heralded as the first such trial of its kind. The *State Journal* speculated that legislators arriving early for the 1929 session might attend the trial to watch "the state enforce its provisions."

Person told the jurors they were deciding questions of "life and liberty" in addition to how many times Mrs. Miller had been convicted. He also pointed out that two of the previous convictions were "treated as misdemeanors." Finally, he said "the entire United States is watching the case." It took the jury only fifteen minutes to count the convictions and return a guilty verdict. Minutes later, Collingwood pronounced the mandatory life sentence.

National publications, including the infant *Time*, labeled Collingwood the "pint for a life" judge. A year later, *Time* chose the story as one of the year's news highlights. The news magazine neglected to report that attorney Person had filed an appeal of the conviction and sentence with the Michigan Supreme Court on January 28, 1929.

It took a year for the court to hear oral arguments in the case—on January 16, 1930. Seymour Person spoke for the defendant and Attorney General Wilber M. Brucker, Ingham Prosecutor John W. Bird and his assistant, Dan McCullough, for the People. Bird had replaced Barnard Pierce as prosecutor and "inherited" the appeal.

Ironically, the chief justice at the time was Judge Collingwood's old circuit court partner, Howard Wiest. Wiest wrote the opinion that reversed Etta Mac Miller's fourth liquor law conviction and set aside the habitual criminal conviction and its mandatory life sentence. The unanimous decision was announced on March 7, along with the granting of a new trial and an order that Miller be returned to the custody of the Ingham County sheriff. The court's order was filed three days later but prison records in the Michigan Archives show that Etta Mae Miller was released March 11 from the Detroit House of Correction without bond.

Wiest, the tough anti-liquor judge for more than twenty years on the circuit bench, must have done some soul-searching to overturn the conviction that had brought national attention to Michigan at the peak of Prohibition. But he arrived at his decision on a strict, simple law interpretation. Wiest noted Miller's defense was alibi and that she testified she was at her Lathrop Street home for the entire afternoon of October 3, 1928, and thus could not have been at a home a block away selling bootleg whiskey to two men. Her alibi was backed up by her sister-in-law and a man waiting to see her son. Collingwood, Wiest noted, neglected to instruct the jury that if they believed the alibi—or even if it raised a doubt in their minds—their verdict must be not guilty. "An alibi," Wiest wrote, "may fail as a substantive defense and yet serve to raise a reasonable doubt as to guilt." Thus, Collingwood, after withstanding considerable scorn for having sentenced a mother of ten to life in prison "over two pints of whiskey," suffered the additional slap of having the entire matter reversed. No record could be found of a Miller retrial and no new convictions were ever added to her prison file.

Judge Collingwood served on the circuit bench for twenty-five years until he was defeated for re-election by Charles H. Hayden in the spring of 1935. He left office at the end of the year and immediately re-entered private practice at age seventy-five. He also was elected president of the Ingham County Bar Association for 1936 but soon became ill and moved to Boston to live with his sister. They later moved to Clearwater, Florida, where he died on February 24, 1937.

Armed service activities in World War I of Ingham County lawyers were not featured in any of the twentieth-century local histories. Mere mention of service records accompanied biographies of some lawyers published in the *Fuller-Turner Historic Michigan*, Volume III, which came out in 1924, but there was no concerted effort to record the war heroics of anyone who fought in France or against the German navy. Newspapers during the war frequently mentioned war service on the home front, particularly the deeds of Walter S. Foster, who served as chairman of the Liberty Bond drive in Ingham and Eaton Counties in 1917 that raised thousands of dollars for the war effort.

Some lawyers who had patriotic blood in their veins but were too old for military service, found ways to contribute to the war effort. Charles F. Haight, in the middle of his second term as Lansing's municipal judge, was one. Haight, a descendant of patriots who fought in the American Revolution, resigned from the bench and joined the YMCA forces for service in France. The organization provided entertainment, recreation, and spiritual assistance to soldiers sent back from the front and in need of treatment for what was then called "shell shock." Haight served overseas for eight months until the Armistice. Then he returned to Lansing and resumed his law practice.

Unable to convince the Lansing City Council of the need for an additional municipal judge, the Ingham County Bar Association in 1918 turned its interest toward supplementing the salaries of the circuit judges, who were still being paid only $2,500 a year when many attorneys were making twice that figure in private practice. The bar finally managed to get the court committee of the Ingham County Board of Supervisors to introduce a motion to supplement the salaries of the county's two circuit judges by one thousand dollars. But the issue lost, fifteen votes to eleven, on January 11, 1919. Jason Nichols, Samuel Rhoades, and a lawyer named Warner argued for the increase. The board of supervisors eventually hiked the circuit judge pay to $6,000 in 1924 after the legislature boosted the base rate to $5,000. The board had already (in 1919) increased the annual salary of the assistant prosecuting attorney from $900 to $1,200.

The decade of the 1920s signaled the end of the single-gender (male) domination of the courts and the legal system in Ingham County. It started at the end of 1919 after Michigan began allowing women to register to vote, a year ahead of those in most other states who had to wait until the Nineteenth Amendment to the United States Constitution was ratified. Michigan women who owned real estate had been allowed to vote on bond issues and expenditures of public funds under the state constitution of 1909. Later constitutional amendments included nearly complete women's suffrage.

In September of 1919, Mrs. Harriet W. Casterlin of Mason became the first woman in Ingham County to be placed on the circuit court jury list. The story of her selection—though detailed—was relegated to an inside page in the September 26 *State Journal*. The story assured male readers that Mrs. Casterlin was a true pioneer with nerves of steel and an ability to think quickly and come up with the right answer.

Juror Casterlin's credits included her being the first church organist in Mason. She also had spent a winter in northern Idaho, substituting for her schoolteacher son. Alone in his mountain home one night, she confronted a marauding coyote that had discovered the buried meat supply. She chased the beast in deep snow in her night clothes, eventually retrieving the food. Another time, she consoled the family of a young miner killed in an accident and then conducted the funeral services in the isolated village. That involved a four-mile sleigh ride in the mountains with the coffin and the community's only organ. Juror Casterlin sat on the first case—called on October 1—a forgery trial, and several others.

Recording the early women attorneys of Ingham County poses a problem. The first woman listed in a directory as a lawyer, of course, was Mary Lucas, whose deceitful career was exposed in the late 1890s by Judge Person years before she was convicted of murder by poison of a neighbor. Lucas was pardoned by Governor Sleeper on December 31, 1921, after serving eight years of her life sentence. Her age, seventy-seven, was listed as the chief factor in the pardon. She reportedly spent her remaining life in Wisconsin.

Another candidate for first woman lawyer in Ingham County would be Eva Akers-Mead. But there's a cloud over her legal career, too. She first came to public attention in May of 1900 when she and her husband, Charles Mead, were arrested and charged with child cruelty in Williamston. The case was never tried and Mrs. Mead was released, clearing her criminal record if not her reputation.

Before that, Eva Mead had been a well-liked school teacher in Mason. In his 1905 *Past and Present of Lansing and Ingham County, Michigan*, lawyer-historian Albert Cowles included Mead's name on a list of 104 attorneys who joined the Ingham bar between 1862 and 1905. Thus, Cowles recorded Mrs. Mead's connection with the profession while apparently declining to pass any judgment on her.

Another early woman lawyer in Ingham County was Alice E. Alexander, a noted tax law expert who served as commissioner of the state Corporation and Securities Commission under Governor Frank D. Fitzgerald in the late 1930s. Alexander had earlier served several years as secretary of the commission. When the corruption division of the Michigan Department of State was established in 1922, Alexander was commissioned to set up its work. She was admitted to the bar in 1928 and came into the legal limelight a few years later by winning the case in which Michigan acquired the right to tax the intangible assets of corporations where they were used. Previously, firms had dodged Michigan intangibles taxes by being incorporated outside the state. Alexander's brother, David H. Crowley, was attorney general under Fitzgerald. Alexander died at age seventy-nine in Detroit on October 30, 1955.

A pioneering woman attorney who ultimately had her name on her firm's door was Caroline Montgomery Thrun. Her career touched six decades. Thrun, a legal specialist like Alexander, was admitted to the bar in 1935 and was immediately appointed an assistant attorney general because of her experience in public school law. She held that position for 20 years, and then helped her husband, Frederick M. Thrun, open a Lansing law office.

Mrs. Thrun received her education wherever her husband served as a professor, at the University of Michigan, William & Mary, and Michigan State University; she also raised three children. When son Robert joined the firm, it became Michigan's only mom-and-pop-and-son law office. Thrun, Maatsch and Nordberg still represented a substantial number of Michigan's school boards in the 1990s.

Caroline, imposing despite her four-foot, nine-inch frame, chuckled when she recalled one of her early divorce cases. Before the case got to the court argument stage, she counseled the couple to resolve their differences and remain together. Result: no fee for attorney Thrun.

The elder Thruns recodified Michigan's school laws in 1955. Caroline did the job alone in 1976, at age seventy-nine. She officially retired in 1981, but was still happy, at age eighty-six, to answer school law questions almost until the day she died—on August 22, 1983.

It is impossible to wrap up the decade of the "twenties" without noting the passing of two pioneer members of the Ingham County Bar Association. Between them, Samuel L. Kilbourne and Frank L. Dodge probably did more than any other pair of Ingham lawyers to foster the practice of local law during ICBA's early years. Both first learned law in the office of a veteran lawyer. Both served in various capacities in Lansing's city government. Both later taught law. Both served in the Michigan legislature. Both were organizers and joiners. Both were devout church-goers. Both frequently exhibited their sense of fairness in legal matters and in their everyday lives. And both were Democrats and successful practitioners in a community known for its Republican leanings during the extensive period in which they were a big part of it.

The final days of Sam Kilbourne's life were sad ones. Late in May of 1925, about a month after his eighty-seventh birthday, he was taken from his home on South Capitol Avenue to the old State Mental Hospital at Kalamazoo. He died on June 14, 1925. In his obituary, the *State Journal* said Kilbourne's was "one of the most brilliant legal minds this city ever knew." It could have added that the ICBA's founder nurtured the organization as its president for its first seventeen years during the peak period of his own career.

Frank Dodge, seventy-six when he died on Christmas Eve of 1929, had practiced law in Lansing for fifty years. He was in the state senate from 1883 through 1885 and a United States commissioner for four years. His city service included the police and fire board, board of education, and city council, the latter for twelve years. He was once president of the council and of the charter commission of the 1920s. He had just been elected president of the State Board of Supervisors when he died at St. Lawrence Hospital after a three-month illness. The Victorian Turner-Dodge mansion in North Lansing, now owned by the city, bears his name.

While Dodge was concluding his long-time legal career, Leland W. Carr was beginning what would become more than a fifty-year association with Ingham County courts.

Carr was born in Livingston County, just east of Stockbridge on September 29, 1883, of parents who were both teachers and farmers. His schooling included the Pinckney public schools, the State Normal College at Ypsilanti, and the University of Michigan Law School.

A young lawyer and one-time assistant Ionia County prosecutor, Carr's career in state government began when he was thirty-three years old and just married; he was appointed in 1913 by Attorney General Grant Fellows to his staff. Six years later, Carr was in the Michigan State Highway Department as deputy commissioner and advisor, where Governor Alex J. Groesbeck spotted him as Wiest's replacement. When Judge Wiest left the Ingham bench for the supreme court in 1921, Carr filled the vacancy. The appointment had the hearty endorsements of such legal notables as Alva Cummins, Harris Thomas, and Walter S. Foster, reported the *State Journal*.

In the 1921 spring election, Carr received 10,485 votes to solidify his seat for the remaining two years of the term. Jason Nichols got two votes, and Seymour Foster one. In eight short years, Leland W. Carr had served notice he was a legal force in Ingham County and in Michigan. His name would become familiar throughout the state in the years to come.

Not only did Judge Carr successfully run for election to four terms on the Ingham Circuit Court bench, but in 1945 he was appointed by Governor Harry Kelly to the supreme court—once again replacing Judge Wiest, who had died in office. Thus, to a quarter of a century of service to Ingham County as a judge was added another eighteen years on the state's highest court. He served three times as chief justice until, at eighty years, age forced his retirement in 1963.

In the middle of his forty-three-year stint as a judge came an extra-curricular assignment for Carr as a one-man grand juror. He headed a criminal investigation team that probed into Michigan's most famous scandal involving bribery of government officials and related charges. All told, there were 115 indictments handed down by the Sigler-Carr grand jury and its successors. The citations included 54 members of the Michigan legislature, a number of whom were convicted.

When he was not writing or studying briefs, presiding in court, or reading up on the law himself, Carr was teaching. He was president, dean, and lone professor of the unofficial Leland W. Carr School of Law, an institution that met after hours in his Lansing City Hall courtroom. Twice a week, from 7:00 P.M. to 11:00 P.M., Carr offered instruction to law school students prepping for the state bar examination and others who "read law" under him because they could not afford formal law school training. Some of Ingham County's leading lawyers in the middle decades of the twentieth century were among the scores tutored by Carr. Over forty of them showed up for his 1963 retirement party, including three program speakers—Lansing attorney Richard B. Foster, ex-Ingham County

Prosecutor Charles R. MacLean, and Dr. LeMoyne Snyder, former medico-legal director for the Michigan State Police and a world-renowned criminologist.

As he predicted at his retirement fete, Carr did not retire from the law. For nearly six more years, the kindly legal giant walked almost daily to downtown Lansing, occasionally dropping in at the new supreme court quarters or meeting long-time lawyer friends for lunch. Judge Carr was eighty-five when he died on Memorial Day, 1969, at the home he built in 1922 at 416 North Sycamore Street.

21

BETWEEN THE WARS

At the end of the first decade of automobile manufacturing in Lansing, it was evident that Michigan's capital city was growing. But most folks still kept a horse for transportation in 1910, and many Lansingites continued to keep their own chickens, and milk their own cow. Lansing had many small town features, but it definitely was a city on the move. As factories continued to spring up in the north end, along Cedar Street and on both sides of the Red Cedar and Grand rivers, there was a surge of residential growth. By the time the census of 1920 was tabulated, Ingham County had 81,558 residents. Lansing could boast that it had 57,327 of them.

In the next ten years, the county's population zoomed to 116,587 and the city of Lansing's skyrocketed even higher, proportionally, to 78,397. The number of lawyers—seemingly lagging behind the 1920 figures—increased considerably between 1920 and 1930. The *Lansing City Directory* for 1920 listed sixty-one lawyers (there were perhaps another ten in Mason, Leslie, Williamston, Webberville, and Stockbridge). By 1930, eighty-seven legal practitioners were listed in the directory. Countywide, there were probably close to one hundred attorneys, most of them members of the Ingham County Bar Association.

With the Great Depression already clamping down on family and business spending, there was precious little legal work to go around. The county's court setup was virtually the same as it had been since 1903, when Lansing opened its municipal court—a single city judge, two circuit judges, and at least two justices of the peace in the smaller communities and townships.

Prohibition's passage in 1919 had put an end to police raids on legal business places that sold liquor, wine, and beer on Sundays or too late into the evening; saloons and taverns literally dried up. It took a while for clandestine watering places to open up for the sale of "bathtub gin," "home brew," "moonshine" and other illicit alcoholic fluids. When bootlegging got into full swing, police had a field day raiding the sales places—and the raids provided some lawyers with work defending the servers and drinkers. Some operators, of course, would pay their fines and be back in business within hours.

Careless operation of motor vehicles gave police—and lawyers—an ever-growing field of operations during the 1920s. Cars were made to go faster and faster, injuries became more serious, and automobile-caused deaths were more frequent. It all translated into additional court time.

Court criminal activity picked up slightly in the 1930s, partly due to the increase in population. A summary of 1934 activity in the Ingham County Prosecutor's office, published in the *Lansing State Journal's* New Year's edition, gives a capsule view of county crime the previous year. It showed complaints and warrants in 823 cases during the year, with sixteen defendants acquitted at trial and 354 convicted. Justices of the peace dismissed 172 cases upon examination, many of them "domestic difficulties," and ten additional cases were nolle prossed.

That quick justice was still the order of the times is shown in a review of the murder of a twelve-year-old girl, whose slayer was apprehended "with the active cooperation of the state police and the Ingham County Sheriff's Department." As a result of the efficient police work, the *Journal* reported, "the murderer was apprehended, made a voluntary confession of guilt, pleaded guilty and was sentenced [to life] on a charge of first degree murder, all within the space of a few hours." Prosecutor Dan D. McCullough praised both departments.

Fifteen coroner's inquests during 1934 were mostly to determine negligence in fatal automobile accident cases. Prosecution of drivers on negligent homicide charges resulted in several convictions. Eighty criminal cases were left over at the end of 1934, so the county's two circuit judges started the new year with twenty-five felony trials facing them.

Much of McCullough's time during December of 1934 was taken up with an investigation of what still is Lansing's worst catastrophe—the December 12 fire at the Hotel Kerns at Grand Avenue and Ottawa Street, now the site of a riverside park. Thirty-four persons, including several legislators, were fatally burned, suffocated, or plunged from windows to their deaths. Eighty witnesses, including Governor Comstock, testified at the coroner's inquest. No prosecution resulted.

Meanwhile, the twenty-first amendment to the U.S. Constitution had sounded the death knell early in 1933 of the "noble experiment," a term attributed to President Herbert Hoover. Prohibition enforcement had never been popular; in fact, in some locales, enforcement had met with indifference, if not hostility. Ingham County weathered the storm without experiencing the racketeering, extortion, kidnapping, and murder that occurred in some parts of the country.

Michigan decided it could control the return of "legal booze" by creating a state liquor control system, administered by a commission appointed by the governor. It was set up and fully operating for all of 1934, with Auditor General

John Stack insisting he be allowed to monitor the commission's books and inventory its stock. The first full year's gross from liquor sales and dealers' licenses was eight million dollars, sufficient to cause the Michigan State Grange to claim that licensees permitted to have dancing and entertainment were "worse than the old saloons."

While Michigan was exploring ways to control liquor sales, Ingham County lawyers were exploring ways to select judges. ICBA members participated in a secret questionnaire on the method of selecting Michigan judges. Since 1850, the judiciary had been elected by popular ballot after local party conventions chose candidates. The method had been ratified in subsequent constitutional conventions, the latest in 1909. But there had been talk in legal circles of switching to a system of appointing judges.

Results of balloting on the question were released by Walter S. Foster, chairman of a bar association committee named to lead a discussion on the matter. Foster reported responses from fifty-four of the association's approximately ninety members showed the majority (forty of the fifty-four) favored a change in the method of appointing trial judges, and thirty-seven favored appointment of supreme court justices. Eight poll participants were in favor of appointing judges and then allowing the electorate to ratify or nullify the appointments.

Another piece of legal news came on June 13, when Edmund C. Shields, a prominent Democrat credited with a large share of President Franklin D. Roosevelt's sweep of Michigan in 1932, resigned as director of the National Recovery Administration in Michigan. Shields at the time was probably Ingham County's best-known lawyer.

The National Recovery Act of 1933 set up codes of fair competition for various businesses and industries. Once the president approved a code, it was binding on the entire industry and code participants were assured exemption from anti-trust laws. The codes outlawed child labor, limited production, and placed controls on prices and sales practices. They also guaranteed collective bargaining, which spurred the labor movement. In less than two years, the NRA was declared unconstitutional by the U.S. Supreme Court. Shields, in announcing his resignation, did not discuss any problems he had with the act itself. But he was upset by an order from Washington that he should remain in his office at all times. In addition to his busy law firm, Shields spent considerable hours as a member of the Board of Regents of the University of Michigan and with county and state Democratic politics.

In retrospect, one wonders if perhaps Ed Shields—though always loyal to his party—possibly sensed that the NRA would be found unconstitutional and figured an early departure as its Michigan director would be personally to his advantage. By no means did he desert the Democratic Party. In fact, when President Roosevelt ran for reelection in 1936, Shields, as chairman of the party's state central committee, was one of the first persons to welcome

Roosevelt when he arrived in Lansing on October 15 on a whistle-stop campaign tour. As he addressed a crowd of twenty-five thousand from the rear of a train at the Grand Trunk station, President Roosevelt was flanked by Shields; Prentiss Brown, campaigning for the U. S. Senate; and Frank Murphy, then high commissioner to the Philippines and candidate for governor of Michigan.

The Roosevelt visit climaxed a twenty-four-hour, double-barreled political blitz for Lansing that was not equaled for fifty-six years. It was preceded by a similar campaign stop the afternoon of October 14 by Governor Alf Landon of Kansas, the Republican standard-bearer. In October of 1992, three presidential candidates—President George Bush, Governor Bill Clinton of Arkansas, and Ross Perot—were in Lansing to participate in a nationally televised campaign debate at Michigan State University's Wharton Center.

By early 1935, the depression was beginning to abate in Ingham County—sooner, probably, than it did in many parts of the country. Lansing's Big Two automotive producers, Oldsmobile and Reo, were turning out vehicles in record numbers and allied industries were running double shifts in some instances to keep up. Both the student body and the instructional staff at Michigan State College were at record levels and state government was on the increase. The attorney general's office, for instance, announced on January 7 the hiring of its twenty-fifth assistant attorney general—Miss Esther Louise Tuttle.

She was one of "the Tuttle girls," daughters of Federal Judge Arthur J. Tuttle of Leslie, Lansing, and then of Detroit. Esther and her sister, Ruth, had made legal history in 1930-31 when they graduated together from the University of Michigan law school, were admitted to the bar, and established Tuttle & Tuttle, the first all-female law partnership in Ingham County. Their office was on the fifteenth floor of Lansing's skyscraper, the Capitol Bank Tower (now Michigan National Tower), in quarters leased from Shields, Jennings, Ballard & Taber.

In a 1989 taped interview, Ruth Tuttle Freeman told how her Republican father, Michigan's leading federal judge in 1931, engineered office space for his daughters in a suite inhabited by the law firm headed by Michigan's most influential Democrat. The deal was based on friendship. It started with a visit by Judge Tuttle and his daughters to the Shields firm's office and a casual mention by the judge that his "girls" were seriously considering forming a partnership in the capital city.

"I never really knew how it came about," Freeman said, "but suddenly they offered us a corner on their floor. A little reception room and two offices. One reason for coming to Lansing was that we couldn't . . . afford a law library [so we planned to use] the State Law Library . . . at the capitol. But then Mr. Shields kindly offered us the use of his wonderful library and we used it all the time we were tenants of his."

Lansing readily accepted two sisters starting up a law practice. The *State Journal* welcomed them with a sizable news story, with pictures of the "attractive

Attorney Sam Kilbourne was one of the founders of the Ingham County Bar Association.

Ingham County's original courthouse was completed in 1844, (Michigan State Archives).

Ingham County's second courthouse was built in 1856, (Michigan State Archives).

Ingham County's third and current courthouse was in construction during the winter of 1904, (Michigan State Archives).

The "Big Four" of the 19th-century Michigan Supreme Court included (left to right) James Campbell, Benjamin Graves, Thomas Cooley and Isaac Christiancy, (painting by John Coppin.)

Attorney Frank Dodge was instrumental in establishing the first circuit court sessions in Lansing.

Orlando Mack Barnes was Ingham County prosecuting attorney in the 1850s before he became one of Lansing's leading businessmen, (Michigan State Archives).

Thomas M. Cooley received national praise for his judicial skills while serving on the Michigan Supreme Court, 1863-85.

Harris E. Thomas was the first secretary of the Ingham County Bar Association and a leading Lansing attorney.

Arthur Tuttle served Ingham County as a prosecuting attorney and circuit court judge, and later as a federal district judge.

Lansing's Edward Cahill served as a justice of the Michigan Supreme Court in 1890.

Ruth and Esther Tuttle pose with their father, Judge Arthur Tuttle. The Tuttle sisters followed in their father's footsteps as distinguished Ingham County attorneys.

Rollin Person served as both an Ingham County Circuit Court judge and a Michigan Supreme Court justice, (Michigan State Archives).

Edmund Shields played baseball at University of Michigan before becoming one of Ingham County's prominent attorneys.

Jason Nichols served in several legal capacities in Ingham County during the 19th and 20th centuries, including probate judge, and was a 70-year member of the ICBA.

Ho Chi Minh, General Vo Nguyen Giap, Allison Thomas and other members of his Office of Strategic Services (OSS) team, taken in July of 1945. Ho, Thomas and Giap are seated front row, third from right, fourth from right and sixth from right, respectively.

Law librarian Charlotte Dunnebacke and Supreme Court Justice John Dethmers research a case in the state law library, (Detroit News).

Shagbark was the country home of Judge Howard Wiest and is located on the outskirts of Williamston, (Photo by Dick Frazier).

Ingham County attorney Leland W. Carr served as Michigan Supreme Court justice, 1945-63.

Three prominent Ingham County Circuit Court judges in the middle part of the 20th century included (from left) Louis Coash, Charles Hayden, and Marvin Salmon.

Ingham County attorneys admitted to practice before the U.S. Supreme Court in 1962 pose with Attorney General Robert Kennedy.

Ingham County Circuit Court Judge Sam Street Hughes also served as mayor of Lansing, (courtesy of the Hughes family).

Lawrence Lindemer of Stockbridge served as a Michigan Supreme Court justice, 1975-77.

Charles MacLean served as Ingham County prosecuting attorney, 1947-50.

Stuart Dunnings Jr. was the first African American to open a law practice in Lansing.

Ingham County Probate Judge Robert Drake played a key role in the establishment of Highfields.

U.S. District Court judges from Ingham County include (left to right) David McKeague, Robert Holmes Bell and Benjamin F. Gibson, (photo by Greg Domagalski).

Both Leo Farhat and Donald Reiseg served as prosecuting attor-
ney and as president of the Michigan State Bar Association.

Naomi Slaughter waits for Ingham County Probate Judge George Economy to give her the signal to
sound the gavel, making her adoption final. (Photo by David Olds, Lansing State Journal).

Members of the Ingham County Bar Association History Committee include (front row, left to right) Rose A. Houk, Richard B. Foster, Allison K. Thomas, Peter S. Sheldon and Susan L. Mallory, and (top row, left to right) Judge Michael G. Harrison, D. Michael Dudley, George W. Loomis, Jack W. Warren, Allan J. Claypool, William L. Mackay and Eugene G. Wanger, (photo by David Olds, 1996).

Ingham County's Circuit Court Bench, shortly after Judge Stell became a member in 1982. Front row, left to right: Jack W. Warren, Michael G. Harrison, James T. Kallman. Back row, left to right: Robert Holmes Bell, Thomas L. Brown, James R. Giddings, Carolyn Stell.

young women," on May 28, 1931. But the paper's editorial writer could not resist a chauvinistic prediction of what their appearance in the county's courtrooms might amount to. The editorial observed that the women's pictures "do not show how much law they know . . . but do convincingly show that they are bound to be interesting citizens." It also wondered how the "gentlemen of the bar" would address the Tuttles "as they speak to each other" (which) "raises something of an interesting speculation." The writer also questioned what the affect on judges would be when "these young Portias" in the face of a judicial blandishment "pout a bit" (and) "in dulcet tones come back with 'Oh, most noble and upright judge'. . . ask yourself, what are the judges to do?"

Concluded the editorial: "The advent of a female doctor, listening to the heart murmurs of a male patient, is as nothing compared to what Lansing is about to experience."

Freeman related the details of an unusual upbringing for her and her late sister. The girls' mother, Jessie Stewart Tuttle, died in 1912 when Ruth was only eight years old. She died unexpectedly of pneumonia fewer than ten days after Tuttle's sudden appointment as federal judge. The daughter said her mother's health apparently worsened in the excitement of the family's abrupt lifestyle change and that her father did not realize she was so seriously ill. The girls grew up with an aunt and at a North Carolina boarding school.

How the Tuttle sisters came to choose law careers is interesting. While they were in the early years of college at the University of Michigan in the mid-1920s, Judge Tuttle was entertaining the Assistant U.S. Attorney General, Mabel Walker Willabrandt, at a dinner in his Detroit home. Mrs. Willabrandt, during the dinner, asked Ruth and Esther why they didn't take up the study of law. Two years later, as a senior, Ruth was day-dreaming in her sorority house when she "suddenly realized I was not going to be back in college the next year." Then she recalled the conversation with Mrs. Willabrandt and within a few weeks, both of the "Tuttle girls" were enrolled in law school.

The nature of their early practice was dictated by the times, Freeman said. Their first client was facing bankruptcy, as were numerous later ones. Freeman said they "took anything and everything" that came in. They did turn down a criminal case involving ten Detroit men, but handled numerous divorce, probate, and collections cases.

Ruth Freeman also recalled her first jury trial as she and her sister represented a young woman suing an automobile driver for personal damages (a fractured pelvis suffered in a collision). The sisters were accustomed to seeking occasional assistance on knotty problems from Byron Ballard, a respected lawyer of the time, and were nervous about the damage case because Ballard represented the driver. Freeman related how she started her final argument by telling the jurors that this was her first case before a jury. They returned a judgment of ten thousand dollars, which the judge immediately set aside as being excessive.

Later, she said, Ballard confronted her, half in jest, with this admonition: "Don't ever pull that on me again, that this is your first trial!"

"It was my first trial," she protests to this day. "I couldn't say that again, so he [Ballard] was safe." Any hard feelings from the trial were soon forgotten.

Freeman, in 1995, still lived in the house Ballard had built for himself on Cambridge Road in Lansing. She married Blair Freeman and Esther was wed to Thomas Bailey (later divorced) in a combined 1936 ceremony. Esther and Blair Freeman both died in 1987.

Esther Tuttle never actually left the firm during her two-year stint with the attorney general's office, joining her sister in the daily operation until they closed it in 1941.

Ruth Freeman remembered a story about veteran attorney Harris Thomas. She described Thomas as "a fine gentleman" who was just leaving practice as she and her sister were starting their careers. One day, she said, she was studying a particularly trying legal problem when she looked up from her table in the Shields firm library and noticed Harris Thomas. "Oh, Mr. Thomas," she recalled saying, "I wish I had all the law in my head that you have." His reply: "Well, I look at you and wish I had all that law in my head that you got from law school. Everything that I have in my head has been repealed."

Judge Tuttle doted over his "girls" long after they had reached adulthood and were married. He frequently wrote letters to them from his Detroit office, addressing each daughter individually if the message was a personal one, or as Tuttle & Tuttle if he was passing on some tidbit of jurisprudence. Sometimes the contents of a letter might even concern advice or queries about the Tuttle apple orchards near Leslie, of which Ruth and Esther were more-or-less resident managers, although Judge Tuttle continued as owner/operator until his death and always took an autumn vacation so he could direct the harvest.

On one particularly touching occasion, the judge sent them, in the form of a four-stanza poem he typed himself, an invitation to "a Valentine dinner on Lincoln's birthday," copying Longfellow's *Midnight Ride of Paul Revere* meter. It was addressed to "my Valentines" and was one of the last letters they received from him. He died, while still on the bench, on December 2, 1944.

Ruth and Esther had closed up their law partnership on June 1, 1941, almost exactly ten years after its formation. The closing was not without some lawyer humor, probably triggered by the announcement sent to all Ingham County lawyers and numerous others. The message, printed on a formal card, had the partners announcing the closing and said they would "thereafter make their principal occupation that of housewifery."

Headline writers had a ball. *The Detroit News* said, "Law Careers Bow to Housewifery" and the *Detroit Times* head was "To the Kitchen." Charles E. Ecker, a lawyer neighbor in what was then called the Olds Tower, penned a poem that concluded with "Good-bye 'Tuttle & Tuttle,' Welcome Housewives."

John R. Dethmers, then an assistant attorney general, later a Michigan Supreme Court justice, said their announcement was the first he'd ever received announcing "intentions to practice the oldest and most noble of all callings, that of housewifery." He credited the "persuasive powers of the respective husbands." Circuit Judge Charles H. Hayden, in a full-page letter, regretted the Tuttles' departure that deprived the bar "of your gentle presence and mellowing influence" although he was pleased they were entering a realm "which far transcends the selfish and material atmosphere of the professional world."

Lawyers Ben Watson and Richard Amerson, who had tangled in court with the sisters, used fewer words in acknowledging "with thanks" the notice, and added that the Tuttles "have at long last recognized that women's place is in the home." Ex-Governor Chase S. Osborn, from his retirement home at Possum Poke in Possum Lane, Poulan, Georgia, sent a charming note to "Mesdames Tuttle and Tuttle," lauding their decision to practice housewifery and commenting that, "If you could inject this idea into the veins and arteries of all the women in the world, it would do many of them great good." He signed the note "Uncle Chase."

The year 1935 was a busy one for political candidates. On January 3, Municipal Judge Sam Street Hughes announced he was a Republican candidate for Ingham County circuit judge. Two weeks later, Republican Charles Hayden also jumped into the race. It marked the first time in twenty-five years that Judge Collingwood had experienced competition—either in a primary or general election—and thirteen years for Judge Carr.

The Ingham County Bar Association could not wait for the spring election, so it conducted a poll of bar members. The results released on February 20 showed Carr far ahead of the field with one hundred votes, Collingwood safely on the final ballot with sixty-five, and newcomers Hayden and Hughes with fifty-one and sixteen votes, respectively. But when the "real" primary was held a month later, Carr was renominated with 6,827 votes, followed by Hayden with 5,011. Hughes was only 230 votes behind with 4,781 and Collingwood, with a quarter of a century of experience behind him and a long record of civic service, was soundly beaten, drawing only 2,953 votes. In the general election on April 1, Carr and Hayden easily defeated Democrat candidates Allan R. Black and Charles F. Hemans, the latter destined in a few years to make more news than his father, Lawton T. Hemans, ever did.

Republican jubilation over victories in the 1935 circuit court race was marred, however, by the loss of Harry A. Silsbee in 1936. Silsbee was a native of Albion, went to Eaton Rapids soon after he graduated from high school, and studied law there under John Corbin. In 1889, at age 19, he came to Lansing and continued his studies under Richard A. Montgomery and Frank L. Dodge, remaining with the firm for seven years and being admitted to the bar in 1895. Silsbee served for a time as clerk of the state house judiciary committee and later as secretary to house speaker Adams. He spent less than a year as an associate of an Ishpeming law firm, returning to Lansing to open a law office with J. P. Lee, and later opening his own law business. Subsequently, Silsbee headed the state's department of escheatable estates for three years.

About 1912, he joined a law firm that included Charles F. Hammond and former Judge Rollin Person and two years later became a partner in the prestigious firm of Person, Shields and Silsbee. Person left the firm for a place on the supreme court bench. When he returned, the firm of Person, (Harris) Thomas, Silsbee and Shields was organized. A later alignment beginning in 1930 included, in addition to that quartet, Byron Ballard and Clayton F. Jennings.

Silsbee was known as an active Republican. He was secretary of the Michigan State Bar from 1912 to 1922, and was president of the Ingham County Bar Association in 1927. He was in his fortieth year as an attorney when he died at age sixty-four.

The 1930s saw the issue of labor relations enter Ingham County courtrooms after the Oldsmobile assembly plant closed down on January 13, 1937, because of a strike. The Lansing plant was shut down because strikes in other Michigan cities—not Lansing—left Oldsmobile with a shortage of parts. Two days later, Governor Murphy called a parley in Lansing and negotiated with United Auto Workers officials and leaders at General Motors Corporation. The deadlock was broken and Michigan automobile workers went back to work.

The labor peace was short-lived. On March 11, Reo workers called a sit-down strike and vowed to remain at the plant, inactive, until management met its demands under terms of the Wagner Labor Act. It was April 7 before the Reo strike was settled following a twelve-hour meeting in the governor's office.

In the meantime, the UAW had attempted to organize workers at the Capitol City Wrecking Company. To get union organizers off company property, the firm's lawyer, S. DeWitt Rathbun, had obtained an injunction from Circuit Judge Leland Carr. Ingham Sheriff Allan MacDonald gave the union until 3:00 p.m. on Thursday, June 4, to comply. By Friday afternoon, Rathbun told MacDonald he was advising Carr that the terms of the order were being violated. MacDonald said he would consult with Carr and Governor Murphy to seek ways to avoid mayhem such as had accompanied a similar situation in Flint.

If Sheriff MacDonald received any advice from Murphy and Carr, he either did not heed it or it didn't work. What he did do was obtain warrants authorized by Prosecutor Thomas Bailey and then ordered a small squad of deputies to start serving them about 1:00 A.M. on the morning of Monday, June 7. Three of the arrests were on bench warrants signed by Judge Carr and charging violation of the injunction, while five were on warrants charging interference with a Capitol City Wrecking employee attempting to go to work. In the latter group were two women—Mrs. Lester Washburn and Vera Christian. Union officials said Mrs. Washburn, wife of the president of Local 182, UAW, was in bed when officers aroused her and took her off to jail, leaving her three young children—aged seven, eight, and ten years—home alone. Their father, who had been in Detroit at a union council, learned of the arrest when he returned a few hours before dawn.

By 8:00 A.M., factory workers and other union sympathizers had blocked all the streets in the center of the downtown area with their automobiles. Union members crowded the aisles inside the city hall and the open spaces around the building, demanding release of the jailed persons. Many left their cars in the street to join the throngs on the sidewalks. Union officials claimed twelve thousand workers in seven plants were participating in the massive snarl of Lansing business and industry. Most retail stores and service firms remained closed, as did bars by order of the state liquor commission.

Governor Murphy arrived on the scene about noon (he had been in Detroit for the weekend) and after a briefing, addressed a crowd on the Capitol lawn from his office balcony. Murphy said he was checking into the legality of the arrests, wanted to know "if a breach of civil liberty was committed," why the warrants were served "the way they were," and "why Mrs. Washburn was arrested the way she was." He promised, "I will take charge and clear up the situation at once."

As state, county and city officials parleyed in the governor's office, a sizable group of union men marched down Michigan Avenue and into East Lansing, bent on closing up East Lansing businesses to add to the stoppages caused by the labor holiday. They were met by a group of defiant MSC students who blocked their way; the students tossed some of the union men into the Red Cedar River.

Calm was restored to Lansing late in the afternoon when five of the arrestees were arraigned in the police chief's office by Mason Justice of the Peace William Seelye and released on their own recognizance. The other three were released earlier on two-hundred-dollar bonds. By Tuesday, the UAW International was saying the Lansing strike was called by Washburn without authority of the international and indicated he would be reprimanded. Bailey refused to drop the charges, but suggested he might consider such action if the complaining Capitol Wrecking Company people so desired. Washburn, attending the Mason justice court trial of five union pickets, including his wife, was arrested on Wednesday in a Mason restaurant on a similar charge of interfering with a working man in pursuit of his vocation and was arraigned on June 9. Seymour Person represented the union defendants.

A month after the labor holiday, Governor Murphy blamed "communists" for the strike. He hastened to stress that he did not believe the union or its leaders were communists, and explained he was referring to "communist cliques."

Meanwhile, the thirty-one-year-old Washburn survived his promised "reprimand" by high union officials by being promoted to the rank of a regional director of the union. He was also convicted by a Mason justice court jury of the misdemeanor charge and assessed costs of one hundred dollars or spend thirty days in jail. Person promptly appealed to circuit court.

Washburn's trial in the upper court began on October 18 in Lansing before Judge Carr. The jury got the case the next day and took only thirty-five minutes to affirm the lower court conviction. Person did not question prosecution witnesses and offered no defense testimony, resting his case once Judge Carr had denied his motion for a directed acquittal verdict.

Carr sentenced Washburn the next day to pay a $250 fine or spend ninety days in jail. Person appealed to the Michigan Supreme Court. One of his appeal arguments was that the Mason justice of the peace, William Seelye, improperly set the first trial for July 14, considerably later than the ten days after arraignment as provided in the statute. The high court ruled in 285 Mich. 119 (June 1938) that the brief delay did not cause Seelye to lose jurisdiction of the case.

Person also claimed the prosecution had not proved Washburn was even present at the picketing site on the day the complainant was interfered with. But the justices ruled his presence was not required, only proof that he was the union's leader and, in fact, had been present other days advising pickets and preventing even the company president from entering his office. The high court also said the statute did not violate state or federal constitutions as to class legislation or civil rights and affirmed the conviction.

Another Ingham legal old-timer, Charles F. Hammond, died in 1937 and the survivors in his firm laid a claim to being the county's oldest law firm. Other firms in recent years have also made similar claims, and it is not the intent of this book to arbitrate the longevity contest if one exists. But what was "the Hammond firm" in those pre-World War II days would seem to have earned the title by then and to have retained it into the mid-1990s.

Jackson-born Hammond (November 10, 1856) came with his parents to Mason soon after he entered public school and attended the University of Michigan Law School for one year in the late 1870s, continuing his studies with Huntington and Henderson in Mason. Admitted to the bar in 1878, he opened a law office in Lansing the next year. He was first associated with J. P. Lee and later shared a suite with Silsbee and former Supreme Court Justice Harry Hooker in the Hollister Building. He kept his office there for nearly three decades.

Hammond's busy political life won him a term as Ingham County prosecutor (1887-89) and later stints as Lansing city attorney, a member of the Lansing school board, and Ingham representative in the Michigan House in 1893-94. He was Ingham County Bar Association president in 1912.

When the American State Bank building was opened in the early 1930s, Hammond and his son, Eugene, moved in as the first tenants. Three years before the elder Hammond's death on November 10, 1937, Henry L. Schram joined the firm. He recalled that octogenarian Hammond rarely missed stopping in at the law office in the morning and offering "to be helpful." Eugene Hammond made Schram a partner after his father's death and the firm continued as Hammond and Schram until Hammond retired. Eugene Hammond died November 11, 1965.

Meanwhile, the firm continued—in the same quarters and under the same name—until Raymond R. Behan joined it as a full partner and the name became Schram & Behan. A later partner was Steven L. Owen, who since has left. Ray Behan's son, Michael, became a partner after Owen left and the firm—117 years old in 1996—continued as Schram, Behan and Behan, still in Suite No. 702 of the American Bank and Trust Company building.

Court activity in the era immediately preceding World War II, especially that having to do with criminal cases, is difficult for a person in the 1990s to contemplate. A summary of 1938 crime, published in a year-end edition of the *State Journal*, reported that crime was on the upswing in Ingham County. Retiring Prosecutor Thomas J. Bailey said his office handled a record 2,400 cases during the year, compared with 2,170 in 1937, also a record. The figure included more than 180 felony charges, only six of which ended with acquittals. The prosecutor's office also represented the county in several civil cases without a loss. Bailey's staff half a century ago consisted of a chief assistant (Leonard B. Crandall); a part-time assistant (Elijah G. Poxson); and a secretary (Norma Triquet). Fifty-five years later, Ingham County Prosecutor Donald Martin's staff included thirty-one lawyers and thirty-six secretarial, case worker, and support staff office employees.

The decade of the 1930s saw the breaking of a tradition that had existed in Michigan for 101 years. Ingham County lawyers and court watchers were especially interested in the event because it was "their" Federal Judge Arthur J. Tuttle who pronounced the controversial capital punishment sentence that resulted in the only legal hanging in the state's history. (Other executions, at least one involving a military law violation, occurred before Michigan—the first state to outlaw capital punishment—acquired statehood in 1837.)

The case involved Anthony Chebatoris, convicted in federal court in Bay City of murdering a Bay City truck driver during a holdup at the Chemical State Savings Bank at Midland. Tuttle sentenced Chebatoris to death under a federal law passed a few months before the robbery. The law was aimed at quelling a 1930s' rash of robbery-connected slayings in banks across the county insured by the Federal Deposit Insurance Corporation. The death sentence was pronounced November 30, 1937, and was carried out in Milan on July 8, 1938.

According to an Associated Press report in the May 28, 1938, *State Journal*, a wealthy Illinois farmer volunteered to bring his "equipment" to Milan Federal Prison and actively participate in the execution without charging a fee. He reportedly had used the equipment at seventy-one hangings over twenty years, but would not spring the device himself, leaving that duty to a U.S. marshal.

Six years after the Chebatoris execution, Tuttle again pronounced the death sentence in a case that attracted national attention. In 1942, Detroiter Max Stephan aided a Nazi flyer, Hans Peter Krug, who had escaped from a prisoner-of-war camp in Canada. Stephan became the first American to be convicted as a traitor to the United States since 1794. Tuttle again pronounced the death sentence, but President Franklin D. Roosevelt later commuted the sentence to life imprisonment.

In 1938, Lansing residents began noticing a "first" that in future decades would become commonplace—a "seeing eye" dog. "Teddy," a female German shepherd, became the constant companion of blind attorney C. LaVerne Roberts. After several weeks of training with the dog, Roberts was accompanied around the business district by his faithful canine law partner, regularly visiting municipal, circuit, and probate courts. The animal was the first of several that helped Roberts keep court appointments until he retired in the 1970s.

22

PAYOFFS AND MURDER

Booth Newspapers reporter Guy Jenkins once remembered when a group of reporters and former Governor Fred Green were viewing photos of Michigan legislators from the 1930s and early 1940s. One of the correspondents remarked about the "fine pictures." Green shot back solemnly, "Yes, sir. That's one of the finest legislatures money can buy."

The temptations of bribery, and the failure of some legislators to resist it, was apparently a serious problem in Michigan before the middle of the twentieth century. Because Lansing was the state's capital city, the majority of the bribes, the investigations, and the resulting criminal prosecutions took place in Ingham County. Lansing area attorneys played prominent roles for both the prosecution and the defense.

The "graft grand jury," as the one-man investigation by Ingham County Circuit Judge Leland W. Carr was called, started out quietly enough, as had half a dozen similar probes of state government in the previous eight decades. The possibility of a state grand jury investigation was first hinted in the halls of the legislature in early August of 1943, when most newspaper headlines were bannering Allied victories at sea in the Pacific Theater, U.S. Air Corps and Royal Air Force bombings of Berlin, and frequent tank battles in the North African desert.

The graft probe rumors, however, became more widespread on August 18 when State Treasurer D. Hale Brake, a 1941 state senate veteran, and William Stenson, a representative from Greenland, added their voices to demands for an investigation. Stenson told Attorney General Herbert J. Rushton that during debate in 1941 on a bill that would ban branch banking, he found one thousand dollars in his topcoat, along with a note urging him to vote "no" on the bill. Stenson said he gave the money to a man whose name he did not know but who, ostensibly, would return it to the person who placed it in his coat.

Brake told of hearing about "a block of votes" for sale for six thousand dollars in the 1943 legislature to help defeat similar anti-branch bank legislation.

The 1941 bill banning branch banks actually passed the legislature, but was vetoed by Governor Murray D. Van Wagoner. Both legislative houses then staged "sit-down strikes," refusing to adjourn unless the governor would promise not to help opponents of the bill when its backers attempted to muster a two-thirds vote to override the veto. The legislature finally adjourned months later after a futile override effort. Early in the 1943 session, the state senate defeated a similar bill.

Rushton eventually petitioned the Ingham County Circuit Court for a grand jury to investigate the legislature. Judge Leland W. Carr, then sixty years old and chief Ingham County circuit judge, was named the grand juror. He began work within hours after the state—on September 1, 1943—authorized $150,000 to fund the probe.

Carr wanted a special prosecutor without strong ties to a political party, so on December 14, 1943, he chose Kimber Cornellus Sigler of Hastings, a member of a Battle Creek law firm, as special prosecutor. Formerly a Democrat, Sigler had switched to the Republican party. The forty-nine-year-old Sigler had the reputation of being an astute courtroom tactician who considered the court a stage and knew how to put on a show for a jury. A former cowboy, football player, and boxer, Sigler loved to dazzle court audiences with his splashy suits. During the next few years, he often strode around Lansing in a Chesterfield topcoat with black velvet collar, pinstripe suit with matching cuff links and tie-pin on a gaudy cravat, colored pocket handkerchief, and a silver-grey vest that matched his flowing mane. Kid gloves, spats, and a walking stick completed the outfit.

Earlier in December, the first grand jury indictee to fall under the Carr hammer was sentenced to prison. State Representative Stanley Dombrowski, who had testified in one of the initial grand jury sessions, walked into Circuit Judge Charles Hayden's chambers one afternoon and repudiated his earlier testimony before Carr that lobbyist Charles Hemans, a lawyer and former member of the University of Michigan board of regents, had paid him three hundred fifty dollars to vote against the anti-branch banking bill in 1941. Hemans was the son of Lawton T. Hemans, the highly respected Ingham County attorney. Once he had denied that Hemans paid him the bribe, Dombrowski begged Hayden for speedy handling of the case—and got it. Within four hours of the time he walked into Hayden's office, the Detroit Democrat was on his way to the state prison at Jackson to serve a sentence of three and one-half to fifteen years on a perjury conviction.

The stiff sentence sent a message to all those connected with government that the Ingham County Circuit Court was not taking lightly its task of disposing of Michigan's governmental graft. And capitol watchers, noting the speed with which Judge Hayden handled the Dombrowski case, wondered if the judge had done the lawmaker a favor by affording him the "protection" of the world's largest prison. Time would show that incarcerated felons could be harmful to the health of cheating legislators no matter where they lived. The next day, Attorney General Rushton, who was present when Dombrowski made his admission, told reporters the lawmaker told him he confessed to the perjury charge "because he feared for his life."

By the end of 1943, the grand jury investigation was taking on a distinct Ingham County appearance. Sigler decided early on that Hemans would become a key figure in the probe. Informers told the special prosecutor that in 1941 and 1942, the witty forty-seven-year-old Hemans had numerous "clients" in and around the Capitol, so many, in fact, that he carefully kept track of all payments he made to legislators in what became infamous as his "little black book." Hemans had retained Seymour Person as his Lansing attorney.

Sigler wanted Hemans—and his book. With some cloak-and-dagger tactics and a measure of charm, the special prosecutor got both. How he did it was related in the *Three Bullets Sealed His Lips* book, an extensive study of the grand jury and its findings by authors Bruce A. Rubenstein and Lawrence E. Ziewacz.

Hemans had offered his legal talents to the U. S. Army. A former Hemans secretary told an investigator that most of his papers were stored at the Hemans family farm near Mason. The sleuth bypassed a caretaker armed with a pitchfork and in a hayloft found boxes of papers and the little black book. Sigler learned Major Hemans had been assigned to the provost general's department in Washington, D.C. Playing a hunch, the special prosecutor went to the nation's capital and, together with his commanding officer, convinced Hemans to return to Lansing. The two men developed an unusual relationship. Hemans started talking—and received between $150 and $600 per month, in cash, from grand jury funds. He lived in a suite in the Hotel Olds, dined, drank, and went out when and where he wished, costing the grand jury over $15,000 during the next two years. Lest "outsider" Sigler might find difficulty or encounter delays acting as a special prosecutor in Ingham County, Prosecutor Victor C. Anderson on December 29 appointed him as an assistant Ingham prosecuting attorney.

Sigler, Anderson, and Carr plunged into grand jury records, Sigler familiarizing himself with what had already been accomplished and preparing for courtroom arraignments of the defendants already indicted. He took time out, however, on Saturday, January 22, to join Carr in announcing a new blanket indictment.

The *Lansing State Journal* informed its readers that twenty-six more graft defendants, including thirteen current members of the legislature and another seven former members, had been named by the grand jury. Sigler told reporters that more than $20,000 in bribe money had changed hands to influence passage of a 1939 automobile financing bill. Six of the defendants were officials of finance firms.

What became known as the "finance company conspiracy case" consumed most of the summer of 1944. In the usually sweltering third-floor courtroom of the Mason courthouse (air conditioning in public buildings was still two decades away), Sigler and Anderson and a dozen defense lawyers toiled away before presenting their findings to Judge John Simpson of Jackson.

The trial began early in June and was in session almost continuously through June, July, and half of August, with only weekend breaks. Hemans was a frequent witness, leafing through his "little black book" and, one by one, naming donors and recipients of bribes.

Testifying under a grant of immunity, Hemans frequently told how he made bribe payments in the bathroom of his hotel suite after inviting the lawmakers to his quarters. He said the bathroom drew legislators "like a magnet." His testimony earned Hemans the name "Baron of the Bathroom" from defense attorneys, who told jurors he lied on the witness stand.

Sigler was the main attraction in the trial and appeared to be making quite a reputation for himself. But two veteran Lansing lawyers, Benjamin Watson and Roy T. Conley, representing the finance company executives, also got in their licks and in final arguments insisted Sigler had used some questionable tactics. Simpson's instruction to the jury consisted of reading one hundred fifteen typewritten pages. When the nine-week trial was over on August 13, all but two of the twenty-two defendants had been convicted. Simpson immediately sentenced the convicted twenty to three to five years in prison.

That evening, Sigler hosted a champagne victory party in his hotel suite. Details of the affair are related in the Rubenstein/Ziewacz book. Two Detroit reporters whose stories had pleased Sigler told the silver-maned crime buster that they "could make him governor." By the time the trial was completed, Sigler knew, positively, that Hemans and his "little black book" were the keys to sifting out the anti-chain bank bill.

On December 2, Carr named Frank McKay, a former state treasurer, in a warrant charging that he conspired with Floyd Fitzsimmons, a Benton Harbor sports promoter and lobbyist, to corrupt the 1943 legislature. The warrant also named William Green of Hillman, a state representative.

Without giving any details of the alleged conspiracy, the warrant simply accused the trio of "wickedly" conspiring to bribe legislators and influence their votes and decisions on a bill regulating the conduct of horse races and parimutuel betting. Carr, it was later revealed, conveyed early on to Sigler that McKay was to be the ultimate target of the grand jury investigation.

An industrialist, financier, and businessman, McKay had been the acknowledged "boss" of Republican politics in Michigan for more than a decade. His word could make or break an aspirant for public office. He was state treasurer from 1925 to 1930, but remained somewhat of a mystery man. Finally, "anti-boss" forces in the party rebelled and muffled his voice in state GOP convention affairs in the fall of 1940. Earlier in 1943, McKay had been acquitted by a federal court jury of mail fraud conspiracy.

Fitzsimmons, one of McKay's political lieutenants, had been a promoter of boxing bouts. He tried for years to make Michigan the capital of the prize fighting game and himself the king of match-makers. Later, he concentrated on lobbying the legislature for bills legalizing pari-mutual betting on horse and dog racing. The bills were invariably defeated after classic battles.

Green, when arrested, was already awaiting trial on a grand jury warrant that alleged he solicited a bribe from Floyd Trumble, a Lansing beauty shop operator, to influence a bill regulating the practice of cosmetology. The horse racing bill upon which the McKay-Fitzsimmons-Green charges centered would have increased state revenues from horse races and required use of special betting machines at the state fair race track in Detroit. The bill had died in the house state affairs committee in the 1943 session.

Before the trio could be examined on the racing bill charges, Carr and Sigler lowered the boom on another thirteen defendants accused of conspiracy and bribery to influence passage of a law favoring naturopaths and other "healing arts" practitioners during the 1939 legislative session. The indictees included Senator Carl F. DeLano of Kalamazoo and four other legislators, four Detroiters associated with healing arts associations, and four others. The bill in question passed the Senate but died in the house public health committee. Had it passed, practitioners would have been given professional status and allowed to use the initials "N.D." after their names.

Sigler said circumstances in the case closely paralleled those in the earlier finance conspiracy case, in which twenty-six acting and former legislators and finance company officials were indicted, twenty of them being convicted. Testimony by Hemans was instrumental in the convictions.

The naturopathy bill graft allegations were the fifth in which the grand jury had issued mass indictments. The week before were the charges against McKay and two co-defendants. Two months before that, the twenty defendants had been convicted of distorting regulatory bills to benefit certain finance companies. All were found guilty of making or taking bribes. Later, fourteen defendants were accused of conspiring to control the form of the state intangibles tax law so as to reduce the burden it would impose on certain large taxpayers.

Carr and Sigler were surprised on December 9 when Senator Chester M. Howell, one of the thirteen defendants in the healing arts conspiracy, asked for a preliminary examination and two hours later changed his mind, asserted that he wished "to help clean up graft in state government," and asked to enter a guilty plea. Howell, re-elected a month before, then huddled with Carr and Sigler and returned to the courtroom to enter his plea. Howell, who published a weekly newspaper at Chesaning, said he hoped "my position may contribute in some small way to keeping this a great state and a great country." Most of Howell's co-defendants, including Martin W. Hildebrand, a prominent Battle Creek chiropractor, demanded examination on the charges. Hildebrand was represented by Lansing lawyer Benjamin Watson.

The next batch of grand jury indictments came on December 16 and named eight lawmakers for bribery and conspiracy in tamperings with the healing arts bill before the 1941 legislature. Seven of the men had also been charged in the earlier indictment. The newcomer was William C. Birk, a former Upper Peninsula senator and ex-mayor of Baraga.

As the new year started to unfold, the grand jury's prospects for more convictions assumed a "good news, bad news" aspect. On one hand, Carr and Sigler could point to their indictments of Green, Fitzsimmons, and McKay on charges of tampering with the horse racing bill. Sigler had obtained a confession from state Representative Warren G. Hooper (now Senator Hooper after a November win in the Ninth District senate race) that McKay had invited him to his room at the Olds Hotel in 1943 and told him he wanted the horse racing bill to remain in committee. Hooper, a forty-year-old Republican from Albion, had worked with the state's leading osteopaths on legislation affecting them and was well known to lobbyists. During his talk with Sigler, he mentioned being offered bribe money by the three men interested in the racing bill and also claimed, according to the *Three Bullets Sealed His Lips* authors, that McKay had attempted to bribe lawmakers to stop passage of the anti-chain banking bill. The latter information must have thrilled Sigler. Now he had all the tools to convict the GOP state boss; he had Hemans's "little black book" of names and bribes offered, along with Hooper's account of how he and fellow lawmakers did the lobbyists' bidding.

On the "bad news" side was the fact that the grand jury coffers were nearly bare and some legislators were wondering if it was in the state's best interest to pump in more funds. Judge Carr had requested another $250,000 to continue the grand jury's work, but he had no assurance that the lawmakers would continue to finance the investigation of themselves.

On Thursday, January 11, 1945, three .38-caliber bullets fired at extremely close range into the head of Senator Hooper on a lonely stretch of Highway M-99 in Jackson County changed the entire course of the Ingham County grand jury investigation. The slugs transformed Special Prosecutor Kim Sigler's star witness into a mute corpse in a matter of seconds. They also served to silence Charles Hemans, touched off a massive police manhunt, and may have induced many prospective witnesses to irregularities in Michigan to think again about coming forward.

Half a century later, Hooper's murderers were still unpunished for the execution-style roadside slaying. Several of the early suspects in the murder plot were later apprehended, tried, and convicted of a conspiracy, but the actual triggerman was never identified in a court action. The best "educated guess," and one strongly suggested in *Three Bullets*, is that convicts were secretly allowed to slip out of the state prison at Jackson, followed Hooper—or picked up his trail from the capitol in Lansing—along his customary route to his home in Albion and waylaid him.

Since the murder occurred in the extreme northwest corner of Jackson County, the Jackson prosecutor and state police from the Jackson post, assisted by headquarters detectives from East Lansing, took charge of the investigation as soon as the victim was identified. Since Hemans was to have been Sigler's star witness, the special prosecutor visited the death scene and conferred with the police as they searched for evidence.

Within a week or so, the murder investigation had become more or less routine. No new suspects surfaced. Hooper was buried and the legislature started working on the bill to pump new funds into the grand jury. Lawmakers also put up a $25,000 reward for information leading to identification of Senator Hooper's killer. And Sigler, suddenly minus a star witness, had the racing bill examination postponed.

In late January and early February, Fitzsimmons was tried separately in Mason before Judge Simpson of Jackson on a charge of offering a legislator $300 for his vote on the 1941 horse racing bill. Sigler prosecuted the case and won a jury conviction. Fitzsimmons was sentenced to three years in prison.

No new leads had developed in the Hooper murder by March. Early in May, however, warrants charging conspiracy to murder Hooper were issued for Harry Fleisher, former head of the "Purple Gang"; his brother, Sam; Mike Selik, a Detroit gunman; and Peter Apostolopoulos, alias Pete Mahoney, a gangster groupie. Their examination, beginning May 11 in Battle Creek, drew a crowd that forced moving the hearing to a circuit courtroom. An array of legal talent at the prosecution table included Sigler and the prosecutors of Wayne, Jackson, Calhoun, and Ingham counties, the latter represented by Victor C. Anderson. One witness told how he and a partner had twice attempted to shoot Hooper in Albion but could not accomplish their mission, which had been contracted by people in Detroit, without endangering Mrs. Hooper or the Hoopers' two sons. Another witness told how he had been offered the task of "wiring" Hooper's car and blowing up the senator, but said he could not find the necessary dynamite.

The hearing went on for four days with Sigler, at his courtroom best, repeatedly battling Detroit defense attorney Theodore Rodgers. When it ended, the four defendants were bound over for trial in July before Calhoun County Circuit Judge Blaine Hatch.

On June 16, Judge Carr indicted GOP boss Frank McKay and seven others—politicians and men connected with the liquor business—on charges of conspiracy to interfere with and corrupt the state liquor control commission. The "others" named in warrants were: William H. McKeighan, former Flint mayor and McKay lieutenant; Fisher L. Layton, ex-state liquor control employee and then administrative assistant to Charles M. Ziegler, state highway commissioner; and Charles Williams, Donald Flory, Charles Leiter, and Isadore Schwartz, whom Sigler said had liquor business connections. At their arraignment, McKay termed the new case "just a rehash" of the federal indictment, which alleged a five-hundred-thousand-dollar shakedown of distillers to ensure the state would buy their liquor. Their examination, with Carr sitting as the magistrate, began on July 6.

The eight defendants were bound over for trial, set to begin January 14, 1946, in Lansing before Judge Simpson. While Sigler vacationed in Florida, two McKay backers—Edwin Goodwin, editor of the *Michigan State Digest*, and Ira Marmon, former head of the Michigan State Police detectives bureau—were arrested for jury tampering. They admitted distributing to prospective jurors copies of articles praising McKay and condemning Sigler. Despite Sigler protests, Simpson moved the trial from Ingham to Jackson County.

Sigler produced essentially the same evidence as he had at the earlier hearing. But as soon as he rested, the defense moved for a directed acquittal verdict on grounds Sigler had proved no crime was committed. Simpson reviewed the evidence for four days and on February 11 read a thirty-two-page opinion that said McKay had a legal right to collect from his salesmen and ordered a verdict of innocence.

After several delays, the murder conspiracy trial finally opened in Battle Creek on July 16, the venue determined by the fact that at least part of the alleged plot was put together at Albion, Hooper's home, in Calhoun County. Harry and Sam Fleisher and Myron (Mike) Selik, former Purple Gang members, and Pete Mahoney, "a swarthy Greek," were the defendants. Sigler was aided by his legal brain trust—H. H. Warner, a lawyer with photographic memory, and Prosecutors Anderson of Ingham and J. J. Dunn of Calhoun counties. Defense lawyers were Rodgers, Edward Kennedy of Detroit, and R. G. Leitch of Battle Creek. Key state witness Sam Abramowitz testified Harry Fleisher told him that he (Fleisher) and Selik would "wipe out" Hooper after several others, including Abramowitz himself, one way or another, botched attempts at the annihilation. The witness said there was a deadline of January 11 on the slaying if the killer was to collect fifteen thousand dollars. He added that Fleisher did not commit the murder and that Selik had gone to St. Louis. Both men lived in Detroit.

To keep the public, and the jury, thinking about a possible McKay involvement in the Hooper murder, Sigler called Anderson as a witness and had him confirm that all graft charges against McKay and others in the horse race bill bribe case had to be dropped when Hooper was murdered. The trial lumbered along in Battle Creek well into its second week until, on July 25, Attorney General John R. Dethmers released the second part of a four-installment report on conditions in Michigan's prison system, especially at the prison at Jackson.

Dethmers's report finally added official weight to a theory that reporters had been hearing for several months—that Hooper's murderer might have slipped out of Jackson Prison to commit the crime and then slipped back behind bars with a "perfect alibi." The report said a ruling ring of big-time convicts practically ran the prison, used prison officials' cars to attend sports events and visit bars, and even attended social events at the homes of the warden and deputy warden. Sigler had officially scoffed at the possibility that the killer came from inside the prison, instead holding to the theory that the slayer was someone to whom Hooper had given a ride.

The news of the prison investigation, which took Dethmers and his staff, aided by state police and corrections department officials, four months to put together, arrived at the Battle Creek courtroom before noon. Sigler exploded and immediately accused Dethmers of timing his report "to steal the show" from the trial and "to help John Dethmers politically." Defense lawyers immediately had Dethmers subpoenaed and at the same time requested a mistrial on grounds that the report was prejudicial to the four defendants. But Sigler claimed the release was actually Dethmers's announcement that he was running for governor of Michigan. (Ironically, within a few months Sigler himself was a gubernatorial candidate.) Before the shouting was over, Sigler had told the court that Dethmers and Frank McKay were "political bedfellows" and intimated Dethmers was seeking help from the beleaguered GOP boss.

The prosecution's summation was vintage Sigler. He told the jury that the state had established "that a diabolical conspiracy of wicked men," including Harry Fleisher and Mike Selik, "undertook to hire killers for 15,000 lousy dollars . . . to rub out a man who had talked too much. They plotted the death of Senator Hooper as if he were a rabbit! They went at it as you would buy a bag of oats!" Sigler reminded jurors that Hooper had given the grand jury damaging testimony against McKay, testimony that was rendered worthless because of Hooper's slaying. On the twelfth day of the trial, the jury came in with guilty verdicts for all four defendants. Judge Hatch sentenced each to four and one-half to five years in prison.

The Ingham County grand jury investigating state government underwent a significant change on September 24, 1945, when the grand juror, Circuit Judge Leland W. Carr, was appointed to the Michigan Supreme Court by Governor Kelly. As he had done a quarter of a century before, Carr replaced Howard Wiest, who had died a few days before while still officially on the bench. Carr, then sixty-two, assured the governor that the grand jury's work would in no way be affected by his departure. Before taking the oath of office on the high court, Carr's final act as circuit judge was to appoint his fellow jurist, Circuit Judge Louis E. Coash, forty-one, as Ingham County one-man grand juror. Coash had been on the circuit bench less than four months.

There were almost immediate rumblings that Sigler and Coash were not hitting it off. Carr had put up with, or ignored, Sigler's flamboyance, his "over dressing," his lavish spending, his apparent personal friendship with Hemans, and his constant references to McKay. Carr claimed that at least Sigler was getting results and was busy most of the time lining up suspects and witnesses for the grand jury. But Sigler's personality and theatrics seemed to bother Coash. And it did not help when Sigler spent most of the autumn after Coash's appointment helping prosecute a case in Oakland County involving some Detroit hoodlums accused of robbing a prominent nightclub frequented by ex-convicts. Several of the defendants were grand jury indictees and/or witnesses, the only excuse Sigler could have had for getting involved in the case.

As the special prosecutor prepared to leave for another Florida vacation, he and the grand jury were blasted from another direction. The state senate created a three-man committee, chaired by Senator Ivan A. Johnston, to probe grand jury expenditures. Judge Coash pledged cooperation, but Sigler bristled and refused to share grand jury secrets with a body that he was scrutinizing.

Answering a Senate subpoena, Coash turned over all grand jury records but asked that Victor Anderson be allowed to attend committee sessions to assure the records' confidentiality. When Johnston refused, both Anderson and Coash notified Sigler in Florida and he left for Lansing immediately to assume command of the battle.

Meanwhile, Johnston started calling witnesses in a public session. George MaDan, grand jury auditor/accountant, reported the grand jury had $400,000 from the legislature and had spent about $325,000 of it. Sigler, to date, had received $69,565, H. H. Warner $36,978, and lawyer Thomas J. Bailey $3,724. The Olds Hotel had received $25,361 for twelve rooms and "services." A grand jury detective testified he had paid Hemans $8,850. The *Lansing State Journal* reported the sum represented "lavish spending . . . for liquor, entertainment and 'special services'" for the prosecution's star witness.

Attorney Roy Conley assisted the committee, without pay, in interrogating witnesses. He elicited from the detective that he cashed checks made out to him and then paid Hemans in cash. At other times, the officer said, he would deposit funds in a Hemans account at Michigan National Bank and give Hemans the receipt.

Sigler returned on Saturday, March 2, and called a news conference to defend the spending and claim the senate was trying to discredit him and the grand jury and squelch the pending bank branch bill indictment.

On Monday, March 4, Judge Coash ordered the temporary suspension of all grand jury operations and the payment of all expenses and salaries of Sigler and his staff. He told Sigler, in a letter, that he had impounded all grand jury records and property until he could personally investigate the situation. He was not "directly or indirectly admitting or recognizing . . . anything irregular in grand jury expenditures." The newspaper, correcting figures published the previous week, said the grand jury had only $46,000 remaining from $425,000 the state had appropriated.

Sigler told reporters he would petition the Michigan Supreme Court to take superintending control of the grand jury. He accused Coash of helping "persons seeking to destroy the grand jury." The special prosecutor revealed he had obtained confessions from "certain members of the legislature in the banking conspiracy" and from some "public officials" relative to an alleged gambling conspiracy. He accused Coash of conferring frequently with Conley and said the judge had admitted talking with Senator Johnston.

Shocked by Sigler's "bitter attack" on Coash, reported the *Lansing State Journal* on March 6, the Ingham County Bar Association met at noon that day and extended a unanimous vote of confidence to the jurist. City Attorney Charles P. Van Note introduced the resolution after saying he'd read Sigler's letter to Coash and that it constituted a personal attack on Coash's integrity and honor. Charles Haight, Coash's former law partner and an ex-municipal judge, said, "There is no more honest nor honorable person in the state, and he is perfectly capable. . . ."

Less than a week later, Coash fired Sigler as special prosecutor and announced a sweeping revamping of the grand jury staff. Richard B. Foster, a former Ingham prosecutor, became the new special prosecutor. Coash, in a letter, ordered Sigler to turn over all documents, records, keys, and other property belonging to the grand jury. Sigler complied within hours. And at a final news conference, he said he would proceed as a private citizen in asking the supreme court to take over the Ingham County grand jury.

Sigler did not stay down long. Buoyed by the support of fifteen weekly newspapers and several dailies pledged to back him for governor, Sigler played it coy for a week, then, heeding a "citizens' call," jumped into the race. Campaigning as a graft buster, he won the June 17 Republican primary handily.

Obviously, it took Judge Coash and Dick Foster some time to go through stacks of transcriptions, interviews, physical evidence, confessions, briefs, information documents, warrants, bills, vouchers, and other evidentiary materials that Sigler and his staff had amassed in twenty-eight months.

Finally, on July 21, Judge Coash handed down indictments naming twenty-eight prominent bankers, lawyers, businessmen, state executives, members of the house of representatives and senate, and manufacturers in connection with 1941 anti-chain banking legislation. It was the biggest prosecutorial move in the three-year existence of the grand jury. And when Coash signed a blanket warrant charging twenty-four of the men with either offering or accepting bribes, he strongly hinted there would be additional warrants in the near future. Four of those involved in the roundup had already agreed to testify against the others, Coash said, and had been granted immunity from prosecution.

The defendants, the indictment alleged, were guilty of conspiracy and a bribe plot involving the bank bill and related legislation passed by both houses of the legislature and vetoed by former Governor Murray D. Van Wagoner. With numerous alterations and modifications, the bill finally was passed and became law in 1945, leading to scores of bank branches throughout the state.

As the preliminary examination began in August, Hemans announced he would not be testifying on grounds that such testimony might incriminate him. He was arrested in Washington, D.C., on a fugitive warrant and was convicted on a federal offense of fleeing across state lines to avoid testifying, fined one thousand dollars and imprisoned for a four-year term. The case dragged on.

Wanting to proceed, Coash and Foster interviewed Hemans in a federal prison in April 1949 and Hemans still insisted he would not testify. Foster promptly moved to quash the bank case and Wayne County Circuit Judge Chester P. O'Hara, who had been assigned the case, dismissed all the defendants. O'Hara refused to dismiss a contempt of court charge against Hemans, but the supreme court eventually dismissed it, ruling that since the main case had been dismissed, Hemans could not be held for declining to testify in it.

Hemans resurfaced two more times. On May 27, 1950—close to seven years after the grand jury was formed—he appeared before visiting Judge Herman Dehnke of Harrisville and entered a guilty plea to a charge of paying a two hundred dollar bribe to then-Representative George O. Harma of Atlantic Mine to influence his vote on an intangible tax measure in the 1941 legislature. It cost him a one thousand dollar fine and five years' probation. Eight years later, on March 8, 1958, Hemans got Victor Anderson, Sigler's former special assistant prosecutor, to help him apply for reinstatement in the state bar. To accomplish this, he was granted a hearing before a grievance committee headed by Lansing attorney Harold Glassen. An official notice of hearing was posted, outlining Hemans' criminal record and seven conditions he must meet to be reinstated. But on the day of the hearing, May 12, Anderson petitioned to withdraw the application, saying Hemans had made a business connection and would not be able to engage in an active law practice, one of the requisites for reinstatement. Hemans later operated an antique shop in Eaton Rapids.

For all practical purposes, the Ingham graft grand jury finished the investigation portion of its task late in 1948. Four years later, Auditor General John B. Martin issued a final accounting that showed the grand jury spent $495,189 in its nine-year existence. Of the total, $228,418 went for attorney fees. In October of 1957, the supreme court ordered all of its records destroyed, and Judge Coash officiated at an incineration at an Oldsmobile Division plant in Delta Township, Eaton County.

After his term as governor, Sigler joined Anderson in a Lansing law firm. Sigler was killed November 30, 1955, when the four-seat airplane he was piloting crashed into a guy wire of a television antenna near Battle Creek. Sigler, Anderson, Carr, Coash, Foster, Hemans, McKay, and most of the others whose lives the grand jury touched have since died.

In late 1994, Rubenstein and Ziewacz came out with a sequel to *Three Bullets—Payoffs in the Cloakroom: The Greening of the Michigan Legislature, 1938-1946.* While they uncovered no new evidence to dissuade them from believing

Jackson Prison inmates were responsible for the Hooper murder, the new book provides an in-depth look at the political intrigue that influenced both the murder and the grand jury investigation. It also features many individuals connected to the Ingham County legal system—Kim Sigler, Richard Foster, Leland Carr, Louis Coash, Roy Conley, Victor Anderson, Charles Hayden, and Joseph Planck.

23

CHANGES IN THE WAR YEARS

Ingham County was rapidly leaving the Great Depression behind as the decade of the 1940s was ushered in. By the end of 1940, real estate and personal tax collections were decidedly up compared with the previous year. In Lansing, Treasurer John F. Webb happily reported a record collection of $1,283,090, representing 93.8 percent of the total tax roll and more than 2 percent higher than the 1939 total at year's end. New construction, both residential and business/industry, was believed responsible for the increased tax payments. More residents were working now, and that also contributed to the increased on-time tax paying.

The construction boom was especially noticeable on the Michigan State College campus, where a state-of-the-art Jenison Fieldhouse was used for the first time in 1940, and where a new addition to the veterinary medicine clinic was almost completed. There was also something else "new" on the campus; John A. Hannah had replaced his father-in-law, Robert Shaw, as president of the nation's first land-grant institution of higher learning.

Municipal court activity in Lansing decreased slightly in 1940, according to the year-end report of Judge Sam Street Hughes, who had just completed his ninth year on the bench. The court handled 8,216 cases during the year, compared with 9,675 the year before. Only 793 were criminal cases, down from 890 in 1938 and 1,710 in 1939.

For Prosecutor Richard B. Foster, 1940 was an exceptionally busy year. Not only did his office handle a customary two thousand or so criminal cases, but also a pair of grand jury investigations. One of the cases involved embezzlement charges arising from indictments growing out of a probe of the publication of state tax notices. After a two-week trial in 1941, a jury found Hyman Levinson, an Oakland County publisher, and Martin J. Lavan, a Brighton attorney and former legal counsel to the auditor general's department, guilty of larceny by conversion. The supreme court, in November of 1942, reversed the convictions.

The other investigation, concerning irregularities in the Ingham County Road Commission, resulted in two elected commission members being indicted and tried on criminal bribery charges after they had been removed by the county's board of supervisors. A commission employee also was charged with embezzlement of public funds. The investigation and subsequent court proceedings resulted in the conviction of Commissioner Archie J. Earl for accepting a bribe. Sentenced to eighteen months to five years in prison by Judge Hayden, he was removed from office. The conviction and sentence were upheld in 1941 by the supreme court.

Of forty-one criminal cases that came to trial in 1940, Foster and his assistants, Paul C. Younger and Marvin J. Salmon, recorded thirty-six convictions, the other six ending in acquittal. The trial load was similar in 1941. By that time, Victor C. Anderson had joined the prosecutor's staff, replacing assistants who had joined the military.

Early in 1941, Lansing Mayor Thomas O'Brien's death left a vacancy in that office. A special election was held and Municipal Judge Hughes was elected to fill the unexpired term. His first official act was to appoint Louis E. Coash to succeed him on the city bench. Coash assumed his duties on April 10, 1941, and was unopposed for re-election in that year's fall balloting. During the year, the city court handled 12,718 cases. To facilitate a busy docket, municipal court moved from the city hall into expanded quarters in the old post office building at Michigan and Capitol avenues. The building would acquire the name of "City Hall Annex" until it was demolished when a new city hall was constructed twenty years later.

Even though Ingham attorneys were extremely busy in the early 1940s, many felt that all people, regardless of their financial status, should have equal access to the judicial system. Carrying out that belief, the Ingham County Bar Association hired John N. Seaman as the first paid "Legal Aid attorney" in 1940. Seaman recalls that the cases taken were primarily domestic relations, housing, and garnishment work. In the next 20 years, attorneys such as John Brattin, Allison Thomas, and William Stapleton followed Seaman in providing legal aid work. Brattin remembers getting paid about fifty dollars a week by the ICBA.

In 1962 the agency was incorporated as the Greater Lansing Legal Aid Bureau and began to receive funding from the Lansing United Community Chest. The first trustees included Theodore Swift, John Dart, James R.B. Hovey, Raymond McLean, Winston E. Miller, C. Laverne Roberts, Donald Reisig, William Stapleton, John Seaman, Lloyd Service, Gladys Spaulding, and George Thornton. Douglas Sweet was hired as the first full-time attorney for Legal Aid in 1963 and George Krause was hired as the second full-time attorney and first executive director in 1964. Subsequent executive directors have included Robert O'Connor, William Kemper, Carl Kaplan, John Schoonmaker, Jay Mitzner, Paula Zimmer, and Douglas Slade.

As 1942 came to a close, the Ingham County Bar Association was paid an honor by the State Bar of Michigan, when it elected veteran Lansing attorney Dean W. Kelley as its new president. As he took over the reins of the state bar, the ICBA gave a testimonial dinner in Kelley's honor at which the senior judge of the Michigan Supreme Court, Justice Howard Wiest, was the speaker. Wiest stressed Kelley's admonition against "the unhealthy growth of bureaus, commissions and agencies [which] are invested with judicial powers without any of the wholesome restraints inherent in the judicial process." Conceding that "the exigencies of war create conditions which make restraints upon civil liberties necessary" and force sidelining of due process, Wiest said it was the "obligation of the members of the bar, without becoming obstructionist, to promote measures to regulate the administrative process."

The end of 1942 marked the close of a state assignment for another prominent Ingham County lawyer. Byron L. Ballard had a varied and widespread career that started in Texas, where he was born in 1890. Son of a physician, he attended public schools in the Lone Star state, obtained his law degree at Washington and Lee University, and his first legal experience in Tennessee, where he was admitted to the bar in 1912. He also practiced two years in Oregon before coming to Lansing in 1916. Ballard was associated with Charles H. Hayden and Harry Hubbard for a time, then with Shields, Jennings, and Taber. A specialist in corporation law, he was counsel to several firms including Motor Wheel, Michigan National Bank, Central Trust, Butterfield Theaters, Michigan State College, Reo Motors, and Michigan Surety. He was on the Michigan State Board of Law Examiners for ten years and served two years as part-time legal adviser to Governor Murray D. Van Wagoner. Ballard died in Hollywood, California, on May 25, 1952.

Legislative action in 1943 increased the financial responsibility of errant Michigan drivers, helped automobile insurance firms and agents by making it mandatory that operators of motor vehicles carry insurance to cover possible claims, and opened a new field for lawyers. Some saw the new law eliminating the role of ambulance chasers—now everyone had auto insurance, and lawyers would no longer be needed to settle accident claims. They had no way of anticipating the future, when juries would award million-dollar judgments in automobile collisions, even in non-fatal cases.

That same year brought considerable changes in personnel in Lansing government. Mayor Hughes joined the U. S. Navy Reserve in mid-year and immediately took a ninety-day leave to enter basic training as a lieutenant senior grade. On completion of his training, Hughes returned to Lansing in August, resigned as mayor, and went on active duty. City Attorney Clay Campbell also resigned. Alderman Edson Bassett, president of the city council, became acting mayor and was almost immediately stricken with a fatal illness. Alderman Ralph Crego was appointed temporary council president and later assumed the mayor's duties in an acting capacity. He immediately appointed Paul C. Eger as city attorney. In the fall, Crego was elected to fill Hughes' unexpired term. In the prosecutor's office, headed by Victor C. Anderson, 1943 again saw approximately 2,000 cases handled by an ever-changing staff. Charles R. MacLean, an assistant prosecutor, enlisted in the U.S. Navy during the year and was replaced by Earl E. McDonald.

The year 1943 also saw the beginning of a long-time ICBA tradition—the "shrimp feed." In his memoirs, veteran Lansing attorney Roy Conley describes the very first shrimp dinner.

> Claude Marshall and Coash [Louis] and me were discussing the possibility of putting on a shrimp feed for the Bar. And, as a result, the three of us organized finding a place to hold it, being the North Lansing Club's hall. Louis agreed to arrange for the purchase of the fish. Marshall to arrange for the help in the kitchen and I to get out the notices to the members of the bar. I had one other duty. I was to arrange for enough beer. That was to be included in the price of "festies."

> Later, when I told Claude and Louie that I had written the Governor, the Attorney General, and the members of the Supreme Court to be our guests, they were amazed and somewhat taken back. However, while the Governor failed to show, three of the members of the Court were there, later informing us they had enjoyed the party and would again like to be invited if we ever did it again.

District Judge Pamela McCabe, former ICBA president, described the continuing tradition in a May 1993 issue of Briefs, the ICBA newsletter. "Over 50 years many rituals and customs have evolved for those loyal volunteers who work at the dinner. As you might expect, there is a hierarchy of jobs; the newest volunteers do clean-up, those with more seniority and the judges dish out the food, a select few dispense the drinks, and preparing the shrimp is an executive rite." McCabe gave credit to Mike Spaniolo and Phil Vilella for their "steadfast guidance" in keeping the tradition alive.

When the United States entered World War II in 1941, many Ingham County attorneys were quick to enlist, and they frequently served with great distinction. Sam Street Hughes, Lansing's mayor, later to become a circuit court judge, held the rank of lieutenant commander and helped re-establish the civil government and public schools in Okinawa, and assisted in restoring fisheries and agricultural industries of the South Pacific island. Other lawyers who interrupted their legal careers to serve their country included Charles MacLean,

Allison Thomas, Richard B. Foster, Archie Fraser, Fred C. Newman Jr., and John Seaman.

McLean was a naval intellegence officer in the Pacific and his final assignment was flying reconnaissance for the Okinawa invasion; Second Lieutenant Thomas parachuted into North Vietnam in 1945, providing technical training to Vietnamese troops and working with Ho Chi Minh; Foster enlisted in the U.S. Army Air Corps just a few days after Pearl Harbor; Fraser was a commissioned officer with an airborne troop carrier unit and served in North Africa, Sicily, and Italy; and Lieutenant Newman served with distinction in the Counter-Intelligence Corps. Lieutenant Colonel Seaman is known for his unusual abilities to learn foreign languages and he put his linguistic talents to good use during World War II. He was awarded the Legion of Honor for his work as a cryptographer, helping to intercept and decipher the German high command's coded messages.

The year 1946 saw one of the nation's most fascinating murder trials take place in Ingham County. The defendant, Clayton Smith, a World War II veteran and a rookie Lansing police officer, was charged with killing his wife with his service revolver. Smith, however, said while changing his clothes, he had hung his holstered revolver on a chair. His one-and-a-half-year-old son Butchie, Smith said, took the gun from the holster with both hands and pulled the trigger. Clayton Smith was released without bond until after the funeral.

Police officials asked Michigan State Police to handle the investigation, eventually led by Detective Sergeant Joe Pearce. Questioning continued for three days, Smith being allowed to go home each evening. Because he gave three conflicting versions—all written and signed by him—flunked a lie detector test, and had a history of a troubled marriage, the officer was charged with first degree murder by Prosecutor Victor Anderson. The prosecutor knew he could not use the lie detector test—administered by physician/lawyer LeMoyne Snyder—in court. But he relied on three police officers who would testify that Butchie could not possibly have been able to fire the gun.

Clayton Smith's parents retained Ben Watson and Roy Conley to defend the officer. Smith insisted the child was "gun crazy" and had fired the weapon. He admitted his own negligence in leaving the loaded revolver where the boy could reach it and and claimed his son had a toy cap pistol that was much harder to fire than the police gun. He said the boy would pick up and pull the trigger on any gun he could reach. With permission from the defendants and with "full knowledge of the police," Conley and Watson searched the bedroom where the slaying occurred and found Butchie's cap gun. Then they got a service revolver from police and had Butchie brought to their office, where the police revolver had been placed on a chair near a window. As the boy's aunt and grandmother talked with Conley, the child wandered about the office and eventually spotted the gun.

"At once he took the gun in his hands, and with a finger from each hand, pulled the trigger, not once but two times, each time saying 'bang, bang'," Conley recorded. His only question was whether Butchie could be expected to repeat his act in a crowded courtroom. At least the lawyers felt some assurance that their client was telling the truth about the little boy's ability to shoot the gun.

The People established the basic facts of the case with testimony of the officers who had first questioned the defendant. His sister-in-law and mother-in-law testified about quarreling and "loud words" the morning before the killing. Three state police officers, testifying as expert witnesses, said they believed it impossible for Butchie to have fired the gun.

The next day Smith responded with convincing answers to the direct examination questions and, though he "danced around" under cross-examination, did not let Anderson destroy him while explaining the various versions of the shooting story. During a recess, Conley picked up the evidence gun from the clerk's desk and put it in his pocket. Outside in a corridor, he encountered two Lansing detectives and a state police gun expert and asked them to accompany him to an empty office to listen to a proposition. As the men trooped down the hallway, Smith's sister, with Butchie in tow, joined the parade. Conley asked the officers to pretend they were not watching the child. Then he placed the revolver on a chair in a corner of the room. "Sure enough, Butchie spotted the gun, picked it up and began pulling the trigger. Now I knew we were 'in,' although I still had other plans," Conley related. Both detectives (the state police officer had not joined the experiment) promised not to alert Prosecutor Anderson to the events in the empty office in exchange for not being recalled to testify. Conley said he trusted the detectives because both were "old fishing companions."

Back in the courtroom, hoping that dramatic presentation of "one good issue" would cause the jury to forget aspects of the trial that went against his client, Conley called Clayton Smith's sister—with Butchie attached—to the witness stand. But instead of spotting his father and rushing to a tearful embrace, Butchie ignored his dad. And when Conley placed the revolver on the corner of the witness stand, the child ignored it, too. Fortunately, he did glance at the jury and began to cry, at least giving Conley a chance to ask for a recess.

When court resumed, Conley got an inspiration. At a whispered session at the bench, he told Judge Paul Eger he wanted to take the judge, Anderson, and Butchie into Eger's chambers for a silent demonstration of the boy's ability to handle the heavy weapon that had killed his mother. Anderson balked, but Eger agreed to the test, promising to explain it to the jury, no matter which way it went. Conley placed the gun on a window sill in Eger's office and Butchie immediately picked it up. Conley told him to "shoot" the taxicab that was passing the window and Butchie aimed the weapon at the yellow car and pulled the trigger three times. Eger was convinced. Anderson was crestfallen. Conley was ecstatic. Eger kept his promise, explaining the happenings in his office as the jury strained to catch his every syllable. The jurors left for the day and Conley recalled several of them had "complacent looks" on their faces. The next day the jurors deliberated briefly before returning a verdict of not guilty.

Conley and Watson combined in another memorable 1940s case, defending Josephine Upton, who with a sixteen-year-old youth by the name of Richard H. Gorman, was accused of the ambush murder of her husband Frank G. Upton, a Lansing factory worker. Upton, returning from work on the evening of August 21, 1947, was gunned down as he walked up a path to his rural home outside Williamston.

Upton was missing for sixteen days before Michigan State Police received information on September 5 from a woman friend of Josephine Upton that Frank Upton had been slain and was buried in a farm dump. Detective Sergeant Joseph Pearce, of the East Lansing Post, learned from the informant that Josephine had first claimed her husband had left her, and she was asking to move in with the informant. When asked what would happen if the husband returned, Josephine said he would not be returning and blurted out her story.

Pearce learned the Uptons had been caring for their own three children and seven others placed with them as wards by the Detroit St. Vincent DePaul Society. The wards included Richard Gorman, his brother Alfred, and their younger sisters. Richard was described by Prosecuting Attorney MacLean in a recent interview as Josephine's "teenaged paramour."

Alfred revealed he had been asked to help his brother Richard and Josephine Upton load the dead man's body into the trunk of her car. Richard denied the murder plot and knowledge of Upton's shooting until, after two hours of questioning, he was asked if there was more than a single shot fired. Then, MacLean said, Gorman told authorities he balanced a rifle on the porch railing of the house on Berkley Road in Wheatfield Township and waited. Josephine Upton, armed with a shotgun, was concealed by some bushes nearby. As Upton walked up the path, Gorman zeroed the gun's sights in on the red ember of the cigarette the man had in his mouth, lowered the sights a few inches and fired. The bullet struck the thirty-year-old victim near the heart and shattered his spine. Gorman was quoted as saying, "He dropped like a dead bull."

Both Gorman and Upton related a sordid tale of how Frank Upton kept the family in almost constant terror with beatings of the older children and threats against all of them. She said his "favorite trick" when he was angry was to hold the sharp blade of a hunting knife against her throat. She said on the morning of the day he died, her husband beat their ten-year-old son Carl because he had driven their tractor into some baling wire.

Several weeks passed before the pair were examined in Municipal Judge Paul Younger's court in Lansing. Probate Judge John McClellan waived jurisdiction so Richard Gorman could be tried as an adult and he was represented by Russell A. Searl, retained by the St. Vincent DePaul Society.

Soon after the defendants were bound over to circuit court, the national detective magazines that were popular in those pre-television days started to show an interest in the case. The trial lasted for three weeks in December, before and after Christmas. Forty-six witnesses testified. MacLean battled Conley and Watson daily, with Assistant Prosecutor Earl McDonald often helping out.

Conley and Watson decided on a plea of self-defense, insisting the defendants feared Frank Upton would injure or kill them in a rage. Josephine Upton's father actually provided the prosecution a break in the case when he testified that he found a knife in the dust of the path the day after the shooting. Both defendants then testified Upton had been brandishing a knife as he came up the path, and that they shot him in self defense. To get around the written statements given to police before the trial, the defense attempted to establish they were coerced.

No mention had been made of the knife before trial. After the defense introduced it, MacLean called together all the witnesses he could round up and asked if any of them could identify the weapon as Upton's. The prosecutor's heart sank when one of Upton's friends said, "Yep, that's his knife all right." But MacLean regained his composure when the witness added: "But he didn't have it on the day he was killed—I had it in the shop putting a new handle on it. I gave it back to Mrs. Upton some time later."

It probably was a case of a bit too much defense testimony and the jury convicted both defendants of first degree murder. The verdict came late in the afternoon of New Year's Eve after the jury deliberated more than four hours. Both defendants showed little emotion when the verdicts were announced, the Gorman youth maintaining the cold indifference he had assumed throughout the trial. He and Josephine Upton were sentenced a few days later to life imprisonment.

Death claimed nearly a dozen prominent Ingham lawyers during the latter months of World War II and immediately after peace returned in 1945. United States District Judge Arthur J. Tuttle died at age seventy-six in Detroit's Henry Ford Hospital on December 3, 1944, after a two-month illness. Although he had been on the federal bench for thirty-two years and served in Detroit as United States District Attorney for a year before that, Ingham lawyers always considered Tuttle one of their own. He was still operating the sizable Tuttle Orchards on the old family homestead site near Leslie at the time of his death.

Early in his political career, Tuttle decided to become acquainted with as many people as possible. He reasoned that joining various organizations was the best way to accomplish this—and to woo voters on a personal basis—so he became a "joiner." He joined lodges, brotherhoods, fraternities, insurance societies, service clubs, and historical and library groups. When he died, Tuttle was an active member in more than forty organizations. He carried a small hand satchel of receipts and "member-in-good-standing" cards to show off wherever he might be.

On his death bed, Tuttle realized he would have to break his record of perfect attendance at Rotary Club meetings for over twenty-five years. College friend Clyde Webster, an Eaton Rapids native who became a Detroit circuit court judge, recalled the moment at a memorial program sponsored by the Wayne County Bar Association in the empty Tuttle courtroom in Detroit's Federal Building. Determined not to hurt his attendance percentage, the dying judge called for paper and a pen, Webster said, and scratched out a letter of resignation from Rotary so that his attendance would remain perfect.

The Detroit News, in an editorial at the time of his death, said Tuttle "had a sternly unyielding sense of right and wrong. He deeply respected the majesty of the law. He demanded an equal respect on the part of others. It made him, in the eyes of those who did not understand his character, something of a courtroom martinet." But to those who understood Arthur Tuttle, his strictness had its bounds. He was a feisty courtroom fighter as a prosecutor, an enforcer of the law as a district attorney, and a courageous judge on the federal bench. He twice pronounced the death sentence, and he once stepped down from the bench and gave a penny to a man he had just sentenced to probation and payment of a one-cent fine.

Earlier in 1944, Simon Roe, the first lawyer to be elected judge of the Lansing Municipal Court after it was created in 1903, died on January 13, 1944, after a law career that spanned half a century. He received his early education in Oneida Township, Eaton County, and came to Lansing about 1898 after a four-year stint as prosecuting attorney of Cheboygan County. He served four years as municipal judge and in private practice occupied the same office in the Dodge Block for thirty-four years.

Joseph H. Dunnebacke, who had practiced law in Ingham County for forty-two years since his graduation from the University of Michigan law school in 1902, died of a heart attack on December 4, 1944, at age seventy-three. He and Tuttle had for a time been law partners in Lansing. After serving several terms as Lansing city attorney, Dunnebacke was appointed U.S. Commissioner in Lansing by Tuttle in 1918, and served fourteen years in that post, most of it during the prohibition period.

Other prominent Ingham County attorneys who died during the 1940s included Jason Nichols, who was a seventy-year member of the ICBA; Alva Cummins, who served as Ingham County prosecutor, was a Democratic candidate for governor in 1922; legendary attorney Edmund Shields; and revered Judge Howard Wiest.

While the deaths of so many prominent attorneys saddened ICBA bar members, another Ingham County attorney achieved national prominence in the 1940s. LeMoyne Snyder, son of Michigan Agriculture College President Jonathon Snyder, was born on the MAC campus in 1898. He first became a medical doctor, graduating from Harvard Medical College in 1923. After several years as a ship's doctor on world-circling steamships, Snyder returned to

Lansing, practiced medicine, and began his study of the law. He frequently spoke of the "joints" where he received his formal education—MAC, Harvard, Vienna, but most important ". . . his study of law at the knee joint of Judge Leland Carr."

Snyder founded the department of police administration at MAC and was medico/legal director of the Michigan State Police. He continually preached the importance of using scientific methods in investigating the causes of violent death crimes, and established the state police crime lab. His textbook, *Homicide Investigations*, was published in 1944, went through thirteen editions, was translated into German, Spanish and Japanese, and was even quoted by a witness in the 1995 O. J. Simpson trial. He became even more famous when he combined with author Erle Stanley Gardner in co-founding the Court of Last Resort, which specialized in freeing unjustly imprisoned persons. Many of the "Court's" cases were featured during the 1940s and 1950s on network radio and television programs.

Snyder practiced legal medicine from an office in downtown Lansing from the early 1930s to the late 1950s, when he moved to California to work more closely with Gardner on Court of Last Resort cases. The law firm of Snyder and Loomis (now Loomis, Ewert, Parsley, Davis & Gotting), founded in 1953 by LeMoyne's brother Plummer Snyder and George Loomis, offered LeMoyne's legal medical services for a number of years. Brother Plummer became an expert in regulatory and public utility law. Clients included electric, gas, telephone, and transportation companies.

While the early history of Ingham County law was largely male dominated, Charlotte Dunnebacke began to make major contributions to the legal profession in the early 1940s. Born in 1908, she graduated from the University of Michigan Law School in 1932, began practicing with her father, attorney Joseph Dunnebacke, and eventually joined the staff of the State Law Library, serving as its director from 1943 to 1978.

Dunnebacke served under eleven governors, twelve attorney generals and thirty supreme court justices. Her uncanny abilities to research questions of law and find little-known legal resources to answer complex legal questions earned her the reputation of being a "walking legal index." It was not uncommon to find Dunnebacke peering over the shoulder of a library user—be it attorney, legislator, judge, or general public—to ask if she could help with the research. She had a delightful sense of humor that charmed even the most difficult library patron. Outside of the library, Dunnebacke served on the Lansing City Traffic Board, the Ingham County Family Services Board, and was a member of the Michigan Association of State Librarians. She died March 15, 1986.

24

GOOD TIMES FOR LAWYERS

The decade of the 1950s was to be "the best of times" for millions of Michiganians—a time when the ravages of the Great Depression and World War II were becoming mere memories, incomes were on the rise, the economy was stable, and all roads pointed toward peace and prosperity.

It was a great time to be alive, especially for a young lawyer. There were the advantages of a bustling economy kept healthy by the proximity of a burgeoning state government that was crying for lawyers, an automobile manufacturing installation (Fisher Body and Oldsmobile divisions) that could not build luxury cars fast enough and a rapidly expanding university in East Lansing that was the newest member of the Big Ten.

After three decades of a Democratic Party strangle hold on the nation's presidency, the Republicans had convinced the recent war's most respected hero that he was one of them and had installed General Dwight D. Eisenhower in the White House. In Michigan, a Democrat, in the form of a lanky ex-U.S. Navy officer named G. Mennen Williams, had beaten "graft-bustin'" Kim Sigler out of the governorship, but most GOP pundits would tell you Williams was a "one-termer."

Like other situations in the private sector, lawyer jobs were becoming easier to find. Many veterans intent on becoming lawyers took advantage of the G.I. Bill of Rights, which provided room, board, tuition, and books.

Numerous attorneys who would eventually lead the Ingham County law profession began rising to prominence in the 1950s. Leo Farhat, for example, opened his law office in Lansing after graduating from the Detroit College of Law in 1952. In memoirs prepared in the early 1990s, Farhat said the first month's rent for his office in the Tussing Building was paid by Bill Tyler, an African American contractor whom his grocery-man father had befriended in the 1930s. His first client, Farhat wrote, was a man seeking to transfer a license for an automobile. The fee was two dollars.

Within a few weeks, Farhat was in court on Tyler's behalf, suing a local restaurateur for six hundred dollars worth of construction work owed the builder. The fact the defendant had once threatened Farhat with a knife "because he learned I was dating his daughter" did not deter the young attorney and he won the case.

But Farhat did not win them all. He lost more early 1950s cases than he won and conceded in his recollections that "all the lawyers were tough to go against," especially because "I didn't know what the hell I was doing." Some of the best lawyers in the county, according to Farhat, were Joseph Planck, Bernard Pierce, Ben Watson, and Roy Conley, the latter "a seat-of-the-pants trial lawyer [who was] absolutely brilliant."

In time, Farhat met James Burns and Ray Rapaport, both slightly more experienced lawyers. Both befriended him. Farhat got a referral eviction case in a Jackson court from a law school friend, but was not sure how to proceed. Rapaport gave him some tips but refused payment for his advice. Farhat finally tried to shove a five dollar bill to him to pay for some long-distance telephone calls, and his mentor still refused, but set up a condition: "Whenever a young lawyer asks you for help in the future, you have to help." Wrote Farhat: "I said I would and I have."

Farhat and Burns became law partners in 1953. The first case that came their way was a lawsuit filed by the Board of Water & Light against a Burns client. Burns cross-complained and collected $1,500 for the client, $500 of which was the legal fee. Farhat happily took his $250 share, "never dreaming there was that kind of money in the law business."

The young lawyer then began to handle traffic and minor criminal cases. Then came a puzzling zoning case in which a Polish immigrant grocer wished to fashion a parking lot behind three stores he owned on Logan (now Martin Luther King, Jr.) Street. The city council turned down his request. Farhat then questioned the constitutionality of the ruling. After a two-day trial, Circuit Judge Louis E. Coash ruled the council denial "arbitrary, capricious, unreasonable and unconstitutional" and the parking lot was built. Farhat became a zoning expert overnight and for the next 15 years had more zoning case offers than he could handle.

When the Ingham County prosecutor position was open in 1956, Farhat decided to try politics. He came in a distant fourth to Jack Warren in the primary, but quickly supported Warren in the November election and became the chief assistant when Warren was elected. Four years later, Farhat won the prosecutor primary race and was easily elected in November 1960. Farhat appointed Don Reisig as his chief assistant, but Reisig left before the term was up to join the Lansing city attorney's staff. Farhat replaced him with Tom Skehan. When Skehan decided to run for prosecutor, he appointed Ray Scodeller as chief assistant; Scodeller eventually succeeded Farhat as prosecuting attorney.

Farhat got some statewide exposure when he was elected president of the Michigan Prosecutor's Association in 1964 after holding several lesser posts in the organization. He was president of the Ingham County Bar Association in 1965, chairman of the Sixth Congressional District Republican Committee from 1967 to 1975, and served on numerous state bar committees and disciplinary committees of the Michigan Supreme Court. And in 1978-79, Farhat was president of the State Bar of Michigan. It was not a boast, but a show of pride in his Lebanese heritage when he commented, "It's not every day that a first-generation American gets to be president of the State Bar of Michigan."

After his days as prosecutor, Farhat had a partnership with Robert Luoma and Peter Treleaven. Michael Stafford later joined. The firm eventually took in Monte Story, Michael Cavanagh, and Leo's brother, Norman. The firm's current (1996) name is Farhat, Story and Kraus.

Baiting Lansing attorney Stuart Dunnings became a favorite Farhat pastime. Once, he wrote, Dunnings called him in a frenzy, complaining that a Stockbridge justice of the peace would not accept a not guilty plea from his client. Answered Farhat: "Well, how in the hell do you think we're going to clean up our backlog if we keep accepting not guilty pleas?" After a moment of silence, Dunnings realized Farhat was again "pulling his leg."

Much more than just being on the receiving end of Farhat's kidding, Stuart Dunnings became, and still is, a force in Ingham County courts. He was the county's first black lawyer. After graduating from UM law school in 1950, he worked hard to make his way into the system, sweeping floors in the old residence where his first tiny office was situated to pay for his rent, and hitch-hiking to courts in East Lansing, Lansing Township, and Mason because he could not afford an automobile.

It was entirely fitting forty years later that Donald Reisig, a former Ingham prosecutor and circuit judge, then stepping down as president of the State Bar of Michigan, should be the one to present the tribute to Dunnings as the Ingham County Bar Association's Outstanding Lawyer of the Year for 1990. The honor had gone to Reisig the previous year. In his remarks, Reisig said Dunnings had brought his fellow lawyers "an appreciation of the need for personal and cultural diversity . . . a renewed understanding of the aspirations of the underprivileged and a greater willingness to comprehend, appreciate and participate in the quest for racial justice in America."

Stuart J. Dunnings Jr. was born on August 21, 1924, at Staunton, Virginia, where his father was a custodian at Staunton Military Academy. His mother, Bertie, took in washing to help keep the family off welfare during the Great Depression. Dunnings graduated from Booker T. Washington High School, an all-black school, in 1942. He saved approximately three hundred dollars while caddying at the local country club during summer vacations and was a freshman at Lincoln University when he joined the U. S. Army in an enlisted reserve capacity that allowed him to remain in school until the next June.

Dunnings, who was a private most of his army career, termed it "the worst experience of my life—I couldn't stand it." He said young white officers treated him and other blacks as if they were "dumb and stupid." His combat engineering outfit fought in France, Luxembourg, Holland, Belgium, and Germany. In a taped interview, Dunnings indicated that most of his army engineering duty was excavating latrines. During the Battle of the Bulge, he recalled, "the damned ground was so hard we had to dynamite [it]" before doing any digging.

Back at Lincoln after the war, Dunnings continued his struggle to finish college. He was aware that the small, segregated high school in Staunton had ill-equipped him for college. "I had to knuckle down and study like hell," he said, to compete with blacks from high schools in the big eastern cities. But he graduated on time—and cum laude—in June of 1947 and that September entered the University of Michigan Law School. He graduated with a law degree in January of 1950.

On the day after Labor Day in 1951, Dunnings opened a two-room upstairs office in a remodeled house on the northwest corner of Kalamazoo Street and Capitol Avenue. His landlord, insurance agent J. Riley Oles, charged him forty-five dollars a month rent. Dunnings paid the rent by talking Oles into letting him clean all the offices in the building once a week. The energetic young attorney "lawyered" from 8:00 A.M. to 3:00 P.M. and then put in eight hours at Oldsmobile. His first "legal secretary" was Romaine Scott, a black high-school senior who worked that first year after school and then full time for the next fourteen years.

His first case involved a man who had picked up a pair of trousers in a department store, then tried to exchange them for money by claiming he'd paid for the goods several days before and was dissatisfied with them. The Dunnings client was in circuit court, charged with larceny from a building. During cross-examination, Judge Marvin Salmon detected an irregularity and called Dunnings to the bench and said, "You can't do that." Answered Dunnings, "Well, judge, this is what Perry Mason does."

At the close of the prosecution's proofs, Dunnings moved for a directed verdict of not guilty, arguing that his client "did not intend to steal the property and deprive the owner permanently of the goods," one of the elements of larceny from a building. As proof of that, Dunnings offered, the defendant returned the goods and never left the store with the pants. "All he wanted to do," Dunnings told his interviewer, "was use the goods temporarily to extort, to get money under false pretenses. Chuck MacLain was prosecuting the case and he offered me simple larceny. My client took it and was satisfied."

Even as early as the beginning of the 1950s, discrimination cases started coming Dunnings's way. One that received considerable publicity involved one of the famed River Rouge High School basketball teams, visiting Lansing for the state tournament at Jenison Fieldhouse on the MSU campus. The team had reservations at the Wentworth Hotel, but when a dozen or so black athletes and their coaches strode into the downtown Lansing hotel, the management refused them rooms.

After the team had won the Class B championship, Dunnings filed suit against the hotel, claiming a civil rights law violation. Circuit Judge Louis Coash awarded a verdict "for nominal damages" of seven cents because Dunnings could not prove any actual damages. That got even more publicity, even in *Jet Magazine*, and Dunnings served notice on every hotel in the area that he'd sue them if they denied rooms to blacks.

Dunnings began to get a reputation as a criminal defense lawyer and tried dozens of cases for both black and white defendants. He became adept at picking appropriate jurors but nearly out-foxed himself in one case. His client was charged with indecent exposure but insisted he was merely relieving himself in a parking lot when two young girls spotted him. "My strategy," he said, "was to get as many farmers as I could on the jury . . . I figured farmers frequently had to relieve themselves out in their fields and would appreciate my client's [predicament]."

Fred Newman was prosecuting the case, and kept trying to get women seated as jurors. Every time Dunnings would excuse a woman on a peremptory challenge, another woman would take her place. As Newman kept seating women, Dunnings felt fortunate to wind up with six male farmers and six women on the jury. He also felt some satisfaction and pride in his jury-picking methods when the jury came in hung—six for guilty, six for acquittal—until the panel was polled and it was determined the women had all voted for acquittal and the men all for conviction.

As busy as he was, Dunnings twice accepted the presidency of the local chapter of the National Association for Advancement of Colored People. During his reign, local schools began hiring black teachers, and stores started to hire black clerks. As an attorney, he won school desegregation cases in Benton Harbor, Kalamazoo, and Grand Rapids. Committees under his direction also documented numerous Lansing school segregation claims that ultimately brought about "cross-town busing" and desegregation in Lansing.

Dunnings practiced alone for fourteen years before inviting another young black lawyer to join him in a partnership. But first, he had to convince Benjamin Gibson to leave the office of the Michigan attorney general and into a slot where he could get some criminal law experience. Dunnings had supported Leo Farhat in the latter's bid to become Ingham County prosecuting attorney. He told Farhat that it was time for a black in the prosecutor's office. Then he talked Gibson into leaving the attorney general and joining Farhat's staff, with the promise that after a year or so, Gibson could join Dunnings in a general practice partnership.

By that time (1964) Dunnings and dentist Clinton Canady had built an office building at 530 South Pine Street. Gibson came aboard and stayed for eleven years at Dunnings & Gibson. Clinton (Joe) Canady III joined the firm about the same time Gibson left to teach at the new Cooley Law School. Gibson re-entered private practice for a few years and then was appointed by President Jimmy Carter to the federal district court in Grand Rapids. The firm currently is known as Dunnings & Frawley.

Archie C. Fraser worked as a Wayne County motorcycle patrolman and a railroad fireman before becoming a full-time attorney. After World War II he was appointed state public administrator by Governor Harry Kelly and later became general counsel for the Michigan Public Service Commission. In 1950, Fraser became a partner in the Lansing firm of Ballard, Jennings, Bishop and Ellsworth. He was known for his expertise in representing public utility companies. His firm today, after a series of partner changes, is one of mid-Michigan's most prominent—Fraser, Trebilcock, Davis and Foster.

Fraser's partners, all who began their careers in the 1940s and 1950s, became equally prominent. Everett R. Trebilcock specialized in litigation and became a Fellow of the American College of Trial Lawyers; James R. Davis specialized in administrative, business, and utility law and won a distinguished volunteer award from the ICBA in 1987; and Joe C. Foster Jr. is known for his expertise in estate planning and trust and tax law, and is listed in *The Best Lawyers in America.* Their firm currently has more than forty attorneys and has had six serve as president of the ICBA.

In 1951, Prosecuting Attorney Paul C. Younger appointed Jack W. Warren as an assistant prosecutor. Warren went on to become a municipal judge, Ingham County prosecuting attorney, Lansing city attorney, and circuit court judge. When he retired in 1986, he had served 20 years on the Ingham circuit bench.

Former Michigan Governor Kim Sigler re-entered the Lansing legal profession in the late 1940s after losing the governor's post to G. Mennen Williams in 1948. Sigler practiced with Victor Anderson and Lee Carr Jr., son of Supreme Court Chief Justice Leland W. Carr, until the ex-governor was killed in a plane crash in late 1953. Approximately five years after Sigler's death, attorney Cassius Street came to Lansing, joining Anderson and Carr. He quickly heard many stories about the flamboyant lawyer and politician. "I understand Kim Sigler would interview prospective clients in the morning, then turn the case over to Vic [Anderson]," Street remembered in a 1992 interview. "Vic would then do all the leg work and brief Sigler before the case went to trial. Sigler would [present the case] to the jury, sounding as if he had been involved in every detail. It was a good marriage between Sigler and Anderson in terms of being able to blend their skills."

The first big client Sigler was able to attract to the firm was MSU (then Michigan State College). "When Sigler died, Anderson and Carr were worried they would not be able to retain MSU as a client," Street said. "But they did, for thirty years, until MSU began hiring in-house attorneys."

While Sigler was active in private practice in downtown Lansing during the 1950s, an assistant attorney general was making a name for herself in the nearby government buildings. Maxine Virtue was considered a national expert on family law, was often quoted in the local media, and gave numerous presentations to Lansing area women's and service clubs. In an October 11, 1959, *Lansing State Journal* article, women's writer Virginia Baird described Virtue as a "diminutive, blue-eyed, snowy headed wife of a university professor and mother of two teen daughters" who has spent years studying the problems faced by metropolitan courts, the structure of the state's children services system, and in surveys of the methods courts use in handling family problems.

"The family is the basic unit of our social and moral culture—the keystone in the arch of our civilization," she wrote in one of several books she authored. "Strong public policy indicates the desirability of preserving viable marriages where they can be saved, even though the parties are so desperate that they seek a divorce."

The Ingham County Bar Association began a tradition of honoring its veteran members in 1951. For the next forty-two years, the practice was continued at the association's annual banquet. The 1951 class of Ingham bar veterans included twenty-two who had thirty-five or more years in the profession. They all received engraved certificates at a luncheon at the Hotel Olds, attended by a record eighty-six ICBA members. Then a *State Journal* photographer lined up the ten most senior and it was discovered they had a total of 509 years at the bar. The "youngsters" in the picture were Judge Leland Carr with forty-five years and Judge Charles Hayden with forty-seven. Others in the photo were O. J. Hood, sixty-three years, and L. B. McArthur, fifty-five, both of Mason; James A. Greene and T. Roger Lyons, both with fifty-one; Seymour Person, fifty; and Charles E. Ecker, Walter S. Foster and Dean W. Kelley, each with forty-nine. Increases in human longevity in the second half of the twentieth century caused the bar association to change the period from thirty-five to fifty years for honoring its veterans.

There were considerably more lawyers practicing in Ingham County, of course, than the 107 listed in the 1950 city directory—probably a dozen or so in the outlying communities and numerous others in state government or employed as company attorneys for business and industrial firms.

Until now, the judicial system had seen few changes. A third circuit judge had been added in 1945 to the Thirtieth Judicial District by a legislative act. With the time-consuming grand jury of the 1940s behind them, the county's circuit judges—Charles Hayden, Louis Coash, and Marvin Salmon—managed in the mid-50s to keep up with the case load of criminal cases referred from close to twenty justices of the peace, and civil matters, ranging from naturalizations and divorces to damage suits and public utility rate wrangles. The circuit judges from 1942 until the end of 1947 were paid $7,000 a year by the state and an additional $2,000 from Ingham County. But by 1951, the state salary had been increased to $9,000 and the county stipend to $2,750.

The county's lawyers also realized that Ingham courts, simply due to their proximity to state government, were assigned more than their share of lawsuits against the state. Hardly a week went by that pairs or groups of lawyers did not discuss the "judge shortage" and wonder among themselves when "they" would do something about the situation. There was also beginning to be talk about getting rid of Michigan's antiquated lower court system—the justice of the peace courts.

This was not the first time that the justice of the peace system had been criticized. Prosecutors as far back as Arthur Tuttle at the turn of the century had come down hard on police and sheriff's officers who insisted on taking criminal cases to the local J. P., without first contacting the prosecutor. Too often, if the defendant decided on a circuit court trial, the prosecutor—who often did not get into the case until the preliminary examination phase—found himself without credible evidence and had to move for dismissal. Frequent complaints were heard that justices issued warrants only to get the $4.30 fee, and there was little the prosecutor could do. In Lansing, the situation had led to a legislative act in 1903 creating a Lansing Municipal Court, with the judge required to be a licensed attorney. Some lawyers, however, possibly because they could "get away with" more in front of a non-lawyer judge, resisted reform and helped prolong any change in the system until after the 1962-63 Constitutional Convention.

Among the better-known justices of the peace in Ingham County in the post-war era were Robert Morris Montgomery and George Hutter of Lansing Township, Roy Adams of Mason and Joe Pearce of Meridian Township. All of them were active in the State Association of Justices of the Peace and were considered personal friends by most of the county's lawyers, although Hutter was the only lawyer in the group.

Montgomery, the oldest, with a birth date in 1901, was probably the best known of the post-war J. Ps. He was the grandson and namesake of Justice Robert Morris Montgomery, who served on the Michigan Supreme Court for nearly twenty years before being appointed by President William Howard Taft to the United States Court of Customs Appeals. The younger Montgomery was a Lansing Township justice of the peace for nineteen years, beginning about 1935. Starting in 1953, for fourteen years, he was the Michigan director of elections, supervising elections at all levels, vote canvasses, recounts, and nominating petitions. Before that, and while still a township justice, Montgomery also represented Lansing Township and part of Lansing for four two-year terms in the legislature, from 1944 through 1950.

When Montgomery left the bench in 1953, he was succeeded by George J. Hutter, an attorney who had practiced in Lansing since 1937 and who won the seat after Montgomery decided to take the elections post. Hutter maintained his court at 2707 E. Michigan Avenue in the same quarters Montgomery had used for two decades. There are stories that both judges occasionally sent next door to Mac's Bar when they came up short of jurors.

Hutter's legal career spanned forty-two years. A native of Hungary, he immigrated to Texas and stopped briefly in Missouri before attending Wayne State University and obtaining his law degree from Detroit College of Law. He was a U.S. legal counsel before he moved to Lansing.

Hutter was active in the State Bar of Michigan and gained wide recognition for his attempts to reorganize the justice court system. He was also consulted during the organization of the district court system, which he did not live to see go into effect on January 1, 1969. Hutter, in the midst of his presidency of the Ingham County Bar Association, died on August 20, 1968.

A busy justice during those years was Joseph Pearce, of Meridian Township, a retired Michigan State Police lieutenant who spent a large share of his career as a detective at the East Lansing post, where he helped prosecute cases.

A popular and versatile magistrate was Roy W. Adams, who occupied the bench at Mason from 1945 to 1968. Adams was the epitome of the old-time justice of the peace. He was eighty-seven when he died on June 28, 1971, less than three years into retirement. He used the same office as had his father, William J. Adams, an earlier justice of the peace. A native of Reed City, where he was born in 1885, Roy Adams moved to Mason with his family when he was three. He had numerous "careers"—first as a railroad messenger between the railroad station and the post office; as a horseback mail carrier when rural postal service was inaugurated in 1903, and later as an automobile-borne carrier.

Adams ultimately became Mason's unofficial historian, a school board member, a Consumers Power Company sub-station operator, a ticket agent for the suburban trolley line, and the owner-operator of two early motion picture theaters in the county seat. Later, he ran successful electric contracting and heating businesses. The justice of the peace also was a correspondent for newspapers in Lansing, Jackson, Grand Rapids, and Detroit, acted in local theater productions and authored a historical novel, *Peg Leg*, in 1950. Adams also played flute and piccolo in the Mason city band and directed the city orchestra.

Joe Pearce, who still lived in his retirement home in Newaygo in 1994, estimated he handled close to 25,000 cases in the almost nine years he served as a J. P. in Meridian Township—from 1959 to 1967. At the time the district court system replaced the J. Ps. in 1967, Pearce was outspoken about the switch, maintaining that "big courts" are too impersonal and that "with a few more controls," the justices of the peace could have been continued as "the courts closest to the people."

Over the years, Pearce handled just about every type of case that existed—overweight trucks, traffic violations, weddings, fence viewing, and "dog cases," including sheep killing, for which farmers received twenty dollars for every sheep killed, the money coming from dog license fees.

In May 1954, circuit court employees and judges slacked off of their daily work schedule to honor the senior circuit judge, seventy-six-year-old Charles G. Hayden. *Lansing State Journal* writer Birt Darling described Hayden as, "The white-haired jurist, who is the personification of the story-book judge interested in everyone's troubles." Hayden had a long Lansing history; he attended Lansing High School and during his youth supported himself with jobs at the Lansing Spoke Works, making wagon rims at one dollar a day for Drury Porter, and working summers at the Michigan Sugar Company. "I really worked my way up in the world, too," he said. "I got to be a field boss at $1.50 a day."

Widely respected as a jurist, Hayden was also known for growing roses, raising dwarf fruit trees, and fishing. Always on his desk was a clipping, stating, "Nobody grows old by merely living a number of years. People grow old by deserting their ideals."

In 1956, the Mason courthouse was once more drawing attention. Harry Howell, the courthouse custodian, was "sprucing up" the inside of the half-century-old building with an apple blossom pink-and-blue color scheme. While *Lansing State Journal* writer Fred Olds admitted the new interior decoration was unusual, he gave it his complete endorsement. Calling it a real "purty" building, Olds wrote that Ingham residents could match their courthouse "against any in Michigan from the standpoint of care and beauty."

In 1958, subscribers to *Time* magazine found Sixth District Charles E. Chamberlain on the cover of an October issue, illustrating an article titled *How to Run for Office.* A former Ingham County prosecutor who was born on a Locke Township centennial farm, Republican Chamberlain won his first congressional seat in 1956, defeating MSU speech professor Donald Hayworth by 3,967 votes. Despite frequent attacks by mid Michigan liberals and an MSU campus-based recall effort, Chamberlain remained in his office until his retirement in 1974. His successor was another attorney—Robert Carr.

25

CHANGING THE CONSTITUTION

It was noon, October 3, 1961, when Michigan Secretary of State James Hare took the podium at the Lansing Civic Center. "May I have your attention please?" he asked the 144 delegates. "By authority invested in me as secretary of state by the Constitution and statutes of the state of Michigan, I hereby call this convention to order." Hare's call to order marked the beginning of almost a year of deliberations that would produce a document to replace the outdated 1908 constitution. "Con-Con" had been approved by a state referendum in April 1961 and delegates representing the state's 34 senatorial and 110 representative districts were elected September 12.

While the delegates were mandated to draft a new constitution, the outcome was uncertain. Only another popular vote would determine whether the new constitution would become law. The delegates came from a range of professions, but attorneys were elected in the greatest numbers—fifty-six. Also named were businessmen, farmers, homemakers, engineers, teachers, college presidents, journalists, police officers, ministers, and real estate agents. A barber, lumber dealer, florist, and printer also served.

Many eventually went on to higher office, including future Michigan Governor George Romney, Detroit Mayor Coleman Young, Michigan Secretary of State Richard Austin, State Controller and Budget Director Glenn Allen, and Court of Appeals Judge Robert Danhof.

Four delegates were elected from the Ingham County area—attorneys Eugene Wanger and Claud Erickson, Michigan State University President John Hannah, and Onondaga Township farmer Charles Davis. Other delegates, including local attorney Tom Downs, moved to the Lansing area in later years. Wanger, who later chaired the Ingham County Historical Commission, was the youngest Republican delegate at twenty-eight years of age.

Wanger says in a 1992 written summary of his Con-Con experiences: "I drafted and submitted twenty-seven proposals, which turned out to be more than any other Republican delegate, and about half-a-dozen of them ended up in the new constitution (not all without change, however). I had no clout or influence in the convention and was able to do this by persuading other, more influential delegates, to go along with me."

Wanger thought at the time of Con-Con his most important contribution to the new constitution was the creation of the state office of legislative auditor general. "This was a very novel and forward-looking concept in state government and it has worked well over the years. . . ." Today, however, he believes his proposal prohibiting the death penalty, adopted by delegates with only three dissenting votes, may have been even more important.

"While we all knew it was more or less significant at the time, it was still just one of many important items we were working on, and I think that probably none of us anticipated the controversy [recent attempts to legalize the death penalty] about it which has arisen during the past fifteen or twenty years."

Other significant proposals adopted by the delegates included the creation of a Civil Rights Commission; extension of the term of office for governor and state senators from two to four years; abolishment of the office of justice of the peace, to be replaced by a district court system; and the centralization of government by consolidating all state agencies into no more than twenty departments. Wanger believes the work of the Con-Con delegates was successful. He says:

> Overall it seems very clear to me that Michigan's government and the rights of Michigan's citizens are in far better shape today than they would be if we were still living under the old 1908 constitution. We made a myriad of changes and improvements which, given the nature of the political process, would never have been adopted by piece-meal amendment.

Con-Con delegate and future Appeals Court Chief Judge Robert J. Danhof, in an article included in the June 1962 issue of *Michigan Challenge*, listed the changes that had significant impact on the Michigan judicial system. Included were:

- The creation of a unified court system which established a single court of justice. The legislature was given authority to create other courts of limited jurisdiction by a 2/3 vote of the members elected and sitting in each house.
- Fixing the number of supreme court justices at seven, with an eight-year term.
- Authorizing the supreme court to select its own chief justice.
- Authorizing the supreme court to determine which cases it wants to hear, eliminating petty and frivolous appeals.
- Making the office of court administrator a constitutional office.
- Requiring the legislature to follow the recommendations of the supreme court when creating new circuits and increasing the number of circuit court judges.

Danhof, who chaired the convention's committee on the judicial branch of government, would later recall that he drafted the provisions that clarified and strengthened property-owner rights in condemnation proceedings and helped create the Michigan Court of Appeals, little knowing he would later serve on it for more than twenty-three years. He was six times elected chief judge of the court and in 1990 served as president of the national Council of Chief Judges of the Courts of Appeal.

Downs was one of the three vice presidents of the convention. Reminiscing later, he recalled that he was primarily responsible for constitutional requirements that legislative committees vote by recorded roll call, that gubernatorial appointments be automatically confirmed if not rejected by the senate in sixty session days, and that initiative laws adopted by the people can be amended by a three-fourths vote of the legislature. He also played a prominent role in getting the death penalty ban adopted.

Under the headline "Mission Accomplished" in the same issue of *Michigan Challenge* that Danhof described the legal changes, Con-Con President Stephen Nisbet said the delegates fully realized the state had been operating under a pre-Civil War document. "The 1908 convention basically largely rewrote and revised the previous constitution [1850] and added a few ideas of their own," he wrote. "The revision provides the state with a strong and coordinated basic law, devoid of ambiguity and yet possessed of sufficient flexibility to enable all government branches to function efficiently under it without the restraints that had become a part of the earlier document over the years."

The 136 days of deliberation included 473 hours of floor debate, 18,920 pages of transcript, and 830 delegate proposals, according to Nisbet. The result was a document 6,000 words shorter than the 1908 version. The new constitution was approved by voters on April 1, 1963.

The State Bar of Michigan periodically identifies important legal events in the state's history as part of its Michigan Legal Milestone program. The only milestone from Ingham County is the 1961-62 Constitutional Convention.

While the new constitution established district courts to replace the justice of the peace system, thirty-two municipalities—including Lansing and East Lansing—that had specially designed municipal courts decided they were not yet ready to give them up. The delay left judges Earl E. McDonald, Charles M. Murphy, and George Sidwell on the Lansing bench and William Harmon on the East Lansing bench until the early 1970s. The county's out-county lower court in Mason, however, was ready to begin business on January 2, 1969. Newly elected District Court Judges R. William Reid and James H. Edgar presided. Reid even took time from his moving-in duties to accept a guilty plea from a California driver who had been ticketed by Michigan State Police for running a red light, the *State Journal* reported.

In 1962, Frank J. Kelley was appointed Michigan's attorney general by Governor John Swainson. Not originally from Ingham County—he was born in

Detroit and practiced law in both Detroit and Alpena—Kelley made mid-Michigan his home, participating in a wide variety of both legal and charitable activities. In the next thirty-three years, Kelley was re-elected nine times, served Governors Swainson, Romney, Milliken, Blanchard, and Engler, and is currently the nation's longest serving attorney general. In a December 1991 article, the *Michigan Bar Journal* praised Kelley for being the first state attorney general to create consumer protection, environmental, and medicaid fraud divisions. It also pointed out that of the more than 2,700 legal opinions issue by Kelley and his office, fewer than 20 had been overturned in court.

A year later, in 1963, Glenn S. Allen Jr. became state controller and, like Kelley, the Kalamazoo native eventually made the Lansing area his home. Before he retired in the 1980s, he had also served as state budget director and spent three terms on the Michigan Court of Appeals.

As Kelley and Allen were beginning their state government legal careers in the early 1960s, Supreme Court Justice Leland W. Carr was ending his. An Ingham County circuit court judge from 1921 to 1945 and a supreme court justice from 1945 to 1963, Carr was honored at a testimonial banquet at the Jack Tar Hotel on November 6, 1963. The speakers and attendees were literally a "Who's Who" of Ingham County lawyers and judges.

ICBA President Charles MacLean was master of ceremonies for an event that combined both humor and respectful tribute. Former Prosecuting Attorney Richard B. Foster reviewed Carr's distinguished legal career, stressing the judge's extensive knowledge of the law. "We used to be impressed and sometimes startled, Judge Carr, by your quotation and citation of cases from memory, including the name, volume and page number, cases that if we were familiar with them we had found only after hours of research. If on such occasions we appeared diffident or nervous it was because of sheer respect for a knowledge that we would never achieve."

Circuit Court Judge Marvin J. Salmon mentioned Carr's poise and dignity on the bench. "Courteous though he was, he could express himself with righteous indignation, and with force and effect. And true to his instincts and character, he always ruled courageously. Judge Carr's prestige as a trial judge in Ingham County is still with us, I assure you."

Physician and attorney LeMoyne Snyder described the classes taught by Carr where hundreds of students learned much of their knowledge of the law.

> At each session Judge Carr would give us a typewritten list of twenty or a couple dozen cases to prepare for the next class . . . and of course you were expected to look these up and make a brief on each one, reciting the facts and the point of law that particular case illustrated. These classes continued for year after year, and then finally the wind-up, of course, was the famous review course that Judge Carr conducted. This

would last for several weeks, and the class would be expanded many times in numbers, and persons would come in from all over the state of Michigan and take up residence here during the weeks . . . prior to the bar examinations.

What sort of a teacher was Judge Carr? According to Snyder, Carr was "an inspiring teacher. He was methodical, he was meticulous, he was patient and understanding. He made sure you understood every point before you passed on to another."

When it came Carr's turn to speak, he assured his audience that he was retiring from the bench but not from the profession of law. "I think it would be impossible for me to do that. I've been at it too long. And I shall simply find my place in it as best I can."

One of the "places" that Carr found was in son Lee Carr Jr.'s Lansing law firm where he consulted with Lee and his colleagues Victor Anderson and Cassius Street. Street remembers learning from the former supreme court justice.

"Occasionally I had a case I had been working on for months, sometimes years," Street said. "I'd go into Judge Carr's office and present the facts to him. He'd sit silent for a few minutes, then ask me to bring my secretary in. He would then dictate a brief from memory, seeming to have more mastery of the facts than I did, articulating points in a short, beautifully concise and accurate way. He would then cite specific cases—often cases he had been involved in as a supreme court justice. His mental capacity and his grasp of legal principles was amazing."

Carr died on Memorial Day 1969 at the Lansing residence he built at 422 N. Sycamore.

While Kelley, Allen, and Carr were making news in Lansing, twenty-nine Ingham County attorneys were making news in Washington, D.C. In April 1962, Congressman Charles Chamberlain presented the twenty-nine to Chief Justice Earl Warren and the associate justices as part of a ceremony admitting the lawyers to the U.S. Supreme Court. Included were Frederick Abood, Raymond Campbell, James Kallman, Marvin Salmon, and Raymond Scodeller. A visit with Attorney General Robert Kennedy followed.

A new juvenile detention home had been under construction on the east side of Ingham Medical Hospital and in early November of 1960 Supreme Court Justice George C. Edwards and Ingham County Probate Judge Robert Drake joined other officials in the official dedication. Edwards said if the home could save even two youngsters from getting a life sentence in prison, it would pay for itself. Drake said the home would house both neglected and delinquent youth but assured the audience that neglected children would have no contact with delinquents.

Pleased with the new dentention home, Probate Judge Drake still believed more resources were needed for troubled youth. Two years later Camp Highfields was created. While Drake has always insisted that Highfields was the result of community action, few would dispute his leading role. In fact, the historical section of one of Highfield's brochures begins, "Highfields was born in the mind and heart of Ingham County Probate Judge Robert L. Drake." Drake had told the Ingham County Board of Supervisors that a year-round youth opportunity camp was needed—a place where juvenile delinquents can be made to feel that someone cares for them and where kids without loving parents, educational opportunities or peer and home relationships can turn their lives around. The supervisors gave their moral support, but could not find the tax money to finance the project. Drake then turned to the community, gave talks to service clubs, showed his ideas to foundations, and, eventually, succeeded.

Camp Ingham, the initial organization with Drake as its president, was formed in 1962. Drake recruited substantial support from the mid-Michigan legal community. Joe Foster Jr., for example, prepared and filed documents for tax-exempt status. Tom McGurrin drew up the articles of incorporation, and James Kallman served as legal advisor. Many other attorneys have served on the Highfields Board of Directors over the past thirty years. Today, Highfields is one of Michigan's premier facilties for treating and caring for troubled youth.

When Zolton Ferency opened his law practice in 1968, few took notice. Over the next two decades, however, the Detroit College of Law graduate was to become Ingham County's most controversial lawyer, known for his escapades both inside and outside the courtroom.

A frequent candidate for office in both state and local elections, the MSU criminal justice professor's courtroom work frequently generated media attention—whether he won or lost. Included in these high-profile activities were his suits to relieve prison overcrowding, his defense of former state Sen. Basil Brown on drug charges, his legal challenge of the Michigan Democratic Party's caucus system, his opposition to allowing the Christian Broadcasting Network on local cable television, and his suit to keep the Tisch tax-cut proposal off the ballot.

It was not unusual for Ferency to provide legal advice without charge. In 1989, for example, when the Michigan Lottery Commission was considering the idea of operating a game based on the results of the National Football League, Ferency issued a press release stating that lottery officials have no authority for conducting games that allow bettors to wager on the outcome of athletic events. "The law in this area is clear," he argued. "A lottery is a game of chance and betting on horse racing, foot racing, boat racing, football and baseball games is not a lottery." Even though Ferency was frequently attacked by organizations and individuals for his often non-traditional ideas, his death in 1993 provoked a seemingly never-ending stream of praise—even from many conservative Republicans who often opposed his causes.

In East Lansing, the late 1960s and early 1970s had provided multiple opportunities for attorneys such as Ferency and John Brattin who were vigorously opposing the Vietnam War. Sometimes they defended anti-war protesters whom city officials believed were too aggressive in their demonstrations, sometimes they penned pro-peace columns for local newspapers, and occasionally they even joined local and national anti-war marches.

It was not just the Vietnam War opponents, however, who were challenging authority in the college town and keeping City Attorney Daniel Learned and City Manager Jack Patriarche working overtime. Even long-time residents who were not joining the peace marches hired attorneys to represent their interests against the city. Camille Abood represented downtown merchants who wanted the city council to decrease restrictions on the size and placement of advertising signs; H. James Starr represented clients upset over the city council's idea to ban non-returnable bottles within the city limits; and James VandeBunte and Donald Hines represented residents upset over possible changes to an alley between Abbott Road and Evergreen Street.

Still, despite the tense times, both attorneys and clients frequently went out of their way to treat each other with respect. East Lansing lawyer Allison Thomas still chuckles when reminded of a "hippie" couple whom he represented in a pro bono assignment in the late 1960s. When the day came for the trial, he met his clients outside the courtroom and was presented with a string of "love beads" the couple insisted he wear for the trial. "I didn't want to offend them by refusing to accept the gift, but I sure as heck wasn't going to face the judge wearing a string of beads," Thomas said.

He appeared without the beads and won the case.

26

COOLEY LAW SCHOOL AND A DECADE OF MURDER TRIALS

It was in the early 1970s that Supreme Court Chief Justice Thomas J. Brennan Sr. decided to act on an idea that had tumbled around in his mind for some time: a law school in the state's capital city. He proposed the idea to the State Board of Bar Examiners, naming it after Michigan's eminent nineteenth-century supreme court jurist—Thomas M. Cooley.

Brennan was born in Detroit on May 27, 1929. He graduated from Detroit Catholic Central High School, the University of Detroit, and the U. of D. Law School, obtaining his law degree in 1952. After practicing law in Detroit from 1953 to 1961, he was appointed a common pleas court judge in 1962 at age thirty-three. A year later he was appointed a Wayne County circuit judge and in 1966 was elected to the Michigan Supreme Court, where he served through 1972.

When word got out about Brennan's idea, numerous members of Michigan's legal establishment assured him that no new law school was needed, or wanted. But a handful of associates and friends encouraged him to push forward. Brennan and his small group of followers began to share the dream of a law school "that would offer a legal education to those traditionally not part of the legal profession's mainstream." Their goal: to prepare "students for entry into the legal profession through an integrated program with practical legal scholarship as its guiding principle and focus."

The school was chartered as a non-profit educational corporation on June 19, 1972. The original board of directors included Ingham County Bar Association members Louis A. Smith, John L. Coté, Robert A. Fisher, John W. Fitzgerald, Jack W. Warren, and Russel A. Swaney. In following years, other attorneys such as Michael F. Cavanagh, Thomas E. Brennan Jr., Benjamin Gibson, Lawrence P. Nolan, and Dorothy Comstock Riley joined the Cooley board. A stretched budget and time pressures resulted in classrooms without furniture as the school's opening neared. President Brennan solved the dilemma by purchasing used "one-armed bandit" chairs from just-closed O'Rafferty High School.

Fitzgerald taught Cooley's first class, a freshman property class, on the night of January 12, 1973. It was four months before class members learned they would be allowed to sit for the bar examination. Accreditation by the American Bar Association came in 1978. Meanwhile, the first class of fifty-nine graduated in January of 1976. The school boasted 6,125 graduates at the end of 1994.

Initially, Cooley classes were held in a former photoengraving shop on South Grand Avenue, the present administration building. In 1973, the law school purchased the old Masonic Temple building on Capitol Avenue and moved classes, the law library, and faculty offices there. Then, in October 1991, Cooley opened its five-story, remodeled state-of-the-art law library in the former J. C. Penney Company department store building at Washington Avenue and Kalamazoo Street. Suddenly, with the purchase of several former retail buildings in the same block as the library, and enrollment for three annual terms topping 1,500 students in recent years, Cooley became Michigan's largest law school. Students come from all over the United States and from twelve foreign countries; about 75 percent are from outside Michigan. Cooley alumni are from every state but North Dakota. Its faculty includes nearly fifty full-time instructors and over one hundred adjunct professors, many of them Ingham County lawyers and bar members.

In a 1986 address to the Rotary Club of Lansing, Judge Brennan said that Cooley had grown to become the twenty-second largest law school in the United States. That was at the time the country was recovering from a recession, and Brennan boldly predicted the school someday would be in the top twenty—or maybe even in the top ten. In June of 1994, Brennan again addressed Lansing Rotarians and proudly announced that Cooley was the fourth-largest accredited law school in the United States, outnumbered only by Georgetown, Suffolk and Harvard. By September, Cooley edged past Harvard to become the third largest law school in the nation. Brennan also reminded the Rotarians they were soon to inaugurate the club's first woman president, Helen Pratt Mickens, herself a Cooley graduate and then associate dean at the school. He said he frequently bragged about Mickens, Governor John Engler, and Speaker of the Michigan House of Representatives Paul Hillegonds, all Cooley graduates.

Meanwhile, Lansing finally decided to open its district court—designated District Court 54-A—in 1971. The first four judges were Charles Murphy, Earl McDonald, Terrence Clem, and James Wood. Maurice E. Schoenberger was appointed district court judge in East Lansing in 1970, while William Reid and James Edgar were the first district court judges sitting in Mason.

During the 1978 legislative session, Ingham County, the Michigan Supreme Court, and the legislature made a deal that gave Ingham two additional circuit judges—and all of the state's court of claims business. The court of claims had existed since 1859, established to hear lawsuits and claims against the state. The law stipulated that the court would be presided over by a circuit judge, but did not indicate from what circuit the jurist would come. In practice, many court of claims cases were directed to Ingham County, just as grand jury cases looking into possible state government wrongdoing had been for over a century. Ingham County officials had frequently contended that they did not have enough judges to hear both county and state cases. With the new arrangement Ingham judges would hear all claims against the state over one thousand dollars except those arising from line-of-duty injuries to state employees. Claims under one thousand dollars were decided by the State Administrative Board.

The two additional judges elected in November 1978, increasing Ingham's circuit court roster to seven, were Robert Holmes Bell and James Giddings. They joined existing judges Jack Warren, James T. Kallman, Ray C. Hotchkiss, Michael Harrison, and Thomas Brown.

Increasing movement of the county's population from Lansing to outlying areas once again prompted discussion as to the proper center of county government. *Ingham County News* staff writer Jim Schutze wrote an editorial for the paper's July 8, 1970, edition that began by again pitting Lansing against Mason. "At some point, Ingham County will have to decide where its county seat really is. The likelihood that the Ingham County Circuit Court will leave Mason permanently within the next two years to sit year-round in Lansing is only one indicator in a larger and graver trend. "Lansing is big; Mason is small; Lansing is slowly pulling government out of Mason and into Lansing."

Schutze suggested, however, that by the year 2000, the 150-year-old fight over the proper location of a county seat may be changed. ". . . county facilities should be located where they are most accessible and noticeable to the populace. That won't mean Lansing. It may not mean Mason. But it will mean a place in the center of the new suburban growth."

While county seat location arguments were confined to inside columns of newspaper, murder often dominated the front-page headlines. Nearly 100 years after the Marble murders took place near the corner of Hagadorn Road and Burcham Drive within the current city limits of East Lansing, another spectacular murder case began less than a mile away. Martha Sue Young, an MSU student who lived with her mother on North Hagadorn Road, disappeared on New Year's Day in 1977. Her boyfriend, twenty-two-year-old Donald Miller, told police he dropped Young at her house around 2:00 A.M. Evidence, including the testimony of a witness who had testified under hypnosis, eventually pointed to Miller as the killer of Young, and Lansing teacher Kristine Rose Stuart—even though no bodies had been found. On February 21, 1979, an Ingham County grand jury, presided over by Circuit Court Judge Michael Harrison, indicted Miller on two counts of second degree murder.

Miller was already awaiting trial on charges of rape and attempted murder in connection with an attack on two teenagers in their Delta Township home. On May 9, 1979, a jury found him guilty of two charges of attempted murder and one of rape. He was eventually sentenced to thirty to fifty years in prison.

The Ingham County case against Miller for the Young and Stuart murders quickly became complicated and would later be described by Prosecuting Attorney Peter Houk as a "bizarre set of murders unequaled in this state for missing bodies and no evidence."

On July 13, Miller led police to the bodies of Young and Stuart, hidden in two separate sites in Clinton County. At a press conference the next day, Houk said Miller would be allowed to plead guilty to two charges of manslaughter in exchange for leading police to the sites. A few days later, Miller admitted two more killings—Wendy Bush and Marita Choquette—and led police and Chief Assistant Ingham County Prosecutor Dan McLellan to the body of Bush. In return for his cooperation, prosecutors agreed not to use the evidence against him.

On August 28, 1979, Miller was sentenced by Circuit Judge Robert Holmes Bell to serve two consecutive prison terms of ten to fifteen years. Prosecutor Houk, who had campaigned on a promise not to plea bargain, found himself criticized for his decision to "strike a deal" with Miller and defense attorney Thomas Bengtson, especially by those who feared Miller would shortly be "back on the streets."

Houk, however, believed he had taken the only responsible course and explained his actions in a September 3, 1979, *Point of View* column in the *Lansing State Journal*. Houk argued that the absence of bodies and the fact that key evidence had been obtained under hypnosis would have made conviction difficult. He also pointed out that the families of the victims had given their approval before any deal was finalized. Houk wrote:

> One means of helping to insure that Donald Miller no longer poses a threat to the community would be judicial review of his mental status whenever he is released from prison. I have already advised the parole board to inform the Ingham County Prosecuting Attorney prior to Miller's release, should he ever be released, so that mental commitment can be initiated then.
>
> The citizens of Ingham County elected me to fill a position that often requires the making of hard decisions. Sometimes those decisions require me to make a choice between rigidly adhering to policies that I believe in and making humane exceptions. I made a humane exception in favor of the families of Miller's victims. I, too, wish a harsher penalty could be imposed on Miller. However, the facts and law do not provide

a likely way to do that. I made a hard decision in the Donald Miller case. I remained convinced that it was the right one for the families of Miller's victims and the community in which I and my family live.

Miller was denied parole in 1997 for the third time.

Three months after Martha Sue Young disappeared, there was another murder in the news. On the evening of March 9, 1977, Francine Hughes drove her four children to the Ingham County Sheriff's Department in Mason, telling officers she had poured gasoline over the bed of her intoxicated husband and ignited it. "I burned him up," she sobbed. Authorities eventually ruled that James B. "Mickey" Hughes died of smoke inhalation. Francine Hughes was charged with first degree murder. The so-called "Burning Bed" case was eventually featured in a book and made into a movie starring actress Farah Fawcett. Feminist organizations cited Francine as a symbol of battered wives and banded together to support the thirty-year-old woman's legal defense. The trial began October 26 in the circuit court courtroom of Judge Ray C. Hotchkiss.

In pre-testimony opening statements, Assistant Prosecutor Martin F. Palus said he would show Francine Hughes was having "an intimate" relationship with an unidentified man. He said that accounted for her actions against her ex-mate.

Lansing lawyer Aryon Greydanus was appointed by the court to defend Hughes. He conceded to the jury of ten women and two men that his client set fire to the home but that the action was not premeditated. Instead, he said, her act was done as she struck back "in the context of her experience" (as a battered woman).

Their marriage had been dissolved in 1971, but Francine had then allowed Mickey to move back in because he needed care for injuries suffered in a motorcycle accident. The prosecution announced it had thirty witnesses lined up and Greydanus promised fifty for his client.

Police officers and the Hughes children testified as to the continual and often violent beatings that Mickey administered to Francine. Mickey's heavy drinking frequently accompanied his violent actions, witnesses acknowledged. Palus eventually introduced evidence of the love affair, apparently discovered when three letters from Francine were uncovered as state police cleaned out the locker of a state Capitol security guard who had committed suicide. Francine testified she had only one date with the security guard, breaking off the relationship because she learned he had a wife and children.

The defense surprised the courtroom by calling Dr. Arnold Berkman, a psychologist and Michigan State University professor, to the stand. Berkman testified Francine was temporarily insane when she killed her ex-husband and was "at the mercy of her impulses." The testimony added an element of temporary insanity to what had appeared to be a self-defense motive.

A prosecution witness, state psychiatrist Dr. Lynn Blunt, testified he did not think Francine plotted her ex-husband's death. He said he felt the act was an "impulsive thing" and did not indicate premeditation. Greydanus immediately moved that the first degree murder charge be stricken, but Hotckiss denied the motion. Francine described her emotional state as trance-like when she poured the gasoline under Mickey's bed and ignited it. "I didn't really feel anything," she testified. "It was like I was watching myself do the things I was doing."

The trial went to the jury on November 3. After approximately five hours of deliberation, the jurors announced that the act was one of premeditation. But, Francine Hughes was not guilty, the jury ruled, because she was insane at the moment she set a fire beneath the victim's bed. Thus, according to Michigan law, all she had to do to win her freedom was to be examined by a state psychiatrist to determine if she required treatment at a state mental facility. Two weeks after the verdict, on November 16, Francine underwent a one-hour interview at the Michigan Center for Psychiatry at Ypsilanti. Afterward, Dr. Blunt said he would inform the court Francine Hughes was not now insane.

Just three months after Hughes set fire to her ex-husband, mid-Michigan was mourning the slaying of Lansing Police Officer Mac Donnelly. His heroism in stopping a bank robber's car in Lansing's Frandor Shopping Center, which contained four Michigan National Bank employees as hostages, and one hundred thousand dollars from the bank vault, led to the capture of the bank robbers and may have saved the life of the hostages. Donnelly was shot in the neck and died at the scene.

The four suspects were quickly dubbed the "Frandor Four." David Bellah, a thirty-year-old Indiana resident, was convicted in Circuit Court Judge Jack Warren's courtroom of killing Donnelly and was sentenced to spend the rest of his life in solitary confinement at hard labor. Two other defendants, both men, were acquitted of killing Donnelly but found guilty on kidnapping and bank robbery charges. The fourth member of the Frandor Four, a twenty-two-year-old Florida woman, accepted a plea bargain deal and pleaded guilty to conspiring to rob a bank. Interestingly, when Bellah was sentenced, Prosecutor Peter Houk stood beside Bellah's defense attorney, Donald E. Martin, as Judge Warren read the sentence. A decade later Martin succeeded Houk as prosecuting attorney.

Not all legal happenings in the 1970s, however, involved violence and complicated court cases. Three key events occurred in that decade that emphasized the commitment of Ingham County attorneys to the mid-Michigan community. On November 29, 1977, a small group of women lawyers met to discuss organizing a regional association affiliated with the Women Lawyers Association of Michigan. A steering committee comprised of Mary Fowlie, Linda Bruin, Karen Bush Schneider, Marsha Woods, Paula Woods, Quenda Story, Paula Zimmer, and Barbara Green was created. On March 20, 1978, the Mid-Michigan Region of WLAM was officially formed, with Zimmer serving as the group's first president. During its approximately seventeen-year existence, the Mid-Michigan Region WLAM has provided increased professional opportunities for women attorneys and participated in numerous community service projects. During the 1981-82 program year, the Mid-Michigan Region hosted the statewide fall conference in Lansing, featuring keynote speaker Gail Sheehy, author of the bestselling *Passages* and *Pathfinders*. Conference attendees also took time to honor two of Ingham County's most prominent women lawyers—school law expert Carolyn Thrun and State Law Library Director Charlotte Dunnebacke.

In 1979, attorneys Clinton Canady and Hugh Clarke founded the Lansing Black Lawyers Association. It originally started as a networking and social organization for black attorneys in the Lansing area, but later evolved into an organization participating in community-based activities, hosting professional development dinners, awarding scholarships to deserving students, providing financial support for meals for needy families, and supporting Thomas M. Cooley Law Students' participation in the Frederick Douglas Moot Court Competition. The annual professional development dinner program was named after the late Otis T. Smith, the first black to serve on the Michigan Supreme Court.

In the spring of 1992, the Lansing Black Lawyer's Association began publishing a quarterly newsletter, prominently featuring articles written by local attorneys that addressed a wide range of legal issues. Authors included in the first issue were District Court Judge John W. Davis; Deborah J. Gaskin, assistant executive director for an Open Profession of the State Bar of Michigan; assistant attorney General Lamont W. Walton; and Helen Pratt Mickens, associate dean at Thomas M. Cooley Law School.

While the black attorneys were organizing, Cooley Law School instructor Fred Baker was founding Sixty Plus, a clinic dedicated to providing senior citizens with the "highest quality advocacy, legal representation and community education." For the first three years it was a volunteer project, featuring Baker and thirteen interns—"Baker's Dozen." One hundred clients were represented in the first year of operation.

In 1981 the clinic was incorporated as a non-profit, 501 (c)(3) corporation by Cooley Law School, the Young Lawyers of the State Bar, and Lansing's St. Lawrence Hospital. At that time, the law school formally adopted Sixty Plus as its live-client clinical law program and provided a two-credit, two-term elective course series for student interns. Since 1981, Cooley professors Dorean Koenig, Kent Hull, Nora Pasman, Jim Peden, and Ann Miller have followed Baker as clinic directors.

By 1995, thirty-two student interns were supervised by four attorneys, under a contract to seven hundred residents of Ingham, Eaton, and Clinton counties each year. Sixty Plus has also been designated the regional legal ser-

vices provider for the elderly under Title IIIB of the Federal Older Americans
Act and the statewide center for Medicare advocacy for elderly residents of nursing homes throughout Michigan. Located in the St. Lawrence Hospital complex, Sixty Plus attempts to "serve those in greatest social and economic need
by prioritizing service so that clients with the highest priority legal needs obtain
the earliest appointments for an initial interview. All persons sixty years of age
and older are entitled to an appointment if they live in Ingham, Eaton, or
Clinton counties.

27

A CHANGING OF THE COURT

Supreme Court Justice Leland Carr had retired from the bench in 1962 but he was still remembered by justices two decades later. Chief Justice Mary Coleman, Michigan's first woman supreme court justice, presided at the 1980 ceremony at the presentation of the unveiling of the Lansing justices portrait that was to be placed in the hallway of the supreme court chambers. She called Carr "big in many ways . . . large in stature [with] a big heart . . . [a mind of] broad compass . . . scholarship with a wide reach . . . and a knowledge of Michigan law [that] was indeed encyclopedic."

She then called on Justice Theodore Souris, whose term overlapped Carr's for three years, to speak. Souris, considerably younger than Carr, recalled, "We never called him Leland . . . It was always Mr. Chief Justice, as it should have been . . . I can remember vividly the day of Chief Justice Carr's retirement from the bench . . . As we walked out of the room, I tried to express to him the feelings of regret I had [of his departure]." At this point the lumbering giant put his arm around his shorter and younger colleague and said, "Mr. Justice Souris, don't you think it's time you called me Leland?"

While the general public's knowledge of the law often comes from the criminal trials that are splashed across the pages of daily newspapers and featured as the lead stories on the local television news, much of the work of the mid-Michigan lawyer involves extensive research that is done far from the media limelight. In 1980, for example, East Lansing attorney Jack Coté represented the families of four men who disappeared in a rented, thirty-two-foot boat while crossing Lake Michigan from Chicago to Muskegon, bringing suit against both the boat's manufacturer and owners. Neither the boat nor the four men were ever found and there were no witnesses to the sinking.

Coté brushed up on his U.S. admiralty law, spent countless hours going over company documents, inspected craft identical to the one that sank, and even attempted to find the sunken boat. To cover all bases, Coté talked with Jacques

Costeau, arranging for the famed underwater explorer's television cameras to be mounted on lake bottom sleds and dragged along the boat's known course.

It took seven years to get a judgment, but Coté eventually established that the boat's air ventilation covers were installed backwards and tended to take on water in choppy seas. He also uncovered proof that the boat was designed without a bilge pump in its stern to remove unwanted water and prevent capsizing. In 1987, nearly a year after the bench trial, U.S. District Judge Wendell Miles ruled that Coté had proven the case of the four plaintiffs' families. The total judgement came to $2.9 million.

The media, however, focused more on criminal than civil matters. Michigan State Trooper Craig Scott was shot to death on February 9, 1982, during a routine traffic stop on U.S. 127 south of Lansing. The trooper was apparently killed because the car's occupants, felons paroled early due to prison overcrowding, thought their recent shoplifting activities might be discovered. The tragedy fueled attempts to reinstate the death penalty in Michigan, led by the trooper's widow, Lydia Scott. The attempt was unsuccessful, but two years later, East Lansing Police Officer James Johnson was killed during an attempted robbery and a neighbor woman was also shot to death. Both of the accused killers were convicted felons and one had served only ten years of a twenty-year murder sentence because of time off for good behavior. Again, cries for the death penalty surfaced, but failed to change Michigan law. Governor James Blanchard was influenced by the killings, however, and refused to give early releases to prisoners under the Prison Emergency Overcrowding Act. Many believe the refusal led to prison overcrowding problems and the significant expansion of prison facilities in the 1980s.

While the Scott and Johnson killings were painful for mid-Michigan residents, another incident on January 15, 1986, had spectators chuckling in the courtroom of Ingham County Circuit Judge James R. Giddings. Giddings was presiding at a jury trial of a Lansing man charged with carrying a concealed weapon when a juror passed word along to the judge that a defense witness "is wearing my shoes." Apparently the shoes had been stolen earlier while workmen were remodeling the juror's house. The juror was able to identify the shoes because of their size, some gray paint spatters and a peculiar fraying of one of the laces. Giddings excused the juror from further duty on the case, had the defense witness arrested, made him remove the shoes and had him booked into the city jail. "It was the darndest thing that ever happened in my courtroom," Giddings told the *Lansing State Journal*.

That same year, attorney Michael E. Cavanaugh experienced a courtroom incident that rivaled Judge Giddings stolen shoes experience. Appearing before the Michigan Supreme Court on October 8, Cavanaugh was representing the State Employees Association in a dispute over an interpretation of the Freedom of Information Act. When Cavanaugh made a humorous statement the justices all laughed. "Justice Levin laughed more heartily than the others," Cavanaugh remembered. "[He] always leans back in his high back leather chair as he hears oral arguments [and he] kept leaning back farther and farther as he laughed. Suddenly he flipped over backwards. As I looked at the court, there were six justices in formal black robes at the bench and one pair of feet sticking straight up in the air. The courtroom had become absolutely silent."

Cavanaugh wondered what he should do. "Justice Levin was going to be very embarrassed by all of this—if he was still alive. Should I just keep talking and pretend I did not notice that one of the justices had just tipped over backwards in his chair? Should I wait?" Chief Justice Williams, who was seated next to Levin, looked down at Levin and without a trace of sympathy in his voice said, "I told you that if you kept tipping back in your chair this would happen someday."

Justice Levin jumped to his feet, put his hands in the air and said, "I'm all right. I'm all right."

The court officer righted Levin's chair, the justice sat down, and in complete seriousness Levin said, "Mr. Cavanaugh, that was a powerful argument."

Two of Lansing's better-known attorneys joined forces in 1980 when Lansing lawyer Ted Swift agreed to become a visiting professor at Cooley Law School. Cooley President Thomas Brennan told the *Lansing State Journal* that Swift was a "gold-tongued jury lawyer and a very persuasive advocate in the appellate court situation. I think he will command the attention of the young people and have considerable classroom charisma."

Swift seemed to "command attention" everywhere he went. University of Michigan alumni knew him as the law student who smuggled a horse through a classroom and into the dean's private garden. The Junior Chamber of Commerce named him Lansing's Young Man of the Year in 1962 for his numerous community contributions. Just before the Cooley appointment, the East Lansing High School graduate gained nation-wide notice for staying a court order by U.S. District Court Judge Noel P. Fox that allowed unlimited gill-netting in Grand Traverse Bay. And later, Swift argued a motion in the Michigan Supreme Court with eleven pages of rhyme.

In 1982, East Lansing attorney Michael F. Cavanagh won election to the Michigan Supreme Court. A brother of former Detroit Mayor Jerome P. Cavanagh, the new justice began his Lansing law career in 1967 as assistant city attorney and served fourteen years as a Lansing District Court Judge. Interestingly, two years later, Cavanagh found himself in Ingham County Circuit Court Judge Jack Warren's courtroom as a potential juror in a manslaughter trial. Cavanagh said he thought it was his civic duty to appear, but Warren excused the supreme court justice upon stipulation of counsel.

Warren retired in 1986, ending twenty years on the circuit bench. He had previously served as a Lansing municipal judge, county prosecuting attorney and Lansing city attorney. Governor Blanchard appointed Ingham County Prosecuting Attorney Peter Houk to fill Warren's seat on the bench. Houk was sworn in by Supreme Court Justice Patricia J. Boyle in a robe he borrowed from Cooley Law School; Houk's new robe was still at the cleaners. Attorney Donald Martin replaced Houk as interim prosecutor, then defeated administrative law judge Edward Rodgers in November for the permanent position.

In 1987, Ingham County Circuit Court Judge Robert Holmes Bell was appointed federal judge in Michigan's Western District. Bell, forty-two years old, had been a circuit judge since 1979, serving previously as a district judge in Mason and as an assistant county prosecutor. Bell had a strong interest in Ingham County's legal history and had compiled an historical chronicle of the county's circuit judges. Unlike many Ingham County judges who were born elsewhere, Bell grew up in Williamston and was elected district judge in Mason in 1972. Bell was often praised by his ideological opposites. Liberal East Lansing attorney Zolton Ferency called Bell conservative but sensitive to human situations. Ferency said Bell was the kind of judge who insists you wear a tie in the courtroom, but who'll slip you one in private to spare your feelings. Once Judge Bell actually did lend defense lawyer Ferency a tie. Bell laughed when a *Detroit Free Press* reporter reminded him of the incident. "I am quite concerned that the court deliver justice and that it appear to deliver justice," he said. "To embarrass or intimidate anyone brings justice down."

The 1980s and early 1990s became the decade of firsts for Ingham County judges. In 1981, Claude Thomas, a former Lansing police officer, became the county's first black judge when he was elected to a district court seat. In 1985, John Davis became the second when he replaced the retiring Terrence Clem as a district judge.

In 1982, Michigan Supreme Court Commissioner Carolyn Stell was elected the county's first woman judge when she won a seat on the circuit bench. Six years later in 1988, Pamela McCabe, an assistant county prosecutor, was appointed by Governor James Blanchard as the county's first woman district court judge.

Then, in 1990, Lansing voters elected Beverley Nettles-Nickerson to the district court bench, making her the county's first black woman judge. A year earlier, she was chosen one of thirty "Leaders of the Future" by *Ebony Magazine*.

The year also saw Ingham County's first husband-and-wife judicial team when David Jordon became district court judge in East Lansing, joining wife Carolyn Stell on the bench.

Judge Stell admitted there was potential for conflict of interest, especially when her husband's cases were appealed to circuit court. "We don't talk about any of his preliminary exams," she told the *Lansing State Journal*. "It has caused some funny incidents. He'll open his mouth to say something and he'll say 'Forget it.' Or else I'll just say 'I don't want to hear about it. But it's really a non-issue."

Also in 1990, Attorney General Frank Kelley appointed Gay Secor Hardy as Michigan's first solicitor general—the first and only woman to hold that position. A 1955 graduate of the UM Law School, Hardy served twenty years as assistant attorney general in charge of the Health Professionals Division. She is credited as being the motivating force for the strict standards of conduct adopted by state regulators for doctors, nurses, pharmacists, and other health care providers. As solicitor general, responsible for all appeals on behalf of the state in appellate courts, she was determined that no assistant attorney general who represented the state of Michigan would be unprepared for any question posed from the bench. She videotaped all practice arguments so assistant attorneys general would be able to see themselves as the appellate judges would, and make appropriate improvements.

In late 1989, delegates to the 1961-62 Constitutional Convention held a reunion at the East Lansing Holiday Inn University Place, reflecting on the convention and the constitution's twenty-five-year history. Former Governor George Romney gave the opening address, while Secretary of State Richard Austin presented concluding remarks. Taking part in panel discussions were Lansing attorneys and former delegates Eugene Wanger, Tom Downs, and Glenn Allen. Downs told the *Lansing State Journal* there were many improvements made in the 1963 constitution, including the strengthening of the governor's office and the elimination of various agencies and commissions. "I think with the Supreme Court throwing out the unconstitutional parts, there has been a net gain," he said.

In the nineteenth century, attorneys such as Orlando Mack Barnes combined legal careers with lucrative business ventures. In the 1980s and 1990s, local attorneys were also using their law training to excel in other professions. Bill Long, for example, used political science and social work degrees, and later a law degree from Cooley Law School, to serve as director of the Michigan Department of Labor under former Governor William Milliken from 1975 to 1981, and later chaired the Public Service Commission from 1985-1991 under former Governor James Blanchard. In the early 1990s, Long went into private practice before accepting the job as executive director of the Lansing-based Michigan Federation of Private Child and Family Agencies in 1993.

East Lansing attorney and University of Michigan Law School graduate Larry Owen served as the chief deputy commissioner of insurance in the 1970s, mayor of East Lansing in the 1980s, and on the MSU board of trustees from 1985 to 1990. Owen ran for governor in 1994, losing in the Democratic primary to Howard Wolpe.

Donald Reisig, a former Ingham County prosecutor and circuit court judge, was appointed Michigan's drug czar by Governor James Blanchard in 1989. As a state official, he coordinated the efforts of thirteen state agencies involved in drug prevention, enforcement, and treatment. Soon after his appointment as drug czar, the Lansing-based *Lawyers Weekly* named Reisig and Lansing attorney George Sinas among the twenty most influential lawyers in Michigan. Interestingly, both men were associated with the Lansing firm of Sinas, Dramis, Brake, Boughton, McIntyre & Reisig.

More recently, in 1993, Michigan State University hired banker/lawyer M. Peter McPherson as its nineteenth president. While some faculty members had argued for a president with a background focusing on other credentials, many believed McPherson's law and business background was a definite plus for a university that had spent the last decade intermittently embroiled in turmoil. Interestingly, one of McPherson's first introductions to Ingham County law came through his jobs as a page and janitor at the Capitol during his MSU student days.

In 1989, the ICBA honored five more of its fifty-year attorneys at its annual dinner. Assistant Attorney General Rose Houk presided, introducing Judge Glenn S. Allen Jr., John Brattin, Fred C. Newman Jr., John N. Seaman, and Allison K. Thomas.

Allen, who began his law career as a clerk to Supreme Court Justice William Potter, was cited for his service as a member of General George Patton's staff during World War II, his time as mayor of Kalamazoo, his work on the court of appeals, and his contributions as a visiting circuit judge in Eaton and Mackinac counties during retirement. Houk added that Allen claimed he was the only judge who goes to work on a boat.

Brattin, who often spent part of Thanksgiving and Christmas delivering meals to shut-ins, was honored for championing the rights of minorities and the poor. Brattin, according to Houk, "has been mentor to many lawyers over the years, always willing to help those who approached him for assistance and advice."

Newman, who practiced many years in partnership with Bill Mackay and was an assistant prosecuting attorney in the 1950s, was known as an excellent lawyer with a great sense of humor. Known to his friends as "Fritz," Houk said Seaman practiced law with a simple creed: "Never try to mislead the jury, be sincere with them and they will do the right thing for you and your client."

Seaman, who founded a partnership with retiring prosecuting attorney Charles MacLean in 1951, was especially known for his expertise in estate planning and served as chairman of the Michigan Civil Service Commission. When he was not practicing law he was learning foreign languages, even becoming familiar with the language of the North American Ojibwa tribe. During World War II, he worked in the intelligence unit that broke the Enigma Code of the German military.

Thomas, an assistant prosecuting attorney from 1947 to 1948, is considered an authority in Asian history. His law specialty included business law, probate, and estate planning.

28

MSU GETS A LAW SCHOOL

It was the summer of 1994 in downtown Lansing and prospective jurors were showing their anti-government disposition as they waited to be called for circuit court duty. "You don't need to come back tomorrow if you're not selected today," said a middle-aged lady. "The court doesn't keep track." An older man agreed. "You really don't need to come back," he said. "They'll never figure it out."

Two days later, some of the jurors who decided to return were sitting in the courtroom of Ingham County Circuit Court Judge Thomas Brown. The judge quickly indicated he had strong feelings that mid-Michigan residents should serve on a jury when called. "It's your duty," he explained. When a local college professor protested he had too many students to counsel, too many classes to teach, Brown reminded him of his civic responsibilities and refused to excuse the professor. When a secretary said her boss could not function without her, Brown again refused to excuse.

After the jury had been selected, the trial concluded and the verdict announced, Brown thanked the jurors for their time. Too many people are failing to appear for jury duty, he said, and we (the court) have not been doing much about it. Brown said he had been given the job of taking action against delinquent jurors and that he was taking his new assignment seriously.

Six months later, the *Lansing State Journal* reported that Brown actually was ordering no-show jurors to appear and explain their failure. Warrants would be issued for those who did not. Chief Assistant Prosecutor Kim Eddie said the judicial system suffers when residents do not answer the call for jury duty. "We try to get a cross section of the community," he said. "If people don't appear, we can't."

Ingham County residents did not need much urging, however, to pay close attention to the legal battles of former football star O. J. Simpson or Detroit doctor Jack Kevorkian. Daily television reports provided extensive coverage of the

Simpson trial, while the print media splashed stories of "Dr. Death" and his insistence that assisted suicide was both legal and humane.

Ingham County had a trial of its own that created national attention when East Lansing dermatologist Gregory Messenger was charged with manslaughter for removing his premature infant son from a respirator on February 8, 1994. Bound over for trial by District Court Judge Patrick Cherry, the early 1995 trial in Circuit Court Judge Michael Harrison's courtroom generated visits from media throughout the country, including the television cameras of CNN, ABC, CBS, and NBC. The prosecution argued that Messenger should have waited for further tests to better determine the baby's condition before disconnecting the respirator. The defense argued that the family had the right to determine what was in the best interests of the child and that Messenger made an appropriate decision.

On February 2, 1995, the jury acquitted Messenger of the manslaughter charge. The verdict immediately stimulated debate in the media. The official Vatican newspaper, *L'Osservatore Romano*, criticized the outcome. "With this sentence, the first headstone has been placed in another monstrous cemetery for the burial of unwanted newborns . . . ," wrote theologian Gino Concetti. Len Fleck, a professor of philosophy-medical ethics at Michigan State University, disagreed. In an interview with *The Detroit News,* he said, "The jury's decision is reasonable, reflects a compassionate perspective and is probably the best that can be expected under the circumstances."

While the attorneys in the Simpson and Kevorkian cases received extensive criticism for their conduct from both colleagues and the media, such was not the case in the Messenger trial. When the trial ended on February 2, 1995, Judge Harrison made a statement, specifically addressing the professionalism of both the prosecution and the defense. He said:

> Before we recess I have several thoughts I would like to express. Number one, I am an individual who appreciates professionalism. I also expect professionalism. And although I am certain that is secondary to the matter which has been tried for the past two weeks, I hope that it does not go untold that this is a matter which was presented in the finest tradition of the legal profession.

> This matter was tried to the jury. The attorneys concentrated on the issues. There was civility to the witnesses and the participants. There was politeness to each other. There were no side shows. The lawyers did their work as expected of them.

> That is not to say that there were not a few rough edges. But they were indeed insignificant as one views the scope of this matter, and those naturally come from advocacy.

But I hope those who are critical observe and offer praise where it is due. And I believe that professionalism was demonstrated here. And I do thank counsel.

Assistant Prosecuting Attorney Michael Ferency and defense attorney Frank Reynolds both thanked the judge for his comments.

Two legal battles, not yet concluded by the end of 1995, kept at least some of the more than eight hundred attorneys listed in the 1995 Lansing phone book busy. Lansing implemented an early retirement program in 1992, allowing top officials the opportunity to leave city employment early with increased benefits. Charges that certain officials helped design the program, got it approved, and then took advantage of the enhanced retirement program, generated multiple legal actions.

The 1992 discovery that monies were being misspent by the Michigan House Fiscal Agency also kept both lawyers and courts busy. The result ended in several criminal convictions, a reorganization of the agency, and a Pulitzer Prize for two *Detroit News* journalists with legal connections—reporter Eric Freedman, a Meridian Township resident, is also an attorney, while his co-winner, former *MSU News* editor Jim Mitzelfeld, recently left the paper to study law at the University of Michigan.

Sam Street Hughes, former Lansing mayor and circuit court judge died on April 26, 1990. Jeanne Schulte Scott, a former Michigan assistant attorney general then practicing law in North Carolina, wrote *Lansing State Journal* columnist John Schneider about Hughes' respect for the "law and fellow human beings." She also remembered a favorite story about Hughes during her time as a public defender. In 1979, Scott was in court for the sentencing of one of her clients— a woman convicted of writing bad checks—for the third time. "Even after the third conviction, Judge Hughes, in Scott's words, "recognized the plight of this young mother with limited skills trying to make her way in a society for which she was ill-prepared by upbringing and education."

The pre-sentence report recommended that the woman be sentenced to three to five years in prison. Scott described the actual sentencing this way: "[Hughes] proceeded to lecture her on her need to improve herself and her life opportunities through preparation and education. He told of his own struggle to prepare himself against great odds." Hughes then made a puzzling reference to a school of cosmetology.

"He told my client," Scott continued, "how after just a couple of years of study and training she could find a job where she could earn her living and contribute much back to society. During his entire discourse, he never once mentioned the words jail, prison or incarceration." Hughes sentenced the woman to three to five years at the school of cosmetology. The school happened to be the Detroit House of Corrections.

"My client turned to me quietly and said, 'Miss Scott, am I going to jail?'" Scott remembered. "When I told her where the school was located, she replied, 'That Judge—he makes going to jail almost seem like fun.'"

Scott said she'd like to think her client stuck with cosmetology and came out of prison a productive member of society. "All things considered," Scott said, "It was the best thing Judge Hughes could do for her."

The Michigan legal community lost another of its most distinguished members when long-time State Bar of Michigan Executive Director Michael Franck died on June 28, 1994. A member of the ICBA, Franck was known as one of the leading authorities on lawyer ethics and discipline. In his memory, the Board of Commissioners of the State Bar of Michigan named their building in downtown Lansing as the Michael Franck Building for the State Bar of Michigan.

In 1992, Michigan Court of Appeals Judge Robert Danhof retired. An East Lansing resident, Danhof had served on the court since 1969. Governor John Engler appointed East Lansing attorney Clifford Taylor as Danhof's replacement. Taylor had served as an assistant Ingham County prosecutor in 1971 and had run unsuccessfully for attorney general in 1990. His appointment instantly made the Taylor family one of Michigan's most powerful legal entities—wife Lucille Taylor then being legal counsel to Governor Engler.

Over the years, Ingham attorneys have had a strong commitment to their community. Harry Hubbard, for example, was a participant and leader in dozens of mid-Michigan volunteer organizations since joining the current firm of Hubbard, Fox, Thomas, White & Bengston in the 1920s. He served as president of the Lansing Lions Club, as treasurer of the Lansing Hospital Expansion Drive, as a United Way board member, and was an active leader in the Lansing Regional Chamber of Commerce.

The tradition continues. In 1994, *Lansing Magazine* featured a story about Ingham County attorneys, past and present, who have made major contributions to their communities. Included were Camille Abood for his work with the Greater Lansing Food Bank; Lyn Beekman for his efforts on behalf of mentally handicapped children; John Bos for his work on behalf of the YMCA, the Michigan Capital Medical Center and the Michigan State University Foundation; Robert Drake for his leadership in creating Highfields; and Charlotte Dunnebacke for receiving the YWCA's prestigious Diana Award in 1975. Others mentioned were Stuart Dunnings Jr. for his efforts on behalf of minorities; Archie Fraser for his work in support of local service clubs; Beverley Nettles-Nickerson for her contributions to the United Negro College Fund and the Michigan Dance Association; and Harris Thomas for his efforts in promoting Lansing as an auto manufacturing center.

In 1995, a local attorney received one of the Lansing area's most prestigious honors—the Lansing Regional Chamber of Commerce's ATHENA award.

Helen Pratt Mickens, associate dean at Cooley Law School, was cited for her long-time involvement in the Capital Area Women's network and for hosting the *It's the Law* television program.

Sometimes the community contributions were not individual but group efforts. The Broom Hockey Benefit, for example, was begun in 1977 by a group of attorneys who decided to challenge the MSU hockey team in a benefit contest for the Boys & Girls Club of Lansing. Lansing District Court Judge Charles Filice worked out the details with Spartan hockey coach Amo Bessone. The 1988 Legal Eagles lineup included such local attorneys as Barry Devine, Phil Dwyer, Mike Otis, Kevin Cole, Phil Vilella, and Ken Frankland. The Legal Eagles apparently took the contest quite seriously, even employing a "ringer" in one of the earlier contests—former Detroit Red Wings star Ted Lindsay.

In January of 1995, a resource group reviewing a possible linkage between MSU and the private Detroit College of Law issued a report supporting the concept of a formal affiliation on the East Lansing campus. Administrators, faculty, students, and alumni had been periodically discussing a law school at Michigan State University for the past three decades with no formal action ever being taken. On February 22, the Detroit College of Law Board of Trustees voted to affiliate with MSU. Then, on February 28, the MSU Board of Trustees approved the merger. MSU had a law school.

Reaction was mixed. Most connected to MSU were jubilant. "We have fought long and hard, wrestling with the feasibility of having a law school," trustee Robert Weiss, a former Genesee County prosecutor, told the *Detroit Free Press*. Trustee Robert Traxler agreed: "This is really a jewel in the crown." Politicians and educators in Southeastern Michigan, however, were generally critical of the merger, opposing the move of the DCL from the Detroit area to East Lansing. Detroit Mayor Dennis Archer argued losing the law school would add to Detroit's problems. An article in the April 14 issue of *The Chronicle of Higher Education* pointed out the problems of a public/private marriage of law schools.

> This kind of affiliation is rare, legal experts say, because folding a private, professional school into a state-supported university can be complicated. "The task is not at all insurmountable, but, as they say, the devil is in the details," said Frank T. Read, deputy consultant on legal education to the Bar Association.
>
> Money and governance most often cause disputes between partners in public-private ventures, experts add. Indeed, state lawmakers with oversight of appropriation and higher education have already raised concerns. They say they will periodically audit Michigan State to insure that no part of the university's lump-sum appropriation is funneled to the law program.

In response, Michigan State President M. Peter McPherson has promised that the law school will operate wholly within its own tuition revenue and donations.

Former MSU President Cecil Mackey, who earned his law degree from the University of Alabama and held law professorships at Florida State University and Texas Tech University, was named the campus facilitator for the affiliation.

In an interview for the August *MSU News Bulletin*, Mackey said the architectural drawings for a four-story law building to be built south of Eppley Center and north of the MSU Cyclotron were near completion. The new structure would house separate business and law libraries, faculty, student and support staff facilities, and classrooms.

Mackey said the current entering class at DCL will spend all of the 1995-96 academic year in Detroit and come to East Lansing the following year. Students accepted for the 1996-97 school year will be part of the first DCL class to spend its entire academic career on the MSU campus. Official ground-breaking ceremonies for the four-story, 184,650-square-foot law building took place November 27, 1995.

"This is a truly momentous occasion," McPherson said. "This alliance between Michigan State University and the Detroit College of Law will benefit the people far into the future."

Another "momentous occasion" happens every year in the courtroom of Ingham County Probate Judge George Economy. Believing that adoption is a great way to start a family, Economy begins the holidays on a positive note by making a "big deal" of finalizing the year's December adoptions. As he completes the legal requirements, the judge lets the adopted children join him at the bench and even pound the gavel. As the press photographers take their photos for the next morning's papers, the children and their new families give each other congratulatory hugs.

"These families learned what others have the past eight years; Santa wears a black robe the last business day before Christmas," the Lansing State Journal reported after the 1995 event. One young adoptee was especially appreciative. "Now I'm happy," he said. "I've got a family that loves me."

APPENDICES

With Introductions by Eugene G. Wanger

APPENDIX A

An Oratorical Appendix

"If I were asked to state wherein the history of the United States differed from the history of all other countries, I would answer, 'In the influence which the art of oratory has been allowed to exercise upon the political and social development of our nation.'" The author of this statement, historian Hendrick Van Loon in his book, *America*, clearly had lawyers in mind; and in the early days most of our country's leading politicians were lawyers. The settling of our broad new land by a people devoted to democratic decision making, before the invention of electrical aids to communication and in the face of a significant amount of illiteracy, demanded—to an extent never before seen in human affairs—leaders with powerful lungs and substantial intellectual energies. And since many of the principal speeches were printed for wide distribution and attentive perusal by those who could read, a speaker's knowledge, understanding and way with words, in addition to his vocal abilities and sheer stamina, were also vital to his hoped-for success.

Making the Eagle Scream

In the time of our great-grandparents most Americans had reason to look forward with pleasure to the 4th of July. For decades an annual picnic that day in nearly every city and town had provided them with the opportunity to celebrate their exuberant patriotism, watch a parade, consume a wide variety of refreshments, listen to band music, dodge exploding fireworks and for the main event hear some notable—often a prominent local lawyer—deliver an oration extolling American independence. If they liked him they would say—alluding to the symbol of our republic—that he had really "made the eagle scream." A speaker's success, it was believed, often had a strong impact upon his future prospects.

In 1859 a thirty-five-year-old former Ingham County prosecutor gave the Lansing Independence Day crowds just such an oration. He was Orlando M. Barnes, who in future years would become mayor, legislator, candidate for governor, Shakespearean scholar and prison reformer; and who, by his business ability, would win—and lose—one of Michigan's great fortunes. His address, which follows, was reported by the press as "one of the best orations it has been our pleasure to listen to, and drew forth the general admiration of the audience."

The Spirit and Principles of the American Revolution

An Oration Delivered at the City of Lansing, July 4, 1859.
By
Orlando M. Barnes
(Reprinted from the 1859 pamphlet edition)

> *"A Free People must recur to the principle of their Liberty."*
>
> ———Montesquieu.

I do not entertain any hope of being able to make myself heard by every member of this vast multitude. I beseech your silence, however, and I shall trust for attention to the interest every American feels in the ceremonies of this day.

I congratulate you, my fellow-citizens, on the happy circumstances under which we have met to celebrate the EIGHTY-THIRD ANNIVERSARY OF AMERICAN INDEPENDENCE. While other nations are swept by desolating wars, and red with the blood of battle, we in Republican America are in the enjoyment of Peace and Liberty, and every individual and national blessing. Providence has kindly apportioned to us our existence at a most fortunate moment—a period when and from which we can estimate its vast importance to us and mankind. Our country has attained a name and a praise in the whole Earth. In every language we are spoken of with admiration. "We stand on commanding ground." Our resources, too, are vastly greater and more varied than those of any other nation—while on the ocean we have the most merchant-ships and the greatest commerce. There rolls not a blue wave of the sea over which our flag does not float; and, better than all else, wherever it floats it commands respect and insures protection. We have more telegraphs and railroads, more newspapers and printing-presses, more schools and colleges than any other People—while the degree of general civilization is higher than was ever attained before in any age or country. The fruits of our Revolution have been ripening and are being gathered. The TREE OF LIBERTY, planted by the toil and watered with the blood of our venerated ancestors, has sprung up and grown to gigantic proportions, so that it now casts its benignant shade over the inhabitants of earth, and the oppressed from all lands come and repose beneath its branches.

Amid all these happy circumstances, we have met to celebrate the American Revolution. I cannot dwell to-day on the events of that Revolution. I cannot speak of the separate glories of Bunker Hill, where the first considerable battle of that Revolution was fought; where our fathers first met face to face, in "battles magnificently stern array," the disciplined troops of England; where our Warren fell. I cannot mention the separate glory of Saratoga, of Yorktown, Trenton, Eutaw Springs, and the hundred other fields of revolutionary contests, where American blood was poured out, and American Liberty won. The blood that once crimsoned them has disappeared forever. The bones of the heroes there cloven down have crumbled to dust. Yet laurels that fade not away bloom on those fields. The snows of eighty-three winters have covered them, and eighty-three springs have melted it away forever; the flowers of eighty-three summers have bloomed over them and eighty-three autumns have cut them down forever; yet the glory of those fields has not passed away, or withered. It is fresher today than when they were covered with gore. Eighty-three years has but added to the luster of the Revolution.

Nor can I pronounce any eulogium on the statesmen and heroes of that time; nor can that be necessary. Our Father-Chief, the venerated General GEORGE WASHINGTON, the Father of his Country, the leader of our heroism, the glory of our nation, the example of virtue so worthy of admiration, I need only name, for he dwells in our memories and lives in our hearts. Nor are his generous associates scarcely less known and remembered. Their names are household words; the American Republic is their monument. So long as a tongue shall exist to utter their names, and a heart lives to which Liberty is dear, so long our Washington, and Jeffersons, and Adamses, and Henrys, shall not need eulogium to insure grateful remembrance. So long as the Republic shall be preserved and perpetuated, so long the men of the Revolution shall not want a monument. And every new State added to that Republic, shall be a stone added to that monument to pile it to the skies. And we trust that that monument shall endure to the end of time, and stand to perpetuate from age to age the memory of that event, and to testify its importance from generation to generation.

Indeed, has America a son whose bosom is not thrilled by her deathless deeds and deathless names? Has she one whose heart does not beat with a new animation in contemplation of her historic recollections? What emotions fill our hearts on reviewing scenes and incidents in our history, or fields of battle rendered sacred by glorious victory! For example, mark the visitor to Bunker Hill; and no matter from what section of this wide land that visitor may come— whether from the sunny South or chilly North, from the Atlantic or Pacific shores; no matter whether the fiery flood of youth, or the cool, tranquil stream of age, courses within his veins; and no matter whether yeoman or civilian, divine or scholar—as the light falls upon his gazing eye from that sublime monument which stands over the battle field, like a sentinel watching over the bones of fallen heroes, his heart beats with new animation; his genius receives inspiration; his soul catches the flame of patriotism; the spirit of the departed takes possession of him; and the man swears thrice again allegiance, and devotes himself anew and forever upon the altar of his country.

What I shall speak of to-day, more particularly, are the Spirit and Principles of our Revolution. It is these that give that Revolution its chief importance. The valor of our fathers would indeed have immortalized their names, but could have been of but little use comparatively, to the world, had it not established certain institutions and principles. A mere victory in battle is of small moment in itself. But if the battle be a battle for truth, the principle established by the victory is immortal, and must operate forever. *The principle of the battle is the soul of the battle.*

Events occasionally transpire which introduce a new state of things and give direction to long trains of events succeeding. Such was the giving of Christianity, the invention of Printing, the discovery of America, the Reformation of Luther, and our own Revolution. Such occurrences open new eras in the world's history, and are forming events having a spirit and principles of their own—creative powers, which they impart to ages following. The new principles form the basis for new action, while the new spirit imparts new life to the actors. Before these the old order of things is powerless and must ultimately pass away. How was it that Luther was able to stand against, and even triumph, over the awful powers brought to oppose him? How was it that our own thirteen feeble Colonies were able to stand against the strongest nation of Christendom? It was because they were planted upon the principles and animated by the spirit of new eras. There was a Divinity that shaped their ends and breathed into their nostrils new life.

Nothing can be more important for a free people, than to keep constantly before them the principles on which their liberty is founded, and to preserve in their bosoms the spirit which animated the men who acquired it. Montesquieu lays it down as a rule, that "A free people must often recur to the principle of their liberty,"—the principles on which its institutions are founded. So long as the nation is guided by the principle on which its liberty has been reared, and is actuated by the spirit which acquired it, the nation must be safe. How shall these be kept alive but by frequent recurrence to them? As time rolls on, a people are apt to be drifted away, by the current of events, from their original position and to loose their original spirit. When Xerxes had been expelled, in disgrace, with the remnant of his vast army, from Greece, by a mere handful of brave Greeks, he accounted for the event by saying that, "so brave and intelligent a people could not be conquered." And so long as Greece preserved her original principles and spirit—so long as she remembered her Thermopylae and Marathon, the declaration proved true. She was unconquerable. But when she had lost the principles that made Greece, *Greece*, and when the spirit of Thermopylae had died away, she yielded tamely to the invader, and the very fields of her glory became the homes of slaves.

Let us, then, on this our Country's Natal Day, recur to the spirit and principles of the event we celebrate.

First among them all I place the American idea of Liberty and Equality. The scholars and philosophers of other times and countries may have had very correct ideas of theoretical liberty; but theoretical liberty is very seldom practical liberty. Locke, the greatest and best philosopher of his age, formed a civil government for the colonies of the Carolinas, which he and his associates supposed embodied the true idea of civil liberty; but so wanting and imperfect was the system found that it died in early infancy. Our liberty cannot be said, in a true sense, to be the work of any man or set of men. It is the work of nature and events— the gift of Heaven rather than the creation of man. It is only where humanity has received a high development; it is only in an enlightened, moral and conservative age that free institutions, like ours, can prosper. The student in geology perceives that, to prepare the earth for the habitation of man, the Great Creator subjected it to stage after stage of progressive development. So it has been with the race, our own ancestors, and our own civil fabric. They had been subjected to stage after stage of progress before they could be deemed fitted by Providence for the happy residence of American Liberty. A people must be trained into free institutions before they can safely exercise them. No people can be transported from a degrading despotism to a state of high civil liberty in a day or a year—it is the work of ages. Our fathers were fitted for liberty by their peculiar discipline in their mother country; by the events of the world that preceded their existence; by the self-dependence, self-control, and culture they acquired as colonists; and above all, by the participation they enjoyed in their local governments. Fellow-citizens, I beseech you, do not put so low an estimate on your liberty as to suppose it at all compatible with barbarism, or ignorance, or immorality. Its holy character would soon be lost amid such associations.

There are two other errors, in regard to this subject common in other countries, and not wholly unknown in this. The one is, to suppose that civil liberty means *freedom from restraint*; and the other, that in a free Representative Republic the majority have *absolute* power. No errors can be more fatal to liberty itself. Freedom from restraint is not freedom; for where there is no restraint, right and security cannot exist. True civil liberty consists rather in the certainty and liberal fitness of the laws; and exists, let it never be forgotten, in proportion as the right is certainly secured, and the wrong is certainly prevented or redressed; in proportion as every man is permitted the just, the right, and the consistent, and is not sacrificed to or injured by others. If freedom from restraint be freedom, then faction-torn Mexico must be regarded as the freest land on earth.

Nor is it true that a majority in a free State have absolute power. If this were so, our form of Government would be an absolutism, as much so as Russia or Turkey. The majority, under our system, have all right to *govern*, but no right to *tyrannize*. They can have no right to take away the rights of the minority; no *right* to do a *wrong*. The rights of a minority are just as sacred, in opposition to a popular majority, as to a Nero or a Russian despot. Unrestrained power, in any form of government, constitutes it an absolutism. In our system, the majority are not supreme and unrestrained. It is confined and limited to legitimate rule. Beyond that, the majority and minority are equal. In any other view, a Republic is the worst form of absolutism, because it is a many-headed tyranny. Such is not the American Goddess of Liberty. She dreads anarchy and absolutism alike. She looks upon every human being as equal, in the rights given by nature, and to secure the weak as well as the strong,—the few as well as the many, she exacts of every human being obedience to the equal laws made to protect them in those rights. She would not, like the false divinity of the French Revolution, deluge the land in blood, in the name of Liberty, till there is not a mountain-top for her ark to rest on; but she delights in peace, equality and security. She requires a high state of civilization, intelligence, moral and religious culture; equality in the laws and in their execution—in their spirit as well as in their letter—and that, when the laws have been pronounced by the proper authority, that they be faithfully administered and faithfully obeyed. Such is American Liberty. Such the liberty received from Heaven by our fathers. It is this for which they toiled, and fought, and perished. This is the view of American Liberty embodied in the immortal Declaration which has just been read to you.—"We hold these truths to be self-evident, that all men are created equal,—that they are endowed by their Creator with certain inalienable rights,—that among these are life, liberty, and the pursuit of happiness—that to secure these rights, governments are instituted among men, deriving their just powers from the consent of the governed." These are principles that were never before the principles of any people. Philosophers, like Montesquieu and Sidney, may have professed some similar views, but it was reserved for the American people to construct institutions upon these principles. It is well for us to often recur to these doctrines of Liberty. There is no offspring of the Revolution from which we are so liable to be drifted the whirling current of events in this rapid age. We hold that all men are created equal—equal in what? Not in wealth, not in the adventitious circumstances that may have surrounded birth, nor yet in their physical, mental or moral endowments, but equal in their natural rights, equal before Heaven, and equally entitled by nature to the joys of earth and the inheritance of Paradise. The feeble man's title to his little strength, and to the avails of his little strength, is equal to the strong man's title to his. The poor man's title to his only dollar is equal to the rich man's title to his million.

Let it not be supposed, however, that because all are equally entitled to, every one therefore is equally fitted and prepared to exercise liberty. Fitness to exercise civil liberty, like fitness for any trade, occupation, or profession, must be the work of education. The inheritor of the largest estate is often found least qualified to enjoy or employ it. And civil liberty—the same as individual property—is liable to be used by its possessor in such a manner as to injure others. We must, therefore, and rightfully may, impose the same conditions on individual liberty that we do on individual property, require every one so to exercise and employ his own as not to injure others. And such conditions must be imposed alike on individuals and classes.

Second. The American doctrine of progress is next to be considered. Our revolutionary fathers were men of progress and lived in a progressive age. They labored in the performance of the journey from despotism to freedom, and from barbarism to enlightenment. But while they were men of progress, they were also strongly conservative. In them conservatism and progress were happily blended. The human mind in the midst of great revolutions, is apt to confound the good and the bad. A nation that has groaned for ages, under the yoke of oppression, is inclined to consider everything ancient as bad and deserving destruction. Thus it was with the French nation in their revolution of 1789. Almost every institution of former times—almost every idea of previous existence, fell before its mad career in an hour, and the people of France were at the time left like a shipwrecked mariner, tost by the wind and waves on some lonely island, bereft of all former means of life, and left to provide new ones as best he may. Far different from this was the conduct of our fathers. They moved forward in their work with the utmost caution. Revearing the hoary age of the past, they sought to preserve everything good and true in it. Interested in the present and anxious for the future, they endeavored, so far as existing institutions did not subserve their ends, to supplant them with new ones. Intensely progressive, they were also strongly conservative. They never regarded it as many would-be reformers seem to do, as the true way for a man to get rich, to first throw away all the property he has already acquired. *"Hasten slowly"* was their rule, and should be ours. Not everything new is useful, while most that has stood the test of long trial, is good and true. Truth never dies—"The immortal years of God are hers." Our fathers knew this well, and practiced accordingly. True progress is not to be made by casting away all the wisdom of ages past, but by adding to the store already laid up. A conservative age, too, is essential to the safety of liberty.

Third. The third characteristic principle of our Revolution was Nationality and Union. The breaking out of our war of independence opened to our ancestors a wider field for the exercise of their powers and patriotism. Previously each colony had been confined to its own local affairs. But a broader field at once broke upon their view; at the same time their separate weaknesses rendered a union of all, essential to the maintenance of the rights of each. These causes brought the colonies together to form the American Union; and the blood shed in its defense cemented them into a Nation. Experience soon demonstrated the utility of union, and rendered that which was at first but a temporary expedient, a permanent state of things. It moulded the colonies into a common brotherhood. Through this instrumentality they gained the war of independence, and placed their country among the nations of the earth; through it America has attained its present greatness and prosperity; through it alone can be preserved our greatness, prosperity, or liberty, and through it alone can we accomplish our future destiny. Standing as it does the instrument by means of which our liberty and greatness have been acquired and through which only these can be continued; dear and consecrated as it is by the recollections of the past and the hopes of the future, accursed be that man who shall bring to the celebration of this day anything less than National Feelings and Union Sentiments. Accursed be that man that will do less than love and cherish it.

Fourth. UNIVERSAL EDUCATION.—Previous to the rise of America there did not exist any system of General Education. The world owes to us the introduction of this institution as one of the public institutions of the country. Since its introduction here, the system has spread far and wide, and is everywhere working out its wonderful results. But its origin is American. The importance of this event to the race cannot be estimated.

Knowledge is power. But in proportion as men are ignorant and rude, physical strength is power. When men fought with swords and spears only, the man of the strongest arm was most powerful. Now all is changed. The man of the least physical strength, armed with the implements of man's invention, is as powerful as the man of greatest strength. Education is a great equalizer. But it is not in contending armies alone that knowledge is power. It is power over matter—it is power over mind. Turn your eyes in whatsoever direction you please, and you will see the power of knowledge over matter. Yonder mills, where our noble river is harnessed to so much machinery, these edifices, these beautiful fields and gardens, and the thousand things, within the scope of vision, are witnesses of its power. Knowledge is Aaron's rod with which the family of man had smitten the barren rock of nature and caused it to send forth its sweet waters for the sustenance of the race.

It was the design of our fathers that every American should he endowed with this power. It is a part of that endowment essential to every being who would be elevated to the noble dignity of sovereign over himself. Like the king on his throne, the sovereign over himself must be crowned. Intelligence and Virtue are the jewels that must sparkle in his diadem or his crown is not fit for his wearing.

The Spirit of the Revolution.—Such, fellow-citizens, are some of the principles of our Revolution. But it had not only principles—it possessed a spirit. Mere principles, without spirit in a nation, will effect but little, and amount to the possession of valuable means without a disposition to employ them. For example, Mexico, in her Revolution, professed to adopt at once all our principles. But she was unable to carry them out. She had not the spirit of our fathers; and you all know the miserable shipwreck she made in her attempt at Republicanism. A nation has a soul, a motive element, and it is that vital principle that preserves the distinct nationalities on earth and leads them to greatness and to glory. When Leonidas was about to close in the battle of Thermopylae, where he knew that he and all his associates must surely perish, he selected from his army but three hundred Spartans, and sending the rest home, he said to them: "Go, tell it at Lacedoeman that we die here in defence of her laws." Then casting a last look upon his beloved land, he exclaimed: "Ye rocks of Thermopylae, free mountains and happy plains, I shall perish, but ye shall remain." During three long days he kept the countless Persian host at bay; but died at last—yet died as the hero dies. The inscription placed upon the monument erected on the battle-field where these heroes fell, testified the appreciation of their countrymen for this battle and these sentiments. Nor has the firm rock of Thermopylae been more endur- ing than the name and fame of Leonidas. When, in after ages, Greece lost her liberty, it was not so much in consequence of the loss of her primitive principles as it was by the loss of her primitive spirit. And the history of Greece would be our history should we loose the spirit of our ancestors.

But we trust the soul of our nation is immortal. Indeed, there seems in nationalties a living principle—a soul. Why is it that poor down-trodden Italy, the renowned ancient mistress of the world—the home of so many mighty men and noble deeds—why is it that she is always, even now while I speak, rising from her bondage and struggling with her chains? It is because the spirit of Ancient Italia—O! most noble name!—is not dead, though it be crushed down.

"Truth crushed to earth shall rise again."

Even in recent times we have witnessed the progress of the Divine Goddess of Liberty through the seven-hilled city, calling up from her very ruins that same spirit that made ancient Rome mistress of the world. But never has there been a people into whom has been breathed a nobler animation than that which char- acterizes our Revolution. Intensity of action and fervency of patriotism were its characteristics. Was there ever a time when the human mind possessed greater activity than during and since our Revolution? Was there ever a time when the people were more ready to sacrifice every personal consideration for the public good? Bunkerhill and Saratoga, and Yorktown and Valley Forge are proofs of their patriotism. The bones of Revolutionary sires, cloven down in the battle for freedom, now reposing on every hillside and in every valley from Maine to Georgia, are proofs of their devotion. Let me present a few examples. Witness the spirit of Patrick Henry, the sublime orator whose soul could not bear to hear the clanking of the chains which were forged to bind his country in bondage, and whose eloquence was tuned to the notes of "Liberty or death," and roused the nation to hostile arms. "I know not what course others may take," said he, "but as for me, give me liberty or give me death." Said Jefferson, the author, and his associate signers of the Declaration of Independence, "And for the support of this Declaration, with a firm reliance on the protection of Divine Providence, we mutually pledge to each other our lives, our fortunes, and our sacred honor." Said John Adams, the strong right arm of Liberty in Congress, and the advocate of the Declaration, "Sink or swim, live or die, survive or perish, I am for the Declaration."

But the field of battle furnished the proof of devotion. Said the brave Col. Campbell, when dying upon the well-fought field of Eaton Springs, where his valor contributed so much to the success of our arms,—said he, as he was told that the shouts that awakened his dying slumbers were the shouts of victory, *"Then I die contented."*

I cannot individualize further. What was expressed by the generous and high-minded General Greene on a certain memorable occasion, was the sentiment of all. When in 1780, that brave man took the command of the Southern Army, he found affairs in a desperate condition. All the South was then under the control of British and Tories. Defeat upon defeat had weakened our cause; disease had invaded our feeble army and thinned its ranks; and in addition to all these, destitution and famine, the gaunt companions of death, conspired to ruin as it seemed the cause of freedom. In the face of every obstacle, Greene, with a feeble band of Americans, almost unarmed and almost destitute of food and clothing, confronted the powerful army of Lord Cornwallis. All but the truest and boldest began to regard the cause of America hopeless. The hearts of men were dying away within them. Greene was remonstrated with for rashness, and entreated to retire and leave the land to the enemy. But his sublime and heroic reply was: "I will save the country or perish in the attempt." And nobly did he redeem his pledge, as the bloody but successful battle of Eutaw Springs soon after evinced. And this was the sentiment that animated all—"I will save the country or perish in the attempt." Even the common soldier felt the inspiration. Even he was great in principle and action. True greatness, gentlemen, is not evinced by place or name, but by the quality and extent of a man's principles and actions. An undertaking too, inspires those engaged in it with something of its own character. It was so with the American Revolution. Great in itself, it inspired greatness in all engaged in it. This the common soldier felt. He felt that he was struggling in a great and righteous cause; and he felt also that something of his country's weal or woe hung upon his own efforts. He felt that centuries past and centuries to come were looking down upon him. These considerations inspired his mind with lofty sentiments and nerved his arm for great exertions; and the devotion he often manifested to his country was sublime. Witness him wounded and dying on the field of battle. When the contest is over, the victory won, and the clash of arms hushed, and he, pierced with the shafts of death, is left on the crimsoned field to die, far even then from losing sight of his country, as his heart's blood flows fast from his bleeding wounds, and the stillness of death is gathering upon his brow, he raises his last feeble glance to Heaven, and with the last breath he heaves from his chilling chest, he thanks the God of his existence that he has given him a life to offer in defence of his country. He dies for his country—but cheerfully dies. Like Leonidas he lies there in defence of his country's cause.

"The lightnings may flash, and the loud thunders rattle;
    He hears not—he heeds not—he's free from all pain;
        He sleeps his last sleep—he has fought his last battle—
            No sound can awake him to glory again."

Let him repose in quiet; let the patriot and the hero sleep; but, his deeds and his memory, they live forever.

Nor let it be supposed that these sentiments inspired the soldiers alone. It burned upon the tongues of the orators—the Henrys, the Otises, the Lees. It moved the hearts of the statesmen—the Jeffersons, the Hancocks, the Adamses. It sat, like the spirit of Inspiration, upon every patriot brow. Nor has it ceased to animate their descendants. Said the Quakeress, when told that Washington was dead, "He is in Heaven now, but I suppose he is looking down upon us, and that his spirit, though unseen, will still lead our armies to victory." The spirits of those Revolutionary sires still live and move among us. In the fields of doubtful battle, wherever the cause of America is endangered, the shades of Washington, and Green, and Marion, glide unseen to the head of the army, and lead it on to victory. In the legislative halls, whenever the cause of liberty is at stake, the venerable shades of Franklin, and Adams, and Jefferson, glide to the side of the champions of freedom, to inspire them with the wisdom of that olden time. "I seem," says Burke, on one occasion in the House of Commons, in England, "I seem to see the shades of our ancestors who once filled this hall, sitting around me." Thus the shades of our ancestors seem to stand around their devoted descendants.

These are the principles, this the spirit of that great event we celebrate. These are what immortalize our Revolution. These are the objects commended to our consideration on this anniversary.

Armed with these sentiments, and animated with this spirit, the Genius of the American Revolution went forth eighty-three years ago to accomplish its mission in the world. It is not the business of a day to recount what it has done. It has extended our borders from the Allegany to the Mississippi, over the Rocky Mountains and to the peaceful Ocean of the West. Our country has become, not a *sea-girt isle*, but an ocean-bound Republic. Its vast and varied resources have been developed with unexampled rapidity. Upon every hill-side have been placed the temples of learning, side by side with the temples of God. Every brook has been made to drive machinery. Steamboats have been put afloat on every river, lake and ocean, and the railroad—that great revolutionizer of modern times—has been and is being constructed through every part of our land, while the nervous system of the country—the telegraph—has been put into operation. The printing press is doing its magical work in every hamlet.

I cannot pass to my conclusion without stopping a moment to contemplate that silent and bloodless revolution which is now taking place in the world. The revolution of 1776 only gave a commencement to the actual revolution which has followed, and is to follow it. Contemplate this latter revolution for a moment, in a single point of view—that of railroad development. Anterior to railroads, nothing but seaside places, or the banks of navigable rivers, were susceptible of high improvement. Every place on the face of the globe that attained much civilization, had the advantage of navigable waters. But not so since that period. Commerce and travel are now passing from the water to the land. The railroad is now the most speedy, and the preferred means of communication. Not even the steamboat can compete with the rail car; the genius of commerce is no longer balked by the appearance of terra firma; but in her rail cars, drawn by her iron steeds, she hurries over the land more fleet than the viewless wind, and clothed in her bright garments of civilization, and laden with the riches of all climes, she bestows her treasures and confers her smiles on every corner of the earth; and I trust it will not be long before our beloved city of Lansing shall awake to the call, and feel the tread of her iron steeds, and share her treasures and rejoice in her smiles. Water communication is no longer necessary or absolutely essential to the growth of a large city; and on this spot, where the forest so lately reared its huge trunks and lofty boughs, may we not expect ere long a great metropolis?

The railroad, too, is a democratic institution. It is a great equalizer of the blessings and productions of earth. It is a great advocate for equality. By its operations the man in the remote interior is placed nearly on the same footing with the citizen of New York City. There is no luxury it does not distribute; there is no necessary of life it does not equalize.

Nor has the influence of the events we celebrate been confined in their operations to America. It has penetrated every corner of the earth and the sea. It has gone south the full length of the American continent, and struggled with more than fraternal affection to lead our southern neighbors to freedom. It has gone westward across the Pacific to the beclouded inhabitants of Asia. It has gone back across the ocean to the home of our forefathers. It struggled long for an abode in the sunny climes of France. It visited the seven hills of the Eternal City. It fought for freedom on the plains of Hungary, against the combined despotisms of Europe. It has visited the graves of Shakespeare and of Milton, of Hampden and Burke, and the parent stock has been instructed and consoled by the youthful descendants.

Europe is indebted to us for her railroads and telegraphs, and many other valuable improvements of the age, and for the elements of a new civilization. Everywhere that influence is now being felt, and in polar cold or tropical heat, it is everywhere leading man to a higher civilization and to freedom.

Go on, then, Genius of our Revolution! Redeem the ocean and the land from the thralldom that has too long reigned over them. Illume the world with the sun of a new civilization. Crown with your altars every island of the sea. Put the song of the redeemed on the tongue of every oppressed nation of the earth.

Hemans Dedicates the Courthouse

In the early days of the republic, and for about a hundred and fifty years, the county courthouse was the political center—and often social center—of the community. It frequently was the only building around with room for large meetings, and being most often centrally located in the county it became the natural gathering place. In many smaller county seat towns this tradition lingers on; and everywhere the status of the courthouse as the symbol of American local government remains. When Ingham County needed a new courthouse in 1902, it took the Board of Supervisors one hundred and eight ballots to choose the design of Edwyn A. Bowd of Lansing. It was completed at a cost of $96,678.00 and dedicated with a grand celebration on May 9, 1905. The principal orator was attorney Lawton T. Hemans of Mason, the most distinguished citizen that the county has ever produced. A Democrat in overwhelmingly Republican territory, Hemans served in many local offices, in the legislature, in the 1908 Constitutional Convention, as state railroad commissioner and twice was candidate for Governor, losing by only a few hundred votes. His *History of Michigan* was used in the state's schools for years and his biography of Michigan's first governor, Stevens T. Mason, established him as a scholar and an authority on the early history of our state and the Old Northwest. The *Lansing Journal*, in reporting the dedication said of Hemans, "He was eloquent and his address was received with every evidence of appreciation."

A Monument of Progress

By
Lawton T. Hemans
(Reprinted from the memorial volume published by the Michigan Historical Commission in 1917)

Mr. President and Fellow Citizens: The occasion that has brought together this body of our people is one worthy of the interest and enthusiasm we are giving to its celebration. It is the vaunting of no vain-glorious pride to say of the county of Ingham that it has become great in all the essential elements of modern progress, and that it represents in its citizenship the ingrained traits of the best traditions of this Republic.

In the dedication of a structure such as this, in reality a temple of justice, a building set apart to civic virtue, surely we should find in reverent thankful hearts the spirit that has brought us hither to become participators in an event calculated to stimulate the elements that have made for past successes, and that in themselves are our best guaranty of the perpetuity of free institutions.

Two years ago, on the 5th day of this present month, we met, and with imposing ceremonies, laid the corner stone of this building. It was a day prophetic of the beautiful structure we now behold, for even then we knew it was to be a monument marking the progress of our people, a progress that has been unfolding and expanding since the day when the first hardy pioneer reared his rude cabin within our borders. There is pleasure and satisfaction in the completion of a good work, but thrice pleasurable and satisfying is the completion of a work that combines utility with the elements of symmetry and architectural beauty, and which in its completeness bespeaks a lesson and a meaning. Within these walls the skill of the artisan may be visible for ages to come; but if the children of the future shall see in it nothing more than spacious halls and an imposing exterior, then shall more than half its cost have been wasted. This edifice is more than rooms and apartments where the treasured records of the people find safe deposit and public servants do official bidding. It is more than trusses of iron, beams of wood, and carven stone, it is a monument to the genius of our people, representative of their past, their progress, their patriotism and their intelligence.

It is told of President Harper of Chicago University, that once, as he contemplated the magnificent buildings of that institution, perfect in appointments and pleasing in design, he said, "All that Chicago University now needs is a past." To the citizen of Ingham County who is filled with love for its people and its fertile soil, this structure will lack no such endearing association, for, though new in point of time, it is none the less indicative of all that has gone before. The county of Ingham has 'been a partaker in no small degree in the progress and development which form the chief marvel of the time. More wonderful than our ultimate achievement is the fact that it is the achievement of scarce a life time, equalling if not surpassing in its total accomplishment the slow growth of former centuries.

It was not until the fall and winter of 1825 and 1826 that John Mullett, Henry Parke and others tore their way through tangled swamps and primal woods to set the governmental limits of our townships; a section which was then a remote quarter in the trackless wild within the then county of Wayne. By an act of the Legislative Council of Michigan Territory bearing date the 29th of October, 1829, the sixteen townships of the county were given territorial entity as the county of Ingham.

If an illustrious name has power to stimulate those who live under it to emulate the virtues of its giver, then it was rare fortune which gave us the name we honor in perpetuating. Samuel D. Ingham, of Bucks County, Pennsylvania, had reached his fiftieth year when his name was given to our county. He was a man of broad culture self-acquired, the heir to a name already honored in his State. On his own merit he had already won distinction in his native State and as a member for many terms in the federal Congress his commanding abilities had received national recognition; in the year of the county's formation he had entered to serve with distinction in the Cabinet of Andrew Jackson as Secretary of the Treasury. To the end of a long life, which did not close until the year 1860, he exemplified to a high degree those traits of character which have ever made for the honor of individuals and the greatness of states.

A few days after the county's creation, and on the 4th day of November, 1829, it and the newly formed county of Jackson were made to form a part of the township of Dexter, and attached to the county of Washtenaw for judicial purposes. Later its territory was attached to the county of Jackson, and not until June 1838 did it become an organized county, with the rights and privileges of the then other twenty-eight counties of the State. At this time less than nine hundred souls had found homes within our borders, but the hardy pioneers had left behind the blazed trail over which increasing numbers were soon to follow. With alacrity the widely scattered settlers organized the congressional townships to participate as such in the new political rights thus bestowed. Although but seven townships had been organized at the election of 1838, eleven were in existence by March 1839. Of the eleven, Alaiedon continued until some years later to comprise the present four northwest townships, while Phelpstown comprised the present townships of Williamston, and Locke, and Brutus, embracing the present townships of Wheatfield and Leroy. Although at the date of the organization of the county, Mason had had an existence of but three months as a platted town, still its few inhabitants, alive to the injunction of the Ordinance of 1787, that "the means of education should forever be encouraged," had made the erection of a schoolhouse their first duty after providing shelter for themselves. It was to this schoolhouse, through weary miles of trackless forest, astride his faithful steed, with saddle bags filled with the legal lore his head did not contain, that on the 12th day of November, 1839, came the Hon. William A. Fletcher, Chief Justice of the Supreme Court of the State, and then and there organized the judiciary of Ingham; a task in which he was assisted by Amos E. Steel of Onondaga, father of the present Sheriff of the county, and William Child as Associate Judges, while Peter Lowe, still remembered by the most of us, officiated as clerk.

The bar of Ingham County may well honor itself by honoring the name of William A. Fletcher. He brought to the trials and hardships of a frontier life the culture and training of an able jurist. At one time his circuit comprised the whole of Michigan outside of the then limits of the county of Wayne. He rendered signal service to the Territory and the State as Chief Justice and Attorney General, and lived a blameless life, a fit example to every man who would prosecute his high calling in the court he organized.

When we recall that the pioneer schoolhouse still stands and that of those who then lived within the county limits and were then of sufficient age to know something of the interest the event occasioned some have been spared to join in the pleasures of this day, we may justly feel that the event of 1839 was essentially modern. Yet from that time some years were destined to elapse before the township of Lansing was even organized or the Indian disturbed in his possession at the junction of the Cedar and the Grand.

Although the county seat had in the beginning been located and established at a blazed tree at the quarterpost between sections one and twelve in what is now the township of Vevay some three miles east of this city, the business of the county had always been transacted at Mason, because its buildings were those nearest to the established seat of justice. To this place it was eventually removed, by legislative enactment, on the sixth day of March in the year 1840. The first location was upon lands entered by Charles Thayer of Washtenaw, who at once upon the establishment of the seat of justice financed the future prospects of his holding by erecting a windowless log structure and creating on paper the ephemeral City of Ingham, which showed school sites, public parks and broad avenues; while it was not destined to become the actual county seat, yet if we are to believe the recitals in early conveyances it was not a losing venture, for several undivided interests were sold in Chicago and other places for considerations aggregating some seventy-five thousand dollars. Surely the lamb and the promoter were abroad in the land back in the days when the honest pioneer found spiritual consolation within the leafy aisles of God's first temples.

At the first general election, 260 voters exercised their franchise, and the county could then boast a full $700,000 of assessable values. A county so pretentious could not be expected long to be satisfied with the cramped accommodations of an 18 by 24 schoolhouse, especially when it, was required to do duty as a meeting-place for the board of supervisors, local meeting-house on

Sundays, and general gathering place for all other local as well as county events. The records disclose that in the year 1840 the County Clerk and Register of Deeds were housed at an outlay of $325, and that at the October session of 1842 by resolution duly adopted, each supervisor was made a committee to sound his constituency on the proposition of erecting a new county building. The agitation bore fruit the following year in the erection of the first county building, the building committee being authorized to contract for a building that should be twenty-eight by thirty-four feet, with eighteen foot posts, and that should not cost to exceed the sum of $800, with the proviso that if so large a building could not be obtained for the sum stated, that they advertise for bids for as large a building as could be built for the money. The committee had the good fortune to meet the requirements of the Board and in due season it stood completed, south and across the street from this edifice. Six hundred dollars of the contract price was paid in State bonds and two hundred dollars in the form of a conveyance of some village lots that had theretofore come into the possession of the county.

It was an imposing structure, surrounded by the halo of a yellow fence, to which James Turner, Hiram H. Smith and John Coatsworth did not put the finishing touches until the board of supervisors had exhausted upon it much serious discussion and earnest effort. When completed, the building was accepted by the narrow margin of 8 to 7. Whether the Board split on the color of the fence, or on the question of columns for the front of the building as proposed by Supervisor Skadan, is a question that may never be settled. For twelve years this building served the needs of the county for the purposes for which it had been constructed.

Not until 1848 had the county found need of that adjunct of civilization known as a county jail. In this year the first one was constructed. Whether there was any connection between this fact and the location of the State capital within the county the year previous, is perhaps a question too delicate to be discussed.

It was at the April election of 1856 that the voters of Ingham County voted the appropriation for the building of what is familiarly known to us all as "The Old Court House," endeared to most of the members of the Ingham bar by many a tender memory and happy association. It was in the old frame court house that John W. Longyear, Orlando M. Barnes and others began their careers of honor and distinction. While the date of its erection is comparatively recent, still in that day we could claim no more than fifteen thousand of population and less than three millions in assessed valuation, and of the funds required for the building of this twelve thousand dollar structure the borrowed portion was obtainable only in New York, where a three-thousand-dollar ten percent bond was of necessity exchanged for twenty-eight hundred dollars in cash. After the negotiation of the loan the Board of Supervisors, as though there might still be some question as to the risk of the loaner, passed a resolution to the effect that the county would pay both principal and interest when due.

The Old Building saw the making of Ingham County. For forty-two years it was the center to which our people came in their civic relations; here people from the more distant townships met, matured and kept alive those warm friendships that were a marked characteristic of the older days; within it young men came to the bar, and by patient judges were enabled to acquire the experience and develop abilities, which in some instances have given to Ingham County names high in the service of the State and nation. Time considered, the Old Court House stood to witness the most far-reaching social and industrial changes that have taken place in the history of the world. It witnessed the inception and growth within county limits of great State institutions bestowing the blessings of a liberal and Christian civilization upon the unfortunate. It saw the great State Agricultural College, and schools less pretentious, come into existence and under a wise State policy enabled to extend their influence to the uttermost parts of the earth. Its brief life went back to the days when Lansing, the capital of the State, was little more than a rude clearing, its population not above the limits of a country village reached only by the stage-coach lines that crossed its bounds from the south and east. It has lived to see it a beautiful city filled with every requirement made necessary by modern life, its thousands of population comfortably housed and sustained by the multiplicity of its industries, and an honor to the State whose capital it has proven worthy to be. The old building lived to be the silent witness of the growth and development of thriving cities and villages within the county limits. It saw the forests melt before the settler's axe, to be replaced in season by blossoming orchards and fields of golden grain, the landscape resplendent with its mantle of emerald, studded with flocks and herds that rejoice the heart of the husbandman. The Old Court House saw the cabin of the pioneer give way to the modern home whose owner owned the soil upon which he bestowed his effort, the fullest realization of free government. The county's valuation of $2,932,857 in 1857 is now exceeded by the amount of a round half million in the second ward of the city of Lansing alone, while the county as a whole shows assessable values close to twenty-six millions and a total population of 43,607 as contrasted with the 15,000 of the earlier date.

As the children of Israel under Joshua threw up a rude monument of unhewn stones beside the river Jordan as a memorial of Divine favor, so this building may be in some measure our monument and memorial to the blessings of our own retreating past. Into it we can truly say there have been built the hardships and privations of former years; that it stands as the memorial of a rough road safely traveled, a monument in which every ward and township of a great county has its part, from which every individual may draw the stimulus of gratitude for what has been so nobly achieved and inspiration for still greater hope and effort; for if this edifice breathes the spirit of our past, it equally enjoins that we as individuals put that spirit into the future. A monument that does not inspire to future glory is wasted effort. The Pyramids, the Parthenon, the Colosseum, mark the past and height attained by the civilization of Egypt, Greece and Rome, but it is a melancholy fact that they mark as well the depths to which they fell. The past of Ingham County teaches a lesson that can not be too often reiterated, a story that can not be too often told, it is the great truth that the rewards and successes of life are the fruits of homely virtues; that temperance, industry and frugality make for collective as well as individual well-being; that the strength of counties and of states rests upon the integrity of their citizenship and the jealousy with which they resent encroachments upon their honored rights and institutions.

If this beautiful building shall stand as a fitting monument for the future, it will be because into that future we shall have as a county and a people projected and transmitted the virtues born of industry and want, and not because upon the fruits thereof our children are content to live in luxury and ease. The lesson of this occasion is individual as well as public in its application. To each and all there comes the injunction that to the altar of civic need we bring the best fruits of our wisdom and our conscience. It enjoins upon every individual that amid new and changing conditions, both social and industrial, we hold to those great basic principles that have brought us the glory of our past.

My friends and fellow citizens, let us not seek the wealth that enervates, nor the power that tempts to wrong. Let us so live and learn that in the building of character, both individual and public, each achievement shall be only an incentive to still further effort; then will our monuments of the future be as have been those of the past, stepping stones from which the children of the future may look to the brighter fields that lie beyond.

Self-government has its tremendous responsibilities as well as its compensations. If each generation shall manfully grapple and solve its problems, then the summit of human achievement lies only beyond the veil; if, in luxury and indolence, we fail in the task assigned, then no matter how grand the monument with which we mark our present, the coming centuries may tenant them with people to whom their true meaning and significance is as foreign as is the mighty temple of Ramesses to the humble Fellah that by chance may wander through its ruined vestibule.

Praising the Pioneers

It should never be forgotten that the men and women who settled Michigan in the first third of the nineteenth century were well aware that they were making history. As the decades wore on, it was natural that those who succeeded—that is to say, those who survived—developed considerable pride in their accomplishments. By the 1870s they and their progeny had a tremendous interest in recording and commemorating their achievements. County histories, replete with paid biographical sketches, were promoted and written; and "pioneer societies" mushroomed across the state. The legislature passed a law allowing counties to spend money for historical purposes and, in 1872, the Ingham County Pioneer Society was organized. At it's fourteenth annual meeting, June 8, 1886, the "orator of the day" was forty-seven year old attorney Samuel L. Kilbourne, whose life is recalled earlier in this book. A graduate from the first class of the law department at the University of Michigan, Kilbourne, a Democrat in a predominantly Republican area, after serving in several lesser offices, was elected to the legislature in 1874 and was an outstanding stump speaker. Here is his address that day, a eulogy to his listeners, as reported by the *Ingham County News.*

An Address to the Ingham County Pioneer Society
By
Samuel L. Kilbourne
(Reprinted from the Ingham County News *of June 17, 1886)*

Providence has smiled on us and the added year sits lightly on the heads of those whose gold and raven locks have taken on purity's emblematic white.

Nature is in holiday dress and has put on its sunniest smile to greet you here to-day as you assemble at one of the earliest and best known of the settlements.

Of what shall we talk? Of the days of the log cabins and winding foot paths that ran around the hills, by the brooks and stream, through nature's deer parks, connecting the little sunlit fields, miles apart, where young wives and husbands were laying the foundations of that unit of civilization, the home, the family, where were found in humble simplicity all the elements of nationality, guided by and enlightened by the sublime teachings of the Book of Books, which never fails to comfort and instruct the humblest and the highest, that wonderful volume so peculiarly the teacher and the solace of man when isolated far from his fellows and a conspicuous object in the home of every pioneer?

Shall be repeat anew the oft told story of the journey westward from granite hills, the seaboard, the Keystone or the Empire state, a story that always interests, that is shaded with a mournful tone or clothed in words of joy as the mind of the speaker leads him or her to brood over the shadows or rejoice in the sunshine of the past?

Shall we stop to talk of ague, chills and burning fevers antidoted with copious droughts of boneset, smartweed, and cherry bark; of hot corn sweats, cold packs, in sheets wrung out in crystal springs, or shall we take the sunny side and dance on puncheoned floor to old Zip Coon and Monnie Musk or lead the blushing girls through opera reel from early eve until the sun glints in to shame the candle light, and the fiddler's chin rests wearily on the violin whose sweet notes flow obedient to the hand that involuntarily draws the resined bow, making myriad liquid strains that make the happy dance unmindful that another day has dawned; or shall we join the husking bee in moonlit fields and feast on luscious pies, by loving hands presented, or raise our small but patriotic flag to azure skies and rouse the forest echoes as we celebrate the nation's birthday.

The pioneer's life was not all trial, gloom and shadow, but rather had its full share of pleasure, uncankered by the jealousy that often comes of growing wealth.

True he had a constant struggle. Was that a hardship? I answer, as you will, "No." The primal law of nature is motion, constant and unending, with the penalty of disease and death imposed on violation of this law. The tree grows strong by struggling with the winds that buffet it. The ocean roars defiance to the raging storms and hurls its waters upward in the Storm King's face. The sparkling brook, checked in its course and held in idleness presents a pool of dead unsightly water. The grain that nature grows for us, struggles to maturity beset by frosts, and armies of winged enemies. All animal life runs the gauntlet of preying foes, and man, the captain of all creation by Divine appointment is here to lead and guide the fight and win victories from every opposing force.

You are all victors here to-day, and all around you are spread out the trophies of your prowess. Well may you look back over the field of battle and exult at sight of the conquest you have made.

Full fifty years ago your skirmish line was deployed and little lodgments made from which with varying success but constant yearly progress the struggle was kept up wild beasts reptiles, miasmatic poison and the dark browed forests, with hills for defenses and almost impenetrable swamps to bar your way, all at last have yielded and your silken banners float above the happy homes of those you lead to conquest.

At New England firesides this, now blooming, Michigan was known only as an ill-defined morass in the limitless "Far west."

Let us take a retrospect by which to measure our accomplishments. Seventy-five years ago only 4,528 people were within our States borders. Fifty years back we find the population had increased to 88,000 and now nearly two million prosperous wolverines uphold the dignity of the Peninsular State.

Our County's first presidential vote was cast in 1840. General Harrison received 265 and Martin Van Buren 261, total 526, showing a majority of four for hard cider.

Your lives were cast in a great age. The age or iron and electricity. The of the annihilation of distance, of the telephone and electric lighting. All these wonders are here and we take them as a matter of course. I suppose daily lines of flying machines will not astonish us next year.

Before departure for the West you had learned of the ordinance for the government of the Northwest territory drafted by Thomas Jefferson and to us an instrument second only in importance to the declaration of independence. The ordinance, you found, secured to the inhabitants of the region the most magnificent educational endowment the world has known, the setting apart forever of the public domain for the establishment of schools that should fit your children for the duties and the blessings of life here and, under Providence, for the life hereafter.

You builded temples of worship and temples of learning, side by side, and from year's end, as the morning's sun half reaches it meridian, bells answering bells all over this great commonwealth, ring out an invitation to the little wards Heaven has placed in our keeping to enter and learn where knowledge is free. $4,600,000 are expended annually now under the law to educate 570,000 children of Michigan.

The educational system is your grandest monument and no state has reared one prouder.

You behold a commonwealth not alone of lands and houses and herds, but of worthy men and women sprung from your loins and enjoying the fruits of your labor.

You cannot be unmindful that with the rank growth of our national tree, false doctrines and political heresies, like enervating suckers at the roots of the national tree, have sprung up and grown luxuriantly and being ungrafted with the buds of liberty have borne not harvests of golden fruit, but stunted, blotched and bitter apples of discord.

You helped found society to be governed by law and under its protecting wings equity and safety may always be found. Although this is a festive gathering I have ventured to allude to some of the things that pass before our eyes and greet our ears at every turn believing that those who reared the temple have the right to stop the hands that mar in the least foundation pinnacle. Public opinion is the great power in this country and that emanating from the society of the pioneer of Ingham Co. will be in the future as in the past enlightened, patriotic, and just to all men.

Shields Recalls "The Cross of Gold"

In 1896 a thirty-six-year-old Nebraska lawyer, at the Democratic Party's national convention in Chicago, delivered what is perhaps the most compelling oration in American history. Supporting Western silver against Eastern gold and ending with the stirring lines, "You shall not press down upon the brow of labor this crown of thorns; you shall not crucify mankind upon a cross of gold!" the relatively unknown speaker won his party's nomination for President of the United States and changed the political history of the country. His name of course is William Jennings Bryan. Attending the convention was a law student from the University of Michigan, Edmund C. Shields, who—as set out elsewhere in this volume—later became one of Ingham County's and Michigan's most important lawyers. Shortly before he died a half-century later, Ed Shields wrote down his recollections of that oration in the following essay.

William Jennings Bryan, The Peerless Orator
By Edmund C. Shields
(Printed from the author's original manuscript)

In 1896 I was preparing to enter the law department of the University of Michigan after having completed the foundation course I laid out for myself in the literary department. I had been a reader of political articles and editorials in the various papers. I was twenty-two years of age and had been following the newspaper debates on Bimetalism. The country was then greatly agitated over the question of free silver at the ratio of 16 to 1 and other monetary issues that tied into that discussion. It seemed divided into two groups: The conservatives allied themselves under the banner of the gold standard for the United States' Government; and those who believed in the issue of gold and silver at the above ratio. The Eastern States and their leaders were committed to the gold standard side of the issue while a part of the Midwest, South and the far West espoused the cause of free silver.

After reading many of the articles and editorials, I decided to go to the National Democratic Convention to be held in Chicago during the second week of July, 1896. There were two things that handicapped me . . . one was the lack of funds to pay my expenses . . . and the other was the obtaining of tickets to the various sessions of the convention. The first dilemma I solved by joining with an old schoolmate and running a stand in my home town on the 4th of July. My share of the profits of this venture furnished me my actual traveling expenses. I overcame the second obstacle much easier than I had anticipated. I went to the city of Detroit several weeks before the opening of the convention for the purpose of conferring with the Honorable Don M. Dickinson, who was then the head of a law firm in Detroit, and who also was one of President Grover Cleveland's close political advisers and was the Postmaster General in President Cleveland's cabinet. I remember well when I arrived in the cabinet member's office of a delay of about two hours while he was conferring in his private office on other matters with other people. The other members of his law firm and his secretaries sought to solve my problem, but I insisted on waiting to see Mr. Dickinson in person. About 12:30, when lunchtime arrived, he emerged from his private office with the others who had been conferring with him. Some of his office force had informed him of my presence. I had never met the gentleman before and cannot speak too highly of his cordial reception. I told him that I had no appointment with him but would be glad to come back any other day if I could get a personal interview, if my appearing that day inconvenienced him. I remember his excusing himself from those who were going out to lunch with him, and inviting me into his private office. I told him I would be very brief in presenting my request. That I had been reading about the great questions that were agitating the country politically and that I was anxious to attend the convention and hear the debate by the country's leaders, but that I could not afford to go to Chicago unless I could procure a ticket to the convention.

We were both standing in his private office . . . he put his arm on my shoulder and said, "You are the first young man in this State to make such a request. I can assure you now that you will have a ticket to every session of the convention. They will be mailed to you some few days before the actual Convention date." I thanked him and had stepped out of the office when he re-called me and said that he could not then make a definite promise to have me act as his messenger in Chicago but he was then considering that and that I would hear from him shortly if that could be worked out. If so, I would have a hotel room next to his suite and would get an opportunity to attend all the sessions. That any work that I did as messenger would not interfere with my hearing all of the Convention procedure.

In due time I received a letter asking me to report at his hotel and stating that he had made reservations for me. It was my duty to remain available where his secretaries could contact me with instructions to take notes or papers to the heads of the various delegations in other hotels in Chicago. My work as messenger generally began shortly after the sessions closed and some nights I remained on duty practically all night. This gave me an opportunity to see how political matters were handled on a big scale and also to hear the motions and speeches of the leading participants in the Convention.

I am perhaps one of the few now living who actually heard all of the famous "Cross of Gold and Crown of Thorns" speech as delivered to the seventeen thousand people that crowded the coliseum auditorium.

Mr. Dickinson favored the gold standard and championed it in subsequent phases of the campaign, so that as his messenger any recitals made here would not be prejudiced, one way or the other and particularly not on the silver side as championed by Mr. Bryan. Mr. Bryan's great speech was delivered on the day before the nominations were made, and of course, had a great deal to do with his being nominated at that Convention as his oratory swept all before him. He had a magnificent physique and a wonderful carrying voice. My recollection is that they did not have loud speakers then but whether they did or not, Mr. Bryan was able to make every word that he uttered, heard by everyone attending no matter where they sat in the auditorium. The above part of his speech was the closing part and the climax. Before that he had laid before the delegates a very strong defense of the laborer and small businessman and their rights.

Naturally, having the backing of Mr. Dickinson, a cabinet member, my seat was in an advantageous position in the center of the auditorium and just back of the delegates. The gold delegates were represented there by Senator Hill of New York; Senator Russell of Massachusetts and others. The silverites were championed by Mr. Bryan; Senator Teller of Colorado; Governor Thomas of Missouri; and, Governor Altgeld of Illinois. Immediately back of me in the Convention, seats had been arranged for a marching group sent there to represent the New York Tammany Group and as representative of the gold standard New Yorkers. By the time Mr. Bryan closed his address, his oratory had swept the entire convention. As an illustration of that I can repeat a conversation carried on by the leaders of the Tammany marching unit. They consisted of about two hundred members. They wore high hats, cut-a-way coats and light trousers and were stalwart giants. When quiet was restored, I remember hearing the leader of the Tammany marching unit say to his associates, "Well fellows, it's all over. We might as well go back to New York. There is the nominee of this convention for President and any effort to stop him would be useless."

Throughout his address, Mr. Bryan called attention to the cleavage between the big businessmen and the small businessmen as his words gained momentum and swelled through the auditorium he charged his opposition in the convention as talking about businessmen, when in reality they were talking about big businessmen and were leaving out the small businessman entirely and using the term business in too limited a sense.

He thundered forth, quoting, "That the man who is employed for wages is as much a businessman as the Corporation Counsel in a great metropolis. . . . The merchant in the crossroad store is as much a businessman as the merchant of New York. . . . The farmer who goes forth in the morning and toils all day, who begins in the spring and toils all summer, and who by application of brain and muscle to the natural resources of his country creates wealth, is as much a businessman as a man who goes upon the Board of Trade and bids upon the price of grain. . . . The miners who go down one thousand feet into the earth or climb two thousand feet upon the cliffs and bring forth from their hiding places the precious minerals to be poured into the channels of trade are as much businessmen as the few financial magnates who in a back room corner the money of the world. We come to speak for this broader class of businessman." As he uttered these words, you could feel that you were being lifted right out of your seat and that even those in opposition were having trouble in maintaining composure. The feeling seemed to be that at last the small businessman and the so-called underdog in life had a real champion in Mr. Bryan, and when he finally reached his peroration, it seemed as if he had assumed the height of a towering mountain peak as he thundered forth, "The Cross of Gold and Crown of Thorns" conclusion in his closing defense of the small businessman and the laborer. As his ringing words faded away it seemed as if everyone of that vast audience had been lifted to the rafters of the coliseum, so spontaneous and electrical was the effect of his delivery.

The following day the convention delegates nominated Mr. Bryan as their presidential standard bearer. When the echos of the speech that nominated him had died down bedlam broke loose in the convention. Delegates grabbed the standards of the various states and started a march around the convention hall. Fist fights prevailed in connection with these efforts but no one paid any attention to the outcome of these encounters because of the wave of enthusiasm that swelled over the convention in favor of Mr. Bryan's nomination.

As I looked from where I sat across the great hall to the top of the coliseum, I beheld a young lady dressed in white who marched down one of the main aisles and selecting one of the States' standards, started a stampede such as I had never before seen, and many convention experts afterward said, had never before occurred in any like gathering. That night there was gloom throughout the hall rooms of the opposition. My sponsor, President Cleveland's Postmaster General, refused to support the Bryan ticket and led a rump defection in the Democratic party that contributed considerably to the defeat of Mr. Bryan for President of the United States. Mr. Bryan appeared to be about forty years ahead of his time, but he laid the foundation for the betterment of the working classes which has led to the present great change for all engaged in business, whether large or small and also led to the spreading of the feeling of cooperation now shown by the heads of big industry to all those employed by them.

In my humble opinion, Mr. Bryan's speech was one of the greatest oratorical efforts of all time. Some skeptical persons may exclaim, "How do you dare venture such an opinion when your experience in such matters must have been extremely limited!" I will refute the charge of *limited experience*, and explain the basis for my contention. It has been a hobby of mine ever since my high school days to read of, study, hear personally, and recently over the radio and television, outstanding orators and preachers.

Anything political can happen in a National Party Convention. This was well illustrated in the Democratic Convention herein reported held in Chicago in 1896. I do not think any delegate to that Convention thought when the Convention opened that William Jennings Bryan had any chance for the Democratic nomination. In a period from 23 minutes to half an hour, Mr. Bryan changed the entire situation when he concluded his address. After his speech the conditions changed entirely, and no one else but Mr. Bryan had a chance for the nomination of his party. Mr. Bryan was not only the assured nominee, but the entire policy of the Democratic party in less than half an hour had been changed, and the control thereof delivered to Mr. Bryan, his friends and political associates for many years to come. He had proved by his magnetic and triumphant utterances that oratory could, and would change the results of the Convention and the history of his party.

APPENDIX B

The Making of a Lawyer

While a modicum of intellectual ability is generally regarded as essential, there seems to be no agreement about what other qualities best fit a person for the practice of law. This lack of agreement is paralleled by a wide diversity among members of the profession, a diversity which is conspicuously revealed in the following articles by two of the county's very eminent and successful attorneys, the late Joseph W. Planck and the still present Theodore W. Swift, indicating some of the things which occupied prominent places in their minds when they were training for the bar. Both articles relate to the proverbial saying, commonly first encountered in law school, that "The law is a jealous mistress," which is usually interpreted by law students to mean that "You won't have time for anything else!" Joe Planck addresses this concept directly and he was, after all, president of the State Bar of Michigan. Ted Swift. . . .Well, you might say that Ted addresses it indirectly, but you must read his article carefully to appreciate—to fully absorb—his point of view.

The Law Is a Jealous Mistress: A Popular Fallacy

By Joseph W. Planck
(Reprinted from the American Bar Association Journal for February 1938)

Blackstone said, "The lady of the Common Law likes to lie alone." To the contrary is the eminent authority of John Seldon: "The proverbial assertion that Lady Common Law must lie alone never wrought with me."

Thus is framed an issue of which Charles Lamb might well have disposed in the Essays of Elia, where he undertakes to disprove certain popular fallacies. The subject might well have proposed itself to one reared, as was he, within the classic walls of the Inner Temple. That the law is a jealous mistress has been heard for several centuries in Anglo-American law. It is, perhaps, time that this venerable ghost were laid.

Thackeray describes a great lawyer, who best exemplifies the fruit of the fallacy, in these terms:

> He was a man who had laboriously brought down a great intellect to the comprehension of a mean subject, and in his fierce grasps of that, resolutely excluded from his mind all higher thoughts of poets, all wit, fancy and reflection; all art, love, truth, altogether so that he might master that enormous legend of law. He could not cultivate a friendship or do a charity or admire a work of genius or kindle at the sight of beauty. Love, nature, and art were shut out from him.

What a libel on a great profession and how utterly false! The horizon of the law is as broad as human life itself, and all culture is its domain. All knowledge and learning is grist for the lawyer's mill. What is the subject of a lawyer? Let us hear the word of *Juvenal*: "Whatsoever it is that mankind does, their hopes, their fears, their angers, their pleasures, their vagaries, their delights, all of these things form the subject of our creation."

Dean Leon Green of Northwestern University Law School wrote as follows in discussing preparation for the bar:

> What formula short of all knowledge can be written? The student cannot slight his own language and its literature for they give him the power of thought and articulation without which he cannot function. Government, economics, and history in their fullness are all basic. Of all studies, they give meaning to law. The natural sciences he must have to give him understanding of the world he lives in, and to break the chains of prejudice which have so greatly hampered his forbears. Psychology, sociology and anthropology are gaining significance as the importance of human behavior and human welfare comes to the fore in the emerging order. And for purposes of a sustaining base, how can the lawyer survive without some integrating philosophy of all learning and all life?

A learned judge, Hon. Merrill E. Otis, holds that,

> To say that he is learned in the law who has committed some or many of its rules to memory, who knows not history and philosophy and science and literature and jurisprudence is to give a poverty stricken meaning to an opulent, ancient phrase.

Indeed, Lady Common Law imperatively requires a host of bedfellows. Some of them are decidedly practical. The law was the first of the social sciences and tends to remain aloof even today. The concept of natural law, immutable and preordained, long delayed the idea that law is a useful, social device. The end of the law may be said to be the attainment of social justice. It is only one of several disciplines striving toward that end. Taxation is now a matter, not only of producing revenues, but of exercising social control. The time-honored theory of the proper sphere of government is in the process of being re-defined in much broader terms. Lawyers today must be political scientists, economists and sociologists, as were Hamilton, Jay and Madison.

One more authority may suffice for the complete refutation of the ancient libel with which we are concerned. Lord Macmillan once spoke to American lawyers in Chicago:

> No lawyer is justly entitled to the honorable and conventional epithet of "learned" if his learning is confined to the statutes and law reports. It is the province of the lawyer to be the counsellor of persons engaged in every branch of human activity. Nothing human must be alien to him. "You are a lawyer," said Dr. Johnson to Mr. Edwards; "Lawyers know life practically. A bookish man should always have them to converse with. They have what he wants." Equally the man of letters has what the lawyer wants, for if he is to fulfill his role usefully and wisely he must have a mind not merely stored with the precedents of the law but possessing that width of comprehension, that serenity of outlook and that catholicity of sympathy which can nowise be so well acquired as from consort with the great masters of literature. In such company is found the corrective for the narrowness of mere professionalism. The lawyer does well from time to time to lift his eyes from his desk and look out of the window on the wider world beyond. There can be a too sedulous devotion to the text-books of the law and I do not commend the example of Chief Baron Palles, who is said to have taken Fearne on Contingent Remainders with him for reading on his honeymoon.

Let us recall a great lawyer created by Sir Walter Scott in Guy Mannering. Colonel Mannering is paying a visit to the study of his counsel, Mr. Pleydell in the High Street of Edinburgh.

"The library into which he was shown," we read, "was a well-proportioned room hung with a portrait or two of Scottish characters of eminence by Jamieson and Caledonian VanDyke, and surrounded with books, the best editions of the best authors and in particular an admirable collection of classics. 'These,' said Pleydell 'are my tools of trade. A lawyer without history or literature is a mechanic, a mere working mason; if he possesses some knowledge of these, he may venture to call himself an architect.'"

Let us prepare a grave both wide and deep and respectfully inter this hoary proverb, that the law is a jealous mistress, to which we have so long paid lip-service. In the same sepulture belongs Thackeray's lawyer. Requiescat in pace!

"There's A Unicorn in the Garden"

By Theodore W. Swift

(Reprinted from the University of Michigan's Law Quadrangle Notes for Fall 1981)

Theodore W. Swift, 1955 graduate of the Law School, is a member of the law firm of Foster, Swift, Collins & Coey of Lansing, Michigan. But he says his "real claim to fame" is the incident described in this article, which occurred in 1952 during his student days at the Law School.

An early grade of "A" in Criminal Law (practical experience) lulled me into the belief that I could continue the extracurricular practices learned in the Marine Corps while still managing to achieve scholastic fame as a 1952 freshman law student. When I succeeded in convincing the elder statesmen of the Ann Arbor chapter of the Veterans of Foreign Wars that my three month tour of duty on Vieques (near Puerto Rico) entitled me to membership, my social success was assured and my academic fate was further sealed. I was entitled to bring "guests" to the "club" which was located on Liberty Street, the closest real bar to the Law School. Evenings and weekends were spent enjoying the pleasures of the "VOOF" with droves of my Law School "friends." My personal popularity has never since reached such a zenith.

The zelous pursuit of happiness and rowdy behavior brought the year-end news that I was no longer welcome as a tenant of the Law Club; my academic standing was also labeled "precarious."

The combined rudeness of the Law School Dean, the formidable proprietress of the Law Club (affectionately dubbed "Little Orphan Annie" because she, like Annie, always wore the same colored dress; her choice was black), and the Law School faculty kindled a sense of bitterness which was not tempered by the blandishments of the good wife that I acquired in the summer of 1953. In those days, before protest marches could be staged for any reason, or no reason, my anger at the system was intense and unfulfilled. There seemed to be no way to cry out against the callousness and injustice perpetrated on the law students, in general, and me, in particular.

A protest vehicle was provided when I was invited to join the Barristers Society, a Law School "honorary," in the spring of 1954. The history of the Barristers Society is murky, at best, but the organization has been on campus, except for various periods of suspension, since 1904. The society has no constitution, no by-laws, no organized alumni, no official status, and no purpose. It persists to this day as a self-styled "honorary" for those who are doomed to be denied any other form of recognition. Each year the 25 senior members of the society tap 10 junior members who, in turn, select 15 more of their classmates for membership during their senior year of Law School. Dedication to the good things in life remains the prime requisite for membership.

I was honored by my invitation. I applied myself to the official functions of the group, to wit, the sponsorship of two dances during the school year and the yearly publication of an insulting and semi-pornographic document known as the *Michigan Raw Review*. The caption and the style of the *Raw Review* was designed to simulate the respected *Michigan Law Review*; the content of the publication was totally dissimilar.

The president of the Barristers Society named me as public chairman for the 1954 spring dance—The Crease Ball. The term originated from a law professor's comment that spring brought "thoughts of love" to law students. The students emerged from winter hibernation with a crease in their pants—the only time of the year this phenomenon was observed. Hence, Crease Ball. I was told to find a gimmick which would attract the attention of the law students, a notoriously lethargic and blasé group. My power was total and absolute; my budget was minimal.

Since I had been given a mandate to attract attention, I also sensed a personal opportunity to vent my frustrations at the forced rigidity of a law student's life.

The Law School was physically designed to allow a student to spend an entire three-year "sentence" within the confines of a singular city block. You were expected to eat, sleep, study, and go to class within that one isolated square of Ann Arbor. All classes were held in Hutchins Hall, the major cocoon within the mother womb of the Law School.

Hutchins Hall is a marvelous architectural achievement complete with terrazzo floors, marble walls, stained glass windows, and classrooms which ascend from a speaker's pit in a steeply rising and ever-widening fan-shaped series of benches. To an outsider, the building signified a reverence for the Law; to the inmates, the minute-jumping clocks, the lock-step sound of changing classes, the "screws" who doled out daily tongue lashings, and the thick walls combined to create the ideal environment for a maximum security prison. Another unique feature served to further the prison analogy; like every good reformatory, Hutchins had a courtyard. Unlike a prison, however, the 1954 inmates of the Michigan Law School were forbidden to set foot in the "yard."

I am told that present enrollees of the University of Michigan Law School are now allowed access to the interior courtyard. This open door policy undoubtedly resulted from the frustrations experienced by the recent dean of the

Law School, Theodore St. Antoine, when he was a member of the Barristers Society at the time of the events related above. St. Antoine will undoubtedly deny such a damaging accusation, but he was, in fact, a pivotal member.

The word "courtyard" does not give justice to the pristine setting which was hidden deep within Hutchins Hall. A more accurate term would be "garden." Lush grass was unblurred by weed or dandelion. Roses of varied hues and fragrance bordered the emerald floor and climbed the magnificent walls which completely surrounded the garden. The symphony of color was available to all, and was magnified by the view through the stained glass windows; but the perfumes of the rich loam, the manicured grass, and the dew-flecked petals were forbidden to the students. Those olfactory delights were reserved for only two mortals who shared the secrets with the hummingbirds or bees who might have been swept into the 50-foot square garden by a passing storm.

The dean of the Law School was ensconced in an office on the third floor of Hutchins Hall overlooking the garden. It was rumored, and later confirmed, that each morning the dean would open his windows wide to gaze down upon the lovely vista. He would then drink deep of the visual and nasal delights. The lone janitor, assigned the task of clipping the errant strands of grass and pruning the sheltered roses, was the only other individual with access to the yard. Perhaps that custodian shared the students' resentment of the garden since it was a compound of labor to which he had been assigned. Whatever his feelings may have been, his work arena was a pleasant one. The area was commonly referred to by the inmates as "The Dean's Garden."

At this time, a James Thurber vignette was experiencing a rebirth of popularity. The ditty, "The Unicorn in the Garden," became the subject of a short cartoon film which was then being shown to enthusiastic audiences in Ann Arbor. This Thurber story was to become the final catalyst for a plot which occupied the time and ingenuity of numerous Barristers—precious few of whom could afford a moment away from their studies.

If great oaks do grow from little acorns, this scenario was spawned by the casual suggestion of a fledgling barrister during an evening of frivolity at the Flame Bar. "Let's put a unicorn in the dean's garden," observed the sodden student. At that instant, an avenue was opened for the venting of myriad Law School frustrations; a device was hatched to protest the exclusion of students from the garden; and a method provided for a "boffo" publicity vehicle to promote the upcoming dance.

The idea was tested the following day in a more sober atmosphere. The appeal remained. Volunteers were enlisted to search for a proper unicorn. The genuine nature of these offers of aid confirmed by the aborning belief that law students were not worldly wise and were not suited to animal husbandry. After convincing our disappointed cohorts that the last live unicorn had been seen centuries ago, we decided to create one. Our research confirmed that a unicorn was simply a horse with a single spiraled horn projecting from its forehead. A beautiful cone, colored in the fashion of a barber pole, was soon created. Barristers were then dispatched to neighboring farms near Dexter and Saline with orders to fit the spike to the head of a willing horse. The initial reports of progress were glum.

Those few farmers who still kept horses seemed generally unwilling to let red-eyed law students attempt to fit conical spikes to the heads of their animals. In the few cases where this owner reluctance was overcome, the horses were found to be even more reticent to participate in such damned foolishness. One shocked city-bred volunteer commented, as he surveyed the newly broken skin on his arm, "I thought horses only ate grass." As defeat piled on defeat, a decision was reluctantly made that the unicorn concept must be abandoned. At the same time, it was determined that the idea of a plain horse in the Dean's Garden, albeit difficult, remained viable. Better yet, a jackass would be obtained, placed in the garden, and a sign would be draped on the beast of burden reading "You Bet My Ass I'm Going to Crease Ball."

This capital idea rekindled sagging spirits and once more loyal Barristers fanned out through Washtenaw County. We found the environs devoid of donkeys, mules, or asses (I don't think we ever bothered to determine the distinctions). This setback was taken with more alacrity than our original unicorn failure. Deductive reasoning, the hallmark of the lawyer craft, surfaced at last. If we, as exalted members of an honorary, could not grasp the distinction between a horse, mule, donkey or jackass, why should we fear that our law school colleagues, to whom the message was aimed, would be any more perceptive? Having bridged this logical gap, we turned our efforts to a search for a mere horse. If we could procure a horse, we would simply label it an ass, and an ass it would be.

As the date of the impending dance drew near, our horse search intensified. The reluctance of the farm folk of Washtenaw County to participate in our great endeavor was appalling. We never resorted to subterfuge or trick, however, and we told the horse owners the exact nature of our plan. We advised them that we could not accurately predict the reaction of those persons in power, and we cautioned as to the element of risk involved—if not to ourselves—then to the horse. We promised that: 1) the name of the owner would never be divulged, 2) no liability would result, and 3) no violence would be precipitated. We even pledged the sacrosanct beer fund of the society as indemnification to the owner in the event the horse was not returned in the same condition as delivered. I don't recall that we ever discussed how we would have utilized the animal if we had been forced to a purchase, but surely our ingenuity would have persevered. We were always big on barbecues.

Then came the news that one of our members had located a farmer with either an advanced sense of humor or an inclination to rid himself of a horse.

We did not question his motive; we quickly closed the deal. We agreed to a day lease of his horse for the sum of $50.00. The farmer, in turn, agreed to deliver the beast to the Monroe Street entrance of Hutchins Hall at 5:30 A.M. on the appointed day, and he also stood ready to transport the jewel back to the farm—assuming survival. In case of illness or accident, we agreed to purchase the animal for the sum of $100.00. Although I did not participate in the bartering for the equine mammal, and was not to see the thoroughbred until the day in question, we had obviously dealt with a shrewd bargainer. When I later viewed the beauty, it was clear that the owner had struck a sharp bargain. Even our paltry lease payment must have far exceeded the best possible offer obtainable from the nearest mucilage works.

Having secured the horse, we now turned to the problem of gaining access to the garden and to the ancillary issue of providing "cover" for the culprits involved. The operation smacked of a covert CIA caper. We may even have had several former CIA agents in our membership; in those days, a tour with the CIA after graduation from undergraduate school was a fairly common and popular sport.

Access to the garden was limited to a single door on the east side of the courtyard. This opening was located approximately 50 feet from the outside entrance to Hutchins Hall facing south on Monroe Street. Although Hutchins Hall remained locked, in its entirety, from early evening until approximately 7:00 A.M., access to the building posed no problem. Certain gifted students, such as *Law Review* editors and Case Club judges, held keys to the building. Sympathetic personages from among those ranks were solicited and a key to the building was readily obtained. But no one, we concluded, had a key to the interior garden door except the janitor-gardener and, possibly, the dean. Our attention, naturally enough, was brought to bear on the janitor-gardener.

We placed a full-time stake-out on the garden in order to determine who was assigned the task of garden upkeep. One of our agents was on duty when the custodian approached the door, opened the same, and proceeded to perform his duties in the courtyard. The key-carrier was thus identified. Further surveillance followed. The other custodial duties of the keeper-of-the-key were duly noted, and his day-to-day routine was carefully catalogued. By the end of a week, we knew where this gentleman could be found at almost any given moment an any given day. We had not yet devised a method for obtaining the key but standard CIA tactics were rejected. Although we were certainly the outcasts of the law school, violence and direct larceny were not in our bag of tricks.

The employee was found to be, from a check on his personal life, a hard working and conscientious servant of the University. He had no discernible drinking habits so the prospect of befriending him at some convivial watering spot was discarded. He did not appear to be particularly fond of law students and it seemed unlikely that we could simply persuade him to part with his key.

Because of his advanced years, however, it was deemed possible that he might be separated from his possession if caught in a stressful moment.

Since the windows of the second floor offices of the Case Club also opened upon the garden, it was decided that our plan to divest the custodian of his key must emanate from that point. During a period of changing classes, we threw open the windows of the Case Club office and heaved a sheaf of papers down into the garden. I then rushed to the aged custodian, told him that my very important term paper had just blown out the window, and begged his immediate assistance in gaining entry to the garden for retrieval purposes. Instead of handing me the key, he volunteered to lead me into the garden and even offered assistance in helping me gather up the papers. I was dismayed. "You have more important duties," said I, "so why not simply loan me the key?" "I would get the papers," I explained, "hurry to my next session, and return the key to him immediately after class." I described for him the first floor classroom where I would be during the next hour. With great hesitancy, he pulled forth his master ring, separated a single key from the collection, and handed me my ticket to the garden. I rushed down the stairs and into the yard, gathered up the useless papers, noted the janitor watching me from the upper window, and sprinted to my class.

My seat selection placed me next to an outside window of the first floor room, and after a proper passage of time, I pushed open the window for a bit of ventilation. When the professor turned to his chalkboard to diagram a "springing use" or some such nonsense, I tossed the key through the open window to a waiting confederate. Within the hour he had procured a duplicate, announced his return by a gentle rapping on the window, and in perfect prearranged harmony, lofted the key back through the window directly into my trembling hands. I exited after class and found the worried keeper-of-the-keys stationed directly outside the door. I thanked him profusely and returned his key. Later that day we fitted the duplicate key to the oaken garden entry and found, to our delight, that we had obtained a workable passport to the sanctuary.

The appropriate sign was made ready for the draping of the horse, and all plans were "go."

In a search of our membership, we found one Barrister who professed expertise in the handling of horses. He was delegated to meet me on Monroe Street at the hour of 5:30 A.M. on D-Day, for the purpose of lending assistance in the negotiation of the horse out of the truck, up a series of steps, into the building, dawn a hallway, and through the door into the garden.

After a restless night in my apartment, I answered the alarm at approximately 5:00 A.M. My wife, gainfully employed at that time as an Ann Arbor teacher, inquired as to my unusually early rising. Apparently fatigued from supporting me, she did not question my ludicrous statement that I was going to log in an early effort at the Law Library. Such a fiction would not normally have passed muster, but in the fog of the early dawn, she merely grumbled, rolled over, and I was on my way to a starting gate rendezvous with "Whirlaway."

I was not a total stranger to the deserted streets of Ann Arbor at 5:00 A.M. since, more often than not, that was the hour when I was winding my way home. In the soberness of this dawn, however, I was amazed by the apparent proliferation of police. As I traversed the distance to the Law Club from our lowly digs at the north end of State Street, I fancied that every passing person was taking notes as to my suspect appearance. I reached the Monroe Street entrance at approximately 5:20 A.M. and duly observed the dawning of what promised to be a glorious spring day. When, at 5:30, neither horse nor confederate had appeared. I recall a moment of introspection when I asked why I had became involved in such folly. The prospect of expulsion, and what it would mean to my wife and parents, teased my mind. Perhaps, I mused, neither horse nor companion would show so that I could cut and run.

As the familiar bile of cowardice backed up my throat, I heard the faraway chug of a vehicle. It was clattering its way from the south and soon came into view as it careened off State onto Monroe. In the gray of dawn, the shape of the vehicle quickly became evident. In earlier days, it must have been a fancy truck, but the vicissitudes of time had made serious inroads. It now appeared as a fender-flapping contraption with high-boarded sides surrounding the flatbed. As the truck lurched to a halt, the baggage in the back was rudely jolted and the quiet dawn was wrenched by a high-pitched and seemingly endless neigh. Except for Tom Mix movies, I had never before been so close to a frightened horse. The sound was ear-splitting, and I was certain that the entire town of Ann Arbor had been signaled to arms by the unexpected reappearance of Paul Revere's steed.

A weather-beaten and bewhiskered man-of-the-sod jumped from the cab of the vehicle (he didn't bother to open the door—there was none) with the frenzied look of a man pursued by the entire FBI. Without greeting, he dashed to the rear of the truck, noisily removed and dropped a back barrier, and backed Whirlaway to the street. Still without a word, he handed me the short rope which tethered the beast, hopped into his antique, and roared away into what was left of the night. As the backfires and clattering faded in the distance, the silence of the Ann Arbor dawn again enveloped me. I took stock of the situation and found myself standing in the middle of Monroe Street holding a piece of rope to which a horse was attached. The poor beast had obviously seen better days. His advanced years belied the label of "frisky," but the unusual hour, the unique surroundings, and the obvious nervousness of his appointed handler had awakened what little adrenaline still pumped through his spavined system. As difficult as it must have been for him, he began to prance and balk. For a brief period, while his spirits surged, he threw his hoofs into reverse and began to back towards State Street. I could not halt this progress, of course, but I knew better than to release him. During all of this time, my mind was racing for a plausible alibi in the event the local police stumbled upon the scene. My favorites, as I recall, were in the nature of "I had a hell of a time running him to the ground, Officer!"; or, "Do you have a report of a missing horse?"; or, "Look what I found—is there a reward?"

Whirlaway soon tired of his strenuous efforts, and returned to a docile state more typical of his octogenarian status. With a few soothing words, I was able to lead him, in a tentative fashion, to the foot of the steps of Hutchins Hall. There we stood for an interminable period. My problem was now purely logistical. I had the key to the outside door in my pocket but the rope was not sufficiently long to allow me access to the door while still holding the end of the rope. This was due to the fact that Whirlaway would not progress beyond the bottom step. In retrospect, I realized that I could have hitched him to a railing, Clint Eastwood style, while opening the door, but this thought never occurred to me that day. Instead, I continued to tug on the rope, and Whirlie continued to balk. During all of this time, my horse expert failed to materialize. I believe that one Ken McConnell, now of Bloomfield Hills, was to be my assistant. McConnell had a demonstrated law school record of being untrustworthy, and he continued his pattern on that day. He never did appear.

The beast and I were still stalemated in our private tug-of-war when help suddenly appeared in the form of a law school acquaintance whistling down Monroe Street on his way to opening the Law Club dining room for breakfast. This cavalier gentleman, Bill Van't Hoft of Grand Rapids, seemed not the least bit startled to find me there at that hour—tied to a horse. The coolness and quickness he displayed on that occasion foreshadowed the great success he has realized in later life. His opening greeting was casual enough: "Hi, Ted, where'd you find the good looking date."

In my frantic state, I had no time to be coy or to advise him that I was now married and no longer dating. Instead, I quickly divulged to him the grand plan and my obvious problems. He was immediately sympathetic to the scheme, and he also claimed experience in matters and manners of horse. He took control of the chaotic scene, issued brisk orders, and the program was back on track.

He first advised me that horses don't willingly climb stairs (a fact that I didn't know, but one which I have never forgotten). He excused himself for a moment, scouted a couple of nearby alleys, and promptly returned brandishing a huge board. When I asked the purpose of the weapon, he politely told me that he was going to give that horse "a swat in the ass." I cringed at such cruelty and remonstrated on behalf of Whirlaway. His reply was terse and to the point. "Do you want to get the damn horse up the damn steps, or don't you." His cruel rhetoric and limited vocabulary appalled me, but I nodded in the affirmative.

We propped open the double doors allowing entry to Hutchins Hall, and I then took a strain on the rope. My confederate slowly circled the unsuspecting beast, and I closed my eyes as I saw Van't Hoft go into his backswing. The noise of the impact was sharp, and the reaction of the recipient was sudden. Whirlaway bolted up the stairs, passed me in a blaze of speed, and clattered headlong into the foyer of Hutchins Hall. I was still tenaciously clinging to the rope as he spurted by, and I followed him without hesitancy—or the need of walking. The noise of those hoofs on the polished mosaic of the gilded hallway remains riveted in my mind to this day. Because the poor beast found it impossible to gain secure footing on the highly polished surface, the sound resembled the *Charge of the Light Brigade* across a shopping center parking lot. I was certain that the two janitors we knew to be on duty would come instantly to determine the source of such a clatter, but again my newfound colleague came to my aid. He rushed to the basement area to engage them in normal 5:30 A.M. idle conversation. Whatever he did, or said, it was sufficient. No one appeared on the scene in response to the sound which flooded the normal funereal surroundings of Hutchins Hall.

Whirlaway did not like the hallway and finally took a firm four-legged stance. I shoved and slid him to the garden entrance and opened the door with my purloined key. When the heavy oak portal swung open, the frightened animal spied the elegance of the dew-covered garden. The rest was easy. With a quick flurry of energy, and a shuffle step of sliding hooves, he projected himself into the center of the garden. I quickly tethered him to a stake set in the middle of the arena, and gleefully noted that the rope was sufficiently long to allow him access to all of the grass and most of the new budding roses. I wished him Godspeed, patted his bruised rump, and beat a hasty retreat.

All of this was done after I had hung on him the appropriate sign announcing the upcoming social event. It was not the blanket of black-eyed susans normally hung on a Preakness winner, but Whirlaway did not seem insulted. He was not accustomed, I am certain, to the usual amenities of the winner's circle.

After a quick breakfast at a local beanery, I returned to Hutchins Hall to survey my work. At 7:45 A.M., with a trace of a smile on his face, Whirlaway was busily engaged in reducing the lawn to a stubble. I posted myself by the Law Club entrance to Hutchins Hall to await the somnambulant students destined to arrive for 8:00 A.M. classes. They came in their usual aimless gait—ladened with books and heavy of eye—retracing, by rote, their steps to the classroom. Most looked straight ahead and, for a moment, I was afraid that no one would glance into the forbidden garden. At last, a more alert specimen appeared. For some reason, he glanced into the garden and his double take was worthy of the late Lou Costello, the master of said gesture. He actually rubbed his eyes first to make certain that he had seen what he had thought he had seen. Once he had determined that his eyes had not failed him, he pressed his face to the window and explained, "I'll be a son-of-a-bitch, there's a unicorn in the Dean's Garden—eating rosebuds!" I could not have written a better line, and but for the profanity, it was an exact quote from Thurber's opening passage. A whisper could normally be heard within the confines of Hutchins Hall at 8:00 A.M., but his exclamation ricocheted through the building. Everyone dashed to the windows to verify the presence of Whirlaway, and the 8:00 classes, as well as all subsequent morning classes, were undercut by the exclamations of delight and surprise. The news of his presence blazed through the Law School and spilled over into the undergraduate ranks. Soon huge crowds were gathered at the courtyard windows to observe Whirlaway at his morning pastoral pleasure.

The Barristers now reached the third and final stage of the operation—The Cover. We had carefully gauged the principals involved, and we had programmed their expected reactions to our heinous deed. The anticipated response set in shortly after 9:00 A.M. when the dean arrived at his office. In accordance with his usual format, he walked to the window, swung it open to enjoy the beauties of the day, glanced into the garden, and became hysterical. Upon regaining temporary control, he issued two orders. The keeper-of-the-key was to be immediately produced in the dean's office as was the president of the nefarious Barristers Society.

Our leader was one James (Buck) Buchanan, and he immediately responded to the edict. The dean was furious and demanded to know why the Barristers Society had committed such a travesty. Buchanan denied any involvement on the part of the society, and joined the dean in condemning the reprehensible misdeed. On behalf of the Barristers, he went the extra mile and volunteered to enlist the membership in removing the offensive animal at an appropriate time. The dean replied that the appropriate time was now. Buchanan countered by saying that immediate removal was impossible since the members were in class and could not possibly be assembled until the noon hour. Noon was not sufficient for the dean and he demanded that the animal be removed by 11:00 A.M., "or else." As Buchanan was about to leave, the dean added this comment: "Not only must the beast be removed, but all of his leavings as well." His reference, of course, was to the numerous road apples that Whirlaway had deposited in apparent violent reaction to his rich and unaccustomed diet of bluegrass and roses.

In his second angry response to the insult of the garden invasion, the dean ordered the immediate firing of the errant key keeper.

By 10:00 the ever aggressive *Michigan Daily* had reporters an the scene. A photograph was taken of Whirlaway in all his splendor. The local correspondent of *The Detroit Free Press* even called to interview the dean. When the amused reaction of the outside world became apparent, the dean's normal unflappable serenity returned. Buchanan was summoned from a second class to again appear before the dean. He was asked how the "removal and disposal plan" was coming, and Buchanan again noted that the time restrictions were too difficult to meet.

"We are trying to locate the owner of this stray, sir, and we're attempting to find volunteers to deal with this animal and his belongings. We need time, sir." The dean relented and in a soft voice, accompanied by forced smile, he said, "I love a joke, but that animal must be out of there by noon and all of those other things must be gone, too."

"Yes sir."

"If the Barristers Society didn't do this, who do you think perpetrated such a criminal act?"

"I really don't know sir, I just can't believe that any law student would be involved in such a thing. That sign about Crease Ball is an obvious attempt to shift the blame to the Barristers Society."

"By the way, what is the Barristers Society?" asked the dean.

"It's a form of study group, dean," said Buchanan in his parting shot.

The rumor was leaked to the *Daily* that the dean, in reaction to the horse, had fired the custodian. When press inquiries began to be directed to the law school, the janitor was promptly told to "return to work with no comment." The anxious farmer was contacted, and the mop-up operation commenced. At noon, a distinguished band of law students began a pilgrimage into the sacrosanct garden. (We were not dumb enough to produce our own key.) We suspected that whoever appeared would be under close surveillance from above, via field glasses, and for this restoration phase we selected our most credible members. Only persons of high academic standing, *Law Review* credentials, or Case Club victors, were chosen to participate. All were attired in coats and ties, the normal dress for serious seekers of the truth. We led with our ace-in-the-hole, Theodore St. Antoine, *supra.* He was then editor-in-chief of the *Michigan Law Review* and winner of the prestigious Campbell Case Club competition. He carried the shovel, and was primarily responsible for removing the "leavings." We even draped St. Antoine with a sign indicating that he, too, was going to Crease Ball. Whirlaway, suffering from indigestion, was led as quietly back to his waiting van as his flatulence would allow. The owner seemed disappointed that Whirlaway was returned in such excellent condition; his dreams of forfeiting our bond had been shattered.

The picture of Whirlaway ran in the *Daily* the next morning with the following caption:

> By 7:00 A.M. yesterday, the horse above had appeared in the courtyard of Hutchins Hall at the Law School to advertise the Barristers Club's Crease Ball . . . Staked in the middle of the courtyard . . . and entirely surrounded by the Law School building, the question of how the horse got into the courtyard remained unanswered.

Although the dean had professed that he could "take a joke," we did not believe that the mere changing of the lock allowing entrance to the garden marked the end of the event. We felt that an investigation was being conducted, and that the dean was determined to resolve the question of how the horse gained entry into his garden. We decided to implement our "cover" scenario to protect the more vulnerable members of the society from disciplinary measures. This plan was designed to obfuscate the trail of the prime suspects and to thwart and confuse the inquisitors who were hot on the trail of those responsible for this deed.

Since a minimal investigation would have revealed my long personal history of anti-social behavior, I mailed a previously drafted letter to the *Michigan Daily*. The letter was printed in its entirety on the 1st day of May, 1954, the morning after the ball. It read, in part, as follows:

> In view of the really serious matters which your editorial page has featured this week, I hesitate in submitting this letter . . .

> I am writing to protest the printing of the picture in Wednesday's *Daily* which featured a horse. Evidently some of the editors of the *Daily* seem to feel that there is something newsworthy about the fact that a modern day unicorn made an appearance in the sanctuary of the Hutchins Hall courtyard. Perhaps there was a certain amount of humour involved in the situation. Be that as it may, I nevertheless stand opposed to any publicity being furnished for this prank.

> Obviously some misguided and juvenile law student taxed his limited mental capabilities to the hilt to perpetuate this hoax. Is such a feat worthy of a picture in your paper? Why do you pump this young rascal's over-inflated ego with indirect praise? Who knows what your coverage may do to spur him on to further deeds of small meaning?

> The University of Michigan's Law School has long shared a reputation with Harvard University as the top legal institution in the land. As such, we stand in a position which commands respect and demands a comparable duty from the students. Such acts do not, needless to say, add to this reputation . . . What serious student faced with choosing his school would consider Michigan after reading of the "Unicorn in the Garden" affair.

> . . . By your poor choice of what is news, you have added to the rush of poorly planned activity which seems to have swept through the Law School as of late.

> Viewed in a serious light, and regardless of the fact that it was placed there to promote Crease Ball (which I shall not attend), the

whole incident is deplorable and should be ignored by all serious students and all self-respecting newspapers. In my eyes you have breached a duty to your University.

—*Ted W. Swift*—

The printing of the letter brought me my only personal contact with the dean during my three years in Ann Arbor. It was not a personal audience, but a phone call in which the dean thanked me for my views and congratulated me on my good judgment. Obviously I had diverted him, at least for the time being.

But we were not done. At that time, in our University of Michigan Junior Law School class, we had two outstanding students in the form of Eugene Alkema and Robert Fiske. Alkema had already attracted considerable attention within the Law School because of his impeccable appearance, diligent study habits, and spectacular academic performance. At that point in his Law School career he had received nothing but "A's." As I was told, the dean himself had been the only previous student to graduate from the Law School with a perfect academic record.

Fiske was running academically only a bit behind Alkema, writing for the *Law Review*, and playing superb hockey for the Law School team. He also carried a certain mystique in that he had graduated from Yale and had chosen to come to Michigan for his law training. While we were curious about his Yale background, the dean revered it. The dean always liked the idea of Yale men coming to Michigan.

Alkema and Fiske, in order to make the subterfuge complete, responded with their own letters to the *Michigan Daily*. Fiske's letter was printed on May 7, 1954. His comments, printed below, were designed to thoroughly confuse our pursuers.

Mr. Swift's letter of April 30th came as a great surprise to me, for I had not expected to find such an attitude in a fellow student. As a law student myself, I found the "Unicorn in the Garden" a highly humorous distraction from the ordinary law school life, and think that the instigator of this ingenious act, whoever he may be, should be highly commended. I don't believe I had ever heard of Mr. Swift until I read his letter, but he obviously appears to be the type of "books for books sake" student who, in his quest for legal dignity, would perhaps have been better off to have chosen the Harvard Law School, where such "juvenile" disruptions of the academic are unheard of. However, since the die has been cast, and Mr. Swift is stuck with Michigan (and vice-versa), all I can do is suggest that he might find life around here a lot more enjoyable if he would occasionally take some time off from his conscientious pursuit of the law, and have a little fun.

—*Robert B. Fiske, Jr., '55L*—

P.S. As for the Crease Ball, I think I can safely speak for all who attended in saying that it was a roaring success—in spite of the absence of Mr. Swift.

While the Dean and faculty were attempting to sort out the confusing Swift-Fiske positions. Alkema joined the media blitz in the May 8 issue of the *Daily*. He went a bit beyond the required, in my view, since he chose to refer to an unfortunate incident of my freshman year involving skyrockets launched from the Law School roof in the general direction of President Hatcher's home. The letter nevertheless served its purpose.

Recently Mr. Ted Swift, in effect, called for the wrath of the dean's office to descend upon the "rascal" who perpetrated the affair of the "Unicorn in the Garden." All I can say is that, occupied as he must be in the Legal Research Building with his outlines and reference works, the incident has assumed exaggerated significance to him. I am sure that few of his less scholarly brethren view the episode as an affront to the dignity and decorum of the Law School. As finals approach, tension mounts, and even the most studious need some diversion. Surely Mr. Swift must agree that leaving a horse in a courtyard for a few hours is more acceptable than shooting skyrockets off the roof of the Lawyers Club (J entry) during a certain football game often held in the Spring. Things have come to a pretty pass when one can't have a little harmless fun without being castigated for it by someone with Mr. Swift's unusual sense of propriety. Thank heaven there are few like him in the Law School. We couldn't take many more!

—*Gene Alkema, '55L*—

After the printing of these letters, and a few more that followed, we had the investigators thoroughly baffled. The prime suspect had assumed the role of a critic, and those least likely to participate had come forward in support of the project. We had done, then, all that we had set out to accomplish, absent our ability to produce a Unicorn, and we had thought that the matter would be given a quiet death. Instead, to our delight, unknown allies assisted our quest for confusion. As was always the case in those days, there were numerous groups and individuals seeking causes. Our exchange of correspondence lured other perennial and vocal student forces into the fray. More letters poured into the *Daily* on this crucial issue. It became, in short, a cause celebré. Was this act a symptom of capitalistic decline? Or was it good clean fun? Was the horse a victim of cruelty? Was expulsion enough for those who were involved or should capital punishment be invoked?

Whenever the sparks would begin to die, some other unsolicited author would rekindle the flame. In all, eight letters were printed on the subject. Seldom was so much written about so little. But all of this was to the good, we thought, since the dean, and the powers of the Law School, would not want to become further involved in what had become such a volatile campus-wide issue. The innovation of discipline would only mean further public scrutiny, and we began to sense that we would be spared disciplinary measures.

The Crease Ball was held with high attendance and a higher casualty rate; the investigations were dropped; and the *Michigan Daily*, in its final letter, indicated that it suspected that it had been victimized by this artificial issue. In short, even the *Daily* had been duped.

For the most part, the story had a happy ending. I personally suspect that there was only one victim of this confrontation, the not-so-innocent Gene Alkema. In his senior year he received his only "B" in Law School. I have always suspected, although he would deny it, that his letter was responsible for the only flaw in his otherwise perfect academic record.

But I do not worry long about Alkema or the shortfall in his quest for perfection. He is alive and well and rich and representing management in a distinguished Grand Rapids firm. I suspect that he is proud of his role in the Unicorn affair and that this pride soothes any residual pain resulting from his lone "B."

Fiske, too, has managed to survive. After a brilliant career as the U.S. district attorney for the Southern District of New York (Manhattan), in the fall of 1979 he retired from public service and returned to the prestigious Wall Street Firm of Davis, Polk & Wardwell. Fortunately, his duplicitous conduct in the Unicorn caper never surfaced while he was in public service; presumably the barons of Davis, Polk & Wardwell are prepared to overlook his checkered past—if they are even aware of the same.

As for me, it was, with the exception of the acquisition of my wife, my only claim to fame during three years in Ann Arbor. Wherever I go in this country, I am greeted by some U-M graduate who says, "Oh you're the guy who put the Unicorn in the Garden." Fame is hard to come by, and is a vapor after all, but I had my moment in the sun, and I wallowed in the adulation which followed. As one of my classmates recently said, "Most of us graduated and went on to success and fame—in your case, Swift, you peaked early."

So be it. At last I can confess to my own form of circa 1954 "Animal House." The Statute of Limitations must surely have run after 25 years.

P.S. And best wishes to you, Whirlaway, wherever you are. I hope that you are surrounded by roses.

APPENDIX C

Two Original Bar Documents

The following two documents from the early years of the Ingham County Bar Association are interesting to read today. The first is its *Articles of Association* of 1909, showing the simple scope of its operation in that less complicated era together with the names of its members. They were drafted by a committee of Chas. W. Nichols, Paul H. King, and Rollin H. Person. Unfortunately, the personally signed Articles called for by Article VI, Section 3, have not been located. Of special note are the provisions for investigating any members of the bar charged with professional misconduct.

The second document is the *Schedule of Minimum Charges for Legal Services of the Ingham County Bar* dated August 1, 1919. Motivated by the desire to prevent what was then all but universally regarded as unseemly competition and supported, no doubt, in an undetermined number of cases by a hope of stabilizing—or even increasing—one's income, the signers bound themselves "in no instance to charge less" on pain of expulsion from the Association for unethical conduct. Such minimum fee schedules, most of them less strict than this, were fairly common throughout the profession until the mid-1970s, when they were finally determined to be price-fixing in violation of the federal anti-trust laws and quietly dropped. It is unlikely that they were ever much enforced and the fear of being called "unethical" probably kept most doubters in line. The last one issued by the Association, dated May 25, 1965, stated that it was only a "Suggested Minimum Fee Schedule" and, moreover, that any lawyer could charge less when "peculiar and unique circumstances" required. Since almost all legal matters contain peculiar and unique circumstances, this made even the "suggested" minimums of doubtful application.

Articles of Association of the Ingham County Bar Association

(Printed from the original manuscript of 1909)

Article I.

Name.

Sec. 1. The name of this association shall be the INGHAM COUNTY BAR ASSOCIATION.

Article II.

Object.

Sec. 1. The object of this association is to maintain the honor and dignity of the profession of the law, to increase the usefulness of the profession of the law, to increase the usefulness of the profession in promoting the due administration of justice, and to cultivate social intercourse among the members of Ingham County.

Article III.

Meetings.

Sec. 1. A regular meeting of the association shall be held annually on the first Monday of December at two o'clock in the afternoon.

Sec. 2. Special meetings of the association may be called from time to time by the president.

Sec. 3. Notices of all meetings of the association shall be given by the secretary. Such notices shall, when not impracticable, be in writing, but may in cases of urgency be given by telephone or other means of personal communication.

Sec. 4. All meetings of the association shall, unless otherwise ordered, be held in the attorneys' room, so-called, in the City Hall, at Lansing.

Sec. 5. A quorum for the transaction of business shall consist of ten members.

Sec. 6. The order of business shall be as follows:

Roll Call.
Reading and Approving of Minutes.
Communications.
Reports of Standing Committees.
Reports of Special Committees.
Reports of Officers.
Notices.
Motions and Resolutions.
Unfinished Business.
Election of Officers.

Article IV.

Members.

    Sec. 1. Membership in this association shall be either active or honorary.

    Sec. 2. The terms and conditions of active membership shall be as follows:

        a. Residence within the County of Ingham.

        b. Active practice at the bar, which shall be deemed the main
           taining an office for the practice of law.

        c. Good character and reputation in and out of the profession.

        d. The payment of annual dues as provided in ARTICLE VII.

        e. Election to membership in the manner herein provided.

        f. The signing of these articles of association as active members.

    Sec. 3. Officers of the judicial department of the state government residing in Lansing, the judicial officers of the county, attorneys-at-law of good character and reputation now resident in the County having retired from the active practice of the law, and active members of this association retiring from practice, may, by a vote of the members of the association, be admitted to honorary membership. Such members shall sign the roll of honorary members, and shall not be subject to the payment of annual dues.

    Sec. 4. Active members of the association only, shall have the privilege of voting.

Article V.

Officers.

    Sec. 1. The officers of this association shall be a president, a vice-president, a secretary and a treasurer.

    Sec. 2. The election of officers shall be held each year at the regular meeting. In the event the regular meeting herein provided for not being held for any reason, the election of officers shall be held at a special meeting to be called for that purpose. All elections shall be by ballot. The term of all officers herein provided for shall begin on the first day of January of the year for which they were elected. If for any reason the association shall fail to elect any or all officers, the officers then in office shall continue therein until his successor or their successors shall be elected.

    Sec. 3. It shall be the duty of the president to preside at all meetings, to call such special meetings as may be necessary, to appoint all committees, unless otherwise ordered by the association, and to perform any other duties pertaining to the office.

    Sec. 4. In the absence of incapacity of the president, the vice-president shall perform the duties of the president.

    Sect. 5. The secretary shall keep a record of the proceedings of the association, shall keep on record these articles of association for signature by both active and honorary members, shall give notice of meetings, attend to any correspondence on behalf of the association, and in the absence or incapacity of the present or vice-president perform the duties of president. He shall make a report at the annual meeting showing the work of the association for the preceding year.

Sec. 6. The treasurer shall collect all dues payable by members, shall be the custodian of the funds of the association, shall make disbursements only on vouchers approved by the secretary, shall keep an account of all moneys received and disbursed, and shall make an annual report to the association as to its financial affairs. In the absence of incapacity of the president, vice-present and secretary, the treasurer shall perform the duties of president.

Article VI.

Committees.

Sec. 1. The following named standing committees shall be appointed annually by the president; a committee on grievances, consisting of five members, of which committee the president shall be ex-officio a member; a committee on membership consisting of five members; and a committee on resolutions and a committee on social intercourse consisting of three members each.

Sec. 2. All charges of professional misconduct on the part of any member of this association or of any members of the bar of the county, whether a member of this association or not, shall be made to the president of the association, and referred to the committee on grievances, and such committee shall within a reasonable time investigate such charges and report upon the same at an annual or special meeting of the association.

Sec. 3. Persons possessing the required qualifications may become members upon filing an application in writing endorsed by two members, and being elected to membership by the membership committee or the association at any regular or special meeting. All active members of the bar may become charter members of the association by signing the articles of association at or before the first annual meeting on the first Monday of December, 1909, without being elected as herein provided.

Sec. 4. The committee on resolutions shall draft such resolutions as on occasion may be necessary.

Sec. 5. The committee on social intercourse shall arrange for such affairs of a social nature as it may deem expedient.

Sec. 6. The president may appoint such special committees as may be necessary.

Article VII.

Dues.

Sec. 1. Each active member shall pay annually to the treasurer at the regular meeting of the association the sum of three dollars. The name of any member in default of dues for two years shall be stricken by the secretary from the roll of members. Such members may by a vote of a majority of the association be reinstated upon the payment of all arrearages. The association may by a like vote remit either temporarily or permanently the dues of any member.

Article VIII.

Amendments.

Sec. 1. These articles may be amended in the following manner: Notice of the proposed amendment may be given at any meeting and a copy of such notice and of the proposed amendment shall be furnished by the secretary to each member of the association. The amendment may then be presented and voted on at any meeting thereafter held, providing that in the call for said meeting reference shall be made to the fact that such amendment will be considered; and if, at such meeting, a majority of all of the members of the association shall vote in favor of such amendment, it shall be declared adopted, and a part of these articles of association.

Samuel L. Kilbourne	C. P. Black
Rollin H. Person	John J. Zimmer
Frank L. Dodge	Clark C. Wood
Arthur J. Tuttle	Edward Cahill
Jason E. Nichols	James Harris
Joseph H. Dunnebacke	Lawton T. Hemans
J. A. Boice	L. B. McArthur
L. B. Gardner	A. A. Bergman
Paul H. King	Geo. W. Bristol
Richard Raudabaugh	Wm. C. Brown
Oscar J. Hood	Charles F. Hammond
John A. Brooks	Elmer S. Avery
John McClellan	Henry R. Roach
Seymour H. Person	Clyde V. King
Eugene T. Hammond	O. C. Trask
Chas. W. Foster	John I. Carpenter
Chas. W. Nichols	George R. Heck
Harry A. Silsbee	S. B. Roe
Samuel H. Davis	E.C. Chapin
Alva M. Cummins	T. Rogers Lyons
Chas. H. Hayden	Harry E. Hooker

Walter S. Foster

Frank Morrill Fogg

W. T. Webb

Henry M. Gardner

Harris E. Thomas

Wm. A. Fraser

W. F. Cairns

J. Earle Brown

Edmund C. Shields

Chas. H. Chase

Carl H. Reynolds

Charles F. Haight

W. J. Carbaugh

Samuel H. Kelley

Spencer D. Kelley

Oliver Spaulding

Adelbert Mosher

Charles E. Ecker

Paul G. Eger

Byron L. Ballard

Dean W. Kelley

Robert S. Ballard

Roll of Honorary Members of Ingham County Bar Association elected as such by the Association.

Howard Wiest

Charles B. Collingwood

Chas. A. Blair

Claudius B. Grant

Frank A. Hooker

Aaron V. McAlvay

Joseph B. Moore

A. A. Keiser

Robt. M. Montgomery

Russell C. Ostrander

Flavius L. Brooke

Chas. C. Hopkins

James M. Reasoner

Thomas A. Lawler

R. W. Cooper

Schedule of Minimum Charges for Legal Services of the Ingham County Bar

(Printed from the original manuscript of 1919)

Conveyancing

Wills,	$5.00
Warranty Deeds	2.00
Mortgage	2.00
Quitclaim Deed	2.00
Land Contracts	3.00
Mortgage Discharge	1.00
Notice to Quit	1.00
Auto Drivers License	1.00
All other Blank forms	2.00
All typewritten contracts, agreements or papers of any kind, whether single or carbon copies	3.00
Examining Abstracts	3.00
Counsel	2.00

Justice Court

Retainer in Civil matters, either for plaintiff or defendant, including drafting papers for institution of suit, to be charged in advance	10.00
Trial of Civil case, including retainer	15.00
Retainer in criminal matters, to be charged in advance	15.00
Trial of Criminal case, including retainer	25.00

Circuit Court

Retainer for plaintiff or defendant, including the drafting of papers for the commencement of suit, except where declaration or bill of complaint warrants additional charge, to be charged in advance	25.00
Criminal case retainer, to be charged in advance	50.00
All uncontested cases, both Law and Chancery including divorce cases, including costs	$75.00
Statutory Petition to Discharge Mortgage	35.00
Daily service charge, half day to count as whole day	35.00
For trial of any Circuit Court case, including retainer	100.00
Minimum of Appeal cases from Justice Court per day	35.00
For trial of any Circuit Court case, including retainer	100.00
Minimum of Appeal cases from Justice Court per day	35.00
Default judgments on notes, etc.	35.00

Probate Court

Probating Estate	25.00

Supreme Court

Appeal	100.00

Circuit Court Commissioner

Appearance	5.00
Trial of cause	15.00

Industrial Accident Board

Contested cases, same as Circuit Court.

Incorporating Concerns

50.00

Income Tax

Making return for corporation	10.00
Capital Stock Tax return	5.00
Individual under $5,000.00	3.00
Individual over $5,000.00	5.00

Collections

Commercial Law League rates as adopted by this Bar Association heretofore.

Mechanics Lien

Preparing Affidavit and Filing   5.00

Office Work

Per hour   5.00

Nothing herein contained shall preclude the taking of cases upon contingent fees, or yearly contracts with clients.

We the undersigned attorneys of the County of Ingham do herewith pledge ourselves to abide by the minimum charges for legal services adopted by the Ingham County Bar Association on August 1st, 1919 as above set forth, and in no instance to charge less than said amounts, and we agree that any violation of these rates after a proper hearing upon complaint before the Grievance Committee of the Ingham County Bar Association, shall be considered unethical and sufficient cause to subject us to expulsion from membership in the Ingham County Bar Association.

Dated: August 1st, 1919.

Harry J. ...   501 Lansing State Sav. Bk Bld

Carl H. M...   Cap. Nat. Bank Bldg

W.F. Carbaugh   704 Lansing State Savings Bank

A.M. Cummins   Lansing Bldg

M.C. Brown   "   "

J.H. ...   Prudden Bldg

H.N. Seelye   Prudden Bldg

Roy M. Shrouch   Prudden Bldg

James Harris   Cap Nat Bank Bldg

F.E. Porter   Cap. Nat. Bank Bldg

Paul G. Eger   502 Tussing Bldg

W.A. Norton   Dodge Bldg

Gail H. Reynolds   510 Tussing Bldg

Chas W. Nichols   502 Tussing Bldg

Dean M. Kelley   608 Lansing State Savings Bank Building

Frank S. Dodge   " Bank Building

J. Earl Brown   608 State Savings Bk

Charles F. Haight   513 Prudden Bldg

D.G. Warner   413 Prudden Bldg

J.G. Bower   310-312 Prudden Bldg

Joseph H. Trinnebake   501-3 Cap. Nat. Bk Bldg

Benjamin D. Emery   205 Tussing Bldg

John McClellan, 312 Cap. Nat. Bk Bldg.
C. H. & H. S. Foster 401 Prudden Bldg
Harry E. Walker 805 Lansing St. Sav. Bk Bldg.
Charles E. Ecker 200 Capital Nat Bank Bldg
[illegible] 319 W Shiawassee
Harris E. Thomas 501 St. Bank Building
John H. Brooks 209 Lansing State Savings Bank Bldg
Frederick E. DeCamp #308 Prudden Bldg Lansing Mich
Howard W. [illegible] 802 Tussing Bldg
Archibald Jones
Richard Raudabaugh
Samuel H. Rhoads 510 Tussing Bldg

[illegible] 118 Allegan St W
[illegible] Keeler 118 Allegan St W
George R. Hyde 210½ Washington Ave S.
Jason E. Nichols 408 Tussing Bldg.

[illegible] 501-3 Prudden B
Thos. H. Hayden 19 Dodge Block
W. H. Ballard 19 Dodge Block
Robert S. Ballard 501 State Savings Bank Bldg
Allan R Black 501 Lansing State Savings Bank B

APPENDIX D

Resolution Honoring Justice Carr

When Justice Leland W. Carr, who had spent more than half a century in the public service, passed away in 1969, he was universally regarded as having one of the finest legal and judicial minds that the county ever produced. A few days later the following resolution was adopted by the Michigan legislature as a tribute to his memory.

HOUSE CONCURRENT RESOLUTION NO. 167
(Reprinted from The Senate Journal of June 4, 1969)

A concurrent resolution of deep sadness upon the death of Justice Leland W. Carr.

Whereas, On Friday, May 30, 1969, former State Chief Justice Leland W. Carr, 85, died at his Lansing home; and

Whereas, Justice Leland W. Carr's career spanned over 50 years of public life before his retirement from the Bench of the State Supreme Court in December of 1963; and

Whereas, Justice Leland W. Carr as a graduate of the University of Michigan Law School in 1906, a private practitioner in Ionia from 1906 to 1913 when he became and Assistant Attorney General and the Legal Advisor to the State Highway Department; and

Whereas, Justice Leland W. Carr gained renowned status as a jurist and an outstanding member of his legal profession when as the Grand Juror in 1945 his work in connection with that of Kim Sigler, Special Prosecuting Attorney, resulted in over 115 people being indicted on bribery and related charges due to alleged corruption in state government; and

Whereas, Leland W. Carr was named to the Ingham county Circuit Court in 1921 and won re-election four times before being elevated to the Michigan Supreme court in 1945; and

Whereas, There are many outstanding Michigan attorneys who were students of Justice Carr as he taught courses in law to young members of the Michigan State Bar; now therefore be it

Resolved by the House of Representatives (the Senate concurring), That the members of the Michigan Legislature not only on their own behalf but on behalf of all the people of the State of Michigan mourn the passing of Justice Leland W. Carr, knowing well that a giant among men, and outstanding jurist, a renowned attorney and a brilliant student of the law has passed from the Michigan scene but that memories of his abilities as an attorney, judge, jurist and student and master of jurisprudence will long be remembered by the profession and the citizens of the State of Michigan; and be it further

Resolved, That a copy of this resolution be transmitted to his beloved wife, Irene Carr, and to the members of his family.

The message informed the Senate that the House of Representatives had adopted the concurrent resolution; in which action the concurrence of the Senate was requested.

Pending the order that, under rule 32 be suspended.

The motion prevailed, 3/5 of the Senators present voting therefor.

The concurrent resolution was adopted by a unanimous standing vote of the Senate.

APPENDIX E

Incumbents Through The Years

(The following lists of those who have held legal positions in Ingham County throughout its history have been gathered together and brought up to date from a variety of sources.)

Supreme Court Justices from Ingham County or with Ingham County Ties

Isaac P. Christiancy	1874-81	Howard Wiest	1921-45
Edward Cahill	1890	Leland W. Carr	1945-63
Robert M. Montgomery	1892-1911	Thomas E. Brennan	1967-73
William L. Carpenter	1902-15	Lawrence B. Lindemer	1975-77
Russell C. Ostrander	1905-19	Michael F. Cavanagh	1983-
Rollin H. Person	1915-16		

Circuit Judges

David Johnson	1852-57	Theodore P. Ryan	1956-57
Edwin Lawrence	1857-70	Sam Street Hughes	1957-72
Samuel Higby	1870-73	Jack W. Warren	1967-86
Alexander D. Crane	1873-75	Donald Reisig	1968-76
George M. Huntington	1876-82	Ray Hotchkiss	1971-82
G. Thompson Gridley	1882-85	James T. Kallman	1973-90
Erastus Peck	1886-90	Robert Holmes Bell	1979-87
Rollin H. Person	1891-99	Thomas L. Brown	1974-
Howard Wiest	1899-21	Michael G. Harrison	1976-
Charles B. Collingwood	1909-35	James R. Giddings	1979-
Charles H. Hayden	1935-56	Carolyn Stell	1983-
Leland W. Carr	1921-45	Peter D. Houk	1986-
Paul G. Eger	1945-47	Lawrence M. Glazer	1987-
Louis E. Coash	1945-68	William E. Collette	1990-
Marvin J. Salmon	1947-73		

Lansing Municipal Judges

Simon B. Roe	1903-06	Louis Coash	1941-45
William A. Fraser	1907-11	Marvin J. Salmon	1945-47
Charles F. Haight	1912-18	Paul C. Younger	1947-50
William A. Price	1918-19	George Sidwell	1950-60
Richard Raudabaugh	1921-22	Earl E. McDonald	1950-63
William Steinkohl	1922-26	Jack W. Warren	1953-55
John McClellan	1926-31	Charles N. Murphy	1956-63
Sam Street Hughes	1932-41		

Probate Judges

Peter Linderman	1838-39	Frank S. Porter	1897-01
Valerus Meeker	1839-43	Jason E. Nichols	1901-05
Henry Fiske	1843-45	Henry M. Gardner	1905-16
Amos E. Steele	1846-47	Jason E. Nichols	1916
Richard Ferris	1847-48		(June 6 to Nov. 16)
Griffin Paddock	1849-53	Louis B. McArthur	1916-37
William M. Chapman	1853-57	John McClellan	1937-54
William H. Pinkney	1857-65	Robert Drake	1956-63
Horatio Pratt	1865-73		1973-85
Mason D. Chatterton	1873-81	James T. Kallman	1963-72
George F. Giliam	1881-85	Ray C. Hotchkiss	1967-70
Quincy A. Smith	1885-91	Thomas L. Brown	1971-75
George W. Bristol	1891-93	Donald S. Owens	1979-
A.F. Cowles	1893-97	Richard George Economy	1985-

54-A District Judges (Lansing)

James Wood	1969-	Claude Thomas	1981-92
Terrance Clem	1970-85	John Davis	1985-95
Charles Filice	1971-	Beverley Nettles-Nickerson	1990-
Patrick Cherry	1975-	Paula Manderfield	1993-

54-B District Judges (East Lansing)

Maurice Schoenberger	1971-74	David Jordon	1990-
Daniel Tschirhart	1974-86	Richard Ball	1993-
Jules Hanslovsky	1987-92		

55 District Judges (Mason)

R. William Reid	1969-80	Thomas E. Brennan, Jr.	1981-
James H. Edgar	1968-72	Pamela J. McCabe	1988-
Thomas R. Roberts	1980-88		

Prosecuting Attorneys

William W. Upton	1851-52	William C. Brown	1915-18
O.M. Barnes	1852-56	J. Arthur Boice	1919-22
George I. Parsons	1857-60	Barnard Pierce	1923-24
Stephen D. Bingham	1861-62	Harry F. Hittle	1925-26
G.M. Huntington	1863-64	Barnard Pierce	1927-28
R.C. Dart	1865-68	John Wendell Bird	1929-32
H.B. Carpenter	1869-72	Dan D. McCullough	1933-36
E.D. Lewis	1873-74	Thomas J. Bailey	1937-38
H.P. Henderson	1875-76	Richard B. Foster	1939-42
Edward C. Cahill	1877-80	Victor C. Anderson	1943-46
Russell Ostrander	1881-82	Charles MacLean	1947-50
Jason E. Nichols	1883-86	Paul C. Younger	1951-54
Charles Hammond	1887-88	Charles E. Chamberlain	1955-56
George Day	1889-90	Jack W. Warren	1957-60
Arthur D. Prosser	1891-92	Leo Farhat	1961-64
Leonard B. Gardner	1893-96	Donald Reisig	1965-68
Alva M. Cummings	1897-98	Raymond L. Scodeller	1968-76
Arthur J. Tuttle	1899-02	Peter Houk	1977-86
Louis B. McArthur	1903-06	Donald Martin	1986-
Walter S. Foster	1907-10	Stuart J. Dunnings III	1997-
Charles H. Hayden	1911-14		

Presidents of the Ingham County Bar Association

S. L. Kilbourne	1894-1910	Harry S. Silsbee	1927
Edward Cahill	1911	John Brooks	1928
Rollin Person	1912	William C. Brown	1929
Charles F. Hammond	1913	Edmund C. Shields	1930
Jason Nichols	1914	Eugene F. Hammond	1931
Unknown	1915	Spencer D. Kelly	1932
Frank Dodge	1916	Walter S. Foster	1933
Alva Cummins	1917	Ernest C. Smith	1934
Unknown	1918	Carl H. McLean	1935
Unknown	1919	Charles Collingwood	1936
Seymour H. Person	1920	Charles E. Ecker	1937
D.G.F. Warner	1921	Joseph W. Planck	1938
Charles F. Foster	1922	Leland W. Carr	1939
Charles H. Hayden	1923	Paul Eger	1940
Seymour H. Person	1924	Wilbur M. Seelye	1941
Joseph E. Dunnebacke	1925	William S. Cameron	1942
Dean W. Kelly	1926	Byron L. Ballard	1943

Harry Hubbard	1944	C. Bruce Kelley	1971
Charles P. Van Note	1945	John N. Seaman	1972
S. DeWitt Rathbunn	1946	Jack W. Warren	1973
Benjamin J. Watson	1947	John L. Coté	1974
Lewis J. Gregg	1948	Peter J. Treleaven	1975
Barnard Pierce	1949	William L. Mackay	1976
Claude J. Marshall	1950	James A. Timmer	1977
Louis Coash	1951	James E. Burns	1978
William H. Wise	1952	Joseph Lavey	1979
Harold W. Glassen	1953	Jack D. Born	1980
Richard B. Foster	1954	Theodore W. Swift	1981
Sam Street Hughes	1955	James Burren Brown	1982
Clayton F. Jennings	1956	Judson M. Werbelow	1983
Roy T. Conley	1957	Thomas R. Roberts	1984
Marvin J. Salmon	1958	Julius I. Hanslovsky	1985
H. Clay Campbell	1959	David E. S. Marvin	1986
William J. Sessions	1960	Webb A. Smith	1987
Fred C. Newman	1961	Peter S. Sheldon	1988
H.H. Warner	1962	Elaine H. Charney	1989
Charles R. MacLean	1963	Allan J. Claypool	1990
Archie C. Fraser	1964	Rose A. Houk	1991
Leo A. Farhat	1965	Stuart J. Dunnings, Jr.	1992
Raymond R. Campbell	1966	Pamela J. McCabe	1993
Allison K. Thomas	1967	Michael E. Cavanaugh	1994
George J. Hutter	1968	Nancy A. Wonch	1995
Roland R. Rhead	1969	Max R. Hoffman Jr.	1996
Thomas J. Sinas	1970	Beverly Nettles-Nickerson	1997

Past Presidents of State Bar of Michigan who were members of the ICBA

Dean W. Kelley - 8th President	1942-43
Joseph W. Planck - 16th President	1950-51
Leo A. Farhat - 44th President	1978-79
Donald L. Reisig - 54th President	1988-89

Former Chairpersons of the State Bar of Michigan Representative Assembly who where members of ICBA

Donald L. Reisig	1978-79
Michael G. Harrison	1979-80
Susan A. Howard	1985-86
Nkrumah Johnson-Wynn	1994-95

APPENDIX F

County Bar Activities

Readers of this book who are not lawyers may be tempted to ask, "Just what does a county or a local bar association actually do?" To help answer this question the following listing has been made to show many of the events and projects which have been carried out by the Ingham County Bar Association over the years.

Ingham County Bar Association Activities through the Years

By Allison K. Thomas

Partial List of Ingham County Bar Association Activities

Celebration of John Marshall Day
Installation of Judges
Naturalization Day Programs
Law Day Celebrations
Assisting Judge Drake in the Founding of Highfields
Assisting in the Formation of the Young Lawyers Section (the Bench and Bar Society)
Assisting Women's Auxiliary
Attending Funerals of Members in a Body
Conducting Memorial Services
Luncheons with Speakers
Educational Programs for Members
Numerous Publications
Shrimp Dinners
Attending Judge Wiest's Ox and Corn Roasts
Assisting Legal Aid and Pro Bono Programs

Promoting the Legal Education of Lawyers

Developing and Assisting the Work of Many Committees—such as the Character and Fitness Committee

Lobbying with City Council and Legislature for Court Rooms and Legislation for Improving Legal System

Forming Sections Such as Probate

Handling Grievances

Lawyers Referral Service

Maintaining Office and Answering Questions from Public

Raising funds for Food Bank

Promoting Hockey Teams and Raising Funds for the Boys and Girls Clubs to Assist the Youth of Lansing

Liberty Bell Award

Awards to Distinguished Attorneys

Distinguished Volunteer Awards

Promoting Mid-Michigan Women Lawyers Association

Promoting Television Programs Such as It's the Law

Promoting Mediation

Promoting Senior Law Fair

Awards to Attorneys Who Have Practiced for 50 Years

Promoting Legal Clinic for Seniors

Promotion of Publication of Book About Legal History

Promoting Bench and Bar Conferences

Assisting in Boy Scout and Explorer Programs

Promoting Essay and Poster Competition in Schools

Horn of Plenty Food and Clothing Drive

Peer Mediation for Elementary Students in Lansing School District

APPENDIX G

Firm Histories

Church, Kritselis, Wyble & Robinson, P.C.

The firm was one of the first to move out of the downtown Lansing area. The office has been located at 3939 Capital City Boulevard at the airport since 1967.

Edgar L. Church graduated from Michigan State University and Wayne State University and retired in 1985. F. Merrill Wyble is a graduate of Valpariso University, Valpariso, Indiana. He is a Fellow of the Michigan State Bar Foundation. He served on the Board of Directors and as president of Family and Child Services, Inc. He is a member of the Michigan Trial Lawyers Association. His practice is in the areas of family law, probate, and real property.

William N. Kritselis is a graduate of Michigan State University and Ohio Northern University. He is a Fellow of the Michigan State Bar Foundation. He has served as chief of the Criminal Division of the Ingham County Prosecutor's Office. He is a member of the Michigan Trial Lawyers Association, the American Bar Association, the Association of Trial Lawyers of America, Hellenic Bar Association, American Academy of Forensic Sciences, American Society of Law and Medicine, and American Judicature Society. His practice is in the areas of medical malpractice, products liability, and law relating to highway defects.

J. Richard Robinson is a graduate of Michigan State University and Wayne State University. He is a Fellow of the Michigan State Bar Foundation, a member of Michigan Trial Lawyers Association and the Association of Trial Lawyers of America, and the American Bar Association. He was chair of the Ingham County Bar Association, Real Property Section. His practice is in the areas of municipal and corporate, negligence, and general litigation law.

James T. Heos is a graduate of Michigan State University and Thomas M. Cooley School of Law. He is a Fellow of the Michigan State Bar Foundation and has served in the Lansing City Attorney's office and in the Ingham County

Prosecutor's office. He is a member of the Association of Trial Lawyers of Michigan, Michigan Trial Lawyers Association, and the American Bar Association. His practice is in the area of auto negligence, personal injury, and medical malpractice. In 1989, he ran unsuccessfully for a 54-B District Court judgeship.

David S. Mittleman is a graduate of Duquesne University and Thomas M. Cooley Law School. He is a registered pharmacist and a member of the Michigan Trial Lawyers Association, American Bar Association, Association of Trial Lawyers of America, American Pharmaceutical Association, and the Pennsylvania Pharmaceutical Association. His practice is in the area of personal injury, medical malpractice, and products liability law.

Neil F. O'Brien is a graduate of the University of Notre Dame and Thomas M. Cooley Law School. He has served as an assistant prosecuting attorney in Ingham County. He is a member of the American Bar Association, Michigan Trial Lawyers Association, and the Association of Trial Lawyers of America. His practice is in the area of personal injury, municipal law, and criminal law. He also is an adjunct professor at Cooley Law School

Dickinson, Wright, Moon, Van Dusen & Freeman

Dickinson, Wright, Moon, Van Dusen & Freeman was founded in 1878 in Detroit under the name of Russel and Campbell. Over the last 118 years, the firm has played a significant role in the development of numerous business, financial, and public institutions. Dickinson Wright is now comprised of 235 attorneys and has offices in seven cities, including Detroit, Lansing, Bloomfield Hills, and Grand Rapids, Michigan, Chicago, Illinois, Washington, D.C. and Warsaw, Poland.

Dickinson, Wright was the first regional law firm to establish a presence in Lansing—opening an office on West Allegan Street in January of 1970. Since 1970, the Lansing office has grown from its initial two lawyers to its present complement of 20 lawyers.

Partners in the Lansing office include municipal finance lawyers James W. Bliss, Kester K. So and Kirk E. Grable; commercial litigation attorneys Joseph A. Fink and Jeffery V. Stuckey; employment relations attorney, Gregory Palmer; Peter S. Sheldon, whose primary areas of practice are business associations and tax; Peter H. Ellsworth, who practices administrative law; David E. Pierson, whose area of expertise is in land use, real estate and related litigation; and Dwight D. Ebaugh, whose practice includes commercial lending and real estate law. Together with specialists in the other offices of Dickinson, Wright, the Lansing office is able to provide a full spectrum of legal services to the Lansing area community.

In 1983, Dickinson Wright signed the first lease for space in The Atrium Office Center. The Dickinson Wright lease enabled the owners to move the renovation of the former Michigan Theatre Arcade from the drawing board to reality. The Atrium Office Center, where Dickinson Wright's Lansing offices have been located since June 1984, is considered an outstanding example of the restoration of an architecturally valuable building for modern use. The offices retain such architectural features as 18-foot vaulted ceilings, leaded glass and ornamental plaster.

Dickinson Wright's Lansing office lawyers have made substantial contributions to the Lansing community. For example, Peter Sheldon and Judson Werbelow, now retired, have served as President of the Ingham County Bar Association. Judson Werbelow chaired the Lansing Regional Chamber of Commerce and the Ingham County Board of Social Services and was the recipient of the 1992 Ingham County Bar Association Distinguished Volunteer Award. Peter Sheldon has headed the Greater Lansing Estate Planning Council and has been actively involved as an officer and director of the Ingham County Unit and Michigan Division of the American Cancer Society.

Joseph Fink has served as a member and officer of the Board of Trustees of Olivet College, as a Board member of Lansing 2000, and as a member of the Michigan State University Press Society. Peter Ellsworth is a member of the Michigan Civil Service Commission and Dwight Ebaugh serves as a member of the Board of the Lansing Symphony Orchestra and as its legal counsel.

Dunnings and Frawley, P. C.

Dunnings and Frawley, P.C. traces its history to 1950 when Stuart J. Dunnings, Jr. opened a law office in the City of Lansing in the month of September as a sole practitioner. The office was located on Kalamazoo Street near the corner of Capitol Avenue. The office at that time consisted of two rooms on the second floor of a small office building which had been converted from a house. Over the years, the law practice created by Mr. Dunnings grew to include other attorneys and three partnerships and associations were formed culminating in the establishment of Dunnings and Frawley, P.C., in December 1985. In the mid 1960s, while Stuart J. Dunnings, Jr., was still a sole practitioner, he entered into a partnership with Benjamin F. Gibson, and they practiced under the name of Dunnings and Gibson, P.C., until mid 1975. Benjamin F. Gibson subsequently became a judge of the U.S. District Court for the Western District of Michigan where he currently serves as chief judge of that district.

In 1975, the firm became known as Dunnings and Canady, P.C. Shortly after formation of the firm, John J. Frawley, who is currently a member of the firm, joined the firm and has remained since that time.

In August 1985, the firm became known as Dunnings and Frawley, P.C., with the departure of Clinton Canady III. The firm has always maintained a practice of dedication to client service by providing the highest quality of legal service. This has resulted in the firm having the highest rating possible by

Martindale Hubbell, a national organization that annually rates lawyers throughout this country. The firm has enjoyed the highest rating which embraces "faithful adherence to ethical standards; professional reliability and diligence" since early 1970. This distinction is a tribute to the quality and commitment which has sustained this firm for over 40 years.

The firm until January 1, 1997, consisted of the following members: Stuart J. Dunnings, Jr.; John J. Frawley, president, who joined the firm in July 1976; Stuart J. Dunnings III, secretary-treasurer, who joined the firm in 1980; Steven D. Dunnings, member of the Board of Directors who joined the firm in 1984. and Shauna L. Dunnings who joined the firm in 1990. The latter three members of the firm are children of the founder of the firm, Stuart J. Dunnings, Jr. On January 1, 1997, Stuart J. Dunnings III took office after being elected Ingham County Prosecuting Attorney.

The firm's clients include individuals, partnerships, corporations, small businesses, estates, professionals, municipal corporations, realtors, and religious groups.

Representation of the firm's clients has involved the firm's attorneys in litigation and business transactions in a variety of situations, including all levels of the court system, both federal and state.

The firm presently represents the Lansing Housing Commission and Lansing School District, and the firm has done defense work for Ford Motor Company and Prudential Insurance Company.

Farhat, Story & Kraus, P.C.

For 45 years, the firm of Farhat, Story & Kraus, P.C., has had the privilege of helping individuals, families, associations and businesses with their legal matters. During those four decades, the firm has brought together a group of attorneys with diverse backgrounds and specialities, carefully selected to serve the varied legal concerns of its clients. The firm is proud to represent a broad range of clients, from individuals and families to partnerships and associations, from small- and medium-sized companies to Fortune 500 firms. Farhat, Story & Kraus, P.C., presently has twelve attorneys and five legal assistants, and practices in a broad range of legal areas, including civil and commercial litigation, administrative agency practice, appellate litigation, tax and business matters, estate and retirement planning, corporate law, real estate matters, pension and profit-sharing plans, health care, mediation, professional and business licensing matters, criminal defense, employment law, natural resources and environmental law, and computer law.

In 1952, Leo A. Farhat and James E. Burns, bound by friendship and a desire to practice law, opened a small office in downtown Lansing. During the early years, the firm of Farhat & Burns engaged in civil and criminal litigation and real estate and business matters. The firm expanded its corporate, business and tax law practice by the addition in 1971 of Monte R. Story, a principal in the certified public accounting firm of Danielson, Story, Lake and Schultz (now Plante & Moran). For almost a decade, the firm was known as Farhat, Burns & Story. The firm proudly includes Justice Michael Cavanagh of the Michigan Supreme Court among its former members. The firm's name was changed to Farhat, Story & Kraus, P.C., in 1986. Its offices were relocated to Beacon Place on S. Hagedorn Road in East Lansing in 1989.

Richard C. Kraus joined the firm upon graduation from law school in 1977 and is the firm's managing director and head of its litigation department. Max R. Hoffman, Jr., joined the firm in 1983 after ten years' service as an assistant attorney general for the State of Michigan. He became a shareholder and director in 1986. Chris A. Bergstrom also joined the firm in 1983 after four years with the Lansing City Attorney's office. In 1984, Kitty L. Groh became a member of the firm upon her graduation from law school.

Charles R. Toy came to the firm in 1984 after clerking for the Michigan Court of Appeals and working in the Ingham County Prosecuting Attorney's office. David M. Platt joined the firm in 1989 after teaching at Michigan State University and acting as general counsel for a nonprofit research institute and subsequently, for a securities broker-dealer and a consortium of financial planning companies. Thomas L. Sparks joined the firm in 1993 after thirteen years' service as an assistant attorney general for the State of Michigan and five years in private practice.

The firm has four associates. Lawrence P. Schweitzer joined in 1988 after obtaining his Master's in Tax Law. Debra A. Geroux joined the firm in 1995 after graduation from Detroit College of Law where she was managing editor of its law review and vice president of her class. Daniel B. Morgan joined the firm in 1996 after working in private practice since 1984. Prior to law school, Mr. Morgan was a high school principal and teacher. Mary K. Robbins-Kralapp joined the firm in 1996 after her graduation from Thomas M. Cooley Law School. Prior to law school, Ms. Robbins-Kralapp was a registered nurse and nursing home administrator.

Foster, Swift, Collins & Smith, P.C.

Foster, Swift, Collins & Smith, P.C. is proud of its heritage in the Lansing legal community, which spans nearly a century. In 1902, Walter S. Foster opened a law office in the 100 block of East Grand River, in an area now known as Old Town. That was then the commercial and business center of the city, and there were only 40 lawyers practicing in all of Ingham County.

Walter Foster remained a powerful force in the firm and an influential leader of the state bar for more than half a century. His son, Richard B. Foster, joined the firm in 1932, followed by Theodore W. Swift and John L. Collins in 1955, and Webb A. Smith in 1963.

From its earliest years, the firm attracted notable cases. In 1912, Walter Foster served as special counsel to a 23-member grand jury in a proceeding that resulted in the conviction and imprisonment of the Michigan State Treasurer for embezzlement. In 1946, Richard Foster served as special counsel to a grand jury proceeding conducted by Circuit Judge Louis E. Coash involving bribery by members of the Michigan Legislature, the subject of the book *Three Bullets Sealed His Lips* by Rubenstein and Ziewacz. Walter Foster and Richard Foster were also the only father and son combination who each served as Ingham County Prosecuting Attorney.

Foster, Swift, Collins & Smith has always been a staunch supporter of the Lansing community—its businesses and activities. All of the firm's lawyers have been and continue to be active in bar associations at the local, state, and national levels. Six of the firm's lawyers have served as president of the Ingham County Bar Association. Two members have received the Leo A. Farhat Outstanding Attorney Award. Several members of the firm have held prominent positions in community organizations and cultural programs, including president of the Greater Lansing Chamber of Commerce; president, Volunteers of America; chairperson, Mid-Michigan Chapter of the American Red Cross; and members of the boards of directors of several charitable and philanthropic organizations.

The firm is very proud of its members and former members who have served in the judiciary—a Michigan Supreme Court justice, a U.S. District Court judge, a U.S. magistrate, a Michigan Supreme Court commissioner, two Ingham County District Court judges and two Ingham County prosecuting attorneys. Members of the firm have also occupied positions of responsibility in local and state government, including a representative to the Michigan House of Representatives; a regent at the University of Michigan; and a Lansing city councilman. At least twelve of its lawyers have been listed in *Best Lawyers in America*, two members are Fellows of the American College of Trial Lawyers, two members are fellows of the American College of Trust and Estate Counsel, one is an academician of the International Academy of Estate and Trust Law, and another is a commissioner of the State Bar of Michigan.

Foster, Swift, Collins & Smith supports and encourages continuing professional development for all employees. Several legal secretaries and legal assistants have served as officers and leaders in the professional activities of the National Association of Legal Secretaries and the National Association of Legal Assistants. At least sixteen are certified professional legal secretaries or certified legal assistants. More than ten of the firm's support staff have received the Lansing Legal Professional of the Year Award. Four have been awarded the Michigan Legal Professional of the Year recognition. Eleven of the firm's lawyers and one assistant administrator have been selected Boss of the Year by the Lansing Legal Secretaries Association.

Over the years, as the firm grew, its main offices have been in several
Lansing locations. Since 1977, the firm has maintained its headquarters in the
Foster Building, a three-story downtown Lansing landmark. The property has
significant history and was the home of the famous Michigan eatery, Home
Dairy, before the firm purchased and proudly renovated the building into its
comfortable and attractive headquarters.

Since its founding, Foster, Swift, Collins & Smith has gradually become
Lansing's largest law firm and is one of the twenty largest firms in the State of
Michigan. In 1990, the firm opened its southeastern Michigan office. Seven
lawyers now reside permanently in that office, and further expansion and
growth is anticipated.

In 1992, during its 90th anniversary year, the firm joined the law firm network known as Great Lakes Law, with other member firms in Chicago,
Milwaukee, Cleveland, Minneapolis, Pittsburgh, Indianapolis, Rochester (N.Y.),
Montreal, Ottawa, and Toronto. The network positions the firm to better serve
the needs of its clients, which are increasingly international in scope.

Fraser, Trebilcock, Davis & Foster, P. C.

The Fraser Law Firm, Mid-Michigan's oldest law firm, traces its beginning
to the solo practice of Michigan State Supreme Court Justice Rollin H. Person
who began the practice of law in 1875 in Howell, Michigan. Justice Person, like
most legal practitioners of that era, was indoctrinated into the legal profession
by studying law under the guidance and teachings of learned and experienced
lawyers. His legal training prepared him well for service to his community and
profession as he was appointed judge of the Thirtieth Judicial District (com-
prising Ingham and Livingston Counties) in 1891, where he served until 1899
when he returned to private practice in Lansing.

Then on August 5, 1913, Justice Person, Edmund C. Shields and Harry A.
Silsbee formed the firm of Person, Shields and Silsbee with offices in the
Hollister Building in downtown Lansing. On July 16, 1915, Justice Person was
appointed a member of the Michigan Supreme Court and in 1917 Harris E.
Thomas joined the firm and the name was changed to Person, Thomas, Shields
and Silsbee.

Justice Person died in 1917 but his partners continued to pursue legal excellence and a commitment to the greater Lansing community. For the next
decade, these lawyers influenced and participated in much of Lansing's early
industrial and community growth.

Harris E. Thomas specialized in corporate law and drafted the incorpora-
tion documents for such local businesses as Reo Motorcar Corporation, Olds
Motor Works, Autobody Company, and Motor Wheel Corp. He was also
President of Lansing Businessmen's Association, predecessor of the Lansing
Regional Chamber of Commerce. It was during his Presidency that the

Association's members solicited funds and personally financed the balance needed to purchase 52 acres in the southwest part of Lansing to give to Mr. Olds so that he would move the Olds Motor Works to Lansing. This property is the current site of the Buick-Oldsmobile-Cadillac, Lansing Car Assembly operation.

Edmund C. Shields, who practiced law from 1896 to 1947, known for his quick wit and keen legal mind, was one of Michigan's most distinguished and able lawyers. One of his many noteworthy accomplishments included his service to the Democratic party where he served as Chairman of the State Central Committee from 1909 to 1916 and was elected Democratic National Committeeman in 1936 and 1940. His efforts for the Democratic party were not with the expectation of appointment, for he was quoted as saying, "I will not deprive any other Democrat of any appointment by taking it myself." His generosity was also felt in the community where he gave of his time in 1920-22 to direct the campaign to raise funds for the construction of Lansing's St. Lawrence Hospital; and at his death he left a bequest of $100,000 to the Hospital.

In more recent history, the lawyers at the Fraser Law Firm have lived up to the admirable standards set by the firm's forefathers and have maintained a commitment to legal excellence, community and profession. Everett R. Trebilcock and Joe C. Foster, Jr. were named Fellows in the American College of Trial Lawyers and the American College of Probate Counsel, respectively. Mr. Foster was also named in 1985 as one of the 34 best tax attorneys in the United States. Civic commitment has been exemplified by James R. Davis who received the 1985 Tri-County Volunteer Week Community Recognition Award for his many years of volunteer service to the community and by Donald A. Hines who served as the 1985 Director of the Lansing Area United Way Campaign. Mid-Michigan's legal community has also been influenced by various members of the firm over the years with Harry A. Silsbee (1927), Edmund C. Shields (1930), Byron L. Ballard (1943), Clayton F. Jennings (1956), Archie C. Fraser (1964) and David E.S. Marvin (1985), having served as Presidents of the Ingham County Bar Association.

From its modest beginning in 1875, the Fraser Law Firm has grown over the years to include 36 attorneys and a 40 person support staff. And though large in number, the firm continues to provide the high caliber of legal service to its clients as has been provided since Justice Person began his law practice over a century ago. The lawyers at the Fraser Law Firm are not unmindful of the valuable contributions made by the original members of the firm to the Greater Lansing Area and continually strive to insure that the community is served by equally capable persons, committed to integrity, professional excellence and community involvement. In these areas the Fraser Law Firm acknowledges a reputable and noteworthy history, along with the confidence that the pursuit of these ideals will contribute to and make Lansing history in the years to come.

Glassen, Rhead, McLean, Campbell, Bergamini & Schumacher

Glassen, Rhead, McLean, Campbell, Bergamini & Schumacher is one of the oldest firms in Lansing: celebrating its 80th year in 1997. The firm has long prided itself on its concentration of serving the people of Lansing area—and not just the major business interests of the community. Records dating back to 1917 indicate that the firm was originally located in St. Johns. It relocated to the then-brand-new American State Savings Bank Building in the early 1920s. The firm then moved to the Davenport Building located at the corner of Capitol and Ottawa streets in 1961. It was the first tenant in this building which is now known as the 200 North Capitol Building. Although the name of the firm has changed fourteen times, as new partners were added and partners died or retired, the firm has changed its Lansing location only once. The firm has also maintained an office in Grand Ledge, Michigan, since 1976.

Harold W. Glassen started with the firm known as J. Earl Brown in 1930. He was a member until his death in 1992. Roland F. Rhead has been with the firm since 1947; Neil A. McLean since 1955; George P. Cambell since 1967; Jaye M. Bergamini since 1981; and Kevin V. B. Schumacher since 1995.

Roland F. Rhead, Neil A. McLean, and George P. Campbell all have ratings of AV by Martindale & Hubbell. This is the highest rating obtainable.

The firm has elected to stay small. It is a community-oriented, close-knit firm that is focused on the people of the Lansing area and their needs. While initially the firm started by J. Earl Brown handled commercial matters only, over the years the focus broadened to include the great variety of legal matters that are encompassed in the general practice. Attorneys who are with this well-established firm are a part of the community it serves—they live, raise their families here and do volunteer work to enhance the community. This firm is proud of the fact that many of its staff have spent a lifetime of their working years with the firm.

Hubbard, Fox, Thomas, White & Bengtson, P.C.

Hubbard, Fox, Thomas, White & Bengtson, P.C., is one of the oldest law firms in the City of Lansing. The firm was originally founded by Charles H. Hayden and Byron Ballard in the early 1920s. In 1924, Harry D. Hubbard joined them and the firm prospered under the name of Hayden, Ballard and Hubbard.

In 1936 Charles H. Hayden was elected to the Ingham County bench, succeeding Judge Charles Collingwood.

Shortly thereafter, Mr. Ballard joined the Shields firm, which became known as Shields, Silsbee, Ballard and Jennings, and Mr. Hubbard continued on with two associates, S. DeWitt Rathbun and Robert Arvidson.

Later, DeWitt Rathbun and Robert Arvidson founded a new firm; Mr. Hubbard was joined by Dan D. McCullough and Donald G. Fox, and the firm became Hubbard, McCullough & Fox. After Mr. McCullough's untimely death,

Allison K. Thomas, following a stint in the prosector's office and four years in the U.S. military, joined the firm. Jack D. Born became a partner for nineteen years and subsequently affiliated with Transamerica Title Company. He is now retired. Mr. Hubbard died in 1983. Mr. Fox and Mr. Thomas continued on as "of counsel." Mr. Fox died in 1992.

Jonathon R. White joined the firm in 1968 and Thomas A. Bengtson in 1973. Judge Charles Hadyen became the personification of the storybook judge, interested in everyone's troubles, which allowed his own old-fashioned philosophy to rub off on litigants. Everybody in town seemed to "know" him. His nephew is following in his footsteps as a judge in California.

Harry D. Hubbard had a great resonant voice and was gifted with a facility in the language. As a young man he won many oratorical contests and won third place in a National Oratorical Contest, in which Chief Justice Taft was the judge. Mr. Hubbard had the pleasure of riding in the same carriage with Justice Taft from the train depot to the Chautauqua where the contest took place.

Present partners of the firm are Thomas A. Bengtson, Michael G. Woodworth, H. Kirby Albright, Peter A. Teholiz, Donald B. Lawrence, Jr., and Geoffrey H. Seidlein.

Present associates are: Ryan M. Wilson, Mark W. Geschwendt, Thomas L. Lapka, Janice K. Cunningham, Joseph M. Stewart, and William R. Theil.

Allison K. Thomas remains as "of counsel."

Latterman and Associates, P.C.

Mark A. Latterman, of Latterman and Associates, P.C., has been practicing law in Lansing for over twenty years. He was born and raised in Pittsburgh, Pennsylvania. He completed his undergraduate work at Michigan State University and received his Juris doctorate from George Washington University Law School in 1966 where he served as an editor on the *George Washington Law Review.*

Mr. Latterman served as a law clerk for the Ingham County Circuit Court Judge Marvin J. Salmon in 1967, and then opened his own practice in Lansing in 1968. At this time, he specialized in divorce and criminal law, and subsequently specialized in general civil practice, real estate development, corporate law, and municipal law.

Mr. Latterman was one the first contract professors at Cooley Law School, and has also served as an adjunct professor for courses in real property law, zoning, and banking law.

He currently serves as co-chairman of the Ingham County Bar Association Court Facilities Committee that is coordinating the development of a comprehensive court facility in Ingham County.

He also serves on various committees of the State Bar of Michigan, including Sections of Corporation and Real Estate. Mr. Latterman has been a member of the American Bar Association since 1970 and serves on several committees, including Uniform Commercial Code, Secured Transactions, and Securitization of Mortgages, and Taxation.

Mr. Latterman has been admitted to practice in the U.S. District Court for the Western District of Michigan, the U.S. Court of Appeals for the Sixth Circuit, and the U.S. Supreme Court.

Loomis, Ewert, Parsley, Davis & Gotting, P.C.

One of Lansing's larger law firms, Loomis, Ewert, Parsley, Davis & Gotting, P.C., occupies the top two floors of the Accident Fund Company Building overlooking the state capitol from the south. Although engaged in the general practice of law for individuals and others, the firm's law practice is heavily business-oriented. Accordingly, its clients include large and small corporations both publicly held and privately owned, governmental entities and municipalities, professional corporations, real estate partnerships, and other forms of associations and enterprises.

During the past four decades of successful practice, the firm has strived to combine its commitment to professional excellence with its commitment to the Greater Lansing community. Firm personnel have sought to extend their roots into the community in every way compatible with good citizenship and to engage in church, public, political, educational, and charitable activities as befits their respective interests and choices. Diverse groups and organizations, including Michigan State University, have been profuse in thanks to firm personnel for such dedicated interest and support.

The firm was founded on July 1, 1953, as a partnership for the practice of law by Plummer B. Snyder and George W. Loomis, formerly Special Assistant Attorney General assigned to the Michigan Public Service Commission. At that time, Mr. Snyder's brother, Dr. LeMoyne Snyder, the world famous legal-medical expert, was special counsel to the firm. The Snyders, sons of former Michigan Agricultural College President Jonathan Snyder, were born on the Michigan State (then MAC) campus, Plummer in 1900 and LeMoyne in 1889. They were men with handsome facial features, sparkling eyes and friendly smiles, and each frequently displayed a uniquely creative sense of humor, both at work and play. They had distinguished careers while active members of the Ingham County Bar Association from the late 1920s through the early 1960s.

Plummer Snyder was an expert in administrative and public utility law and recognized as such by his peers in some of the nation's largest and most prestigious law offices. Firms in Detroit, Chicago, New York, Washington, D.C., and other large metropolises regularly recommended the hiring of Plummer and his firm for important regulatory cases arising in Michigan; and electric, gas, telephone and transportation companies came to his office from all points in Michigan and from various points outside the State, seeking wise counsel on rates, services and other regulatory matters. Plummer and his partners special-izing in utility law (such as George Loomis, Quentin A. Ewert, and William D. Parsley) tried a number of landmark cases before the Michigan Supreme Court which clarified regulatory statutes and defined permissible regulatory actions within constitutional limitations. See, for example, *General Telephone Company of Michigan v Public Service Commission*, 341 Mich 620; 67 NW2d 882 (1954) and *Huron Portland Cement Company v Public Service Commission*, 351 Mich 255; 88 NW2d 492 (1958).

LeMoyne Snyder, a physician (MD) as well as an attorney-at-law, special-ized in legal medicine. Both he and Plummer took their undergraduate college studies at MAC. Plummer was then graduated from Harvard Law School in 1925 and, following graduation, worked several years for the League of Nations in Geneva, Switzerland. LeMoyne was graduated from Harvard Medical College in 1923, did his internship and residency in surgery in New York City, and then spent two years as a ship's doctor aboard ships steaming around the world. The Snyder brothers returned to Lansing and East Lansing, commencing practices in law and medicine in 1928.

As an attorney, LeMoyne specialized in legal medicine and, in 1940, became Medicolegal Director for the Michigan State Police. After further study of legal medicine at the University of Vienna, Austria, he became world-renown in his specialty. In 1944, his book *Homicide Investigation* was published. Designed as a manual and text for police officers charged with the investigation of mur-der, manslaughter, and violent or suspicious deaths, this book soon became the "Bible" for investigative techniques and procedures in such cases, not only throughout the United States, but in other parts of the world. Its thirteen suc-cessive editions were continually updated to match scientific progress and trans-lated into foreign languages, including German, Spanish, and Japanese.

LeMoyne always spoke highly of the "joints" at which he had received his formal education: MSU, Harvard, Vienna, but most importantly ". . . Law at the knee joint of Judge Leland Carr." LeMoyne received the degree of Doctor of Laws from Michigan State University in 1977 for his ". . . distinguished career in legal medicine . . . assistance to victims of injustice. . . ."

The firm has grown significantly since 1953 and, in 1991, became a profes-sional corporation. Firm management is under the direction of an executive committee, presently composed of five of the firm's strong members: Jack C. Davis, Karl L. Gotting, Harvey J. Messing, Kenneth W. Beall, and Howard J. Soifer. Working by example and leadership, they have sought to achieve total quality management and have encouraged all personnel continually to fulfill the firms's dual commitment to professional excellence and community involve-ment. The firm's continued community involvement embraces a host of signifi-cant public service activities performed by firm attorneys, such as Jack Davis's present service as president of the Greater Lansing Chamber of Commerce and Karl Gotting's former service as president of the Lansing YMCA.

George Loomis, Quentin A. Ewert, and William Parsley are presently counsel to the firm. Messrs. Ewert and Parsley joined the firm shortly after it was formed. Mr. Ewert had previously practiced law as member of the Ingham County Bar and for a term as Grand Ledge City Attorney. Mr. Parsley went directly into the U.S. Army after graduation from law school and joined the firm on his discharge. Attorneys with the firm, in addition to those mentioned above, include, as shareholders, David M. Lick, James R. Neal, Michael G. Oliva, Jeffrey W. Bracken, Catherine A. Jacobs, Ronald W. Bloomberg, Michael H. Rhodes, Jeffrey L. Green, and Gary L. Field. Sherri A. Wellman heads the list of associate attorneys.

A firm brochure, available upon request, sets forth the branches and specialties of law in which firm members have had extensive experience and briefly details each attorney's education and credentials.

Newman and MacKay

On January 1, 1955, Charles E. Chamberlain became the Ingham County Prosecuting Attorney. The best thing he did was hire me as an assistant to keep his office on even keel. Some of the other good men who joined us were Peter Treleaven, William Austin, Joseph Lavey, with certain changes during the two-year period, namely Fred C. Newman, became a chief assistant prosecutor after Joseph Lavey, chief assistant, left for the private practice of law. After Fred returned to private practice, I became the chief assistant prosecutor until the end of our term on December 31, 1956.

After we left the prosecutor's office, in which Donald A. Jones did our appellate work, we decided to form a law firm entitled Newman, Chamberlain, Jones and Mackay. We started our practice on February 1, 1957. In January of 1957, waiting for the new firm to commence, I hung around the office doing most anything. At that time there was no explosion of litigation, at least it didn't explode near my office. So Newman, Chamberlain, Jones and Mackay began. We continued to practice as a firm until Charles Chamberlain, who had been elected United States Congressman from the 6th Congressional District, decided to leave for Washington, D.C..

Few people know that Donald A. Jones was afflicted with rheumatoid arthritis, which incapacitated him, but never his mind. Don told me that he drove to the University of Michigan Law School, turned around, parked his car in the garage, turned the ignition off because he just didn't feel he could make it physically through law school. But as he sat there he told me he said to himself, "I'm going to do it if it kills me." He returned to the University of Michigan and distinguished himself academically. His vocabulary was unsurpassed, and his legal ability was well-known to all those who knew him. Suddenly, after practicing with us for many years, he retired to his home and practiced out of his refurbished garage for several years before he died. He was blessed with an excellent sense of humor.

It was then that we formed the firm of Newman and Mackay. Fred and I practiced law for over 20 years. We had no written agreements, partnership agreements or audits. Fred had a superb sense of humor that maybe a lot of people didn't know about or understand. He was a superb trial lawyer. I can assure you it was my pleasure having had the opportunity of working with him and knowing him.

When we decided to "close down" Newman and Mackay, we did it simply. You keep what you have and I'll keep what I have, and that's the way it ended, as it should. Fred lives in Tucson, Arizona, and is retired. My wife and I had the opportunity of visiting with him last year in Durango, Colorado.

During the years that Fred and I practiced together we were considered general practitioners. However, as events began to develop, we became known as insurance company defense lawyers. I, of course, continue my career and I refer to myself as a "fender bender defender."

That, my friends, is the capsulized history of Newman and Mackay.*

Rapaport, Pollok, Farrell & Waldron, P. C.

In October of 1942 Raymond H. Rapaport left his position as law clerk to Michigan Supreme Court Justice Emerson R. Boyles to become chief attorney for the Lansing rent control office. In 1944, he joined John Leighton, and, on August 31, 1946, he opened his own office in the Tussing Building.

Rapaport began his lifelong relationship with organized labor in 1944 when he was endorsed by the C.I.O., A.F.L. and the U.A.W. in a losing race for Circuit Court Commissioner. He was retained by the C.I.O., A.F.L., U.A.W. and Teamsters to represent their locals in mid Michigan. From 1944 through 1957 Rapaport represented almost every labor union in the Lansing area. According to the Lansing State Journal, "there are a lot of union locals in central Michigan. But if they ever have needed a lawyer you can bet the family jewels that Rapaport got the call. The name Rapaport for the Lansing halls is as symbolic as a union label."

When the A.F.L. and C.I.O. merged in 1958, many State Federations refused to join. Litigation arose between the A.F.L.-C.I.O and the State Federations of Labor regarding ownership of Federation assets. George Meany, the president of the A.F.L.-C.I.O., decided that Michigan would be the test state and that Rapaport would be the attorney. In an interview at the time, Rapaport said, "It may mean a fight, but I never run from a fight." The litigation ended with the Michigan Federation of Labor being dissolved and $271,000.00 of assets being turned over to the A.F.L.-C.I.O. As a result of the Michigan test

---

* William MacKay wrote this history prior to his death in 1996.

case, the other Federations disputing the A.F.L.-C.I.O. merger all gave up their claims and the merger was completed. Rapaport's speedy resolution of the case further cemented his position as a "union attorney."

Over the years a number of attorneys would work for Rapaport. These would include Robert A. Siegrist, Michael E. Miatech, Gerald Oade and Thomas P. Mitchell. Future District Court Judges R. William Reid and James Edgar and former Circuit Court Judge Theodore P. Ryan were also employed by the firm. After he served as a delegate to the State Constitutional Convention, Joseph F. Sablich joined the firm in 1965.

During the 1950s, 1960s, and 1970s the firm became a prominent Workers Compensation law firm. The firm made law in the Supreme Court on many occasions. Joseph Sablich represented the plaintiff in *Burke v Ontonagon County Road Commission*. The resulting decision paved the way for injured workers to obtain benefits for the loss of industrial use of their legs. According to Sablich, the day he received the decision from the Supreme Court was one of the proudest in his life.

Raymond Rapaport died in 1975 and Joseph Sablich took over the firm. Sablich hired Roger A. Rapaport in 1975, Steven J. Pollok in 1977 and Mark S. Farrell in 1979. Roger Rapaport left the Sablich firm in 1981 and started "Roger A. Rapaport, P.C." Pollok and Farrell left the Sablich firm in 1984 and joined Rapaport to form "Rapaport, Pollok & Farrell P.C." The new firm specialized in the Workers Compensation, Social Security and Negligence fields.

By 1988 Donald Waldron Jr. was working for Joseph Sablich and the law firms of "Sablich and Associates, P.C." and "Rapaport, Pollok & Farrell P.C." merged to become "Rapaport, Pollok, Farrell & Waldron, P.C."

The firm has continued its influence in the Workers Compensation field. Beginning in 1981, Rapaport taught Workers Compensation law at Thomas M. Cooley Law School. After Rapaport taught thirty-one straight terms, Pollok joined him at Cooley teaching alternate terms. Between them, they have taught Michigan Workers Compensation to more than 1800 future lawyers. With Pollok's election in 1995, he joins Ray Rapaport and Joe Sablich as firm members who have chaired the Workers Compensation Section of the State Bar.

When asked to discuss his most memorable case, Roger Rapaport had no hesitation. "Without a doubt it is *Barnes v Double Seal Glass*." The case involved a sixteen-year-old boy killed by falling glass. According to the child's parents, many lawyers (including F. Lee Bailey) rejected the case before they were referred to Rapaport in Lansing. "When they came to see me, virtually every workers' compensation attorney in Genesee County had rejected the case because of the exclusive remedy provisions of the Workers' Compensation Act. I was incensed that an incident like this would be allowed to occur."

Rapaport sued the employer in circuit court on behalf of the parents alleging intentional infliction of emotional distress. After the Circuit Court dismissed the case, he appealed to the Court of Appeals. The Court issued a decision allowing the intentional tort claim and saying that the parents had an independent cause of action which was not barred by the exclusive remedy provisions of the Workers' Compensation Act.

According to Rapaport, "I think about the Barnes family often. Every year on the anniversary of Tim Barnes death I review my file. It always renews my answer against that type of workplace. After looking at the file I am ready to spend another year fighting that type of employer."

Every case is not a matter of life or death and some of a law firm's history involves humorous matters. For Mark Farrell, his first days working for Joe Sablich almost brought disaster. Farrell knew when he was hired that the firm represented workers and had close ties with labor unions. An employee at a local factory needed an attorney in a land contract and, wanting to make a good impression, he wrote a scathing letter to the "deadbeat" purchaser. He threatened everything up to and including foreclosure and made no effort to be civil or charming.

A few days later Farrell received a telephone call from the president of a very large local union who not only happened to be one of Joe Sablich's best friends but was also the "deadbeat." He told Farrell that he was through referring people to the firm and that he was through with Joe Sablich. According to Farrell, "My legal career passed in front of my eyes. Fortunately for me, Joe Sablich thought the whole incident was humorous." He was able to soothe the ruffled feathers of the local union president. The land contract was brought up to date and the union president kept referring clients.

For Donald Waldron Jr., his most memorable case was also a learning experience. The case began with an early Sunday morning phone call from a woman whose brother needed representation for driving on a suspended license. Waldron took the case (his first criminal matter). The client said the warrant was a mistake, the license was not suspended but he did have some outstanding tickets. According to Waldron his big mistake regarding the client was that, "I believed him."

After vigorous negotiations the prosecutor agreed to reduce the charge to a civil infraction. With the plea agreement Waldron "felt like Clarence Darrow."As he turned to leave the prosecutor asked Waldron if he wanted to talk about the other eleven Ingham County charges and several in East Lansing. These included two counts of indecent exposure and one for possession of a controlled substance.

One year and several trials later, Waldron's client plead guilty to the traffic offense and the others had all been dismissed. According to Waldron, after the last of the fourteen charges against his client had been resolved, "the next time I received a phone call on a Sunday morning I just let it ring."

Steve Pollok recalled the suicide of an educator with twenty-seven years of experience. He was falsely accused by a student of improperly touching her upper leg. When the Ingham County prosecutor issued a warrant, the teacher killed himself. He left a suicide note saying that he did not commit the crime but that the allegation had ruined his career and that he could not face the trial and suspicions raised by the wrongful accusation.

Pollok filed an application for workers compensation for the widow. He alleged that the teacher's suicide arose out of his employment with the school district. Prior to his suicide, the teacher had consulted with Leo Farhat. Pollok utilized Farhat's expertise in the field of criminal law to prove that the prosecutor lacked probable cause to issue a warrant. Farhat's testimony was taken shortly before his death and, according to Pollok, "it was the strongest expert witness testimony I have ever elicited." During Leo Farhat's testimony he became very emotional and it was quite obvious that he felt very strongly that an innocent and caring educator of long standing had been crushed by the false accusation.

The Workers' Compensation Magistrate awarded Pollok's client Workers Compensation death benefits. The decision was upheld by the workers' Compensation Appellate Commission. The case is currently on appeal at the Michigan Court of Appeals.

The law firm of Rapaport, Pollok, Farrell & Waldron P.C. has gone through many changes over the past fifty-plus years. The names and faces may be different, but the policy of representing workers, their families and organized labor has not changed.

Schram, Behan & Behan

Schram, Behan & Behan is one of the oldest law offices in the Lansing area. Records dating back to the nineteenth century indicate that the practice was first established by Charles F. Hammond, and has been in continuous existence ever since. Mr. Hammond, who also served as Ingham County Prosecutor for a brief time during his early days in practice, was joined in practice, in 1907, by his son Eugene T. Hammond, with whom he remained associated until his retirement in 1934. The Hammonds practiced together for a number of years in the Hollister Building. However, upon completion of the American State Savings Bank Building in 1917 (now the First of America Building), the firm relocated to that building, where it remained as a tenant until the building was closed in 1996. In 1934, Henry L. Schram joined the firm, and by 1937, following the death of Charles Hammond, the firm became known as Hammond & Schram. Mr. Schram had originally come to Lansing as the local attorney for the Home Owners Loan Corporation, a federal agency engaged in refinancing distressed home mortgages. Throughout his years in practice he maintained a keen interest and expertise in the practice of real property law, serving, in fact, as a founding member of the state bar's committee on land title standards. Following the retirement of Eugene Hammond, Raymond R. Behan joined Mr. Schram in practice in 1965, and the firm became known as Schram & Behan. A graduate and present trustee of the Detroit College of Law, Mr. Behan, a former bank officer with the American Bank and Trust Company, was joined in the practice of law by his son, Michael R. Behan, in 1991. The firm now exists under the name of Schram, Behan & Behan and is located in the Eastbrook Plaza at 4127 Okemos Road, Okemos, Michigan.

The Sinas-Dramis Law Firm

In 1951, Thomas G. Sinas, the son of Greek immigrants, became one of the first attorneys of Greek descent to practice law in Lansing. Soon after, Tom's college friend, Lee C. Dramis, a decorated World War II Marine (Silver Star) returned to Lansing to practice law. When these two friends decided to combine their friendship with a business venture, the Sinas-Dramis law firm was born.

In the years that followed, Tom and Lee worked with and came to respect Richard J. Brake, who was employed as an associate with one of Lansing's larger law firms. Dick, the son of a law professor, and a 1950 graduate of the University of Michigan Law School, joined the Sinas-Dramis law firm in 1954.

In those early years, Tom, Lee and Dick did not "specialize" in anything but hard work for a wide variety of clients. In time, however, Tom drew upon his father's restaurant background and friendships with many restaurant and tavern owners to develop a licensing and real estate clientele to compliment a growing divorce practice. Lee initially did bankruptcy and divorce work, but ultimately gravitated to plaintiffs' personal injury work. He became one of Michigan's best and most respected trial attorneys in that field. Dick's practice evolved to real estate and probate work.

Since these early years, several bright young lawyers have joined the firm. Some have become partners. Others have gone on to distinguished careers with other firms or in public life. All have, to some extent, made significant contributions to the law firm's development.

In 1959, most Lansing law firms were located in downtown office buildings. The Sinas-Dramis partners, feeling confined as tenants, decided to buy a large home at 515 North Capitol Avenue and convert it to office use. The firm remained at that location until January 1976, when it constructed the office building at its present location of 520 Seymour Avenue.

In 1964, Barry D. Boughton, a recent graduate of the University of Michigan Law School, joined the law firm and soon distinguished himself as partnership material. Barry became a disciple of Lee Dramis, honing his trial skills in the area of personal injury litigation. When Lee assigned Barry a particularly difficult liability case with minimal damages for "educational purposes," he made a point of explaining to the young lawyer how such cases allowed one to develop a "romance" with the law.

In 1969, Kenneth "Red" McIntyre joined the firm after serving with the Civil Rights Division of the U.S. Department of Justice prosecuting civil rights cases in the South. He also served as chief investigator for the president's Commission on Campus Unrest in its investigation of the shooting deaths of four students at Kent State University in 1970. For what seemed to be an eternity from the mid-1970s and early 1980s, Red was chief trial attorney for Farm Bureau, responsible for the defense of hundreds of PBB contamination claims. Since then, he has devoted his practice to complex litigation and criminal defense.

In 1976, Donald L. Reisig ended a distinguished public career as Lansing City Attorney, Ingham County Prosecutor, and Chief Ingham County Circuit Court Judge to begin private practice as a partner with the law firm. Don's addition to the Sinas-Dramis law firm represented a milestone in the development of the firm's practice. In 1988-89, he served as president of the State Bar of Michigan. Even before that term expired, Governor James Blanchard appointed him as the newly created Drug Agencies Director for the State of Michigan where he served until the end of Blanchard's term.

In the more recent era, new partners have risen from the ranks. Most notably, and to the great pride of his father, George T. Sinas weathered the storm of Lee Dramis's "learner cases" to become a well-respected personal injury attorney having served as president of the Michigan Trial Lawyers Association and as chairperson on the State Bar Negligence Law section. From the time that George joined the firm in 1975, until Tom's untimely death in 1985, George and Tom Sinas were able to enjoy the spirited relationship that comes with father-son law practices.

Timothy J. Donovan joined the firm in 1976. He began his career engaged in a general practice of commercial and general civil litigation, complete with the customary allotment of Dramis "learners." In more recent years, Tim's practice has evolved primarily to personal injury law.

In 1987, Bernard F. Finn joined the law firm as a partner after nine years of successful practice with a smaller Lansing firm. Bernie has devoted his practice over those years to real estate matters, domestic relations law, and as defense counsel in hundreds of complex felony cases.

Michael E. Larkin joined the firm in 1988. After obtaining his degree at the University of Arizona in 1982, Mike practiced with a prominent Tucson, Arizona, personal injury law firm from 1982 until he joined the firm in 1988. His practice is exclusively devoted to the field of personal injury litigation.

Debbie Deprez, after several years of litigation experience with one of Lansing's largest law firms, joined Sinas-Dramis in 1989 and is its most recent parnter. Debbie's practice focuses upon worker's compensation and personal injury law.

In addition to its partners, the firm has had the valuable contribution of numerous past and current associate lawyers who contribute their skills and energy to the firm's practice. Included among the current associate staff is

Catherine Groll, who, after three years of practice with another Lansing firm, joined Sinas-Dramis in 1955 and practices personal injury law.

Lee Dramis died in 1981. His last year was filled with an active, vigorous, and enthusiastic practice of law despite his illness. Tom Sinas died in 1985. He too never lost his zest for life, the law, and his family. Those of us who knew Tom and Lee believe that their commitment to excellence and their legacy of honesty, integrity, humor, and compassion lives on in the way the Sinas-Dramis law firm serves its clients and the community today.

Thomas M. Cooley Law School

In 1971, Michigan Supreme Court Justice Thomas E. Brennan proposed a bold idea to the State Board of Bar Examiners. He envisioned the creation of a new law school in Lansing. No new law school had been established in Michigan in 50 years. Many members of Michigan's legal education establishment assured Judge Brennan that no new law school was needed, or wanted. Judge Brennan redoubled his commitment to establish an innovative law school and he was bolstered by the encouragement of a handful of people. The late Stanley E. Beattie, the chairman of the State of Board of Bar Examiners, was one of those people who supported Brennan's efforts. Thomas M. Cooley Law School's founders dreamed of a law school that would offer a legal education to those traditionally not part of the legal profession mainstream. The law school's mission statement reflected that goal: "The mission of the Thomas M. Cooley Law School is to prepare its students for entry into the legal profession through an integrated program with practical legal scholarship as its guiding principle and focus." The school has not deviated from that original purpose.

Thomas M. Cooley Law School was chartered as a non-profit, educational corporation by the State of Michigan on June 19, 1972. The law school was founded by a group of active judges, practicing attorneys and experienced businesspersons. The first Thomas Cooley Board of Directors were Brennan and Ingham County Bar members Louis A. Smith, John L. Cote', Robert A. Fisher, Honorable John W. Fitzgerald, Jack W. Warren, Russel A. Swaney; and members of the Detroit bar, J. Bruce Donaldson and Honorable James L. Ryan. Other Ingham County Bar members who have served on the Thomas Cooley Board of Directors include: Honorable Michael F. Cavanagh, Honorable Thomas E. Brennan, Jr., Honorable Benjamin F. Gibson, Lawrence P. Nolan, and Honorable Dorothy Comstock Riley.

Michigan Supreme Court Chief Justice John W. Fitzgerald presided over the first freshman Property class on the night of January 12, 1973. These pioneer students did not even know if they would be able to sit for the bar until April 1973 when the State Board of Law Examiners unanimously approved Thomas Cooley as a reputable and qualified law school. This endorsement ensured that Thomas Cooley graduates would be allowed to sit for the Michigan

Bar examination. Provisional accreditation by the American Bar Association came in 1975. The law school gained permanent accreditation status in 1978.

The first class of 59 students graduated on January 12, 1976. Classes were initially held in the present administration building at 507 S. Grand Avenue. The law school purchased the old Masonic Temple building on Capitol Avenue in June 1973 and classes, the library, and faculty offices were moved there. Original faculty members included: Lt. Governor James Brickley, Fitzgerald, Donald Reisig, George Warren and Roger Needham, to name a few. Today, the law school employs 66 full-time professors, and over 100 adjunct faculty members from all facets of the Michigan bar.

In Thomas Cooley's early years, the average student was 30 years old, held an undergraduate degree, and was a commuter. Today, the average student is 28 years of age, and about 80 percent are from outside Michigan.

Judge Brennan was Thomas Cooley's first acting dean. Coincidentally, the law school's namesake, Justice Thomas McIntyre Cooley, was dean of the University of Michigan Law School while he served on the Supreme Court of Michigan. Don LeDuc is the current dean.

Much has changed at Thomas Cooley since those early years. The student body grew in 1996 to over 1,800. Thomas Cooley's trial and practical skills teams compete successfully in regional and national competitions. Recently, the Moot Court team won the Region VI portion of the National Moot Court Competition. Thomas Cooley's nationally recognized clinical program, the Sixty-Plus, Inc., Elder Law Clinic, offers legal services to tri-county area senior citizens, free of charge.

The law school's latest challenge was the completion of the new $10 million library. The 65,000 square foot, five-story library, located at the corner of Kalamazoo and Washington Avenue, is the twenty-first largest law school library in the nation. It blends technologically and advanced research facilities with a traditional book and periodical collections.

Thomas Cooley's future is promising. Its alumni include Michigan's Governor John Engler, state legislators, private practitioners, judges, public servants, federal government appointees, law professors, business people, and community leaders. Thomas Cooley Law School is an important part of the local and Michigan's economy. Statistics show that the law school's 1,800 students pour about $19 million into the state's economy, $15 million of which is spent in the tri-county area. The law school's wages and salaries paid, its goods and services purchased, and its plant and equipment maintained, bring $18 million into Michigan's economy, $16.3 million of which is spent in the tri-county area. First and foremost, Thomas Cooley is dedicated to preparing men and women to serve as skilled and knowledgeable members of the legal profession. Adhering to its original mission, the law school will continue to prepare its students for entry into the bar with practical legal scholarship as its guiding focus.

Thrun, Maatsch and Nordberg, P.C.

Thrun, Maatsch and Nordberg, P.C., succeeds a firm founded by Fred Thrun in 1946. The practice originally focused on school law, public finance, and municipal charters. Caroline M. Thrun joined the firm in 1955 after leaving her twenty-year post as assistant attorney general. She had also been staff legal advisor to the Superintendent of Public Instruction for ten years, responsible for education matters throughout Michigan. Robert M. Thrun joined the firm in 1959. The growth of the firm since that time has been concentrated in general school law; municipal law; elections, public finance; labor management relations and employment law; insurance, construction, and civil rights law and litigation. The firm has also been extensively involved in the drafting of amendments to the School Code, Community College Act, Public Employment Relations Act, General Property Tax Act, and finance statutes.

Timmer, Jamo, and O'Leary

The law firm of Timmer, Jamo, and O'Leary traces its origin to 32 years ago when it was formed by George H. Denfield and James A. Timmer, both of whom, at that time, had considerable insurance defense experience, which emphasis has been continued since that time. During the 1960s and 1970s, David M. Seelye was a partner representing most of the major oil companies in Michigan. Mr. Seelye passed away in 1972, at which time Clifford W. Taylor joined the firm, and the firm name of Denfield, Timmer and Taylor existed for the next 20 years until Mr. Taylor's appointment to the Michigan Court of Appeals in 1992.

All of the then-partners had military experience, Mr. Denfield having been a naval officer in World War II, Mr. Timmer having served in World War II with the 82nd Airborne Division in Europe, Mr. Seelye with a parachute unit in Korea, and Mr. Taylor as a naval officer during the Vietnam era.

Also, the three principals were all former assistant prosecutors, and all served as officers of the Ingham County Bar Association. Mr. Denfield as its secretary, Mr. Timmer as its secretary and president, and all three as members of the Board of Directors. Each partner was an elected member of the Michigan Bar Foundation.

In 1980, John W. Cotner joined the firm, as did James S. Jamo in 1984. When Mr. Cotner left the Lansing area in 1988, Kathleen A. Lopilato became a member of the firm. In 1992, after Mr. Taylor's appointment to the Michigan Court of Appeals, James S. O'Leary joined the firm after serving as the head of the Lansing office of Plunkett Cooney. Mr. O'Leary also served in the army in Vietnam.

The firm represents a varied law school background, with Mr. Denfield a graduate of the Detroit College of Law, Mr. Timmer of the University of

Michigan Law School and Mr. Taylor of the George Washington University Law School, Mr. Cotner of Indiana University Law School (Bloomington), Mr. Jamo a graduate of the Thomas M. Cooley Law School, Mr. O' Leary from the Detroit College of Law, and Ms. Lopilato from Wayne State University Law School.

The firm has had a Martindale Hubbell "A" rating for many years and is listed in *Best's Directory of Recommended Insurance Attorneys*. Each of the attorneys is a member of various insurance defense organizations, and the firm was selected by the Bar Register of Pre-eminent Lawyers shortly after that organization was formed and this listing continues. The insurance defense specialty has also continued over the past 30-plus years, with essentially an unchanged client base.

BIBLIOGRAPHY

Documents

Alaiedon and Aurelius, Mich., Township of. Petition to Honorable Ira Jennings from the inhabitants. State of Michigan Archives, RG 44, Box 221.

Ingham County Bar Association. Articles of Association of the Ingham County Bar Association, Lansing, Mich., November 1, 1909.

Ingham County Circuit Court. Excerpt of Proceedings, *People v. Messenger*, Docket No. 94-67694-FH, Ingham County Circuit Court, February 2, 1995

_____. Calendar, Vol . 94. September 29, 1876. State of Michigan Archives.

_____. Case Files 1839-1920, State of Michigan Archives, (335 boxes).

_____. *State v. Eva-Akers-Mead*, Case No. 68, Box 192, 1900.

Michigan, State of. *1990 Judicial Compensation and Fringe Benefit Survey*, State Court Administrator's Office, 1991.

_____. *State of Michigan Constitutional Convention 1961, Official Record*, Vols. 1 & 2, Austin C. Knapp, Ed.

_____. *Laws of the Territory of Michigan*, Vol. 2, printed from original handwritten documents. W.S. George and Company, State of Michigan, 1874.

_____. Executive Acts 1835-1846, State of Michigan Archives, RG 83-42, Vol. 8.

_____. Acts of the Legislature of the State of Michigan, passed at the adjourned Session of 1837 and the Regular Session of 1838, John S. Bragg (printer), 1838.

Michigan Department of Corrections. Prison Card for Arthur C. Rich, 1926.

Petition to Legislature of the Territory or State of Michigan, Ingham, December 2, 1836, Michigan Archives RG 44, Box 221.

Manuals and Reports

Lansing City Directories, 1874-1995

Legislative Manual of the State of Michigan, Secretary of State, Lansing, 1891-92, 1893-94, 1895-96.

Michigan Manual, Lansing, Mich., 1867-1995

Michigan Reports—Official Publication of the Decisions of the Michigan Supreme Court

Published by Lawyers' Cooperation, Lansing, Michigan.

Twitchell v. Blodgett (13 Mich. 127), January 1865

Stuart v. School District of Kalamazoo (30 Mich. 69), July 1874

The People ex rel Detroit and Howell Railroad Co. v. the Township Board of Salem (20 Mich. 452), April 1870.

The People v. Emily U. Marble (38 Mich. 117), submitted October 10, 1877, decided January 15, 1878

Willard Chapman v. The People (39 Mich. 357), opinion filed October 15, 1878

People v. George W. Burt (51 Mich. 199), July 2, 1983

John W. Whallon v. Circuit Judge for Ingham County (51 Mich. 503), submitted October 4, 1883, denied October 5-17

People v. Hammond (132 Mich. 422), 1903

People v. Pratt (133 Mich. 125), 1903

Vol. 159, Page 528, Decided Feb. 1910

Vol. 172, Page 150, Decided 1912

People v. Etta May Miller (250 Mich. 72), 1930

Vol. 285, Page 119, Decided June, 1938

People v. Martin J. Lavan and Hyman Levinson (303 Mich. 394), 11-1942

Books

Adams, Mrs. Franc L. *Pioneer History of Ingham County.* Lansing, Mich.: Wynkoop Hallenback Crawford Co., 1923.

Bald, F. Clever. *Michigan in Four Centuries.* New York: Harper & Bros., 1954.

Barfknecht, Gary W. *Murder Michigan.* Friede Publications, 1983

Bours, Allen L. *Laying of the Corner Stone of the New Capitol of Michigan*. Lansing: W.S. George & Co., 1873.

Campbell, James V. *Outlines of Political History of Michigan*. Schober & Co., 1876

Catton, Bruce. *Michigan*. New York: W.W. Norton & Co., 1976

Ceasar, Ford Stevens. *The Bicentennial History of Ingham County, Michigan*. Ingham County, 1976.

Cowles, Albert E. *Past and Present of the City of Lansing and Ingham County*. Lansing, Mich.: The Michigan Historical Printing Assoc., 1910.

Dain, Floyd R. *Education in the Wilderness*. Lansing: Michigan Historical Commission, Department of State, 1968.

Darling, Birt. *City in the Forest*. New York: Stratford House, 1950.

Disbrow, Donald W. *Schools for an Urban Society*. Lansing: Michigan Historical Commission, Department of State, 1968.

Dunbar, Willis Frederick. *A History of the Wolverine State*. Grand Rapids, Mich.: William B. Eerdmans Publishing Co., 1965.

Durant, Samuel W. H*istory of Ingham and Eaton Counties Michigan*. Philadelphia: D.W. Ensign Co., 1880.

Edmunds, J.P. *Early Lansing History*. Lansing, Mich.: Franklin DeKleine Co., 1944.

Fine, Sydney, *Frank Murphy: The Detroit Years*. Ann Arbor: University of Michigan Press, 1975.

_____. *Frank Murphy: The New Deal Years*. Chicago: University of Chicago Press, 1979.

Fox, Jean. *Fred Warner: Progressive Governor*. Farmington Hills, Mich.: Farmington Hills Historical Commission, 1988.

Fuller, George N., Ed. *Historic Michigan Land of the Great Lakes*. Vols. I and III. National Historic Association, Inc., 1924.

_____, ed. *Messages of the Governors of Michigan*. Vol. 3. Michigan History Commission, 1927.

Fuller, George N., and Frank M. Turner. *Historic Michigan*. Vol. III. National Historic Association, Inc., 1924.

George, Sister Mary Karl, *Zachariah Chandler: A Political Biography*. East Lansing: Michigan State University Press, 1969.

Gilpin, Alec R., *The Territory of Michigan*. East Lansing: Michigan State University Press, 1970.

Hare, James M., *With Malice Toward None: The Musing of a Retired Politician.* East Lansing: Michigan State University Press, 1972.

Hemans, Lawton T. *Life and Times of Stevens T. Mason.* Lansing: Michigan Historical Commission, 1930.

Heyden, Patricia. *Behind the Badge: The History of the Lansing Police Department.* Lansing, Mich.: Stuart Publishing, 1991.

Kern, John. *A Short History of Michigan.* Lansing: Michigan History Division, Michigan Department of State, 1977.

Kestenbaum, Justin L., Ed. *The Making of Michigan 1820-1860.* Detroit, Mich.: Wayne State University Press, 1990

._____. *Out of a Wilderness: An Illustrated History of Greater Lansing.* Woodland Hills, Calif.: Windsor Publications, 1981.

Kuhn, Madison. *Michigan State: The First Hundred Years.* East Lansing: Michigan State University Press, 1955.

Manassah, Sallie M., David A. Thomas, and James F. Wallington. *Lansing: Capital, Campus and Cars.* East Lansing, Mich.: Contemporary Image Adv., 1986.

McNaughton, Frank. *Mennon Williams of Michigan.* New York: Oceana Publication, Inc., 1960.

Michigan Historical Society. *Michigan Biographies.* Vol. II. Lansing: Michigan Historical Society, 1924.

Mid-Michigan Genealogical Society. *Combined Ingham Co. Mich. 1874 & 1895 Atlases.* Lansing: Mid-Michigan Genealogical Society, 1988.

Nye, Russell B., *Midwestern Progressive Politics.* East Lansing: Michigan State College Press, 1951.

Portrait and Biographical Album of Ingham and Livingston Counties. Chicago: Chapman Bros., 1891.

Quaife, M.M., and Sydney Glazer. *Michigan: From Primitive Wilderness to Industrial Commonwealth.* Prentice-Hall, 1948.

Riddell, William Renwick. *Michigan Under British Rule: Law and Law Courts 1760-1796.* Michigan Historical Commission, 1926.

Rubenstein, Bruce A., and Lawrence E. Ziewacz. *Payoffs in the Cloakroom: The Greening of the Michigan Legislature, 1938-46.* East Lansing: Michigan State University Press, 1995.

_____. *Three Bullets Sealed His Lips*, Michigan State University Press, East Lansing, Michigan, 1987.

Seale, William. *Michigan's Capitol: Construction & Restoration.* Ann Arbor: University of Michigan, 1994.

Sheldon, E.M. *The Early History of Michigan from the First Settlement to 1815.* Detroit: Kerr, Morley & Co., 1856.

Sommers, Lawrence M., ed. *Atlas of Michigan.* East Lansing: Michigan State University Press, 1977.

Streeter, Floyd Benjamin. *Political Parties in Michigan 1837-1860.* Lansing: Michigan Historical Commission, 1918.

Thompkins, C. David. *Senator Arthur H. Vandenberg: The Evolution of a Modern Republican, 1884-1945.* East Lansing: Michigan State University Press, 1970.

Vandercook, Roy C. *The City of Mason: Its Past and Present Life.* Mason, Mich.: News Job Print, 1897.

Weeks, George. *Stewards of the State: The Governors of Michigan.* Detroit News and Historical Society of Michigan, 1987.

Williams, Frederick D., ed. *Northwest Ordinance: Essays on Its Formulation, Provisions, and Legacy.* East Lansing: Michigan State University Press, 1988.

Wilson, Mary Jane McClintock, *The Watch of the Capitol.* Lansing: Michigan Department of Education, 1979.

Writers Program of the WPA, *Michigan: A Guide to the Wolverine State.* New York, 1941.

Articles

Beal, W. J. "Old Seals and State Seals of Michigan," *Michigan Pioneer and Historical Collections* 30 (1894): 337-38.

Danhoff, Robert J. "Judicial Branch: Revised Constitution Provides United Court System." *Michigan Challenge* (June 1962): 22.

Edwards, Judge George. "Why Justice Cooley Left the Bench: A Missing Page of Legal History." *The Wayne Law Review* 33 (5) (1987).

Fortino, Jackie. "'Monte' Thrun Talks About Schools & Law." *Michigan School Board Journal* (January 1982): 12-13.

Harper's Weekly. "A Fine Structure." February 15, 1879.

Healy, Patrick. "Michigan State U. Adopts a Law School From Detroit." *The Chronicle of Higher Education* (April 14, 1995): 57.

Lansing Metropolitan Quarterly. "George Washington Peck: A Man of the Time." (fall 1988).

Linkages. "Long-term Political Activist Dies." Michigan State University College of Sciences, (spring 1993).

Michigan Bar Journal. "State Bar Executive Director Michael Franck Dies in Lansing at Age 61." (July 1994): 630.

_____. "Frank J. Kelley: The Dean of State Attorneys General Celebrates 30 Years of Distinguished Service." (December 1991): 1281-82.

_____. "State Bar Dedicates 10th Michigan Legal Milestone." (June 1989): 466.

Nisbet, Stephan. "Mission Accomplished." *Michigan Challenge* (June 1962): 6.

Wise, Edward W. "The Ablest State Court: The Michigan Supreme Court Before 1885." *The Wayne Rewiew* 33 (5) (1887).

Miscellaneous

Allen Jr., Glenn, biographical data provided to the Library of Michigan by Mr. Allen, April 1963

Carr, Leland, transcript of testimonial banquet honoring Carr at retirement, November 6, 1963.

Thomas M. Cooley Law School, Catalog, Lansing, 1994.

Cooley, Thomas M., collection housed in the Bentley Historical Library, Michigan Historical Collections, Collection Thomas M. Cooley, Box 6.

Drake, Robert L. "Highfields: A Mission Possible." 12-page typed paper written by for the organization's tenth anniversary, June 1977.

Fraser, Archie, hand-written recollections of legal career compiled by Mr. Fraser, 1992.Fraser, Trebilcock, Davis and Foster, typeset history of law firm, undated.

_____. Summary of Ingham County Circuit Court cases appealed to the Michigan Supreme Court from 1890 to 1899, 1991

Freeman, Ruth Tuttle, taped interview by Allison Thomas, 1989.

Hammond, C.F., memorial read in Ingham County Circuit Court, November 1937.

Highfields, Inc. "Highfields: Youth Opportunity Camp" 12-page brochure, 1980.

Houk, Rose. Transcript of speech honoring members of ICBA with 50 years service at 1989 ICBA annual dinner.

Hubbard, Fox, Thomas, White & Bengston, P.C. Law firm history, typed ms. N.D.

Ingham County Board of Commissioners. Road Map of Ingham County, Michigan, 1982.

Lindemer, Lawrence B. Biographical data supplied to the Library of Michigan by Mr. Lindemer, n.d.

Mackay, William L. Synopsis of life of Fred C. Newman, Jr., prepared October 11, 1989.

McWilliams, Melvin S. "President's Message." *Lansing Black Lawyers Association Newsletter* (spring 1992): 8.

Michigan Committee Against Capital Punishment. "Michigan's Historic Ban of Capital Punishment." One-page paper. Lansing, April 1974.

Michigan, Department of State. "How Michigan Became a State." News release from the Bureau of History, 1987.

Michigan Historical Society, *Michigan Pioneer and Historical Collection.* Vols. 11, 18, 21, 28, 29.

Michigan State University, News Bureau. Packet of press releases and newspaper articles pertaining to the Detroit College of Law at Michigan State University, 1995.

Montgomery, Robert. Genealogy record of Montgomery family compiled by James Bruner for his wife, Viola Montgomery Bruner, at Middletown, Ohio, 1992.

Planck, Joe. Script of presentation of history of Ingham County Circuit Court Judges to 1962. Annual meeting of Ingham County Bar Association.

_____. Typed record of interview with Planck, December 4, 1973.

Reisig, Donald. "Tribute to Stuart Dunnings, Jr." Annual meeting of the Ingham County Bar Association, October 24, 1990.

Sixty Plus, Inc., Organizational statement, 1995.

Spaniolo, Mike. "History of the Ingham County Bar Association Annual Shrimp Dinner." n.d.

Strudley, Florence M. Type-written biography of Edmund C. Shields, December 25, 1943.

Street, Cassius. Taped interview pertaining to Kim Sigler, by Allison Thomas, 1992.

Tuttle, Arthur. Transcript of memorial service in Detroit, December 20, 1944.

Warren, Jack. Personal career history supplied by Judge Warren, n.d.

Wiest, Howard. Personal Papers. Bentley Historical Library, University of Michigan, Ann Arbor.

Pamphlets

Michigan, Department of State. *A Brief History of Michigan*, n.d.

The Confederate Congress. *Government of the Northwest Territory*, July 13, 1787. Reprinted from the original by the U.S. Government Printing Office, n.d.

Ingham County Historical Commission. *Historic Courthouses of Ingham County*, n.d.

Michigan Historical Commission. *Messages of the Governors of Michigan*. Vol. 1. Lansing: Michigan Historical Commission, 1925.

Michigan State Court Administrative Office. *One Court of Justice.* Lansing: Michigan State Court Administrative Office, n.d.

Letters—Official Records of the Ingham County Bar Association

Barnett, Leo. Letter about the 1864-74 docket of a former Vevay Township justice of the peace.

Broom Hockey Benefit, program, February 2, 1988.

Bruin, Linda. Memo concerning history of Women's Lawyer Association of Michigan, February 8, 1994.

Cavanaugh, Michael E. Letter concerning Michigan Supreme Court anecdote, September 21, 1989.

Danhoff, Robert J. Letter concerning Con-Con, August 24, 1995. Downs, Tom. Letter concerning Con-Con, August 30, 1995

Houk, Rose. Memo concerning famous murders in mid-Michigan, July 8, 1995.

Hughes, Sam Street. Taped interview by Allison Thomas at Burcham Hills Retirement Center, November 17, 1988.

Ingham County Bar Association. Memorial service program for Sam Street Hughes presented by the, Lansing Civic Center, December 13, 1972.

Latona, Carl. Letter concerning history of Camp Highfields, July 30, 1994.

Loomis, Evert, Ederer, Parsley, Davis and Gotting. History of law firm, 1992.

Mallory, Susan. Memo concerning history of Women's Lawyer Association of Michigan, October 19, 1995.

MacLean, Charles. Letter about personal career, June 22, 1991.

McWilliams, Melvin S. Letter concerning history of Lansing Black Lawyer's Association, July 21, 1994.

Pierce, Joseph. Letter describing experiences of justice of the peace, November 30, 1989.

Reisig, Donald. Script of remarks at Sam Street Hughes' retirement banquet, Lansing Civic Center, December 13, 1972.

Schram, Henry. Letter describing Schram law firm, May 22, 1989.

Thomas, Allison. Letter about former Ingham County justices of the peace and other subjects, October 20, 1989.

Wanger, Eugene. Letter concerning Con-Con, February 19, 1992.

Newspapers

The Battle Creek Inquirer & News, March 18, 1947; March 8, 1958; May 12, 1958.

Chicago Times-Herald, September 13, 1898.

Chicago Tribune, September 13, 1898.

Detroit Free Press, December 4, 1944; July 23, 1986; November 9, 1994.

The Detroit News, 1931-94.

The Detroit Times, July 7, 1946.

Flint Journal, December 14, 1975.

Grand Rapids Press, December 1, 1953.

Ingham County Democrat, December 8, 1898.

Ingham County News, August 29, 1866; September 7, 1866; June 17, 1886; January 18, 1894; July 26, 1894; October 22, 1896; December 24, 1896; July 22, 1897; December 31, 1959; January 28, 1960; July 8, 1970.

Lansing Journal, 1887-1911.

The State Republican, 1886-1911.

Lansing Republican, 1855-85.

Lansing State Journal, 1911-96.

Towne Courier, October 11, 1972; December 20, 1972.

INDEX

Huntington, George M., 79, 311, 313
Huntington, Joseph L., 46
Huth, Joseph, 26
Hutter, George J., 220-21, 314
Hyde, Almerin (Almeron), 51

I

Indian law, 2
Indiana Territory, 7
Ingham County: associate judges of, 26;
circuit judges of, 311; courthouse in,
21, 25, 46-47, 137-39, 140, 146, 169,
222, 263, 267-68; crime in, 141, 178,
187; delegates to 1868 constitutional
convention, 82; district judges, 310;
early court quarters of, 17; early
women attorneys in, 154, 173-74,
180-82, 212; establishment of, 1, 9,
10, 265; financial support of railroads, 85; first black judge in, 242;
first black lawyer in, 215; first civil
rights case in, 117; first county building of, 20, 26; first federal judge
from, 62; first female judge in, 242;
first female juror in, 172-73; first
female lawyer in, 154, 173; first
malpractice suit in, 91-92; first presidential vote of, 276; grand juries in,
132, 133, 148-49, 189, 190-200; jail
in, 46, 267; juvenile detention facilities in, 227-28; labor relations issue
in, 184-86; liquor laws in, 91, 153;
lynching in, 79-81; naming of, 10,
265; Native Americans in, 2-3; natural resources of, 2-3; number of
lawyers in, 46, 75, 76, 177, 219;
organization of, 16; placement of
county seat of, 16, 20, 92, 233, 266;
population of, 16, 26, 75, 85, 177,
265; probate judges of, 312;
prosecuting attorneys, 187, 313; tax
collections in, 203; temperance
movement in, 91, 153

Ingham County Bank, the, 63
Ingham County Bar Association, the
(ICBA): annual banquet of, 128,
148, 219, 244; articles of association
of, 165-66, 300-4; ceremonial functions of, 126-28, 129, 134, 139, 205,
226; and creation of municipal
court, 129; first officers of, 123, 124;
founding of, 123, 124; and funerals
and memorial services, 126, 127-28,
129, 162; and judicial relief issue,
124-25, 128, 150, 166; and judicial
salary increase, 172; incorporation
of, 124; and James H. Thompson
disbarment proceedings, 158; and
Legal Aid, 204; and Marshall Day
celebration, 126-28; member
advocacy of, 126, 199; members
who are former chairpersons of the
Michigan State Bar Representative
Assembly, 314; members who are
past presidents of the State Bar of
Michigan, 314; and method of
selection of judges, 179; objectives
of, 123-24, 165; political functions
of, 125, 150, 152, 166-67, 172, 183;
presidents of, 313-14; reorganization
of 1909, 165; social functions of,
128, 134-35, 148, 206, 244; and the
State Association of Circuit Judges,
128, 148; veteran members of, 219
Ingham County Circuit Court: court
rules of, 19; daily schedule of, 50;
judges of, 311; overload of, 124; sessions in Lansing, 106-10; stages of
evolution of, 48, 65, 150
Ingham County News, the, 81, 91, 106, 233
Ingham County Pioneer Society, the:
establishment of, 272
Ingham County Prosecutor, 187, 313
Ingham Township, establishment of,
13-14
Ingham, Samuel D., 10, 265
inheritance law, Michigan, 159
interurban, the, 146

J

Jackson, Andrew, 14
Jackson, Lansing & Saginaw Railroad, the, 85
Jay Treaty, the, 5
Jefferson City murder, the, 50-51
Jefferson City, 20
Jefferson, Thomas, 7
Jenison Fieldhouse, 203
Jenkins, Guy, 189
Jennings, Clayton F., 184, 314
Jipson, Henry, 34
Jochim, John W., 131, 132, 133
Johnson, David, 26, 311
Johnson, James, 240
Johnson-Wynn, Nkrumah, 314
Johnston, Ivan A., 198, 199
Jones, Coe, 24
Jones, Whitney: and John McKinney trial, 55
Jordan, David, 242, 312
Joslin, Carrie, 141, 142, 143, 144
Joslin, William, 141
judicial relief, 150, 166, 220
judicial salaries, 88, 89-90, 219-20
justice of the peace courts, the, 48, 220, 224, 225

K

Kalamazoo Case, the, 71
Kallman, James T., 227, 228, 233, 311, 312
Kaplan, Carl, 205
Kedzie, Robert, 40-41, 142, 143, 144
Kelley, C. Bruce, 314
Kelley, Dean W., 205, 219, 313, 314
Kelley, Frank J., 225-26, 243
Kelly, Harry, 175, 218
Kelly, Spencer D., 313
Kemper, William, 205
Kennedy, Edward, 196
Kennedy, Robert, 227
Ketchum, Catherine, 118-19
Ketchum, Levi O., 51, 119
Kevorkian, Jack, 245-46

Kilbourne, Joseph Henry, 15, 31, 36, 37, 38, 59
Kilbourne, Louisa F. Burchard, 24, 39
Kilbourne, Samuel L.: address to Ingham County Pioneer Society, 272-74; candidacy for circuit court judge appointment, 150; and the Civil War, 38; and creation of municipal court, 129-30; death of, 41, 174; and the Dodge Bill, 108; early life and education of, 37-38; election as Ingham County Bar Association president, 123, 124, 127, 129, 165, 313; and establishment of Ingham County Bar Association, 123, 124; functions as Ingham County Bar Association president, 126, 128-29, 148; and instruction of students in law, 75; and judicial relief issue, 125, 150; marriage of, 24, 39; and Michigan liquor law, 39; and new courthouse in Mason, 138, 139; noted cases of, 39-41, 101, 102, 104, 117, 132; party affiliation of, 38, 174; and William H. Pinckney, 127-28; as writer and speaker, 76
King, Louise, 169
Kirchner, Otto, 103
Koenig, Dorean, 237
Krause, George, 204
Krug, Hans Peter, 187

L

Landon, Alf, 180
Lansing: attempts to attain county seat status, 92-93, 105, 106-7, 137, 138, 233; city hall in, 137; city water in, 113; depression of 1893, 168; difficulties with early transportation to/from, 35, 45-46, 49; early retirement program controversy in, 247; electric lighting in, 113; entertainment in, 114; financial support of railroads, 85; fire in, 52-53; first European visitor to, 4; first judge in, 28; first law

Warren, Jack W.: as circuit court judge, 218, 233, 311; and Cooley Law School, 231; and David Bellah murder trial, 236; as Ingham County Bar Association president, 314; as Ingham County prosecutor, 214, 218, 313; as Lansing municipal judge, 218, 312; retirement of, 241-42
Washburn, Lester, 185, 186
Washburn, Mrs. Lester, 184-85
Washington Avenue, early grading problems with, 60-61
Washtenaw County, establishment of, 9
Watson Benjamin J., 214: noted trials of, 192, 193, 207, 209, 210; as president of the Ingham County Bar Association, 314; and Ruth and Esther Tuttle, 183
Wayne County (Indiana Territory), 7
Wayne County (Michigan), establishment of, 9
Wayne, "Mad Anthony," 5
Webb, John F., 203
Webb, W. W., 118, 120
Webster, Clyde, 211
Weiss, Robert, 249
Weller, Augustus F., 33, 99
Wells, William P., 107, 109
Werbelow, Judson M., 314
Whallon, John, 108-9, 110
Whipple, Charles W., 25
White, Emmons, 20
Wiest, Howard: as circuit court judge, 150, 151, 311; and Dean W. Kelley, 205; death of, 197, 211; and Hazen Pingree, 126, 135, 167; and James H. Thompson disbarment proceedings, 158, 160, 161, 162-63; and judicial relief issue, 166; as Michigan Supreme Court judge, 134, 166-67, 311; and military uniform scandal, 133, 134, 135; and new Ingham County courthouse, 139; noted trials of, 143, 144, 149, 154, 171; proposed appointment of as U.S. District Court judge, 152; and recall of

judges, 152; and the State Association of Circuit Judges, 128
Wigle, J. N., 118, 119, 120
Wiley, Delos, 38, 39, 75, 77, 81
Willabrandt, Mabel Walker, 181
Williams, Charles, 195
Williams, G. Mennen, 213, 218
Williams, George M., 99
Winchell Amaziah, 16
Wing, Austin E., 22
Wise, Edward M., 66, 71
Wise, William H., 314
Wisner, Charles, 125, 126
Witherall, Benjamin F. H., 32
Wo Non Quit, 20
Wolpe, Howard, 243
Women Lawyers Association of Michigan, the, Mid-Michigan Region, 236-37
Women's Christian Temperence Union, the (WCTU), 119
Wonch, Nancy A., 314
Wood, James, 232, 312
Woodbridge, William, 11, 18, 21, 23, 29
Woodhouse, Lemuel, 82
Woods, Marsha, 236
Woods, Paula, 236
Woodworth, Elijah, 17
Workman, Amos, 17
Wyley, Ann, 4

Y

Young, Coleman, 223
Young, Martha Sue, murder of, 233
Younger, Paul C., 204, 209, 218, 312, 313

Z

Ziegler, Charles M., 195
Zimmer, Paula, 205, 236